THE USES OF JUSTICE IN GLOBAL PERSPECTIVE, 1600–1900

The Uses of Justice in Global Perspective, 1600–1900 presents a n[illegible]rspective on the uses of justice between 1600 and 1900 and confronts prevailing Eurocentric historiography in its examination of how people of this period made use of the law.

Between 1600 and 1900 the towns in Western Europe, the Kingdoms in Eastern Europe, the Empires in Asia and the Colonial States in Asia and the Americas were all characterised by a plurality of legal orders resulting from interactions and negotiations between states, institutions, and people with different backgrounds. Through exploring how justice is used within these different areas of the world, this book offers a broad global perspective, but it also adopts a fresh approach through shifting attention away from states and onto how ordinary people lived with and made use of this 'legal pluralism'.

Containing a wealth of extensively contextualised case studies and contributing to debates on socio-legal history, processes of state formation from below, access to justice, and legal pluralism, *The Uses of Justice in Global Perspective, 1600–1900* questions to what degree top-down imposed formal institutions were used and how, and to what degree, bottom-up crafted legal systems were crucial in allowing transactions to happen. It is ideal for students and scholars of early modern justice, crime and legal history.

Griet Vermeesch is a fellow of the Research Foundation Flanders at the Vrije Universiteit Brussels, in Belgium. Her research relates to urban history and to access to justice in the Low Countries during the early modern period.

Manon van der Heijden is Professor of Urban History at Leiden University and a member of the Academia Europaea. She is author of *Women and Crime in Early Modern Holland* (2016).

Jaco Zuijderduijn is Associate Professor at the Department of Economic History at Lund University, Sweden. His main research interest is the development of economic exchange and conflict resolution. He previously published *Medieval Capital Markets: Markets for Renten, State Formation and Private Investment in Holland (1300–1550)*.

THE USES OF JUSTICE IN GLOBAL PERSPECTIVE, 1600–1900

Edited by
Griet Vermeesch, Manon van der Heijden and Jaco Zuijderduijn

Routledge
Taylor & Francis Group
LONDON AND NEW YORK

First published 2019
by Routledge
2 Park Square, Milton Park, Abingdon, Oxon OX14 4RN

and by Routledge
52 Vanderbilt Avenue, New York, NY 10017

Routledge is an imprint of the Taylor & Francis Group, an informa business

British Library Cataloguing-in-Publication Data
A catalogue record for this book is available from the British Library

Library of Congress Cataloging-in-Publication Data
Names: Vermeesch, Griet, editor. | Heijden, Manon van der, 1966- editor. | Zuijderduijn, C. J. (C. Jaco), editor.
Title: The uses of justice in global perspective, 1600-1900 / edited by Griet Vermeesch, Manon van der Heijden, and Jaco Zuijderduijn.
Description: Abingdon, Oxon ; New York, NY : Routledge, 2019. | Includes index.
Identifiers: LCCN 2018039516 | ISBN 9781138476783 (hardback : alk. paper) | ISBN 9781138476790 (pbk. : alk. paper)
Subjects: LCSH: Law—History. | Justice, Administration of—History. | Legal polycentricity—History.
Classification: LCC K160 .U823 2019 | DDC 340.09/03—dc23
LC record available at https://lccn.loc.gov/2018039516

ISBN: 978-1-138-47678-3 (hbk)
ISBN: 978-1-138-47679-0 (pbk)
ISBN: 978-0-429-02233-3 (ebk)

Typeset in Bembo
by Swales & Willis Ltd, Exeter, Devon, UK

CONTENTS

ILLUSTRATIONS

Figures

Map

Tables

ACKNOWLEDGEMENTS

Financial support by the Netherlands Organisation for Scientific Research (NWO), Research Foundation Flanders (FWO), Leiden University, and the N.W. Posthumus Institute is gratefully acknowledged.

CONTRIBUTORS

Elizaveta Blagodeteleva is a research fellow of the Institute for Social Policy at the National Research University Higher School of Economics in Russia. Her PhD, which she obtained in 2013 from the Moscow State Pedagogical University, examined professional group formation at the Moscow Bar Association between 1866 and 1914.

Donald Fyson is full Professor in History at the Département des Sciences Historiques, at the Université Laval, in Quebec. His expertise lies in the social, socio-legal and socio-political history of Quebec from the eighteenth to the twentieth century. He has extensively published on the history of civil and criminal justice in Quebec.

Katherine Godwin is a PhD-student at the University of Illinois where she writes a dissertation on legal culture and daily life in sixteenth-century Rouen, focusing, in particular, on civil litigation.

Philip C.C. Huang is Professor emeritus at the UCLA and has published extensively on the history of China, including a recently enlarged and updated three-volume study of civil justice from the Qing to the present, and a three-volume study on rural society and economy of the Ming and Qing.

Dries Lyna works as a lecturer at the History Department of the Radboud Universiteit in Nijmegen, the Netherlands. His current research relates to the social functions of colonial justice in the cities of Colombo, Galle and Jaffna in eighteenth-century Ceylon.

Tomás A. Mantecón is Professor of Early Modern History at the University of Cantabria. His main research fields relate to the seventeenth- and eighteenth-century history of violence, social inclusion and exclusion, confessional conflict, social struggles and urban history.

Alexandr Osipian is a guest scholar at the Leibniz Institute for the history and culture of Eastern Europe at the University of Leipzig. His research relates to the Armenian trading diasporas and to discourses and practices of the social construction of the past.

Bianca Premo is Associate Professor at Florida International University and researches a wide range of topics in Latin American history. Her most recent book, *The Enlightenment on Trial: Ordinary Litigants and Colonialism in the Spanish Empire*, is a comparative study that reveals how ordinary, often illiterate litigants made law modern in the courtrooms of vast regions of the eighteenth-century Spanish empire.

Nadeera Rupesinghe obtained her PhD in history at Leiden university, the Netherlands, in 2016 for her thesis titled 'Negotiating Custom: Colonial Lawmaking in the Galle Landraad.' She currently works as director general of the Department of National Archives in Sri Lanka.

Alicia Schrikker is senior university lecturer at Leiden University. Her research focusses on society-state interaction in colonial contexts in Asia in the eighteenth and nineteenth centuries. Her regions of expertise are Sri Lanka, Indonesia, South Africa and India.

Manon van der Heijden is full professor of Urban History at Leiden University and a member of the Academia Europaea. She is author of *Women and Crime in Early Modern Holland* (2016).

Aries van Meeteren obtained his PhD in history at the Erasmus University in Rotterdam, in the Netherlands. His research is related to the uses of justice in late-seventeenth-century Leiden.

Griet Vermeesch is a fellow of the Research Foundation Flanders at the Vrije Universiteit Brussels, in Belgium. Her research relates to urban history and to access to justice in the Low Countries during the early modern period.

Jaco Zuijderduijn is Associate Professor at the Department of Economic History of Lund University, in Sweden. He publishes on the development of economic institutions in pre-modern Europe.

1

THE USES OF JUSTICE IN GLOBAL PERSPECTIVE, 1600–1900

Manon van der Heijden and Griet Vermeesch

Introduction

This volume builds on recent strands in historiography on European socio-legal history of the early modern period, and extends it to a globally comparative scope, and to the period up until 1900. To date, historians have amply demonstrated that European early modern society was highly litigious, and have identified such as a unique feature of Western civilisation (e.g. Kagan 1981; Brooks 1986). In Western Europe, an extensive grid of law courts vested in local, regional, national and international power networks was the main contact point between the early modern state and ordinary people. Insight into the ways those courts were used is therefore crucial for a proper understanding of European history.

Relatedly, new strands in socio-legal historical research increasingly examine judicial infrastructures from the perspective of their users and explore how the law and normative frames were shaped from below in response to the ways litigants actively brought the law into play (see for instance Hindle 2000; Castiglione 2005). The instrumental ways ordinary people took legal recourse – that has been conceptually denoted as 'the uses of justice' – is consequently a central element in current socio-legal historical research (Dinges 2004). This approach ascribes agency to ordinary people, and acknowledges the existence of what Émile Durkheim called the *conscience collective*: the system of beliefs and sentiments underpinning mutual relations and held in common by the members of a society (Durkheim 1997). This system determined to what degree ordinary people went beyond informal forums of conflict resolution and turned to formal law courts. The interaction between subjects and state has for instance been fruitfully explored by Lauren Benton in her study on legal regimes and colonial cultures. Benton argues that the colonial state emerged in part out of a legal politic engaging both colonisers and colonised (Benton 2002).

Alleged European litigiousness seems to echo a supposedly unique feature of Western European social history, which was described in the seminal work of Max Weber: the prominence of contractual relations between non-related individuals as forms of solidarity. Weber emphasised major distinctions between European cities on the one hand and Asian cities on the other, as communal ideas and practices differed vastly. In Western cities, communal interests that transcended kin relations were at the basis of social relations, while kin relations informed communal relations and models of solidarity in Asian cities (Weber 1978). The dominance of contractual relations would have informed the apparently unique litigation patterns in Western Europe, while elsewhere networks of kin first and foremost mediated interpersonal conflicts. In the best-studied case of China, the state mainly intervened in conflicts to punish disturbers of social peace (see for instance Bodde and Morris 1967). In other words: the domination by kinship in Chinese society discouraged the development of civil laws that protected people against theft, assault or fraud. Comparisons between the legal system of the West and China have been heavily debated *and* contested. Archival research on courts during the Qing period (1644–1912) has shown that Chinese local courts did protect ordinary litigants and that Chinese people could use the courts to defend their personal interests (Buxbaum 1971; Huang 1996, 2001; Sommer 2013). Clearly, the Weberian paradigm idealised the West and ignored important nuances in the Chinese legal system and the access of ordinary people to the local courts (Sommer 2013).

This volume does not take the 'West and the Rest' as a starting point, but focuses on the variety of trajectories in the uses of justice by ordinary people in the historical contexts of Europe, Asia and the Americas. As such, it counterbalances the assumed uniqueness of litigation patterns in early modern Europe. In addition, the volume aims to further explore the prevalent concept of 'uses of justice', by connecting it to the debates on legal pluralism and examining it in a global contextual framework. In short, the overall objective of the volume is to confront the prevailing Eurocentric historiography on the uses of justice with elaborately contextualised case studies of legal plurality elsewhere.

While contributing to debates on socio-legal history, the volume similarly aims to enrich at least three related historical debates. The first important debate is related to processes of state formation from below. The law and the law courts were key points of contact between state elites on the one hand and ordinary people on the other in the preindustrial context. Analysis of contemporary uses of justice – who used the law and the law courts in what way – consequently comprises a privileged angle from which to examine interactions between state and society and between rulers and ruled in the past. Such analysis has already been carried out successfully for early modern Western Europe. A number of chapters in this volume help to extend such analysis to the colonial, non-European context as well as to Eastern Europe. The volume contains elaborate discussions on the ways ordinary people negotiated (colonial) state infrastructures to their advantage, and thus contributed to processes of shaping the state.

The second relevant debate concerns the notion of access to justice. Analysis of the ways in which the law was used is intimately connected to the question of who had access to judicial infrastructures. Considering who had access to justice in a non-Western European context helps to assess the extent to which the (colonial) state penetrated society. This also links up with the alleged uniqueness of Western European patterns of litigation. Did ordinary people in non-Western European contexts meet more barriers so as to call in the state to arbitrate and settle inter-personal conflicts? And if so, did this create impediments to transactions, or did informal forums of conflict resolution work just as well? How did official and non-official bodies of conflict management collaborate or interact?

The third important theme is the notion of 'legal pluralism': the co-existence of various legal systems within an area, as well as different legal infrastructures, including formal, semi-formal and informal forums of conflict settlement. The instrumental ways the law was used in the daily social and economic affairs of ordinary people were much connected to the complex and mutually overlapping judicial infrastructures that characterised the preindustrial state. By approaching the law from the perspective of its users, this volume contributes to a better understanding of legal pluralism from below. It also hopes to provide the reader with a better idea of how informal legal systems that were a part of indigenous culture may have substituted formal legal systems, and thus interfered with processes of state formation.

This introduction discusses the concepts and questions related to the central themes of this book. We will start with an explanation of the concept of 'the uses of justice', and the way it has been used by scholars working on early modern Europe. Second, European historiography on the topic of access to justice will be discussed, as a context for the chapters in the volume. Then, we elaborate on the concept of legal pluralism in relation to the debate on the uses of justice, and explore the most important findings in various parts of the world. In the last part, we will briefly discuss the historiographic complications in practising global comparative history that stretches beyond the history of colonialism.

The uses of justice

The starting point of this volume is the concept of *Justiznutzung* or the uses of justice, as introduced by the German historian Martin Dinges in 2000.[1] Dinges aimed to shift the attention of crime historians from a top-down perspective of social control to a more nuanced bottom-up approach. The concept was a response to the general notion among crime historians that in Europe in the course of the modern period a process of *Verrechtlichung* or *juridification* had occurred, notably that people increasingly came to rely on formal criminal court procedures to settle their disputes (Lenman and Parker 1980). Bruce Lenman, Geoffrey Parker and others found that bottom-up forms of social control within communities were gradually taken over by the social disciplining of authorities that increasingly began to regulate moral behaviour. As a result, official authorities and the courts increasingly decided which cases should result in prosecution, rather than the victims or others who had brought the case forward. However, by looking at court cases from the perspective of the actual plaintiffs, Dinges came to a totally different conclusion. He argued that institutions of justice might be seen as instruments in the hands of the authorities, but they might as well be viewed as instruments of people using the judicial system to help settle a personal conflict. In the early modern period, people could opt for many other forms of conflict resolution, and those who filed a complaint had chosen to use the court for solving their conflict. In this line of reasoning, the filing of a complaint was merely one of myriad possibilities for making oneself heard in a conflict that had started out of court.

There are two important arguments that support the concept of the uses of justice as explained by Dinges. First, the types of crime handled and the kinds of people prosecuted by the courts were as much determined by the authorities as by the (mostly urban) population. Secular and ecclesiastical authorities may have set up rules and formulated laws, the numbers of cases they dealt with largely depended on the willingness of the population to bring their conflicts to the court (Farge 1986; Castan 1980; Garnot 2000, pp. 103–120; Shoemaker 1991; Van der Heijden 2012, pp. 94–100). German historians Joachim Eibach and Gerd Schwerhoff have argued that early modern justice was an instrument of regulation as well as an agent of moral discipline (Schwerhoff 2004, p. 223; Eibach 2007, p. 173). This implies that not only the interests of the authorities were served, but also the concrete interests of the person lodging a complaint. Following Keith Wrightson's notion of 'two concepts of order' Dinges argued that 'the authorities could hardly realise their own concept when the most prominent sections of the population pursued different interests' (Wrightson 1980; Dinges 2004).

Second, the many different judicial options and extrajudicial forms of conflict settlement existing in the early modern period suggest that the criminal court was only one of many options available to ordinary people. As Shoemaker's study on seventeenth-century London and Middlesex and examinations on the early modern Low Countries have revealed, most people preferred to settle their conflict outside the criminal court and opted for non-judicial forms of conflict regulation (Shoemaker 1991; Grey 2009; Vermeesch 2015b; Van der Heijden 2016). In addition, the myriad of formal, semi-formal and informal options gave ordinary people the opportunity to strategically use the various possibilities and choose the form of settlement that would serve their interests best. Martin Ingram was the first to plead for a more integrated approach of social control that compares a range of secular and ecclesiastical jurisdictions over a longer period of time (Ingram 1999, p. 95, pp. 87–103). Dinges took this a step further by suggesting the inclusion of formal as well as informal or semi-formal institutions of justice. In order to disclose and explain to what extent people had access to and how they used the courts, scholars need to look not only at criminal, civil and ecclesiastical institutions, but also at other agents of social control such as the family, the neighbourhood and guilds.

Interactions between people, the law and the courts

The judicial pluralism that existed everywhere in early modern Europe was characterised by a complex mixture of personal and institutional interests of the parties involved in conflict regulation.[2] The various forms and functions of secular, ecclesiastical and civil institutions of conflict regulation partly overlapped and church courts and criminal courts sometimes competed for similar cases (Van der Heijden 2012). Furthermore, criminal and civil courts and consistories may have supported the dominance of husbands and fathers in patriarchal households, but could at the same time serve as agents of support to women. Particularly German crime historians have looked at such interactions. The works of Eibach and Rebekka Habermas on early modern Frankfurt show that men's dominant behaviour was as much controlled in the sense that women brought misdemeanour to the marriage courts which supported women against domestic violence (Habermas 1992; Eibach 2007, p. 186). In her study on early modern Basel, Susanna Burghartz found that recourse to justice and the strategies of the courts were not static elements, but subject to change. Between the sixteenth and seventeenth centuries the marriage court of Basel shifted from a forum directed at conflict regulation between husbands and wives to an institution that was aimed at the disciplining of all irregular sexual behaviour (Burghartz 2004). Although processes of professionalisation and juridification may have occurred in the course of the early modern period, scholars agree that in most European towns infra-juridical mechanisms remained vastly important (Denys 2010).

Dutch historians have begun to use the concept of the uses of justice for explaining interactions between law, people and the courts. Adopting Ingram's suggestion to compare secular and church jurisdiction, Van der Heijden found that social control mechanisms in early modern Holland were the outcome of the interaction of aims and objectives of judicial institutions and the way people made use of those institutions. While criminal courts particularly took into account the financial burden of the urban community in their sentencing of marital cases, Protestant consistories focused on controlling sin and morality, and the reputation of their parish. As the urban population was aware of these differences, the business of consistories and criminal courts was selectively influenced by the complainant's preference. Accusers preferred to take certain complaints to the consistory rather than the criminal court, and vice versa (Van der Heijden 2004). These preferences indicate that ordinary people knew what judicial options were available to them, and they seem to have weighed the consequences attached to each of these options. Such options also gave legal agency to social groups that historians generally assume to have had little or no agency. In early modern Holland, women were for instance quite reluctant to bring their abusive and adulterous husbands to the criminal court because prosecution could lead to banishment or long-time imprisonment, and that would endanger the family income. Instead, they asked neighbourhood masters to discipline their husbands, and when those attempts failed, they rather made use of the so-called 'confinement of request' offered by the civic authorities and reconciliation practices by the Protestant consistories.

The latter options provided women much more with the ability to take matters into their own hands (Van der Heijden 2013).

Although most research on the early modern uses of judicial systems has focused on criminal courts, ordinary people were probably much more likely to use civil courts to settle a dispute.[3] Examinations on early modern cities in England, France, Germany and Holland reveal that civil procedures provided women legal agency against the alleged father of their illegitimate child (Evans 2005; Cliche 1988; Walker 2003, pp. 227–237; Hayhoe 2005; Vermeesch 2016). Vermeesch found that in eighteenth-century Leiden single mothers took strategic actions to hold the alleged fathers of their children accountable, and they used the courts, consistories and communities as agents in their defence. Both single mothers and putative fathers who belonged to the Dutch Reformed community were encouraged by the Protestant consistories to take legal action. Furthermore, the judges of the civil courts were markedly lenient to single mothers in granting them free legal aid and by delivering favourable verdicts. Vermeesch also points to the social and cultural barriers between single mothers and the courts that held back many women from starting a lawsuit over their illegitimate child. A recent comparison between unwed mothers in Germany and Holland by Ariadne Schmidt and Jeannette Kamp reveals differences in the social disciplining of authorities as well as remarkable similarities in the uses of justice by women. Although the authorities in the German territories seemed to keep stricter control over the regulation of moral conduct than their Dutch counterparts, in both regions women were able to strategically use instruments of social control and legal forums. These findings confirm the conclusions of Vermeesch about the support of single mothers by third parties; women were able to use judicial institutions to their own advantage with the help of family, neighbours, midwives and consistories (Schmidt and Kamp 2018).

Access to justice

The recent focus of historians on bottom-up approaches, myriad uses of justice and legal agency may, however, also lead to false impressions about the scope of legal agency of the majority of ordinary people in early modern Europe. Tim Stretton has warned historians that assessing the social position of litigants might be 'a risky endeavour', especially if social identification is to be based on information given by parties themselves during their trial, in view of the likely strategic purpose of their disclosures (Stretton 1998, p. 92). Also, as the above comparison of Germany and Holland shows, there were important differences between regions within Europe. Sheilagh Ogilvie argues that there were dissimilarities between the mechanism of social control between the Western part of Europe and the part east of the Elbe. In early modern Bohemia, there seems to have been no display of social disciplining by either the authorities or by ordinary people using the courts. Instead, Ogilvie found that courts in the eastern part of Europe were primarily used by local elites and male householders who wanted to control the behaviour of the lower social strata, outsiders, women, migrants and deviants (Ogilvie 2006).

Apart from spatial variation in the extent to which broad groups in society took recourse to law courts, there was marked variation through time as well. In fact, the period between roughly 1450 and 1850 witnessed vastly changing patterns of litigation that are thus far insufficiently understood or explained. Although insufficient research exists so as to simply accept the universal nature (in Europe) of these patterns, a subsequent rise and decline of litigation has been assessed for a wide range of law courts. Thus, a sharp increase of case load characterised law courts during the long sixteenth century (Kagan 1981; Muldrew 1998; Outhwaite 2006; Wollschläger 1990). In all probability, this was due to population growth and the emergent dominance of market relations. From the mid-seventeenth century, however, the case load of numerous courts drastically fell, to reach an all-time low during the eighteenth century. This decline has been assessed for English, Dutch, French, Spanish as well as German law courts, on all institutional levels. This changed again in the nineteenth century, concomitant with the rise of the modern state and the industrial revolution (Champion 1997; Kaiser 1980; Wollschläger 1990; Le Bailly 2011; Ranieri 1985). These litigation patterns are still insufficiently understood. It is unclear, for instance, whether a litigation decline indicates a decrease of the number of interpersonal disputes, or rather a waning of the inclination to invite law courts into such disputes. These fascinating patterns warn the historian not to simply assume that legal recourse was evident for contemporaries. The decision to go to court was vastly context-dependent.

Possibly, the approachability of law courts decreased during the early modern era, for instance due to rising fees, increasing complexity of legal procedure and the related growing need to employ legal spokesmen. That brings us to the important theme of the relative accessibility of law courts in Europe during the early modern era and the nineteenth century. This accessibility was decisive for the uses of justice, and the place of law courts in society. Nonetheless, it has thus far received fairly limited historiographical attention. The concept of the uses of justice helps to shed new light on this import topic. Complaints of contemporaries regarding the problematic availability of courts often related to court cases that were fully settled by way of adjudication, thus cases that involved the promulgation of a verdict, a procedure that more often than not took much time, energy and money. The large majority of cases that came before law courts were, however, ultimately resolved outside the courts, or involved infrajudicial intervention by notaries, officials or other intermediaries. In fact, it might be argued that the very expensiveness and impenetrability of legal recourse helped the summoning of a counter party to be even more forceful and thus effective in enforcing a settlement out of court.[4]

Analysis of the daily uses of law courts elucidates the remarkable leeway they left for arbitration and settlements, which did not necessarily involve complex, money- and time-consuming juridical reasoning and procedures. Such forms of conflict settlement pertained to the phenomenon of 'infrajustice'. The concept originates in French historiography (Soman 1982; Garnot 1996), yet is becoming used in research outside France as well (Härter 2012), as is also evidenced in this volume. Infrajustice relates to the alternative strategies that were employed to settle differences, mostly in the sphere of crime, that operated on the peripheries of formal law courts. In 2000, the influential French historian Benoît Garnot elaborately discussed the specificity of infrajustice, and called for a not-too-broad definition, so as to preserve the explanatory power of the concept. Infrajustice involved arbitration by notaries or other intermediaries who boasted a certain amount of social authority. An essential aspect, according to Garnot, is the (semi-)public nature of these instances of mediation. Therefore, not all forms of intermediation are to be considered as infrajudicial. Garnot coined the term 'parajustice' for strictly private interpersonal settling of differences. 'Extra-justice', lastly, related to forms of arbitration that complemented legal recourse (Garnot 2000). These concepts may seem somewhat complex, yet they illuminate the notable complexity of conflict settlement in a preindustrial era, where (local as well as central) governmental institutions did not necessarily prevail over other instances of conflict resolution, and where complex dynamics between law courts and non-state bodies defined the shaping of the law. Evidently, the uses of justice are pivotal in this complex mixture of conflict-settling bodies.

Legal pluralism

The essays of this volume are connected to another much more debated concept of judicial plurality, that of legal pluralism. Legal pluralism is commonly understood as the multiplicity of legal orders, a situation in which two or more legal systems coexist in the same social field (Griffiths, J. 1986; Merry 1988; Griffiths, A. 2002, 2011, 2013). Contrary to the studies on the uses of justice, which focus primarily on European regions in the early modern period, legal pluralism has been used in a much broader sense, both chronologically and geographically. Although some scholars use legal pluralism to describe coexisting and overlapping bodies of law and legal norms in early modern Europe, the notion of plural legal orders has primarily been adopted in colonial history and the history of empires in order to fully comprehend the legal complexity of colonial and postcolonial societies (Roodenburg and Spierenburg 2004; Tamanaha 2008; Benton and Ross 2013).

The 'uses of justice' and 'legal pluralism' are part of two entirely different historical debates and are implemented in quite different ways, but the two concepts bear important resemblances. First, both concepts are a response to the deeply rooted idea that legal orders are determined by the state as a reflection of state formation or state centralisation. They present a much more nuanced view that takes into account multiple legal entities, including state law as well as non-state law. Second, both concepts intend to correct the common assumption that state law became increasingly important in the course of the early modern period, at the cost of other forms of law, such as customary law, indigenous law, religious law and other legal arrangements. Finally, acknowledging that societies contain multiple legal systems or normative orders implies that people can – at least to some extent – select and choose from these systems and use them to serve their private interests.

Legal pluralism and uses of justice stand for opportunities, options and possibilities, and thus for individual and collective self-realisation through law.

Adopting the terms 'uses of justice' or 'legal pluralism' helps scholars to find a more nuanced and layered understanding of how state law, other normative orders and people living within these orders interacted. The terms also confront scholars with similar problems regarding the exact meaning of 'law' and 'legal order'. In a very clear overview on the adoption of the term legal pluralism Paul D. Halliday warns us that pluralism has become an umbrella concept that is often described as 'diversity' and therefore reduces the 'analytic force the term may once have possessed' (Halliday 2013, p. 273). The problem of definition has its roots in the pioneering work of John Griffiths who described legal pluralism as 'the state of affairs, for any social field, in which behaviour pursuant to more than one legal order occurs' (Griffiths, J. 1986, p. 34, 38). This broad definition enabled Griffiths to correct the deeply rooted view that state law is central to all legal orders. Accordingly, he successfully shifted the debate on law in colonial societies from the concept of 'legal centralism' to a broader understanding that involved self-regulation and semi-autonomous normative orders (Griffiths, A. 2002, 2013). However, by not clearly distinguishing between law and norm, legal pluralism became as much a celebrated as a heavily debated concept.[5] After all, what *is* law if it includes all sources of law, rules and codes?

Several scholars have sought the solution for the definition problem of legal pluralism in the distinction between state law and non-state law. Sally Engle Merry and Brian Tamanaha suggested that legal pluralism refers to various kinds of norm-making orders, though state law is to be distinguished from other normative ordering (Tamanaha 2008; Merry 1998). For Tamanaha the major pitfall of scholars studying legal pluralism is twofold. First, legal scholars tend to put the state above all other normative systems. Second, social scientists assume too easily that other legal or normative systems are parallel to state law (Tamanaha 2008, p. 410). Lauren Benton and Richard Ross added another important problem in connection to legal pluralism: many scholars tend to view legal pluralism a-historically without accounting for local changes and careful analyses of specific understandings of legal complexity (Benton and Ross 2013, pp. 4–5).

The same reason why legal pluralism is such an appealing concept confronts scholars with theoretical problems: in different times and places, historians, lawyers and anthropologists see coexisting legal orders that overlap and clash, but it seems impossible to find a clear-cut and universal definition of these legal systems. Moreover, the focus on theorising law and defining legal pluralism seems to hinder the actual and concrete historical study of legal systems. Indeed, as Merry put it: 'the concept of legal pluralism can press too quickly toward analyses of systems to the neglect of the variation in particular places' (Merry 1998, p. 891). Others have argued that these difficulties should not hold back scholars from attempting to differentiate between various types of social control. As Woodman put it: 'the conclusion must be that law covers a continuum which runs from the clearest form of state law through the vaguest forms of informal social control' (Woodman 1998, p. 45).

To resolve the difficult discrepancies between the theory of legal pluralism and the empirical study of specific contexts of legal pluralism several scholars have suggested shifting the focus of study. Benton and Ross proposed to focus on patterns of jurisdictional conflicts, because jurisdictions circumvent problems related to the definition of law, distinctions between state and non-state, and between private and public (Benton and Ross 2013, pp. 5–6). Such an approach could more smoothly incorporate different types of conflict regulation, such as those provided by religious institutions, guilds, neighbourhood associations or trading companies, which can exist both in premodern and modern times. In line with Benton's argument Halliday suggested shifting the attention from the model of legal pluralis*m* to the particular and concrete histories of pluralities (Halliday 2013, p. 267). By looking at pluralities in different times and places rather than pluralism, scholars can improve the understanding of how concepts of legal orders were defined in specific historical contexts, and how people actually made use of coexisting legal orders in those contexts.

This volume is connected to such new strands of research, and aims to focus on historical practices of legal plurality and the interactions between those making use and providing legal plurality.

Legal pluralities in practice

Thus far, studies of legal pluralism have focused on theorising law and political imagination of the law, and paid much less attention to the history of the everyday practices of actors using legal plurality. Our objective here is not to present a comprehensive overview of studies of everyday practices of legal pluralism, but to highlight some historical works that demonstrate the importance of a 'uses of justice' approach. Important work has been done on the working of institutions and the interaction between various courts in the British, French, Spanish and Dutch empires in Asia, the Americas and Africa.[6] Still little is known about how slaves, freed men and women, convicts, merchants, wives of colonists, and officials made use of the plurality of institutions that provided conflict regulation. Recently, Victor Olcina Pita found that in fifteenth-century Christian Valencia, Muslim Granada and North Africa, and Christian, Muslim and Jewish merchants made use of the courts and laws of other religions to enforce their commercial contracts (Olcina Pita 2017). Several scholars have started to examine the varieties of criminal justice experienced by slaves in the Americas between the seventeenth and the nineteenth centuries. Some scholars have raised the issue of 'agency' of slaves in criminal law. However, as Nathalie Zemon Davis rightly remarked, 'Historians of European criminal law and prosecution have rarely made the crime and punishment of slaves in the colonies part of their story'. Even less has been said about how slaves and freed men were able to use plural legal orders to their own advantage (Zemon Davis 2011, Rupert 2013; Forret 2015; Fatah-Black 2017).

The case of the Ottoman Empire proves to be particularly relevant to the study of legal pluralities in conflict settlement. Ido Shahar was one of the first to discuss the interrelations between Islamic kadi courts and other non-shari'a tribunals in the Ottoman Empire. He also paid attention to the phenomenon of forum shopping, and raised the question of whether litigants were free to choose the legal forum of the judge who served their interests best. By doing so, he shifted the focus of attention to the litigants' perspective (Shahar 2008). He argued that throughout the history of the Ottoman Empire state-sponsored and institutionalised legal pluralism dominated in many Muslim societies, but in this context the co-existence of kadi courts and other courts probably increased the freedom of litigants to choose. For instance, in sixteenth-century Ottoman Jerusalem, Jews often preferred to bring their matters to the Islamic kadi courts instead of the Jewish rabbinical court (Shahar 2008, p. 124).

Karen Barkey examined people's access to and use of multiple court systems in the Ottoman Empire as well. Like Shahar, she wants to know if subjects could choose between various legal traditions, but she also carefully analyses interactions between the politics of the dominant state and communities with regard to social control (Barkey 2013). Barkey argues that the Laws of Umar (rights and restrictions on non-Muslims) effectively created more legal choices for Jews and Christians, because they could use their own courts as well as the Islamic kadi courts to litigate personal and family legal matters. Jews and Christians could settle conflicts among themselves before their own court or the Islamic jurisdiction. Although Jewish communities in the Ottoman Empire had their own law court based on Jewish law and Christians had their church courts based on canon law, both groups made frequent use of the Muslim court to settle disputes. This was particularly the case in large merchant towns, such as Kayseri, Aleppo, Damascus and Sofia. In addition, Islamic courts were particularly used by non-Muslim women in marital cases, because the kadi courts followed different rules regarding divorce and inheritance. Barkey argues that 'The availability of multiple religious jurisdictions allowed for forum shopping, permitting individuals to search for rulings more to their own advantage' (Barkey 2013, p. 95). This legal pluralism seemed to have been less advantageous to Muslims who were more limited, because they could be accused of losing the Muslim faith.

There were several reasons why non-Muslims would prefer the Islamic kadi courts instead of the courts of their own religion. First, as Najwa Al-Qattan explains, the Muslim courts' efficiency and reliability was appreciated by non-Muslims. As argued by Halil Inalcik in his work on the Ottoman Empire, this refutes the Weberian assumption that kadi justice in the Islamic system was not rational nor predictable (Inalcik 1973, p. 75; Barkey 2013, p. 91). Second, the decisions of the kadi courts incorporated religious, secular and customary traditions and practices, so Jews and Christians felt that the court respected their norms. Third, transactions and agreements involving property registered by the kadi courts were less likely to be contested by Muslims. This made the kadi courts particularly relevant to traders, merchants or others who had disputes over property. Law suits over trade or other kinds of property conflicts between Muslims and non-Muslims and among non-Muslims themselves were frequently brought to kadi courts.

The question is why so many Jews and Christians litigated private matters in the Islamic courts, as such cases fell under the jurisdiction of their own courts (Al-Qattan 1999, p. 433). Bruce Masters has suggested that Christian women would use the kadi courts to start divorce proceedings against their husbands (Masters 2001, pp. 34–35). Similar conclusions have been drawn by Al-Qattan in her study on eighteenth- and nineteenth-century Damascus. She found that Jewish and Christian men and women frequently went to the kadi courts to deal with issues concerning marriage, divorce and inheritance. The Muslim courts provided Christian and Jewish women opportunities of divorce that were not available to them according to their own rules. Moreover, they sometimes also preferred the Muslim rules regarding dowry, inheritance or support after divorce (Al-Qattan 1999). Barkey, however, is less convinced that such actions by non-Muslims were motivated by free choice and personal interest. She admits personal motives might have played a role but believes that most law suits were motivated by 'internalised cultural messages' about the legitimacy of the Islamic courts. She argues that it is important to look at the specific context of Ottoman cities, in which kadi courts represented the power and legitimacy of the Ottoman state and the Muslim faith on a local level. In order to maintain social order and legitimise state power, kadi courts incorporated rules and customs of both Muslim and non-Muslim subjects of the Ottoman Empire. As Barkey concludes: 'The Muslim's court attraction was based on its message of power and domination but also on its practice of justice' (Barkey 2013, p. 97–99).

In sum, studies of legal pluralities in colonial and cultural diverse societies demonstrate that between 1600 and 1900 various social and religious groups, including women, made use of the legal options available to them. Such choices might in part reflect the legal power of (colonial) authorities, but as court cases show, legal pluralistic systems also offered people agency and the opportunity to select alternatives that served their interests best.

Comparing uses of justice globally

How can notions of uses of justice and legal pluralism be used in a comparative and global way? Weberian concepts about 'the West and the Rest' have led to elaborate debates about differences between Europe and Asia with regard to sustained economic growth, since the work of Kenneth Pomeranz often referred to as 'The Great Divergence' (Pomeranz 2000). These debates include fundamental differences between legal systems in Europe and Asia and suppositions that China's lack of civil societies may have contributed to the divergence in economic growth (Vries 2015; Rowe 2012). However, such studies seldom include comparative legal history.

As the works of Matthew Sommer and Philip Huang have demonstrated, Weberian notions of Asian legal systems rather led to biased assumptions about the Chinese justice system and accessibility of the Chinese courts in the Ming (1368–1644) and Qing (1644–1912) period (Huang 2002; Sommer 2013). The Weberian paradigm has tempted historians to focus too much on modernisation, while ignoring any kind of change that *did* happen in China. Sommer argues that 'such approaches may ultimately tell us more about how some scholars fantasise about the West than about Qing itself' (Sommer 2013, p. 118). A more fruitful approach has been offered by Huang, who identified three realms in the Chinese justice system during the Qing period, which operated according to different principles and procedures. The first and most often used type of justice was the 'informal realm' of mediation by local notables. The second form of justice was the 'formal realm' of the county *yamen* court that handled law suits according to the Qing code in formal court hearings. The third realm was an in-between form of justice, in which litigants would file lawsuits while continuing negotiation outside the court through mediation (Huang 1996, 2001; Sommer 2013). Whether this system reflected an integrated justice structure or that different realms represented opposite forms of law (formal law of the imperial state versus informal dispute regulation based on customary norms) is still under debate. The studies of Bradly Reed, Christopher Isett, Sommer and Huang himself seem to suggest that in many cases *yamen* courts adjusted their decisions to local social practices and norms, instead of strictly enforcing the Qing code (Sommer 2013). To what extent Chinese people made use of the various forms of law when settling their disputes is a question that remains unanswered yet (Hinchliffe 2013).

What the case of Qing China above all shows is how difficult it is to make helpful comparisons between legal systems in various parts of the world. In a review article, the editor of *Comparative Legal History* Seán Patrick Donlan argues that comparative analyses might help legal historians to understand respective legal systems, to test hypotheses and to explain changes across time and geographical space. However, he acknowledges that the work of most comparative legal historians centre around European or Western cases. For Donlan, the value of comparative analyses lies in the disentanglement of various legal norms and non-legal social orders (Donlan 2010; 2014). His approach links up to the uses of justice and legal pluralism debates as discussed above, but leaves open the question of how legal historians can successfully apply comparative methods in a global world.

The most important conditions for comparative studies are extensive knowledge of legal sources and of the local contexts in which justice systems have developed. But, even if sources are globally accessible, very few historians have the language skills and depth of knowledge that is needed to compare complex justice systems in various parts of the world. As the Qing case demonstrates, big comparisons easily produce European centric assumptions and misunderstandings about legal systems outside Europe. There are exceptions, such as Marie Seong-Hak Kim who adopted a comparative approach by looking at the legal systems in China, Japan and Taiwan to find out how those jurisdictions impacted Korean law. Whereas most Western studies emphasise coercion under colonial rule, Kim shows that the Chinese Great Ming Code was adopted willingly as a form of self-colonisation. In addition, Koreans seem to apply Confucian ideals far stricter than the Chinese did (Kim 2012; Chen 2013). Other legal historians adopted a global approach, using various case studies to explore global legal processes and the interaction of various legal institutions and practices (Berman 2007; Halpérin 2014). Yet, most legal historians lack the availability of sources and the skills to undertake a similar research project.

International collaborative research projects might solve these problems, provided that researchers ask the same questions, use the same definitions and categories, and adopt the same methodological approach. David Ibbetson pleads for such collaborations, though here again, most comparative research projects on legal history focus on comparisons within Europe (Ibbetson 2012, 2013). A good recent example of such an approach is the book *Cultures of Conflict Resolution in Early Modern Europe* edited by Stephen Cummins and Laura Kounine. Their volume shows the broad variety of contexts and everyday practices of conflict resolution in various European regions. In his afterword Stuart Caroll expresses the wish that legal historians stay focused on John Bossey's 'idea of a social history which would be a history of actual people' (Caroll 2016; Bossey 1983).

The recent volume by Lauren Benton and Richard J. Ross, *Legal Pluralism and Empires, 1500–1850*, does look at pluralistic justice systems in different places across the world. Benton and Ross aim to shift the study of legal pluralisms from conceptual debates to actual practices of jurisdictional conflicts. The contributions to their volume cover the French, British, Spanish, Dutch and Ottoman empires and show vivid examples of how legal pluralism was conceived and practised. As the focus lies on the political imagination, the studies examine polities across empires, the construction of imperial jurisdictions and the representation of legal pluralism. The articles of Linda M. Rupert on slaves and jurisdiction in the early modern Caribbean and the one by Karen Barkey on the Ottoman Empire also demonstrate how slaves and immigrants could take advantage of legal plurality (Barkey 2013, Rupert 2013, see also Fatah-Black, 2017). Overall however, the contributions to the highly valuable volume of Benton and Ross pay much less attention to the everyday use by people of pluralistic legal norms and orders. Our volume on *The Uses of Justice in Global Perspective 1600–1900* is a first attempt to fill the gap in legal history, as it focuses on the use of justice by actual people across the globe.

Scope and content of the volume

The volume intends to bring the scholarship on the uses of justice and legal pluralism between 1600 and 1900 a step further in two ways: (1) by adopting a global approach to bottom-up processes (2) by focusing on everyday practices of uses of justice in Europe, Asia and the Americas.

The concept of 'uses of justice' has not yet been examined in a globally comparative way. This volume offers contextualised studies, framed in a historiographical framework that bridges the divide between socio-legal historians and political and economic historians. Although the latter have identified legal systems as an important explanatory variable in understanding varying development paths across the globe, their focus has been mainly on formal forums of conflict resolution, and as a result the presence of Western institutions has come to be regarded as crucial for development. Our 'uses of justice' approach allows us to question to what degree such top-down imposed formal institutions were used and how or to what degree bottom-up crafted legal systems were really crucial in allowing for transactions.

The essays in this volume have been arranged geographically and cover the various topics that have been discussed in this introduction with diverse emphases. The essays on Western European cases as well as the article of Bianca Premo on the Spanish world especially engage with the topical debate on the uses of justice. Tomàs Mantecón offers a discussion of the concept of 'infrajustice' to reconsider older, teleological interpretations of the early modern Spanish legal system. In historiography, Spanish justice has been depicted as weak, considering the many civil cases that remained unresolved, and a criminal justice system that brought into play orchestrated cruelty so as to deter crime. Mantecón asserts that examination of judicial practice offers another picture of Spanish justice, where local judges – who perhaps lacked knowledge of formal law – successfully mediated and arbitrated conflicts between neighbours, by building on communal ideas of justice. His essay calls for attention to the peripheral areas of the law, where the state and society interacted and influenced processes of modernisation. His reading of Spanish legal history is reinforced by Bianca Premo's analysis of the way litigants engaged courts in a semi-formal manner in the Spanish Empire, thus entering an area of the law contemporaries commonly denoted *lo extrajudicial*. Premo stresses the extensiveness of this sphere of legal practice that was interactive with formal law. To describe manifold examples of such legal practices, she draws on eighteenth-century archival traces of court cases that never went further than the initial stages of a trial, as such cases are most likely to reveal ordinary litigants' legal practices. These cases are not to be considered as external to legal history, as has often been done, but as an integral part of it. Her research persuasively calls into question strict conceptual divisions between 'native' and 'modern' and between 'law' and 'society', that pertain to a myth of modernity.

To elaborate the concept of 'uses of justice', van Meeteren and Vermeesch discuss the usage of a wide range of conflict-settling forums in the late-seventeenth-century Dutch city of Leiden. They describe how the late-sixteenth-century city government, confronted with sudden demographic growth, made efforts to institute infrajudicial institutions and encourage extrajudicial institutions to serve as shifters to handle some of the rising number of conflicts. Analysis of the actual usage of the various forums shows how litigants often ignored the envisioned order in which inhabitants were first and foremost expected to speak to neighbourhood supervisors, before turning to the Commission for Neighbourly Disputes, the Peacemakers or the court of aldermen. Contrary to the arrangement intended by the city government, many litigants used the court of aldermen as a first-instance court and ignored the requirement to first try and reconcile before the Peacemakers. On the other hand, analysis of notarial documents, and notably so-called attestations, in addition shows how a mass of conflicts never reached the urban law court.

That court, however, was vastly important to interpersonal conflicts, even if it did not intervene, as the mere threat of a formal lawsuit had an impact on adversaries. All in all, van Meeteren and Vermeesch show how litigants made their own choices in their legal dealings, and thereby helped to shape the urban institutions for conflict settlement. The article by Katherine Godwin on early-sixteenth-century Rouen delves deeper into the vital role of notaries in conflict settlement to reconsider the place of law courts in the legal system and in society at large. Her study calls for broadening the standard set of sources utilised when studying the legal system, since the role of formal law courts in resolving disputes was comparatively small. After having discussed formal legal procedures based on 40 cases that were waged during the year 1510, Godwin shifts attention to a sample of 210 notarial documents that performed important roles on conflict settlement, both before and after the urban court had stepped in. She asserts that notarial records should be read alongside civil court records to understand the practice of civil disputes, and appreciate its notable fluidity.

The importance of non-governmental, informal forums for conflict settlement is, however, not confined to Western Europe. In his essay, Philip Huang reconsiders the Sinitic justice system, and emphasises the vastness of informal civil justice in China under the Qing dynasty. He corrects the common misapprehension that Chinese law only involved criminal law by asserting that such dominance of penal law thrived on a massive informal system that dealt with civil disputes. The formal system only stepped in when informal mediation had failed. Formal and informal justice systems were complementary and jointly made up a comprehensive property rights justice system. As social mediation did not always succeed at settling disputes, a growing number of civil provisions were included in codified law after the Tang dynasty, as responses to social change and practical need. This new understanding of the Sinitic justice system in the past centuries also helps us to reconsider the historic continuities between Qing and Republican law. Huang's essay convincingly shows how examination of legal practice is necessary for looking beyond official representations and moralistic discourses of the law.

The topic of access to justice is especially at the fore in the articles of Elizaveta Blagodeteleva on the Russian case, and Nadeera Rupesinghe on the case of eighteenth-century Sri Lanka. Blagodeteleva discusses the role lawyers played as intermediaries between the general public and the law in the context of late-nineteenth-century Russia and suggests that the communication with lawyers then constituted an important element of the popular experience of law in the metropolitan areas of the Russian Empire. She focuses on complaints of clients against their sworn attorneys to expose popular litigiousness in late-nineteenth-century Russia, and finds that litigants from all walks of life were rather knowledgeable about the law and used it for resolving everyday conflicts. In addition, people of diverse social backgrounds showed similar attitudes in their dealings with legal practitioners. Nadeera Rupesinghe examines indigenous usage of a colonial law court, the Landraad, in Galle, a Dutch-controlled region in southern Sri Lanka, during the late eighteenth century. Using a sample of 99 cases involving 243 litigants in the years 1778–1779, as well as a sample of 264 witnesses during the years 1779–1781, she uncovers that litigation relating to land issues dominated the Landraad caseload brought by Sinhalese, and that especially litigants who lived close by the court were inclined to take recourse to it. Nonetheless, quite a few litigants and witnesses appeared to have crossed considerable distances to court. It also appears that the male-dominated Landraad did not scare away female litigants. About a quarter of litigants involved in land litigation were women, who were less legally subordinated to their husbands as compared to their counterparts in Holland. They, however, scarcely appeared before the court as witnesses, as the Landraad considered their word less convincing. Lower social groups habitually made use of the court, but were similarly less active as witnesses.

Legal pluralism, lastly, is at the core of the contributions by Alicia Schrikker and Dries Lyna on early modern Ceylon; by Donald Fyson on eighteenth-century Quebec; and by Alexandr Osipian on early modern Poland. The latter examines the functioning of Armenian courts in the Polish juridical landscape and reconsiders longstanding interpretations of declining Armenian judicial autonomy, by bringing the actions and the choices of ordinary Armenians into the equation. By observing legal pluralism from below, Osipian goes beyond the mere examination of competing Christian and Armenian elites, and exposes the impact of less powerful litigants. His examination of Armenian courts in three diverse urban contexts shows the tensions, interactions and jurisdictional conflicts between city governments, the Polish king, the Armenian elites and ordinary Polish and Armenian litigants. Some Armenian courts appeared to lose clientele because the so-called *Magdeburg* jurisdiction was often more attractive. Ordinary Armenians thus made other choices than their elders would have liked them to, and thus impacted juridical infrastructures. The essay by Alicia Schrikker and Dries Lyna provides a discussion of the striking interweaving of legal pluralism and everyday legal practice in the eighteenth-century Dutch colonial context. By considering a range of Ceylonese (Sri Lankan) cases, their text provides a research agenda regarding the analysis of the everyday interactions of local populations with colonial normative institutions, which acted as social arenas. These institutions developed in interaction with established local legal practices. For instance, the bureaucratisation of colonial institutions – including the progressive registration of people and property, and a growing emphasis on written over oral evidence in court – tapped into existing local traditions of registering deeds and using them in interpersonal disputes. Use of Dutch colonial institutions appears to have been a strategy of locals to settle local disputes. A sample of cases that were waged at the Raad van Justitie in Colombo between 1758 and 1788 indicates how at least a third involved parties that were not (directly) employed by the VOC. Schrikker and Lyna emphasise the notable agency of Sinhalese to adopt foreign justice systems to further their own interests. Donald Fyson, lastly, examines legal pluralism in Quebec, after the British conquest, resulting in the hybridisation of law involving the intermingling of indigenous, French and English legal traditions. Whereas such hybridisation has been extensively evidenced in the area of civil law, legal pluralism in criminal legal procedures has been understudied and even negated. Fyson therefore considers legal pluralism in criminal legal practice from below, by discussing four topics: the adaptation of English laws and institutions to a French colony; the influence of French norms on English penal practices; the progressive abolition of special legal status for Quebec's Indigenous peoples; and the influence of American legal precepts and norms. It appears that whereas the normative context suggests the dominance of English criminal law, examination of daily legal practices evidences the hybrid nature of criminal law, and the flexible ways it was used or done without by indigenous or *Canadien* inhabitants.

The different articles in the volume are fairly diverse in terms of thematic approach, and geographical and chronological delimitation. They, however, all examine the uses of justice from daily practice, and from the perspective of the users of justice systems across the globe in the years between 1600 and 1900. As such, the volume hopes to offer valuable contributions to current debates on socio-legal history across the globe.

Notes

1 The idea was first published in a German-language article (Dinges 2000, pp. 503–544). Based on this article Dinges introduced the concept in English in 2004 (Dinges 2004).
2 For a state of the art see:Vermeesch 2015a, pp. 210–216.
3 See for instance: (Kagan 1981; Sharpe 1985; Brooks 1986, 1998). For an overview of the literature see:Vermeesch 2015a, pp. 208–216.
4 This historiography has been discussed extensively in:Vermeesch 2015b.
5 See for this debate: Benton and Ross 2013, pp. 3–7; Halliday 2013, pp. 262–267.
6 See for instance the volume of Benton and Ross (2013). For contemporary examples, see the articles in the *Journal of Legal Pluralism.*

References

Al-Qattan, N. (1999). Dhimmis in the Muslim court: legal autonomy and religious discrimination. *International Journal of Middle East Studies*, 31(3), pp. 429–444.

Barkey, K. (2013). Aspects of legal pluralism in the Ottoman Empire. In: L. Benton and R.J. Ross, eds., *Legal Pluralism and Empires, 1500–1850.* New York: NYU press, pp. 83–107.

Benton, L. (2002). *Law and Colonial Cultures: Legal Regimes in World History, 1400–1900.* Cambridge.

Benton, L. and Ross, R.J. (2013). Empires and legal pluralism: jurisdiction, sovereignty, and political imagination in the early modern world. In: L. Benton and R.J. Ross, eds., *Legal Pluralism and Empires, 1500–1850.* New York: NYU press, pp. 1–17.

Berman, Paul S. (2007) Global legal pluralism. *Southern Californian Law Review*, 80, pp. 1155–1238.

Bodde, Derk and Morris, Clarence (1967). *Law in Imperial China: exemplified by 190 Ch'ing Dynasty cases.* Cambridge.

Bossey, J., ed. (1983). *Disputes and Settlements: Law and Human Relation in the West,* Cambridge: Cambridge University Press.

Brooks, C.W. (1986). *Pettyfoggers and Vipers of the Commonwealth: the 'Lower Branch' of the Legal Profession in Early Modern England.* Cambridge: Cambridge University Press.

Brooks, C.W. (1998). *Lawyers, Litigation and English Society since 1450.* London: The Hambledon Press.

Burghartz, Susanna (2004). Ordering discourse and society: moral politics, marriage and fornication during the Reformation and the Confessionalisation Process in Germany and Switzerland. In: H. Roodenburg and P. Spierenburg, eds., *Social Control in Europe. Volume 1, 1500–1800.* Columbus OH: The Ohio State University Press, pp. 78–98.

Buxbaum, D. (1971). Some aspects of the civil procedure and practice at the trial level in Tanshui and Hsinchu from 1789 to 1895. *Journal of Asian Studies*, 30(2), pp. 255–279.

Caroll, S. (2016). Afterword. In: Stephen Cummins and Laura Kounine, eds., *Cultures of Conflict Resolution in Early Modern Europe.* Farnham: Ashgate, 2016, pp. 281–287.

Castan, Nicole. (1980). *Justice et répression en Languedoc à l'Époque des Lumières.* Paris.

Castiglione, C. (2005). *Patrons and Adversaries: Nobles and Villagers in Italian Politics, 1640–1760.* Oxford.

Champion, W.A. (1997). Recourse to law and the meaning of the great litigation decline 1650–1750. In C.W. Brooks, ed., *Communities and courts in Britain 1150–1900.* London: A&C Black, pp. 179–198.

Chen, L. (2013). Book review. *Comparative Legal History*, 1(2), pp. 277–281.

Cliche, M.-A. (1988). Filles-mères, familles et société sous le Régime français, *Histoire Sociale*, 21, pp. 39–69.

Denys, Catherine (2010). The development of police forces in Urban Europe in the eighteenth century. *Journal of Urban History*, 36(3), pp. 332–344.

Dinges, M. (2000). Justiznutzungen als sozialle Kontrolle in der Frühen Neuzeit. In: A. Blauert and G. Schwerhoff, eds., *Kriminalitätsgeschichte: Beiträge zur Sozial- und Kulturgeschichte der Vormoderne.* Konstanz: Universitätsverlag Konstanz.

Dinges, M. (2004). The uses of justice as a form of social control in early modern Europe. In: H. Roodenburg and P. Spierenburg, eds., *Social Control in Europe. Volume 1, 1500–1800.* Columbus OH: Ohio State University Press, pp. 159–175.

Donlan, S.P. (2010). Histories of hybridity: a problem, a primer, a plea, and a plan (of sorts). In: E. Cashin-Ritaine, S.P. Donlan and M. Sychold, eds., *Comparative Law and Hybrid Legal Traditions.* Basel: Schulthess, pp. 141–160.

Donlan, S.P. (2014). Review article. Comparative legal histories, pluralities, and empires. *Comparative Legal History*, 2(2), pp. 325–334.

Durkheim, E. (1997 [1893]). *The division of labour in society* (ed. 1997). New York: Free Press.

Eibach, J. (2007). Der Kampf um die Hose und die Justiz – Ehekonflikte in Frankfurt im 18. Jahrhundert. In S. Kesper-Biermann and D. Klippel, eds., *Kriminalität in Mittelalter und Früher Neuzeit: Soziale, rechtliche, philosophische und literarische Aspekte.* Wiesbaden: Harrassowitz, pp. 167–188

Evans, T. (2005). *Unfortunate Objects: Lone Mothers in Eighteenth-Century London.* Basingstoke: Palgrave Macmillan.

Farge, Arlette (1986). *La vie fragile: Violence, Pouvoirs et Solidarités à Paris au XVIIIe Siècle.* Paris.

Fatah-Black, K. (2017). The usurpation of legal roles by Suriname's governing council, 1669–1816. *Comparative Legal History*, 5(2), pp. 243–261.

Forret, Jeff (2015). *Slave Against Slave: Plantation Violence in the Old South.* Baton Rouge.

Garnot, B. (2000). Justice, infrajustice, parajustice et extra justice dans la France d'ancien régime. *Crime, History and Societies*, 4, pp. 103–120.

Garnot, B., ed. (1996). *L'infrajudiciaire du Moyen Âge à l'époque contemporaine. Actes du colloque de Dijon 5–6 octobre 1995.* Dijon: Editions Universitaires de Dijon.

Grey, Drew (2009). *Crime, Prosecution and Social Relations: the Summary Courts of the City of London in the Late Eighteenth Century*. Basingstoke.

Griffiths, A. (2002). Legal pluralism. In: R. Banakar and M. Travers, eds., *An Introduction to Law and Social Theory*. Portland, OR: Hart Publishing, pp. 289–310.

Griffiths, A. (2011). Pursuing legal pluralism: the power of paradigms in a global world. *Journal of Legal Pluralism and Unofficial Law*, 43, pp. 173–202.

Griffiths, A. (2013). Reviewing legal pluralism. In: R. Banakar and M. Travers, eds., *Law and Social Theory*. Portland, OR: Hart Publishing, pp. 269–286.

Griffiths, John (1986). What is legal pluralism? *Journal of Legal Pluralism*, 24, pp. 1–55.

Habermas, R. (1992). Frauen und Männer im Kampf um Leib, Ökonomie und Recht. Zur Beziehungder Geschlechter im Frankfurt der Frühen Neuzeit. In R.van Dülmen, ed., *Dynamik der Tradition*. Frankfurt: Fischer, pp. 109–136.

Halliday, P.D. (2013). Law's histories: pluralism, pluralities, diversity. In: L. Benton and R.J. Ross, eds., *Legal Pluralism and Empires, 1500–1850*. New York: NYU press, pp. 261–277.

Halpérin, J.-L. (2014). *Five legal revolutions since the 17th century: an analysis of a global legal history*. Heidelberg: Springer.

Härter, K. (2012). Konfliktregulierung im Umfeld frühneuzeitlicher Strafgerichte: Das Konzept der Infrajustiz in der historischen Kriminalitätsforschung, *Kritische Vierjahresschrift für Gesetzgebung und Rechtsprechung*, 95, pp. 130–144.

Hayhoe, J. (2005). Illegitimacy, inter-generational conflict and legal practice in eighteenth-century northern Burgundy. *Journal of Social History*, 38, pp. 673–684.

Heijden, M. van der (2004). Punishment vs reconciliation: marriage control in sixteenth- and seventeenth-century Holland. In: H. Roodenburg and P. Spierenburg, eds., *Social Control in Europe. Volume 1, 1500–1800*. Columbus OH: Ohio State University Press, pp. 55–77.

Heijden, M. Van der (2012). *Civic Duty: Public Services in the Early Modern Low Countries*. Newcastle upon Tyne: Cambridge Scholars Publishing.

Heijden, M. van der (2013). Women, violence and urban justice in Holland, c. 1600–1838, *Crime, History & Societies*, 1(2), pp. 71–100.

Heijden, M. van der (2016). *Women and Crime in Early Modern Holland*. Leiden.

Hinchliffe, S.A. (2013). Mediating foreign norms and local imperatives: intellectual property 'law' between the East and the West, from Imperial China to 'modern' times. *Comparative Legal History*, 1(2) pp. 155–185.

Hindle, Steve. (2000). *The State and Social Change in Early Modern England, 1550–1640*. Basingstoke, Hampshire.

Huang, P. (1996). *Civil Justice in China: Representation and Practice in the Qing*. Palo Alto: Stanford University Press.

Huang, P. (2001). *Code, Custom, and Legal Practice in China: the Qing and the Republic Compared*. Palo Alto: Stanford University Press.

Huang, P. (2002). Development of involution of eighteenth-century Britain and China? A review of Kenneth Pomeranz's *The Great Divergence*: China, Europe, and the making of the modern world economy. *The Journal of Asian Studies*, 16(2) pp. 501–538.

Ibbetson, D. (2012). Comparative legal history: a methodology. In: A. Musson and C. Stebbings, eds., *Making Legal History: Approaches and Methodologies*. Cambridge: Cambridge University Press.

Ibbetson, D. (2013). The challenges of comparative legal history. *Comparative Legal History*, 1(1) pp. 1–11.

Inalcik, H. (1973). *The Ottoman Empire: the Classical Age, 1300–1600.* New Rochelle NY: Aristide Caratzas.

Ingram, M. (1999). History of sin or history of crime? The Regulation of Morality in England, 1450–1750. In: H. Schilling and L. Behrisch, eds., *Institutionen, Instrumente und Akteure sozialer Kontrolle und Disziplinierung im frühneuzeitlichen Europa.* Frankfurt am Main: Vittoria Klosterman.

Kagan, R. (1981). *Lawsuits and Litigants in Castile, 1500–1700.* Chapel Hill.

Kaiser, C. (1980). The deflation in the volume of litigation at Paris in the 18th century and the waning of the old judicial order. *European Studies Review*, 10, pp. 309–336.

Kim, Marie Seong-Hak (2012). *Law and Custom in Korea: Comparative Legal History.* Cambridge: Cambridge University Press.

Le Bailly, M.C. (2011). Langetermijntrends in de rechtspraak bij de gewestelijke hoven van justitie in de Noordelijke Nederlanden van ca. 1450 tot ca. 1800. *Pro Memorie*, 13, pp. 30–67.

Lenman, B. and Parker, G. (1980). The state, the community and the criminal law in early modern Europe. In: V. Gatrell, B. Lenman and G. Parker, eds., *Crime and the Law. The Social History of Crime in Western Europe since 1500.* London: Europa Publications Limited, pp. 11–49.

Masters, B. (2001). *Christians and Jews in the Ottomon Arab World: the Roots of Sectarianism.* Cambridge: Cambridge University Press.

Merry, S.E. (1988). Legal pluralism. *Law & Society Review*, 22(5), pp. 869–896.

Muldrew, C. (1998). *The economy of obligation: the culture of credit and social relations in early modern England.* Houndsmills: Palgrave Macmillan.

Ogilvie, S. (2006). 'So that every subject knows how to behave': social disciplining in early modern Bohemia, *Comparative Studies in Society and History*, 12, pp. 38–78.

Olcina Pita, V. (2017). Commercial litigation across religious borders: rendering justice for Valencian merchants in fifteenth-century North Africa and Granada. *Comparative Legal History*, 5(1), pp. 88–106.

Outhwaite, R. (2006). *The rise and fall of the English ecclesiastical courts, 1500–1800.* Cambridge: Cambridge University Press.

Pomeranz, K. (2000). *The Great Divergence: China, Europe, and the Making of the Modern World Economy.* Princeton: Princeton University Press.

Ranieri, F. (1985). *Recht und Gesellschaft im Zeitalter der Rezeption: eine rechts- und sozialgeschichtliche Analyse der Tätigkeit des Reichskammergerichts im 16. Jahrhundert.* Cologne: Böhlau Verlag.

Roodenburg, H. and Spierenburg, P. (2004). An introduction. In: H. Roodenburg and P. Spierenburg, eds., *Social Control in Europe. Volume 1, 1500–1800.* Columbus OH: Ohio State University Press, pp. 1–24.

Rowe, W.T. (2012). *China's Last Empire: the Great Qing.* Cambridge, Massachusetts.

Rupert, L.M. (2013). 'Seeking the Water of Baptism': fugitive slaves and imperial jurisdiction in the early modern Carribean. In: L. Benton and R.J. Ross, eds., *Legal Pluralism and Empires, 1500–1850.* New York: NYU press, pp. 199–231.

Schmidt, A. and Kamp, J. (2018). 'Getting justice': a comparative perspective on illegitimacy and the use of justice in Holland and Germany, 1600–1800. *Journal of Social History*, 51(4).

Schwerhoff, G. (2004). Social control of violence, violence as social control: the case of early modern Germany. In: H. Roodenburg and P. Spierenburg, eds., *Social Control in Europe. Volume 1, 1500–1800.* Columbus OH: The Ohio State University Press, pp. 220–246.

Shahar, I. (2008). Legal pluralism and the study of the shari'a courts. *Islamic Law & Society*, 15, pp. 112–142.

Sharpe, J.A. (1985). The people and the law. In: B. Reay, ed., *Popular Culture in Seventeenth-Century England*. London: St. Martins Pr, pp. 244–270.

Shoemaker, Robert (1991). *Prosecution and punishment: petty crime and the law in London and rural Middlesex, c. 1660–1725*. Cambridge.

Soman, A. (1982). L'infra-justice à Paris d'après les archives notariales. *Histoire, économie et société*, 3, pp. 369–375.

Sommer, M.H. (2013). The field of Qing legal history. In: Z. Haihui et al., eds., *A Scholarly Review of Chinese Studies in North America*. Ann Arbor: Association for Asian Studies, pp. 113–132.

Stretton, T. (1998). *Women Waging Law in Elizabethan England*. Cambridge: Cambridge University Press.

Tamanaha, B.Z. (2008). Understanding legal pluralism: past to present, local to global. *Sydney Law Review*, 29, pp. 375–411.

Vermeesch, G. (2015a). The social composition of plaintiffs and defendants in the Peacemaker court, Leiden, 1750–54. *Social History*, 40(2), pp. 208–229.

Vermeesch, G. (2015b). Reflections on the relative accessibility of law courts in early modern Europe. *Crime, History & Societies*, 19(2), pp. 53–76.

Vermeesch, G. (2016). The legal agency of single mothers: lawsuits over illegitimate children and the uses of legal aid to the poor in the Dutch town of Leiden (1750–1810). *Journal of Social History*, 50(1), pp. 51–73.

Vries, Peer. (2015). *State, Economy and the Great Divergence: Great Britain and China, 1680s–1850s*. London.

Walker, G. (2003). *Crime, Gender and Social Order in Early Modern England*. Cambridge: Cambridge University Press.

Weber, Max (1978 [1922]). *Economy and Society: an Outline of Interpretative Sociology*. Berkeley, California.

Wollschläger, C. (1990). Civil litigation and modernisation: the work of the municipal courts of Bremen, Germany, in five centuries, 1549–1985. *Law and Society Review*, 24, pp. 261–82.

Woodman, G.R. (1998). Ideological combat and social observation. *Journal of Legal Pluralism and Unofficial Law*, 30(42), pp. 21–59.

Wrightson, Keith (1980). Two concepts of order: justices, constables and jurymen in seventeenth-century England. In: John Brewer and John Styles. Eds. *An ungovernable people: the English and their law in the seventeenth and eighteenth centuries*. London: pp. 21–46.

Zemon Davis, N. (2011). Judges, masters and diviners: slaves' experience of criminal justice in colonial Surinam. *Law and History Review*, 29(4), pp. 928.

2

THE SINITIC JUSTICE SYSTEM, PAST AND PRESENT – IN A GLOBAL PERSPECTIVE[1]

Philip C.C. Huang

Introduction

The aim of this chapter is to attempt a broad overarching view of the Sinitic justice system, past and present. This is really my first sustained attempt at such a thing since completing my three-volume study of China's civil justice system of the last four hundred plus years. I use the term and concept of 'justice system' because 'system' is broader than 'institutions' and 'codes'; it includes also how things actually worked. And 'justice system' is broader than 'legal system', because the latter tends to focus on the formal institutions and codes, to the neglect of the informal.

My two main foils in this chapter are what I consider to be two common misconceptions about the Sinitic justice system: one misconception is that it is mainly a criminal justice system, with little or no attention to civil justice; and the other, that the Sinitic tradition today is largely dead and irrelevant, replaced by the wholesale copying of Western laws. I discuss these misconceptions by addressing six points about the Sinitic justice system: (1) the central importance of societal mediation in the Chinese justice system; (2) how the justice system as a whole changed over time from interactions between the informal and formal parts of the system; (3) the essential continuities in the system, up until today; (4) how the Sinitic justice system gave rise to a larger East Asian justice system; (5) how the informal, semiformal and formal parts of the system operate together in present-day China; and (6), how the Sinitic (and East Asian) legal tradition differs from the Western legal tradition and the problems of comparing and measuring the very different justice systems.

The informal justice system

The first point I want to make has to do with the vast informal civil justice system that operated alongside the criminal justice system, and it has crucially to do with just what 'Confucianization of the [Legalist] law', which took place in the Former Han Dynasty (in the two centuries BC), meant. Past scholarship has emphasized either the addition of Confucian status differentiation to Legalist law (Ch'ü T'ung-tsu [Qu Tongzu] 1961) or the addition of Confucian propriety (*li*) to Legalist law (Ma Xiaohong 2014). I want to point out that what was even more important was the establishment of a vast informal justice system to deal with civil disputes.

For legal history research, what is different about the Qing, the last dynasty spanning roughly the period 1600–1900, is that we have much richer materials (case records) about the actual operation of the justice system than are available for earlier dynasties, materials that permit us to see not just the codified texts of the law, but also judicial practice; at the same time, oral history materials allow us to see the informal justice system not simply in terms of idealized *li* 礼 or 'harmony' 和谐, but its actual operative workings. We can thereby arrive at a truer picture of the entirety of the informal and formal justice systems working together.

We need first to see that the reason traditional codified law could focus 'mainly on punishments' is that it could rely on the immense and effective informal system to deal with the majority of civil disputes among the people. We have rich materials that show us that in the late Qing and the Republic, virtually every community in society had an organized mediation mechanism that dealt with disputes among the people. Generally speaking, mediation was undertaken among the disputants by respected members of the community or kin group, who would intermediate between the two sides and either bring one disputant to admit wrong and apologize or both disputants to compromise and agree on a settlement. Only when such mediations could not resolve a dispute would the formal system enter in. Over time, the successive legal codes added new provisions and adjustments in order to better handle such unresolved disputes.

For example, from the Qin and the Han dynasties on, Chinese society had adopted for more than 2,000 years the custom of equal partition of familial property among sons. From the detailed Qing-period materials, we can see that most families would first divide the family property into equal shares, and then use a system of chance (like drawing lots) to decide which son would get which share, in a process witnessed by kin and or respected community members, with a formal document (specifying land boundaries and house sections) to verify the process. This had long proven to be an effective method of household division. As for codified law, it specified in this connection simply: 'The division of familial property and land. . . , will be in equal portions according to the number of sons', without any mention of punishments (*Da Qing lüli*, Sub-statute 88-1; Xue Yunsheng's (1970) commentary noted: this was in the Ming [1368–1644] code).

We can see from the example of household division that property rights were implicit in custom and in law. Inheritance as well as buying, selling and leasing of land had in fact operated with stability and security across the centuries. (If there were not secure property rights, how could one speak of inheriting, buying-selling and leasing?) To be sure, the Great Qing Code did not express property rights in positive terms but rather only stipulated under the statute 'Stealing and Selling

Land and House' 盗卖田宅 that 'stealing, selling, exchanging, falsely claiming, falsely contriving a price and drawing up a deed, conditionally selling or occupying others' land and house' would all be punished, by degrees of severity according to the amount of land involved (Statute 93). In actual operation, the formal justice system without question in fact protected such 'rights'. We need to see that the formal legal system took the informal justice system as its given precondition; only thus will we be able to understand that the informal and formal systems in fact made up a comprehensive property rights justice system.

This reliance on informal justice was not some 'pre-legal', 'pre-state' or 'primitive' characteristic of the justice system, as some legal scholars have maintained, but was rather a deliberate choice made by the highly developed legal and state system of the Former Han in the two centuries before Christ. Indeed, it might even be seen as a 'post-legal(ist)' formulation. The Confucians thought that the Legalist system was too harsh and too formalistic and procedural in emphasis, and had to be mitigated by Confucian morality, most especially the informal societal mediation system.

Changes in the justice system over time

The second point I want to make is about changes over time of this justice system governed by such a Confucian principle. The preference for society to settle its own civil disputes (minor affairs) does not mean that it always succeeded in doing so – and the state had to intervene when societal mediation failed. And that led to increasing numbers of civil provisions in codified law.

As an example, the multi-generation family was always a Confucian moral ideal. Even so, in real social life, brothers and their wives often had difficulty getting along with each other and needed to divide up the household before the parents died. In the Qing code, we can see that codified law, on the one hand, espoused the moral ideal of the multi-generation family: 'If the grandparents and the parents are alive, and the children-grandchildren should establish a separate household and divide up the property, [they should be] punished by one hundred blows with the heavy bamboo 杖' (Statute 87). However, in light of actual societal needs, later the following provision was added in a sub-statute: 'If the parents permit it, then it should be allowed' (Sub-statute 87-1). We know that the Ming dynasty Code that preceded that of the Qing dynasty already had such a provision. We can see from Qing case records and Republican-period oral history research that household division while the parents were still alive had become common among many families. This example illustrates both the moralized ideal of codified law and its adaptation to social practices. What it illuminates is how the formal and the informal justice systems interacted and worked together.

It was such combining of the informal, mainly civil, and formal, mainly criminal, justice systems that lends concrete substance to the uniting of Confucianism and Legalism in a single justice system. Whether on the level of conceptualization or of actual operation, such coexistence, mutual reinforcement and interactive relationship of the civil and criminal justice systems are the key to the Chinese justice system (as well as to Confucian 'minimalist governance'). If we ignore either part, we cannot fully understand the other.

The informal civil system was conceived as the societal precondition for the formal criminal system. Without it, the Sinitic legal tradition would not have been able to rely 'mainly on punishments for crimes' for its formal law. A failure to grasp this point means we will not be able to understand the true nature of the codified law that focused mainly on crimes and punishments, nor be able to grasp what is truly distinctive about the Sinitic legal tradition.

The view of some scholars that China had no civil law originates from the failure to see the mutually reinforcing and interconnected relationship between the informal justice system and the formal. The Sinitic legal tradition in fact always dealt with large quantities of civil disputes, most of them through societal mediation; when society could not resolve the disputes, the formal system would enter in with its civil provisions. The two together constituted a civil justice system of immense scope.

In the sphere of inheritance, traditional Chinese society observed very strictly both the custom and the statutory law of equal partition by sons, to the extent of effectively eliminating almost any possibility of a father trying to deprive a son of his 'right' to inheritance. Codified law in fact went on to provide that 'without regard to whether the son is born of the wife, the concubine or a maidservant, division will be equal according to the number of sons' (Sub-statute 88-1). We can see among Qing case records multiple examples of birth sons filing suits against adopted sons, and sons of concubines and maidservants against sons of wives, to assert their legal right to inheritance. The fact is, though traditional Chinese law did not have the term 'rights', it in fact had the operative reality of protecting a host of rights, to the extent that no father could really deprive a blood son from inheriting his property.

Only if we consider the entirety of the traditional civil justice system, both its informal and formal parts and both its practice and its discourse, can we comprehend the substantial continuity between the contemporary and the traditional Chinese justice systems. To overlook the modernity of the past and the traditionality of the present is to be unable to grasp either fully. The key to breaking through the artificially constructed walls between the two is not to fall into either simple modernism or simple antiquarianism.

'Confucianization of law' meant also that official representations and discourses of the law tended to be highly moralistic, even if judicial practice actually deviated from those. More specifically, in the Qing code, the statutes, *lü* 律, tended to state the moralistic ideals, while the sub-statutes, *li* 例, tended to be more concrete guides for actual legal practice. The sub-statutes, we might also say, served as intermediators between moral representations/discourses and social reality.

As mentioned above, case records of the Qing period, plus oral history research of the early twentieth century, have enabled us to see how the informal justice system overlapped with and worked in conjunction with the formal justice system.

Minor civil disputes – especially over land boundaries, marriage, buying-selling (including conditional selling, *dian* 典) of land, debts and such – could almost all be resolved through societal mediation. However, there was always a certain number that could not be resolved, when despite the intercession of a middle person both sides stuck to their positions and refused either to apologize or compromise, causing the conflict to exacerbate to the extent of one party taking matters to court to seek coercive government intervention. In those situations, the state had to enter into such disputes. The result was that over the centuries, on the basis of actual legal practice, statutory law in fact came to incorporate more and more civil provisions.

For example, in the five and half centuries of the Ming and Qing dynasties, the law allowed those who were forced by poverty to sell conditionally (*dian*) their land to redeem such land when they became able to do so – this was something that was sanctioned both by popular custom and by the courts, and tells both about popular custom to protect the poor and the (Confucian) moralization of statutory law. The law therefore provided in a statute that 'if the *dian*-holder should find excuses and not allow the redemption of the land, he will be punished by 40 lashes 笞 with the light bamboo' (Statute 95). However, along with socioeconomic changes in the Qing period, land prices in some areas rose continually and some *dian*-makers therefore threatened to redeem their land unless the *dian*-holder made an additional payment (equal to all or part of the difference between the original *dian* price and the current market value, called a *zhaotie* 找贴), and some went so far as to demand such payments repeatedly. In the face of such social phenomena, the law added in 1730 the sub-statute that only 'one such payment will be allowed on the basis of impartial assessment by a middle person' (Sub-statute 95-3), and a further sub-statute in 1753 that where the original *dian* deeds had not specified that the deal was a 'final sale' 绝卖, redemption would be allowed for only a maximum of thirty years (Sub-statute 95-7). Both new sub-statutes had been recommendations made by judicial officials on the basis of experience in judicial practice, and had then been made into law. They are examples of the adding of new sub-statutes as responses to social change and practical need. Societal practice changed as a result. What these two new sub-statutes show is that, when tensions arose between moralistic legal representations and social reality, judicial practice would first be altered to adapt to social change, leading thence to statutory change, and finally also to changes in social practice (for detailed documentation and analysis, see Huang 2001, Chapter 5).

At the same time, only by distinguishing between practice and text can we see how the civil and criminal justice systems interacted. In fact, the main dynamic for change over time in imperial Chinese statutory law came not so much from changes in its fundamental theoretical framework (e.g., combining informal and formal justice), because that had pretty much become fixed by the middle of the Han with the full Confucianization of law, but rather mainly from accumulated experience in judicial practice and the responses positive law made to the needs of practice. In the Qing period, those changes were manifested mostly in the additions of new sub-statutes, even as the statutes themselves remain unchanged.

It was such changes that over time added more and more to the civil content of the Qing code. In the late Qing, under the 'Statutes on Revenue and Household' 户律 section of the code, the four key chapters of 'Household and Corvée' 户役, 'Land and House' 田宅, 'Marriage' 婚姻 and 'Money and Debt' 钱债 contained a total of 46 statutes and 130 sub-statutes (Xue 1970 [1905]; Huang 2001, p. 21), amounting to a civil code of substantial content. Precisely for that reason, the early Republic could, before the completion of the drafting of a new civil code modelled on those of the West, use the revised Qing code's 'portions of effective relevance to civil affairs' 民事有效部分 (after abolishing the penal packaging) as the civil law of the land for twenty years. Herein we can see the continuity between imperial law and Republican civil law. Had the Qing 'criminal' code not included a considerable amount of positive civil law, it would not have been possible for the Republic to use its 'civil portions' of 'effective relevance' as the temporary civil code for two decades.

Essential continuities in the system

The third point I wish to make is that these fundamental characteristics of the justice system have remained down to the present, albeit with significant changes and reconfigurations. We can see this by a quick review of the informal and semiformal justice systems in contemporary China.

The informal justice system of China today consists first of all of the mediations conducted by villagers' mediation committees 村民调解委员会 and urban residents' mediation committees 居民调解委员会, together termed 'people's mediation' 人民调解. In the late reform period of 2005–2009, these committees mediated an average of 10.3 million disputes each year, of which 5.3 million (52 percent) were successfully resolved. To be sure, these committees today are somewhat different from the mediators of the past, who were mainly the informal, respected members of the community, while today's mediation committees include some community cadres. Even so, their work comes very close to the mediations of the past: mediations are basically voluntary, are conducted through third-party intermediaries, and involve little resort to coercive pressures.[2]

Compared to the early reform period, there has not been much absolute increase in the number of disputes but there appears to be a substantial decline in the success rate of mediations, from a very high reported rate of 89 percent earlier to just 52 percent today. This decline in the reported success rate is due in part to the one-sided emphasis on mediation in the Mao Zedong era and the exaggerations in the reported data. At the same time, community mediations of the earlier period had been undertaken mainly by the most important cadres of the community (such as the village party secretary or the village head) who wielded considerable prestige and authority, but today it is done mainly by common (even lowly) cadres and respected community members, so that it is largely or entirely voluntary.

Moreover, given the rise of massive numbers of peasant migrant workers (270 million), most villages have changed from the earlier (traditional and collective era's) tightly-knit 'communities of the familiar' 熟人社会 to today's 'communities of the semi-familiar' 半熟人社会, in which social relations are much more externalized and multifaceted. Not surprisingly, therefore, the success rates of mediation have declined. Even so, there can be no question about the important role that 'people's mediation' still plays today. Of every two disputes, one is resolved by such mediation. This fact alone tells about the continued importance of informal justice today.

Outside of mediations that are purely (or largely) voluntary, there are also semi-formal mediations in which state organs (and state authority) play a role. There are 'administrative mediations' 行政调解, the first of which are mediations undertaken by the legal services entities of basic-level governments, such as the judicial office 司法所 and the legal services office 法律服务所. Those entities still emphasize the voluntary settlement of disputes, but they are governmental or semi-governmental organs and their mediators are either state judicial officials or quasi-officials who wield a certain measure of official authority. These entities also account for a significant number of mediations – an average annual total of 700,000. Precisely because they wield a certain amount of state authority, their reported success rate is high, 90 percent (more below).[3]

Then come the new-style consumer associations that have been organized under the State Administration for Industry and Commerce to meet the needs that have come with the rise of marketization and a consumer society. These too have come to play a fairly large role, handling in 2005–2009 on average 750,000 cases a year, resolving a high proportion of them (89 percent), comparable to the legal services offices of the basic-level governments. This is something that evolved from the interaction between the traditional, completely voluntary mediation system and the modern, revolutionary party-state system. In its actual operations, even though a certain amount of governmental pressure is used, it still aims at resolutions that are acceptable to both the consumer and the producer/manager through its intermediation (Zhu 2011, pp. 408–417).

Then there are the 'Public Security mediations' 治安调解 that involve an even higher degree of intercession of governmental authority, in the Public Security (police) bureaus' mediations of mainly light crimes (beating another and causing light injury, theft, gambling and such). This is a category of considerable size, amounting to 2.47 million cases (29 percent) of the total of 8.40 million cases handled by the Public Security entities each year. Of course, the handling of such cases involves more governmental authority than consumer disputes. Even so, they are not simple matters of adjudging or commanding certain terms of settlement, but rather do attempt to get both sides to agree 'voluntarily', and should be seen as a method of dispute resolution that involves a definite degree of mediation. To be sure, there are also many instances in which 'mediation' serves merely to soften in name what is in reality arbitrary use of police authority.

Finally, there are mediations done by the courts 法院调解, also called judicial mediations 司法调解. Such mediations of course also carry a definite degree of coercion, because they are mostly seen through the lens of statutory laws, and rely to a considerable extent on the authority of the court – all disputants know that if the mediation fails, the same court will go on to adjudicate, which makes the system very different from Western mediation, which insists on the complete separation of the mediatory procedure from the adjudicatory (more below). Even so, actual case examples show that the courts do try as much as possible through the intermediation of the judge to reach a settlement amenable to both sides, especially in cases involving the terms of property settlements in divorce cases, the distribution among brothers (and sisters) of the burden of maintaining parents in their old age, the amount of compensation to be paid in tort cases, the actual arrangements for repaying a debt, the distribution of obligations and liabilities in a contractual dispute and so on (Huang 2010, pp. 204–212). These also make up a large category, with the courts successfully resolving a third (1.68 million) of the average of almost 5 million (4.92 million) civil cases they handle each year.

The key categories of mediation are community mediation, which, we have seen, still resolves one of every two recorded disputes, and court mediation, which resolves one of every three lawsuits. Clearly then, informal justice remains a major dimension of the contemporary Chinese justice system.

The Sinitic and 'East Asian justice system'

The fourth point I wish to make is that the essential features of the informal justice system have remained not just in China, but also in Japan and Korea, to make up a distinctive feature of what might be termed an 'East Asian justice system' closely connected with the Sinitic justice system of the past.

Looking back at history, Japan had already in its Nara (702–810) and Heian (810–1185) periods 'brought in' China's Tang code as the model for its government and justice systems, and adopted Chinese administrative and legal institutions. Later, in the Tokugawa period (1603–1868), it further adopted Song Confucianism (*Shūshigaku* 朱子学 in Japanese) as its ruling ideology and the guide for its justice system. Like China, Japan has over the centuries relied mainly on its community and clan mediation systems to deal with civil disputes among the people – only when such mediations failed would the case enter into the formal system of the state. Also like China, state laws emphasized mainly criminal law and punishments, albeit also with subsidiary civil provisions (Henderson 1965, pp. 48–49, 55, 61).

What was at once similar and dissimilar to the Chinese justice system was that Japan already in its Tokugawa period had established a quite highly formalized (institutionalized and proceduralized) 'conciliation' (*chōtei* 调停) system, requiring that the petition to the shogunate court bear the seal of the village head and the approval of the local *daimyō*, that conciliation be undertaken before adjudication, that conciliations be limited to a maximum of six times and that summary judgment be undertaken only after conciliation had failed. (For detailed analysis and case examples, see Henderson 1965, pp. 131–66.) Those features were not present in its contemporary Qing court system for dealing with 'minor matters', evincing thereby distinctively Japanese characteristics. Nevertheless, the system resembled on the whole what China today calls 'court mediation', which is very different from Western Alternative Dispute Resolution (ADR) mediation that separates out completely the mediation and trial procedures (more below).

Later, in the modern and contemporary periods, the Japanese justice system, in addition to relying still on societal informal mediation as the given precondition of the court system, added to court mediation the distinction between 'mediation [compromise]' (*wakai* 和解) and 'conciliation' (*chōtei* 调停); the former relies mainly on compromise, while the latter includes more of an adjudicatory or didactic content. The disputant/litigant is allowed to opt out of court procedures with mediation to be conducted by a committee, but may also opt to have the judge undertake the mediation. Furthermore, even when involved in either of the two compromise/conciliation procedures, the litigant may still choose at any time to opt out and enter into a trial procedure (Henderson 1965, pp. 183–87). Clearly, the modern-contemporary Japanese system shows both continuities and departures from the Sinitic Tokugawa system of the past.

Today, the incidence of litigation in Japan is far lower than in the United States (just consider the fact that there are 365 attorneys in the United States for every 100,000 people, but only 16 in Japan – the U.S. ratio is 23 times that of Japan; see Magee 2010, Table 1), clearly because of its wide resort to community mediation as well as mediation in all kinds of social-economic entities (Callister and Wall 1997; Wall et al. 1998), and also because of the compromises and conciliations undertaken in the court system (Henderson 1965, pp. 6–12, 37–43, 48–49; Ficks n.d.). When faced with a dispute, the first choice of most Japanese is for mediation, not adjudication. Even after filing a complaint in the court system, twice as many choose the compromise or conciliation paths as opposed to a trial and, among the former, 55 percent are successfully concluded (Baum 2013, pp. 1079–1080; Henderson 1965, pp. 191–201). That is to say, of every two civil cases entering the court system today, one is successfully mediated. This is a ratio even higher than that in present-day China (one out of three), both of them exceeding by a wide margin what mediation has been able to do in most Western countries.

As for Korea, suffice it to say that, like Japan, it early on adopted the justice system of the Sinitic legal tradition as its model and that today societal mediation still plays a major role in its communities and social-economic organizations (see Sohn and Wall 1993; Wall et al., 1998). At the same time, in part due to Confucian influence, in part to the influence of Japanese occupation, court mediation is quite pervasive today.

'East Asian' mediation vs. Western 'Alternative Dispute Resolution'

The fifth point I wish to make is that this East Asian Sinitic legal system was and is often confused with Alternative Dispute Resolution (ADR). The ADR of the West and Chinese mediation are in fact very different systems. First, we need to distinguish within (Western) ADR between that which comes from a simplifying and discounting of the adversarial court system, such as 'arbitration' and 'out-of-court settlements', and that which comes from a rejection of the adversarial system to result in a mediation procedure that is completely separate from the court system. The Council of Europe, for instance, reached agreement already in 1998 on certain basic principles of mediation, requiring that it be completely voluntary, completely separate from the adjudicatory procedure of the courts and that the mediator must not serve as the judge of the court case (Committee of Ministers of the Council of Europe 1998). In the United States, the operative principles of mediation are substantially the same, and the right to file a lawsuit is a constitutional right that may not be obstructed (Kulms 2013, p. 1257, 1283). Such principles completely exclude what is called 'court mediation' in China, as well as the government's resort to the policies of requiring mediation as a prerequisite for court acceptance of a case, or simply removing certain types of cases from the courts' purview.

Some students of ADR have mixed up the two different systems of ADR outlined above: one evolved out of the adversarial court system and operates largely within its framework; the other, by contrast, has come from a rejection of that system and operates outside of it. To mix up the two, calling them both ADR, and then to equate ADR with the very different Chinese informal and semiformal systems, can only lead to serious misunderstandings. We need to examine first the two different strands of ADR, and only then compare them with the Chinese system.

We first look at the Western mediation system that is completely distinct from its court system. In the United States, because mediation laws vary from state to state (see the separate narrative of different state laws and systems in Kulms 2013), and also because of the strictly informal nature of mediation, we are hard put to find systematic statistical data, even less the kinds of nationwide data that we have for China. At present, I am only able to offer the state of Virginia as an example, because it has a particularly well-developed system of court-recommended (but otherwise completely separate) mediation, and hence has fairly systematic data. From those data we can see that of a total of 1.28 million civil cases handled by the state's courts in 2002, those resolved by mediation totalled just 9,457 cases, mainly pertaining to the 'custody, visitation, and support' of children. That is primarily because familial disputes are the most obvious types of cases that cannot be handled or understood simply in a right/wrong adversarial framework. These data mean that only 0.7 percent of all civil cases were mediated to resolution, very different from China (Virginia Judicial System 2003, Part A, pp. 50, 64, 112, 116, 131; for a more detailed discussion, see Huang 2010, pp. 220–21).

The state of California, considered one of the most advanced in its development of mediation, tells a similar story. Custody, visitation and support rights in divorce disputes are the major area; there is also some use in some small-claims cases, (adversarial proceedings over) bankruptcy, and mortgage foreclosures (Kulms 2013, pp. 1258, 1299–1305). There is little in the way of community-based mediation; the main form of mediation has been 'court annexed' (though conducted entirely separately) mediation (Kulms 2013, p. 1258). Overall, the use of mediation is clearly severely limited by the requirement that it be strictly voluntary; it plays only a very minor role in the total justice system, a far cry from the situation in China.

In addition to mediation, some researchers include under ADR American out-of-court-settlements, and on that basis compare it to China's mediation (for example, Hopt and Steffek 2013, p. 95; Subrin and Woo 2006, Chapter 10). In actuality, US out-of-court settlements are mainly the result of litigants and their attorneys who, after entering into the court process, basing themselves on calculations of litigation costs and 'risks' (i.e., prospects for victory or defeat), reach an agreement to settle, in a situation and process very different from mediation. To be sure, Marc Galanter's research shows that many judges intervene to some degree outside of the court 'in the shadow of the law', to help guide or facilitate the process of such settlements (Galanter 1985). But such out-of-court-settlements are very different in nature – in operative principles and mechanisms – from both Chinese informal and semiformal mediation: there is no consideration of 'harmony' and peaceable resolution of matters as in Chinese 'people's mediation', nor is mediation a part of the formal process of the court, generally initiated and driven by the judge, as in Chinese court mediation. US out-of-court-settlements are mainly decided upon by the litigants and their attorneys, often through gamesmanship, without much concern for 'peaceable resolution' 和解.

To be sure, Galanter in a later piece about 'the vanishing trial' has demonstrated that only less than 2 percent (1.8 percent) of federal civil court cases (distinguished from those of the state courts) actually go to trial (Galanter 2004, p. 459). Some researchers have on that basis argued that ADR carries tremendous import in the U.S. (Hopt and Steffek 2013, pp. 94–95). But actually, Galanter himself explains that ADR cannot explain the decline in the incidence of trials – because that decline has been across the board involving all spheres of civil justice, whereas ADR operates only in 'some sectors and places' (Galanter 2004, p. 517). He goes on to explain that trials have nearly vanished because of their ever-rising cost, with ever more expensive and complex and specialized procedures, becoming ever more a choice that only corporations can afford to make (Galanter 2004, p. 517). We need to see that the U.S. civil court system has long since become a stage for the gamesmanship of horrifically expensive attorneys, having less and less to do with justice. This problem of skyrocketing litigation costs is something that Weber pointed to already early in the twentieth century (Wei Bo 2005, p. 225). The main reason that U.S. lawsuits today rarely end in an actual trial is because its costs have far exceeded what common people can bear. That is the main dynamic behind 'the vanishing trial' – something that really should not be equated with the US's own mediation system nor with China's mediation system.

Some scholars further include arbitration under ADR and thereby lump it with mediation (see, for example, Subrin and Woo, 2006, Chapter 10). But arbitration in the United States is in fact mainly discounted and simplified adjudication (staffed by a retired judge, using a conference room or classroom rather than the court, and so on). In the majority of cases, arbitration still arrives at a clear-cut winner and loser, the 'prevailing party' and the losing party (which has to bear the legal costs – arbitration and lawyers' fees – of the prevailing party). For example, in high-frequency construction disputes in California, the so-called prevailing party is the one that ends with a larger total claim, even if just by one dollar, after all claims of both sides have been examined and decided upon by the judge. It is a system that drives both sides to try to contrive as many claims as possible in order to become the prevailing party and not bear the (still very) expensive costs of the arbitration court. Such arbitration clearly bears the deep imprint of the adversarial formal justice system, and also should not be equated with mediation.

Comparing the U.S. ADR system with China's mediation, we need to see first the historical background and origins of people's mediation in China – it had been developed on the basis of the long tradition of moral values and social customs of a society under the governing influence of Confucian thought, and it came from a justice system that made societal mediation the preferred precondition of formal law, which was the central characteristic of the Sinitic legal system. The American ADR system, on the other hand, comes not from society's customs or ideal of harmony, but rather from ever-rising litigation costs, which has produced two kinds of reactions: one that seeks to reduce costs within the established adversarial formal system, as in the arbitration and out-of-court-settlement systems, and the other that goes outside that system to an 'alternative' way of resolving disputes. The former is very different from China's mediation system; the latter is only something marginal and of limited use – very far from the role mediation has played in China.

But the Western world of jurisprudence today has grown accustomed to lumping mediation, arbitration and out-of-court settlements all under ADR, and of grouping China's mediation system under ADR, or even simply equating ADR with China's mediation system. Doing so is first to scramble together the simplifying-discounting of the adversarial system with the entirely different mediation system, which is distinct from it and a reaction against it. The scrambling together of the two has caused some people to way overestimate what genuine mediation has meant in Western societies. What such unrealistic estimation shows is not the reality of mediation in the United States, but rather the profound dissatisfaction of many with the existing formal system and their wish for a genuine alternative to it. To mistakenly equate such a scrambled-up ADR with Chinese mediation can only lead to even worse misunderstandings. The result is an inability to grasp either the reality of mediation in the United States or the distinctiveness of Chinese mediation.

Mediation has played so much larger a role in China than in the West because of its deep roots in Chinese tradition and society. People had long grown accustomed to the ideals, moral values, and operative mechanisms of mediation, and hence have accepted readily today all varieties of mediation, including its extension into semiformal mediation (administrative and judicial mediation). The ADR system that has arisen in the West in the past half-century, by contrast, comes from an opposite background. It has grown up in a society long accustomed to a highly formalized and adversarial justice system. The American out-of-court-settlement system and arbitration system are mainly simplified and discounted uses of the adversarial court system, while the genuinely alternative mediatory system remains of very limited and marginal use. We must not draw a simple equation between ADR and Chinese mediation. Even less should we think that the West's ADR is the more 'developed' and 'modernized' system that China must imitate, as some misguided Chinese scholars have insisted.

Understanding and measuring differences

The sixth and concluding point I wish to make is a question: how might one take into account such basic differences between the Sinitic and the Western legal traditions in an attempt to develop a globalized index for measuring the justice systems of the West, such as that attempted by The World Justice Project?

The World Justice Project (WJP) was established in 2006 by William H. Neukorn in his capacity as president of the American Bar Association, as a major project of that association, and is funded mainly by U.S. foundations and legal firms, and headquartered in Washington DC. Nevertheless, it has a globalized side as well: it attempts as much as possible to arrive at an objective evaluation of the 'rule of law' based on a global selection of countries (102 by 2015), and is seriously concerned with actual operations of the justice systems and not just certain ideologized values. For example, in its rating of eight major primary 'factors', it includes the practical categories of 'absence of corruption', 'order and security', and 'regulatory enforcement', and among its forty-four subfactors ones that are from the point of view of the users of the system, including 'accessibility and affordability', 'no unreasonable delay', and 'effective enforcement'. Such a point of view is close to the 'legal pragmatism' alternative to the 'classical orthodoxy' theoretical tradition of American jurisprudence, linked in part to the fact that the WJP is established more by practitioners than 'ivory tower' scholars and theorists of the law. Even in its evaluation of the political system, it has not stuck rigidly to some formalistic standard like elections or a multiparty system, but has rather focused on whether governmental power in actual operation has been effectively checked by legislative and judicial entities. Thus, in its 2015 'Rule of Law Index', it has ranked Singapore, relatively authoritarian and to all intents and purposes long under one-party rule, no. 10, well above the United States at no. 21. Even Hong Kong, with its chief executive appointed by China, has been placed at no. 19, also above the United States (WJP 2015). At the same time, it has adopted the broader concept of 'justice' over just 'law', which tends toward a focus only on codified law. And it has adopted 'informal justice' as the ninth of its primary factors (though it has yet to include this factor in the actual computation of its index) (WJP 2015, pp. 13, 160).

At present, China is ranked overall a relatively low no. 71 among 102 nations of the world. The reason has to do mainly with three key primary factors (out of a longer list of factors): (1) 'constraints on governmental powers' is concerned mainly with whether governmental authority is effectively limited and checked: China is scored a relatively low 0.41, ranking no. 87/102. Then, factor

(3) 'open government', concerned mainly with transparency and popular participation: China is scored also a low 0.43, and ranked also no. 87/102. Finally, factor (4) 'fundamental rights', concerned with human rights and freedom of speech, belief and assembly: China is scored a very low 0.32, and ranked no. 99/102 (WJP 2015, p. 76). I will not deal with these issues of political systems and human rights here, but concentrate rather on the discussion of informal justice and its interrelationship with formal justice.

For now, WJP seems to have settled on the practice of placing the evaluation of East Asian mediation under the rubric of its seventh factor, most specially ADR as understood in the West. Its method of scoring is to rely on sample surveys (by face-to-face interview, by telephone or by email), first of 1,000 people drawn from the three largest cities of each country. And, in addition, by surveys of an average of 25 selected 'experts' for each country. The first group is termed the 'representative population polls' (RPP), the second 'qualified respondents' questionnaires' (QRQ). In the computation of the Rule of Law Index, the two groups are treated as of equivalent weight, which means that the few experts are given the same weight as the 1,000 people of the general population surveyed. But at present, the WJP's set of China experts is clearly still rather meagre, consisting of just eight identified individuals (others are ostensibly unlisted), compared to the average of twenty-five for other countries. Among the eight listed, there are two employees of Hewlett Packard, two of foreign law firms, two NGO personnel, and just two Chinese professors (both of the Chinese University of Political Science and Law 中国政法大学). There is not one practising Chinese attorney, judge or judicial official, nor any legal scholars from the numerous law schools that rank much higher than the Chinese University of Political Science and Law (WJP 2015, p. 173). It is clearly a less than ideal makeup.

Then there is the problem of the WJP's obvious bias in favour of developed nations. The crucial weakness here is that the surveys are limited to the urban population, based on a sampling of the three largest cities of each country. This may not be a crucial issue for countries like the United States, where the agricultural workforce totals less than 1 percent of the population, but it is clearly a big problem for developing countries like China and India, and represents major oversights of reality. To ignore small peasant farmers, as WJP does, is a major failing, enough to cause us to question the objectivity of the entire enterprise. WJP itself has to some degree acknowledged the problem, and has declared that it will seek to include rural people in its future surveys (WJP 2015, p. 169; Botero and Ponce 2010, pp. 26–27). But just whether and how that intention will be implemented remains to be seen.

It needs to be explained here that WJP's research method appears to have been inspired by the World Bank's many development indices, including its use of the Gini coefficient method for measuring social equality, and a Worldwide Governance Indicators measure. The problem is, the bank's measurement of social equality in terms of the Gini coefficient (and the different countries ranked on that basis) is based on income data of the different countries, but what the WJP relies on instead are qualitative questionnaires. More concretely speaking, its RPPs are mostly based on questions about hypothetical situations that the respondents are asked to adjudge. For example, the first question in the questionnaire asks: 'Please assume that the government decides to build a major public works project in your neighborhood (such as a railway station or a highway), how likely are the people in your neighborhood/members of your community to be given the opportunity to express their opinions on the project?' Answer: 'very likely 1, likely 2, unlikely 3, very unlikely 4'. As for the QRQ, in the sphere of civil and commercial law, the first question is: 'Please assume that the Environmental Protection Authority in your country notifies a plant that it is polluting a river beyond the legally permitted levels, which of the following outcomes are most likely: (a) the company complies with the law (either voluntarily or through court orders, fines, or other sanctions); (b) the company bribes or influences the authorities to ignore the violation; (c) absolutely nothing happens; (d) don't know/not applicable'. (Botero and Ponce 2010, p. 55ff) The WJP's final Rule of Law Index is based on assigning numbers to and then rank ordering such information. Obviously, there is of necessity considerable subjectivity in the respondents' replies to the questionnaires as well as in the researchers' assignment of numbers to those. To express such data in terms of numerical measures to the second decimal point (0.00 to 1.00), and on that basis to place 102 countries into a precise rank order, might convey the impression of a higher degree of accuracy of the original information than is justified.

To be sure, the WJP's 'rule of law' ideal has been made as broad as possible (incorporating global comparisons), and its use of the concept of 'justice system' (broader than 'law') is relatively inclusive and objective, which are commendable as well as important. What I wish to do here is not to reject completely the WJP endeavour, but rather to point out some of its weaknesses. Its neglect of informal justice is linked to its disregard of rural peoples, and the main reason for its inability to comprehend accurately a country such as China. At the same time, those oversights tell also about the degree to which the modern Western justice system has neglected and or lacked a fuller informal justice system. To move further toward the actual implementation of its stated ideal, WJP needs to reconsider some of the basic concepts and methods it has employed with regard to these aspects of justice.

To give an example of a possible direction for modification, if one follows out the train of thought outlined in this article, one can imagine the following way of measuring informal justice: it might proceed from given social realities – such as the extent of social conflict, measured in terms of numbers of disputes per thousand people – and then examine separately how effective the informal (and semiformal) and formal justice systems have been in dealing with them. The reason for starting with existing degrees of social conflict is that those may have little to do with the justice systems but are rather connected more to such factors as scarcity of resources relative to population, drastic reforms and social change, social inequality, racial tensions and so on.

China and Japan, both with deep heritages from the Sinitic legal tradition, obviously differ greatly in their respective historical and social situations from one another, not to mention from the United States. We want to ask: how successful (what proportion of disputes) has their respective informal justice system been in resolving societal disputes? And further, among all civil litigations, to what extent has semiformal justice (court mediation) been successful in mediating cases? How do we take into account the very sharp differences between the United States and Japan in terms of frequency of litigation?

As for criminal justice, one could conceivably also start with frequency of criminal litigation (e.g., measured in terms of violent major crimes per 100,000 people, taking appropriate account of numbers of prisoners and of executions and, of course, also whether there is effective gun-control), and examine separately the effectiveness of informal and formal justice in dealing with crimes. We might attempt to measure to what extent informal justice has been able to reduce or prevent crimes, which types of crimes, and to what extent. Considerations such as these might help us to better understand and measure the roles of informal justice, which has for so long been so central to the Sinitic legal tradition.

Conclusion

Historically, Chinese legal thought has held consistently that disputes among the people over 'minor matters' 细事 that do not involve criminal offences should preferably be handled first by society itself, with the state intervening only when society is not able to resolve the matter. Past scholarship has emphasized the 'Confucianization of law' in the Han (206 BC–AD 220), referring especially to its incorporation of status differentiation (relations between superior and inferior) (Ch'ü 1961) and its incorporation of Confucian moral values (Ma 2014), but has not paid much attention to the informal justice system – namely, the preference for settlement of disputes by the morals and customs of society itself rather than by law. Precisely for that reason, Chinese codified law of the Han period retained the emphasis 'mainly on punishments for crimes' 以刑为主 that had been in place since the Qin (221 BC–207 BC). This reliance on informal justice was not some 'pre-legal', 'pre-state' or 'primitive' characteristic of the justice system, as some legal scholars have maintained, but was rather a deliberate choice made by the highly developed legal and state system of the Han. Indeed, it might even be seen as a 'post-legal(ist)' formulation.

Even so, because society itself was of course not able to resolve all of its disputes through its informal dispute resolution system, the intervention of state authority was often required. Since the Tang (618–907) at least, the successive legal codes came thereby to incorporate more and more 'civil' content. Nevertheless, codified law retained its earlier penal framework, and packaged most provisions about civil matters with punishments – though not all and, in actual judicial practice, the courts in fact seldom employed punishments in minor civil matters. Although civil provisions in traditional Chinese legal codes appear rather meagre when compared to modern civil codes of the Continental legal tradition, if seen in conjunction with the informal justice system for resolving disputes there can be no doubt that together they formed a vast civil justice system of very broad application.

Entering into the modern and contemporary periods, China has adopted the Western legal discourse of 'civil law' and 'criminal law', and its justice system therefore appears to have completely ruptured with the past. Some observers have therefore arrived at the position that 'modernization' of justice in China must mean 'wholesale Westernization'. But in point of fact, even in China today, the justice system in actual operation has retained the fundamental conceptual framework of the past – namely, that disputes among the people should as much as possible be dealt with by the informal justice system of society itself. The contemporary Chinese state continues to rely on popular/societal mediations as well as a host of semiformal justice systems standing midway between the formal system of the state and the informal system of society. Furthermore, the contemporary justice system speaks more explicitly of using informal (and semiformal) justice to reduce the burdens on the formal justice system. The express logic is: societal mediation of disputes among the people minimizes 'contradictions' (conflicts), thereby preventing many disputes from becoming lawsuits or criminal offences. Such a view is in truth a modernized explication of the traditional principle that societal mediation was to take precedence over the formal justice system. It bears obvious continuities with the past, continuing to view the civil and criminal justice systems as overlapping and interactive parts of a larger whole.

Some scholars have tended either to overlook the informal aspect of the contemporary Chinese justice system, or believe that informal justice is a backward system that must be discarded eventually. They therefore do not grasp the basic continuity between the contemporary and the past justice systems. I have argued that only if we grasp the history of China's informal justice system can we understand what is truly distinctive about the Sinitic legal tradition and its position among the world's major legal traditions, as well as its similarities and differences from the present-day system that has been constructed on the basis of massive importations of Western legal theory, laws and legal discourse. Without such an understanding, we will not be able to comprehend the entirety of the justice system of China today, much less envision or chart out anything like a justice system that embodies not just modernity but also Sinitic distinctiveness.

This applies not only to Chinese justice today, but also to the Japanese and Korean systems. They continue to show the crucially distinctive dimension of the Sinitic justice system: namely that civil justice should be handled as much as possible by society itself, most especially through mediation. Only when societal mediation fails should the formal legal system intervene. That is in fact the key to the much lower incidence of litigation in Japan and in Korea than in the US.

Unlike the Chinese system, the modern Western Continental and Common Law traditions have long been much more highly formalized and proceduralized. If we view the Chinese system only in terms of such jurisprudential theory, we can easily overlook the distinctive emphasis of the Sinitic system on informal justice. In this respect, the influential WJP of the past few years, with its Rule of Law Index that gives quantified measurements of the justice systems of 102 nations of the world, is a good illustration. On the one hand, WJP has wisely adopted the broader concept of 'justice', instead of limiting itself to just codified law, and in that respect is similar to my use of the category 'justice system'. It is also similar to my conception in that it places considerable emphasis on judicial practice, maintaining that one must consider the 'rule of law' from the perspective of the common citizens using the law. Those are its strong points. However, to this day the Rule of Law Index in its quantified computations still includes only eight factors of formal justice, without incorporating informal justice at all. And for now, it seems to be evaluating the East Asian informal justice systems mainly in terms of Western ADR conceptions.

At present, one apparent obstacle the WJP faces is the inclination among some Western as well as Chinese legal scholars to equate the ADR system that has arisen in the West in recent decades with the Sinitic system's informal justice. I have argued that we need to clarify the differences between Western ADR and the informal justice systems of nations with deep roots in the Sinitic legal tradition – i.e., nations of 'East Asian civilisation' (especially Japan and Korea, in addition to China) – before we can make more accurate and telling comparisons between them and the Western justice systems.

Notes

1 The arguments in this chapter are explained and documented much more fully in my article 'The past and present of the Chinese Civil and Criminal Justice Systems: the Sinitic legal tradition from a global perspective', *Modern China*, 42(3) (May 2016), pp. 227–272.
2 For detailed discussion and documentation, see: Huang 2010, Chapter 2.
3 Statistics cited here and below are from: Zhu 2011.

References

Baum, H. (2013). Mediation in Japan: development, forms, regulation and practice of out-of-court dispute resolution. In: K.J. Hopt and F. Steffek, eds., *Mediation: Principles and Regulation in Comparative Perspective*. Oxford: Oxford Univ. Press, pp. 1011–1094.

Botero, J.C. and Ponce, A. (2010). Measuring the rule of law: World Justice Project, working papers series, no. 001. http://papers.ssrn.com/sol3/papers.cfm?abstract_id=1966257 (accessed 2015).

Callister, R.R. and Wall, J.A. (1997). Japanese community and organizational mediation. *Journal of Conflict Resolution*, 41(2), pp. 311–28.

Ch'ü T'ung-Tsu [Qu Tongzu瞿同祖] (1961). *Law and Society in Traditional China*. Paris: Mouton.

Committee of Ministers of the Council of Europe (1998). European principles on family mediation. www.mediate.com/articles/EuroFam.cfm (accessed July 2005).

Ficks, E. (n.d.). Models of general court-connected conciliation and mediation for commercial dispute in Sweden, Australia, and Japan. www.zjapanr.de/index.php/zjapanr/article/view/215/222 (accessed 2018).

Galanter, M. (1985). 'A settlement judge, not a trial judge': judicial mediation in the United States. *Journal of Law and Society*, 12(1), pp. 1–18.

Galanter, M. (2004). The vanishing trial: an examination of trials and related matters in federal and state courts. *Journal of Empirical Legal Studies*, 1(3), pp. 459–570.

Henderson, D.F. (1965). *Conciliation and Japanese Law: Tokugawa and Modern*. 2 vols. Seattle: Univ. of Washington Press.

Hopt, K.J. and Steffek, F. (2013). Mediation: comparison of laws, regulatory models, and fundamental issues. In: K.J. Hopt and F. Steffek, eds., *Mediation: Principles and Regulation in Comparative Perspective*. Oxford: Oxford Univ. Press, pp. 3–130.

Huang, P.C.C. (1996). *Civil Justice in China: Representation and Practice in the Qing*. Stanford, CA: Stanford University Press.

Huang, P.C.C. (2001). *Code, Custom, and Legal Practice in China: the Qing and the Republic Compared*. Stanford, CA: Stanford University Press.

Huang, P.C.C. (2010). *Chinese Civil Justice, Past and Present*. Lanham, MD: Rowman & Littlefield.

Kulms, R. (2013). Mediation in the USA: alternative dispute resolution between legalism and self-determination. In: K.J. Hopt and F. Steffek, eds., *Mediation: Principles and Regulation in Comparative Perspective*. Oxford: Oxford Univ. Press, pp. 1245–1328.

Ma Xiaohong 马小红 (2014). 中华法系中'礼''律'关系之辨正 – – 质疑中国法律史研究中的某些'定论' (Differentiating 'propriety-morality' and 'legal statutes' and clarifying the relationship between them – questioning certain 'fixed conclusions' in Chinese legal history research). 法学研究 1, pp. 171–189.

Magee, S.P. (2010). The optimum number of lawyers and a radical proposal for legal change. http://buckleysmix.com/wp-content/uploads/2010/10/Magee.pdf (accessed July 2015).

The Qing code – *Da Qing lüli* 大清律例 – is cited according to Xue Yunsheng's读例存疑, as edited by Huang Jingjia, and by the statute and sub-statute numbers he added.

Sohn, D.-W. and Wall Jr., J.A. (1993). Community mediation in South Korea: a city–village comparison. *Journal of Conflict Resolution*, 37(3), pp. 536–543.

Subrin, S.N. and Woo, M.Y.K. (2006). *Litigating in America: Civil Procedure in Context*. New York: Aspen Publishers.

Virginia Judicial System (2003). www.courts.state.va.us/reports/2003/SECTIONa.pdf (accessed 2009).

Wall Jr., J.A. et al. (1998). Mediation in the US, China, Japan, and Korea. *Security Dialogue*, 29(2), pp. 235–248.

Wei Bo 韦伯 [Max Weber] (2005). 法律社会学 (Legal sociology). 康乐、简惠美译, 韦伯作品集, IX. 桂林：广西师范大学出版社.

WJP [World Justice Project] (2015), *Rule of Law Index 2015*. Washington DC: World Justice Project.

Xue Yunsheng 薛允升, ed. (1970 [1905]). 读例存疑 (Doubts remaining after perusing the sub-statutes). 黄静嘉编校, 五卷. 台北：中文研究资料中心.

Zhu Jingwen 朱景文, ed. (2011). 中国法律发展报告2011：走向多元化的法律实施 (Report on China's legal development: toward the multifaceted implementation of law). 北京：中国人民大学出版社.

3

THREADS OF THE LEGAL WEB

Dutch law and everyday colonialism in eighteenth-century Asia[1]

Alicia Schrikker and Dries Lyna

Introduction

In May 1788 Michiel Gomes died bankrupt in Batavia (present-day Jakarta). Six years earlier this Sinhalese man had left his family behind in Colombo, to travel 3000 kilometres to the highest appellate court of Dutch Asia.[2] Back home he had lost the trial before the Dutch *Raad van Justitie* against his brother-in-law Nikolaas Fonseka, owing him over 2000 guilders. When he had arrived in Batavia, Michiel Gomes surprisingly pushed his appeal over the expiration date. In the meantime he pledged some of his property (including two slaves), took his money and left creditor Fonseka frustrated back on the island of Sri Lanka.[3]

In the course of seventeenth and eighteenth centuries the Dutch East India Company (VOC) founded a variety of legal institutions in its factories and colonies, with Company servants acting as judges and persecutors. While these *Stadsraden, Landraden* and *Heemraden* carried distinctive Dutch names, in their daily operation they were highly localized institutes, serving litigants all across the religious and ethnic spectrum. Civil cases on debts, divorces and inheritances demanded an understanding of local customary laws. Despite the fact that the VOC set up these institutions to ensure social control, they simultaneously functioned as sites of mediation and conflict resolution in local societies (Schrikker, 2015; Rupesinghe, 2016). Furthermore, these Dutch judicial bodies operated within and alongside existing legal orders in local society. The story of Michiel Gomes illustrates the thorough intertwinement of legal pluralism and everyday experience in the eighteenth-century Dutch colonial context: why did two Sinhalese men opt for a Dutch court to settle their family feud? Why did Gomes ignore his appeal deadline after travelling across the Indian Ocean to Batavia? And what do intercultural processes such as these reveal about the social function of colonial law courts?

Over the past twenty years law and legal practice have gained prominence in the study of colonial and global history, with Lauren Benton's work on legal pluralism and colonial cultures as a crucial incentive (Benton, 2002; Benton, 2009; Benton and Ross, 2013). Research has gradually shifted from a more descriptive focus on rules and regulations to a more dynamic perspective on the use of legal institutions as means of control and resistance. Scholars used the prism of legal pluralism to emphasize the imposition of difference in colonial empires, while others have focused on international law- and boundary-making as instances of colonial exertion of power (Benton and Clulow, 2015). In this contribution the concept of legal pluralism itself is not the object of enquiry, but rather used to describe the intersection of and interaction between indigenous and colonial legal bodies and norms. By focusing on the users of justice as actors within the legal web that the VOC created, this contribution will provide insight into legal pluralities at work, both at the institutional and normative level. This approach is inspired by the basic question raised by John Comaroff of why colonial regimes put in place such institutions and kept them operational, a phenomenon which he called 'expensive, expansive and far in excess of functional requirement' (Comaroff, 2001). The real challenge, he pointed out, remained to understand how these institutions worked in day-to-day practice and shaped society–state interaction. In 2015 Yannakakis critically questioned the way historians so far have employed the – European-produced – archives to study law-making in these courts. More particularly, she called for a deeper understanding of the local in the process of crafting legislation and in legal practice, even when engaging in global debates on colonial law (Yannakakis, 2015).

This contribution aims at doing just that by studying the social function of the Dutch legal system in eighteenth-century Asia in general, and the everyday interaction of local populations with colonial normative institutions in particular. In contrast to its Spanish, British and (to a lesser extent) French counterparts, studies of legal practice in Dutch colonial Asia are more limited. The Dutch-Indonesian historiography does offer a number of important leads though. On the one hand the debates among the colonial legal scholars of the early-twentieth-century school of Van Vollenhoven have left a strong influence on this literature (Hooker, 1975; Ball, 1982; Burns, 1989). They focused on law and regulation to reconstruct local customary law (*adat*) among diverse cultural groups in the archipelago. This rich scholarship has highlighted the pluralistic character of both the procedures and laws at work in Indonesian courts, but in general questions were not raised about the practical workings of the law in court and society in the colonial past. Social historians on the other hand have employed early modern legal cases to reconstruct the diverse social relations in port cities such as Batavia, the Cape and Makassar, bringing to light the wealth of everyday societal information these sources contain (Ross, 1983; Worden, 1985; Niemeijer, 2005; Sutherland, 2009). The work of Kerry Ward on the forced migration of criminal convicts and political exiles has showed the extent to which the VOC employed its spatial network across the Indian Ocean to create an effective punishment regime (Ward, 2009). However, the actual function of Dutch colonial law in local societies has received little attention so far.

For too long historians considered colonial law predominantly as a means to regulate the social and political order, ultimately to sustain the empire itself (Roy and Swamy, 2016; Yannakakis, 2015). This contribution therefore aims to set an agenda for a socio-legal approach to Dutch colonial law in the early modern period, with a focus on civil cases. Conceptually this research was inspired by Dinges' concept of 'uses of justice', to understand how legal courts took root in a society where varieties of dispute resolution existed side by side (Dinges, 2004). In addition, Franz and Keebet von Benda-Beckmann further strengthened our perspective in the horizontal process of law-making with their term 'forum shopping', which they coined to describe their observations of the contemporary interplay of the *adat* and Islamic law among Minangkabau region in West Sumatra. They witnessed a highly dynamic process of interaction between different legal cultures, without one of them imposing on the other. Litigants reverted to either one of these according to their specific needs and societal position (von Benda-Beckmann, 1981; von Benda-Beckmann and von Benda-Beckmann, 2012). The basic question we raise – 'Why did people in Asia opt for Dutch colonial courts?' – mirrors in some way the work of Karen Barkey. In her excellent article on the workings of legal pluralism in the Ottoman Empire she analyzed why Christians and Jews used Muslim Qadi courts to settle their disputes. Barkey first shows that the pluralistic character of the Qadi courts made this possible, as it included secular and local customary law. Secondly, she discusses the role that the courts had in authentication of transactions of commercial goods and land. And thirdly she argues that the Qadi courts could have particular advantages for litigants who preferred to escape the social hierarchies or normative pressures within their own community (Barkey, 2013).

Building on Barkey, Dinges and von Benda-Beckmann, we view the litigators in eighteenth-century Dutch Asia as consumers who had options to settle their civil disputes. This allows us to explore the choices they make both in terms of the venues they utilize and the strategies they pursue. This, in turn, necessitates a re-thinking of the institutions themselves, as they derived a substantial part of their power and legitimacy by structuring and accommodating consumers' choices. This contribution therefore argues for a socio-legal approach that conceptualizes colonial courtrooms not only as instruments of social control, but also as public stages where colonial inhabitants could use them to enforce a social sanction on their peers, and at the same time renegotiate their own social standing within local society.

In order to do so two hundred civil court cases and notarial records from the seventeenth and eighteenth centuries in the Sri Lankan and Indonesian VOC archives are studied. The primary focus is on the judicial courts of Colombo and Makassar (South Sulawesi), but sample material from Batavia and Ambon is introduced as well. Although the analysis relies for the larger part on the qualitative study of several court cases, quantitative explorations on the users of these courts corroborate these first findings. The Indonesian and Sri Lankan court documents provide us with an entry into the world of colonial legal practice, and thanks to existing studies by regional experts they could be thoroughly contextualized within a broader socio-institutional context. In an effort to answer the questions raised above by the case of Michiel Gomes, this article addresses three themes: the first part zooms in on the evolving relationship between Dutch colonial courts and local law systems, both in terms of overlapping jurisdictions and in terms of interaction of norms. The second part highlights the processes of colonial bureaucratization and registration that reinforced the emergence of a Dutch legal culture across Asia. Finally, the focus will move to the particular strategies of local litigators in navigating Dutch institutions to mediate local conflicts on different sides of the Indian Ocean.

Legal pluralism, encroachment and codification

From the early seventeenth century onwards the Dutch East India Company struck root in diverse cultural environments in monsoon Asia, and the character of the Company's presence in any locality could differ greatly. The Dutchmen acted as mere trading agents in places like Surat in North-West India and Canton in South China, or they controlled fortified port towns like Nagapattinam in South India and Makassar in South Sulawesi. Elsewhere in Asia they claimed territorial sovereignty, and set up fiscal and legal structures geared to ensure revenue from land and labour, with examples such as Banda, Sri Lanka, the Cape and increasingly so Java. Wherever the VOC set up normative institutions, they had to account for both existing native and Portuguese legal heritage (e.g. Cochin and Colombo). These VOC civil courts therefore functioned differently from one region to another, without an absolute blueprint; in addition, they were highly dynamic as the Dutch further encroached upon local societies over time. However, within this moving web of legality that the VOC spanned across the Indian Ocean, a fixed judicial hierarchy existed between the several minor and more central localities, with Batavia as the centre of VOC power in Asia. While the numerous port cities had *Civiele Raden* and appellate *Raden van Justitie* of their own, the *Raad van Justitie* in Batavia functioned as the ultimate court of appeal in Asia.

The legal history of the VOC displays two contradictory tendencies. On the one hand there were attempts to centralize and universalize judicial practices, through the central publication of ordinances (*plakkaten*) and through authorization of Roman Dutch law from Batavia to the factories and settlements (van Kan, 1940; Ball 1982; van Wamelen, 2014). On the other hand these outposts proclaimed ordinances themselves in response to specific norms and practices, and included codification and integration of local customary laws. Such local ordinances were printed not only in Dutch, but also in the relevant local languages (Hovy, 1991). The legal web that the VOC created through its institutions and its Batavian ordinances might have taken the appearance of a relatively uniform legal space; it was in fact a network of plural legal practices that were highly localized in function. To complicate matters, VOC institutions never operated in a legal vacuum, but rather alongside other local normative institutes of conflict mediation, such as royal courts or village councils. The process of law-making in the Dutch empire in Asia should therefore be understood not only as a vertical process of bottom-up and top-down interaction, but also as a horizontal process where different normative institutions operated simultaneously in the social, cultural and religious sphere (Tamanaha, 1993, 2008, 2010).

Historic examples of the way such legal pluralities played out in the early modern Indonesian archipelago are found in Wellen's insightful study of Wajoq in South Sulawesi, a coastal mercantile polity bordering Makassar. Her research is built upon on palm leaf manuscripts in the Wajorese language (*lontara*), complemented by the VOC archives. She argues convincingly that the commercial orientation of this sultanate and its diaspora resulted in a strong legal culture geared towards regulating local commerce. She extensively discusses the Wajorese law code (*Ammana Gappa*), and argues that conflict mediation among the Wajoq functioned well. Interestingly though, Wellen found evidence that Wajoq merchants also made use of legal institutions in neighbouring Dutch Makassar, but not for the intra-Wajoq disputes. In cases over debt the colonial *Raad van Justitie* in Makassar facilitated litigation between Wajoq merchants and parties of different cultural backgrounds, such as Makassarese or Chinese traders, and often involved trade partners on other islands in the archipelago. The VOC court in Makassar was used in particular in such cross-cultural and -regional litigation (Wellen, 2014).

This does not necessarily mean that the laws applied by the Dutchmen presiding in this Makassarese court were always Dutch. In 1785 the village chiefs and family members of two young boys, Tapan and Tjanga, accused several local men of abducting the two boys and selling them off as slaves. More than a month later the children were found living enslaved in Makassar in the house of a European man. As the village fell formally under the authority of the Company and the culprits were not from the village, the chiefs had asked the Company to apprehend them. Once caught, they explicitly asked the Dutch councillors of justice to try the men according to local custom, which they did accordingly. While it was rather unusual that Dutchmen chased slave raiders on behalf of local families, this case exemplifies local people using justice at Dutch legal institutions, and it highlights the fact that these colonial courts could apply – even uncodified – customary laws in an ad hoc manner.[4]

In fact, the Batavian ordinances also reveal fragmented codification of Chinese, Muslim and Hindu family law that was published in the mid-eighteenth century, suggesting a degree of cultural adaptation at work in these courts. Interestingly, these Javanese codifications travelled the archipelago and beyond, with the Muslim code even sent to Colombo (Schrikker, 2015). Thus, even the Batavian ordinances then were not only the product of top-down regulation enforcement, but were also shaped in an interactive process within a Dutch legal web that spanned across the Indian Ocean. Dutch historiography still remains somewhat unclear on how this legal knowledge was produced and who exactly had agency in its production. Research on British India, however, has shown how particular groups in local society benefitted from the collaborative act of legal codification (Cohn, 1996). The same seems to have been true in Dutch Jaffna (North Ceylon), where the codification of Hindu law (*Thesewalamai*) in 1706 served the interest of the Tamil elites of the *Vellalar* caste (Arasaratnam, 1981; Schrikker and Ekama, 2017). A second question that needs to be answered is whether such codifications were actually used in court, and by whom; a first survey of civil cases from the Batavian

Schepenbank archives and the Jaffna *Landraad* suggests that little actual reference was made to these codes in court proceedings.[5]

When the VOC took over territorial power beyond the walls of cities such as Batavia, Makassar or Colombo, the Dutchmen became further entangled in local legal cultures. Java specialist Mason Hoadley has researched the encroachment of Dutch legal culture in the eighteenth-century Priangan region south of Batavia, which resided under the Mataram sultanate of Ceribon (Hoadley, 1994). For legal historians Ceribon is an interesting case, as here too the VOC officials had codified local custom (*Pepakem Ceribon*) in the 1760s. Yet, Hoadley did not focus on the *Pepakem Ceribon* as such, but instead produced a detailed study of legal cases and petitions from the surroundings of Ceribon in the eighteenth century, when the power of the Mataram-court over Ceribon dwindled in favour of the Dutch.[6] Studying a large number of civil and criminal cases from the Ceribon region scattered throughout the VOC archives, Hoadley questioned to what extent the VOC built on local legal structures, and to what extent this intervention resulted in institutional change. In the end Hoadley chose not so much to focus on whether or not local substantive laws were in place (i.e. *Pepakem Ceribon*), instead he found that procedural law witnessed the most striking changes over time. In the early eighteenth century the Dutch developed the practice in Ceribon of organizing a *Landraad* or rural court, which would meet on a yearly basis to settle land and other civil disputes and to try minor criminal offences. Other offences were tried by the Dutch resident in Ceribon, assisted by local advisors. Hoadley argued that over time the local judge (*Jaksa*) lost ground and became a marginalized figure in the court; instead the local regents (Javanese nobility) closest to the Company gained positions as advisors in legal cases. This process resulted in the empowerment of particular noble families. Ravensbergen has shown how this process continued in the nineteenth century and how the actors operating within the institutions were constantly being balanced out vis-à-vis each other and vis-à-vis the state and society (Ravensbergen, 2018). Rupesinghe highlights a similar power play at work between the VOC and the *mudaliyars* (headmen) in the *Landraden* in Galle (southern Sri Lanka) in the eighteenth century (Rupesinghe, 2016). The work of Hoadley, Ravensbergen and Rupesinghe warrants the inclusion of the local actors involved in the operation of the courts in the analysis of the social function of colonial courts in local societies.

This discussion of legal pluralism, codification and colonial encroachment underlines once more that the VOC courts never operated in a legal vacuum. The Dutch were well aware of this, by both translating and codifying indigenous texts and practices. Codified customary laws like the *Ammana Gappa* in Makassar, *Pepakem Ceribon* in Priangan and the *Thesewalamai* in Jaffna (Ceylon) give an impression of the norms at work in non-colonial institutes as well, a theme that certainly requires further comparative research. At the same time such norms were also shaped in interaction with the colonial institutions, as we saw in the Makassarese case against the slave raiders. The VOC courts and offices of registration provided for yet another arena for potential litigants. Thus, the indigenous agency for which Yannanakis calls should not only be looked for in the production of codified law, but also in the way the Dutch courts were used by local people in relationship to alternative venues of conflict settlement, very similar to Dinges' concept of 'uses of justice'.

Colonial institutions, bureaucratization and the creation of a Dutch legal culture

However, the indigenous agency interacted with the historical evolution of the colonial law system, and their use of justice adapted to changing circumstances. A 1773 case-study from Dutch Ceylon illustrates the internal dynamic of the Dutch legal institutions, with a special role for the growing bureaucratization. In that year Sinhalese villagers Kierie and Poentje Nainde appeared before the *Raad van Justitie* in Colombo, the highest appellate court in Dutch Ceylon. They wanted to take up their mother's appeal from thirty years earlier, to reclaim her husband's land. After their father's death in 1745 another villager, Wijeendre, had somehow obtained this land with an official letter of donation from the Dutch governor, despite the fact that the Dutch land registration of 1721 (*thombo*) had pointed out Kierie's and Poentje's father as the owner. Their mother had gone to two Sinhalese heads of the district to solve this problem (both the *coraal* and *mudaliyar)*. But after they had become aware of Wijeendre's Dutch letter of donation, they had declined jurisdiction and told the mother to take the case to the colonial *Landraad*. In 1746 the mother lost this trial, but she wanted to take the case before the appellate *Raad van Justitie*. However, first the rural unrests leading up to the Kandyan wars (Dewasiri, 2008) and later on her passing away made sure that this appeal would never materialize. However nearly 30 years later Kierie and Poentje continued their mother's effort. They insisted that the letter of donation was handed out by the Dutch under false pretences back then, and tried to counter Wijeendre's children with an authenticated transcript of the 1772 Dutch head and land registration (*thombos*) to prove their ownership once and for all.[7]

Similar to the Ceribon example the strengthening and re-instalment of *Landraden* in the 1740s by Ceylonese governor van Imhoff went hand-in-hand with a renewed Dutch interest in this pre-existing land registration (*thombos*). Both were a means to an end for the Dutch East India Company in their search for a more efficient system of land revenue and labour extraction (Dewasiri, 2008; Rupesinghe, 2016). However, the growing importance of the *thombos* for the Dutch was not merely continuing colonial encroachment on everyday village life. This increased Dutch attention for land registration strengthened the legal agency of those same villagers, who could invoke it as evidence in a lawsuit. Kierie and Poentje referred back to a register from 1721 to prove their father's ownership of the land; and at the end of the proceedings they brought in the 1772 head and land *thombos* as a *deus ex machina*. Wijeendre's children on the other hand built their case on the Dutch letter of donation (*giftebrief*), which had caused the local chiefs to redirect the Sinhalese feud to the colonial court, rather than settling it themselves.

The growing importance of the *thombo* registration on Ceylon must be understood within a broader framework, as historians often characterize the Dutchmen in Asia for their rationalistic craze to regulate daily colonial life, while cataloguing and categorizing the inhabitants of their factories and colonies (Raben, 1996, p. 77). The land registration and the *Landraden* were thus but one part of a larger network of normative colonial institutions, fond of thorough registration. The Protestant Church can be seen as the other backbone in the Dutch legal culture of eighteenth-century Ceylon, as their registered marriages, births and deaths could therefore produce evidence in court. Rural Sri Lankans who had access to the Protestant Church would consequently also have a better chance at success in litigation than others. Local claimants tried to get their share of an inheritance with an official proof of marriage, or hoped to persuade the court to deem an inheritance invalid because a baptism was not registered before the Church (Kok et al., 2018).

The influence of these normative institutions ran parallel with a growing emphasis on written over oral evidence in court, as Hoadley already noted for the eighteenth-century sultanate of Ceribon (Hoadley, 1994). For Jaffna too preliminary research strengthens this hypothesis, as in the surviving legal documents of the *Landraad* from the 1740s and 1750s the debate most often came down to a discussion over the evidence. The *Thesewalamai*, codified some four decades earlier, was not explicitly referred to; apparently the court continued to rely on the advice of local members of the *Landraad* on questions about local customs. The available court cases often revolved around discrediting witnesses and each other's evidence. The local Tamil record keepers, or schoolmasters as they were called, of the Dutch Reformed parishes were key persons in the production of this required evidence, be it over slave ownership or land transactions. They were called schoolmasters because they were appointed at the village church to teach children the catechism. But as village recordkeepers they were crucial figures and provided access to justice, through registration and authentication of privately created *ola* (palmleaf) deeds. This situation will surely have given them a powerful position in the parish.[8]

Whereas these *Landraden* mainly served villagers in their uses of justice with the *thombos* as crucial written evidence, the legal courts in the Company port cities catered towards the need of urban and mercantile communities. The *Schepenbank* in Batavia for example was hearing court cases and simultaneously functioned as a notarial office, dealing with the registration of property through the authentication of wills, property transactions and manumission deeds. In addition, Batavia had registered notarial offices as well, that expanded up to six in the middle of the eighteenth century. The extensive notarial records suggest that there was good business in registering. These notarial records were used by many different groups in Batavian society, the growing Chinese population in particular (Kanumoyoso, 2011). A first sample survey into the civil cases from the *Schepenbank* in Batavia in the 1770s–1790s shows that these notarial records, but also *onderhandse* (private) deeds and wills on paper and in different languages and scripts, were used in court as evidence. Here too, just like in Jaffna, the larger part of the legal process was dedicated to discrediting the authenticity of the documents of the opposite party. Colonial law in Batavia has to be understood in relation to the local notarial practices and the functioning of other institutes involved in forms of registration, such as the parish and the *wees-* and *boedelkamers*. In each colonial setting such inter-institutional relationships will have functioned differently. A question to be further researched is to what extent Dutch practices in registration replaced, complemented or influenced the practice of other local institutes that regulated people and property, such as the mosque or the Chinese council.[9]

The notarial archives of Ambon already point towards a mutual reinforcement between existing registration practices in South-East Asia and the bureaucratization of Dutch institutions. Among the Ambon notarial papers we found transaction notes written in Malay and authorized by the local raja and village elders. Some time afterwards (up to years) these notes were brought before the Dutch notaries, with the request to register and authorize such notes 'for eternal memory'.[10] Boomgaard has argued that registration of debt was already common legal practice in South-East Asia in the early modern period (Boomgaard, 2009). These pre- and co-existing traditions could explain why local inhabitants easily found their way to the Dutch notarial offices in the first place. The importance of registering all sorts of civil documents before Dutch colonial institutions (and notaries) thus seemingly increased all over Asia as the eighteenth century progressed, tapping into existing local practices. In a way this mirrors the process that Barkey has observed for the Ottoman Empire, when she argues that the capacity of the courts to authenticate and authorize transaction deeds was one of the reasons that drew non-Muslims to the Qadi courts (Barkey, 2013).

Navigating the threads of the Dutch legal web

Turning to Dutch colonial institutions thus seems to have been a particular strategy of local inhabitants, reinforcing the hypothesis to study them as users of justice. A first survey of the 111 cases brought before the *Raad van Justitie* in Colombo between 1758 and 1788 reveals that local inhabitants such as Sinhalese, Chetties and Moors made up the lion's share of litigators in Dutch Ceylon, even before this highest appellate court of the island.[11] This high degree of localization of the Dutch legal institutions in Ceylon is perhaps surprising, given the fact that the last available Dutch census indicates that these groups only made up about 10 % of the 3352 inhabitants of the fort and the Old Town in 1694. However, even back then the immediate hinterland, known as Four Gravets, were already social melting pots for Sinhalese and other settlers, such as Chetties, South Asian Muslims (called Moors by the Dutch) and manumitted slaves from South and South-East Asia. Throughout the eighteenth century their number probably rose considerably in these suburbs, where the (partial) liberalisation of the trade ensured a growth of especially the Muslim and Chettiyar communities (Raben, 1996).[12]

In Colombo both the local Sinhalese as well as the Chetty and Muslim traders thus made conscious use of the Dutch legal system in Ceylon not just to fight oppression by the colonial power, but also as a third-party mediation to resolve inherent local disputes, as in our introductory case of the Sinhalese family feud. Between 1758 and 1788 the *Raad van Justitie* was confronted with a third of all suits where both accuser and defendant were not directly employed by the Company, nor bore Dutch last names. Gomes and Fonseka themselves were avid 'return customers' of the Dutch courts. It turns out that this dispute between two brothers-in-law was not the first feud of the Gomes–Fonseka family that was brought before the *Raad van Justitie*, starting with a lawsuit over the inheritance of Michiel's great-grandfather in the late 1740s. Furthermore, Nicolaas Fonseka returned to the *Raad* ten years later claiming money from Sinhalese and Chetty traders.[13] And after Michiel's passing the family proved to be keen users of justice, when his nephew Joan Fonseka sued the executors of the estate of a late captain Jongbloet in 1793 over a debt.[14]

The *Schepenbank* in Batavia corroborates the Ceylonese story of a high degree of localization, with litigators from a great variety of backgrounds involved in legal disputes, both inter- and intra-community (Blussé, 1986; Raben, 1996; Niemeijer, 2005). In the course of the eighteenth century the population of Batavia and its *Ommelanden* doubled to about 150000 inhabitants, with an exponential growth outside of the city walls. While the numbers of Europeans gradually declined, the share of various groups such as the Chinese, Malay and (former-) enslaved people from the archipelago and the broader Indian Ocean region grew considerably as the century progressed (Raben, 1996). The costs of litigation in Batavia were relatively low, and access to justice was therefore not confined to wealthy entrepreneurs alone (Niemeijer, 2005). In this vibrant ethnic melting pot it was therefore not uncommon that manumitted slaves sued their former masters over property and that Muslim women fought their in-laws over the inheritance of their husbands' estates.

Makassar too functioned as a forum for cross-cultural litigation, even if the relative share of non-Europeans in this court was somewhat lower than in in Colombo and Batavia. Of the litigants involved in the 76 remaining civil cases before the *Raad van Justitie* for the period 1727–1796, around two thirds were European, followed by the Chinese, Makassarese and other local litigants.[15] Makassar was a relatively small Dutch Company town, with about 2500 inhabitants in the fort and nearby service community of Vlaardingen throughout the eighteenth century. However, while its 'European' population consisting mainly of Company officials, their families, Burghers and slaves remained relatively stable at 500 to 700, the Chinese and Malays in the neighbouring kampong rose from about 6000 in 1730 to over 7500 in 1790 (Sutherland, 2010). Sutherland discusses in particular a number of cases from this expanding Chinese community, pointing out that despite the fact that this community had its own provision for conflict resolution, its members increasingly used the VOC courts to settle their disputes. Sutherland puts forward two explanations for this situation that are reminiscent of Barkey's study on the Qadi courts. One is that the VOC institutes could have been attractive for relative outsiders in the communities, or people of lower descent. A second is that because cases brought forward often included commercial transactions in other ports in the archipelago and China, the VOC network could be used to provide evidence from these different spaces (Sutherland, 2009). The Makassar cases involving Wajoq merchants discussed above further stresses this cross-regional aspect as a particular element in the use of VOC justice (Wellen, 2009, 2014).

Cross-regional litigation was also at work in the Colombo *Raad van Justitie*, and pulled in litigators from the Indian coast. In the summer of 1772 the Dutch court of Colombo received an indictment of Muslim trader Rama Najeker of Nagipattinam, a town on the Coromandel coast. Via his local representatives Rama Najeker claimed 5000 kilos of areca nuts from Frans Quintaal, a businessman from French Pondicherry who resided in Colombo at the time. Over the next year and a half the members of this Dutch court who dealt with this commercial dispute encountered Sinhalese *mudaliyars* (chiefs), Muslim moneylenders, African slaves, Tamil translators and Company personnel, connecting coastal towns under both French and Dutch colonial rule in India and Sri Lanka.[16] Sirks and Hallebeek suggest that the conflict played out in this VOC court because of the role of the VOC in registered transactions and cross-regional remittances (Sirks and Hallebeek, 2010).

This last element points to the importance of the Dutch web of legality that spanned across the Indian Ocean, and probably attracted commercial communities to the Dutch courts. However, the existence of such a legal web equally allowed individual litigators to follow the transregional threads all the way up the centre. Returning to our opening story, the Sinhalese Michiel Gomes went above and beyond the Dutch Ceylonese institutions by appealing in Batavia, seemingly without hesitation and immediately after his sentence was formulated in Colombo. Although some may consider it a desperate tactic to escape his creditors, Gomes showcased his agency as a Sinhalese to adopt an inherent foreign legal system and made effective use of the existing Dutch system of appeal. Gomes was certainly not the only one who climbed the legal ladder up to Batavia; in 1793 a woman named Helena who was claimed as slave by a Chetty trader appealed to Batavia, after the *Raad van Justitie* in Colombo decided against her (Schrikker and Ekama, 2017). The Dutch legal web then was not only shaped by the Batavian ordinances that travelled the Indian Ocean to keep control over the diverse populations under Dutch rule; individual litigators could also use these inherent foreign rules and regulations to further their own interests before VOC courts, which in turn contributed to the further expansion of the Dutch legal web.

Conclusion

Returning to our opening case on Michiel Gomes and his brother-in-law, it seems this can only be understood if we perceive them not as mere victims of a Dutch colonial legal apparatus striving for social control, but as active users of justice in a complex system of legal pluralism. The case of Kierie and Poentje Nainde further strengthens the hypothesis that the Dutch court was hardly the only available venue for conflict settlement, as their mother first turned to two local mediators, and one of them referred her to the *Landraad*. Colonial subjects could thus consciously choose to opt for the Dutch legal system, which held certain benefits for different interest groups. Surely, this situation of legal pluralism at work was not unique to the world of the VOC, and in the article we have drawn parallels with the situation in the Ottoman Empire and the British Raj. We argue that understanding the workings of legal pluralism in and around the world of the VOC allows us to ask new questions that are relevant to local and global history.

The increased bureaucratization of Dutch normative institutions ran parallel with a growing importance of written over oral evidence in the courts. Colonial registration of marriages, deaths and land ownership unwittingly increased the legal agency of local inhabitants, who could invoke these Dutch documents to support their family feuds and inter-community cases. Dutch efforts to structure the diverse rural and urban societies under their rule should therefore not be analyzed as the mere end result of a fixed power relationship, but as an ongoing negotiation process, which spurred the development of specific colonial legal cultures. The observed connections between institutions of law and registration provide us with a new vantage point to study local society. Qualitative research into both the colonial case files of legal and religious courts as well as the census registers allow us to reconstruct the paths of particular families – such as the Gomes–Fonsekas – in their encounter with the Dutch legal web. A connected quantitative approach to registers and court cases can complement this narrative approach and provide insight in the nature of society-state interaction as a whole and assess the impact this had on family life.[17]

Moreover, the localized legal systems across Dutch Asia were interconnected, with the centrally published Batavian ordinances tying the web together. Foreign commercial communities such as the Chettiyars and Muslims around Colombo, the Chinese and Wajorese of Makassar and tradesmen from all over maritime Asia in Batavia saw the opportunities provided to them by the Dutch web of legality that spanned the Indian Ocean and incorporated partially codified Chinese, Muslim and Hindu family law. In addition, notarial documents and colonial registration could be relatively easily transported between Dutch port cities to serve as evidence in the court of law. Even non-commercial litigators proved to be clever navigators of this transregional network, with the appeal option towards Batavia as a legal strategy to escape local prosecution and, in the case of Helena, enslavement. While the Dutch legal web was spun across the Indian Ocean and forced migration of convicts and exiles away from the centre, simultaneously colonial subjects moved along its threads towards the centre in their uses of justice.

Notes

1 This article is written in the context of the NWO funded project 'Colonialism inside out: everyday experience and plural practice in Dutch Institutions in Sri Lanka, 1700–1800', which is carried out in cooperation between Leiden University, Radboud University Nijmegen and the Sri Lankan National Archives. We would like to thank Nadeera Rupesinghe, Kathryn Wellen and the editors of this volume for their valuable comments.

2 Sri Lanka National Archives (SLNA), 1/4484–4485 and 1/4513: *Documents related to the estate of Michiel Gomes*. In the documents Gomes and Fonseka are both referred to as Sinhalese, the latter as a *wasser* (Dutch name for the *radā* caste). Their Portuguese last name probably refers to an ancestor who was baptized, rather than an actual Portuguese lineage.
3 After Gomes died, his widow in Colombo offered the *Raad van Justitie* a composition to try and cede her husband's inheritance, in order to be freed of his debts, which spurred a new legal suit with Joan Fonseka, Nicolaas' son. In the end the widow was freed of further persecution and could turn to poor relief, and Fonseka and other creditors were compensated for their losses. SLNA, 1/4484.
4 ANRI (Arsip Nasional Republik Indonesia) Makassar, 341/7.
5 SLNA 1/6018–6020; ANRI Schepenbank, 504–608; Merve Tosun, '(Im)Practical pluralism: legal pluralism in Batavia and its environs: from codification to practice (*c*.1750–1800)' (MA thesis Leiden University, May 2018.).
6 In the nineteenth century Priangan became the economic centre of the Dutch colonial agricultural venture, as it was here that they developed a system of labour extraction that was to be converted into the Cultivation System (*cultuurstelsel*).
7 SLNA 1/4405: *Kierie and Poentje Nainde – heirs of Wijeendre Nainde*.
8 A.F. Schrikker, *Litigation and colonialism in eighteenth-century Jaffna: a first exploration*, paper presented at AISLS 'Histories from the margins' workshop in Colombo, 1–2 February 2018.
9 For the latter example, future research can rely on the kong-koan archives, part of the eighteenth- to twentieth-century administration of the Peranakan Chinese community in Batavia, which carries documents relating to conflict mediation over family affairs and business disputes at work within this mercantile community (Blussé and Chen, 2003)
10 ANRI Ambon 911/1/515 and 531.
11 To be precise, of the 111 unique court cases brought before the *Raad van Justitie* between 1758 and 1788 only 38 % of the accusers (n = 42) and 27 % of the defendants (n = 30) were (a direct relative of) Company personnel. The preponderance of local consumers of justice in lower Dutch courts was probably even higher, given the fact that the *Raad van Justitie* in Colombo only took civil lawsuits worth at least 300 rixdaalders, or appeals from the *Raden van Justitie* in the Galle and Jaffna judicial districts.
12 In the eighteenth century the population in and outside the fort grew considerably in size, although exact figures are not available at this point. To give an impression; the 1824 census lists around 5600 inhabitants in the fort and Pettah and another 25000 in the immediate surroundings (Peebles, 2015, p. 86).
13 Nicolaas Fonseka sued Frans Gomes, his father-in-law, in 1749. Six years later his mother-in-law sued the children of her late husband Frans Gomes, among others Anthony Gomes. Nicolaas Fonseka and Michiel Gomes were thus brothers-in-law. SLNA 4265: *Fonseka and Gomes – Gomes*; SLNA 4325: *Fonseka – Fernando and Chenassadij Poelle*.
14 SLNA 1/4493: *Fonseka – executors of the estate of captain Jongbloet*.
15 ANRI Makassar Inventory. The civil cases are listed under the names of the litigants.
16 SLNA 1/4389: *Narajene Pulle and Moettoe Rame – Paans Quintaal*.
17 For a more in-depth overview of the proposed approach, see the project website: www.universiteitleiden.nl/en/research/research-projects/humanities/colonialism-inside-out#tab-1.

References

Arasaratnam, S. (1981). Social history of a dominant caste society: the Vellalar of North Ceylon (Sri Lanka) in the 18th Century. *Indian Economic & Social History Review*, 18(3–4), pp. 377–391.

Ball, J. (1982). *Indonesian Legal History, 1602–1848*. Sydney: Oughtershaw Press.

Barkey, K. (2013). Aspects of legal pluralism in the Ottoman empire. In: L. Benton and R.J. Ross, eds., *Legal pluralism and empires 1500–1850*. New York: New York University press, pp. 61–75.

Benton, L. (2002). *Law and Colonial Cultures: Legal Regimes in World History, 1400–1900.* Cambridge: Cambridge University Press.

Benton, L. (2009). *A Search for Sovereignty: Law and Geography in European Empires, 1400–1900.* Cambridge: Cambridge University Press.

Benton, L. and Clulow, A. (2015). Legal encounters and the origins of global law. In: J.H. Bentley, S. Subrahmanyam and M.E. Wiesner-Hanks, eds., *The Cambridge world history, volume 6: the construction of a global world, 1400–1800 CE, part 2: patterns of change.* Cambridge: Cambridge University Press, pp. 80–100.

Benton, L. and Ross, R.J. (2013). *Legal Pluralism and Empires, 1500–1850.* New York: NYU Press.

Blussé, L. (1986). *Strange company: Chinese settlers, mestizo women and the Dutch in VOC Batavia.* Dordrecht: Foris Publications.

Blussé, L. and Chen, M. (2003). *The archives of the Kong Koan of Batavia, Sinica Leidensia, v. 59.* Leiden: Brill. Available at: https://books.google.be/books?id=WTnrUMIpwIYC&printsec=frontcover&dq=isbn:9789004131576&hl=nl&sa=X&ved=0ahUKEwjp6KqH6OvYAhUBJVAKHYV-BL0Q6AEIKDAA#v=onepage&q&f=false (Accessed: 22 January 2018).

Boomgaard, P. (2009). Following the debt: credit and debt in Southeast Asian legal theory and practice, 1400–1800. In D. Henley and P. Boomgaard, eds., *Credit and Debt in Indonesia, 860–1930: from Peonage to Pawnshop, from Kongsi to Cooperative.* Leiden: KITLV Press, pp. 61–79.

Burns, P. (1989). The myth of Adat. *The Journal of Legal Pluralism and Unofficial Law*, 21(28), pp. 1–129.

Cohn, B.S. (1996). *Colonialism and Its Forms of Knowledge: the British in India.* New Jersey: Princeton University Press.

Comaroff, J.L. (2001). Colonialism, culture, and the law: a foreword. *Law & Social Inquiry*, 26(2), pp. 305–314.

Dewasiri, N.R. (2008). *The Adaptable Peasant: Agrarian Society in Western Sri Lanka under Dutch rule, 1740–1800.* Leiden: Brill.

Dinges, M. (2004). The uses of justice as a form of social control in early modern Europe. In: H. Roodenburg and P. Spierenburg, eds., *Social Control in Europe (1500–1800).* Columbus: Ohio State University Press, pp. 159–176.

Hoadley, M.C. (1994). *Selective judicial competence: the Cirebon-Priangan legal administration 1680–1792.* Ithaca, NY: Cornell University Press.

Hooker, B.M. (1975). *Legal Pluralism: an Introduction to Colonial and Neo-colonial Laws.* Oxford: Clarendon Press.

Hovy, L. (1991). *Ceylonees plakkaatboek: Plakkaten en andere wetten uitgevaardigd door het Nederlandse bestuur op Ceylon, 1638–1796. Volume II.* Hilversum: Verloren.

Kan, J. van (1940). Bataviasche statuten en de Buiten-comptoiren. *Bijdragen Tot de Taal-, Land- En Volkenkunde van Nederlandsch-Indië*, 100, pp. 255–282.

Kanumoyoso, B. (2011). *Beyond the City Wall: Society and Economic Development in the Ommelanden of Batavia, 1684–1740.* Leiden: Leiden University.

Kok, J. et al. (2018). Contested conjugality? Sinhalese marriage practices in eighteenth-century Dutch Ceylon. *Annales de démographie historique* (forthcoming).

Niemeijer, H. (2005). *Batavia. Een koloniale samenleving in de 17de eeuw.* Amersfoort: Balans.

Paranavitana, K.D. (2001). *Land for Money: Dutch Land Registration in Sri Lanka.* Colombo.

Peebles, P. (2015). *Historical Dictionary of Sri Lanka.* Lanham: Rowman & Littlefield.

Raben, R. (1996). *Batavia and Colombo: the Ethnic and Spatial Order of Two Colonial Cities 1600–1800.* Available at: www.academia.edu/715645/Batavia_and_Colombo._The_Ethnic_and_Spatial_Order_of_Two_Colonial_Cities_1600-1800_Ph.D._thesis_Leiden_1996_. (Accessed: 28 May 2018)

Ravensbergen, S. (2018). *Courtrooms of conflict: criminal law, local elites and legal pluralities in colonial Java*. Leiden: Leiden University.

Ross, R. (1983). *Cape of Torments: Slavery and Resistance in South Africa*. London: Routledge & Kegan Paul.

Roy, T. and Swamy, A.V. (2016). *Law and the Economy in Early Modern India*. Chicago: University of Chicago Press.

Rupesinghe, N. (2016). *Negotiating Custom: Colonial Lawmaking in the Galle Landraad*. Leiden: Leiden University.

Schrikker, A. (2015). Conflict resolution, social control and law-making in eighteenth-century Dutch Sri Lanka. In C. Antunes and J. Gommans, eds., *Exploring the Dutch Empire: Agents, Networks and Institutions, 1600–2000*. London: Bloomsbury Publishing, pp. 227–240.

Schrikker, A. and Ekama, K. (2017). Through the lens of slavery: Dutch Sri Lanka in the eighteenth century. In: A. Strathern and Z. Biedermann, eds., *Sri Lanka at the cross-roads of history*. London: UCL Press, pp. 178–193.

Sirks, B. and Hallebeek, J. (2010). Uit het Archief van de Raad van Justitie te Colombo: Rechtsbedeling in Ceylon in de 18de eeuw. *Fundamina*, 1, pp. 390–412.

Sutherland, H. (2009). Money in Makassar: credit and debt in an eighteenth-century VOC settlement. In P. Boomgaard and D. Henley, eds., *Credit and Debt in Indonesia, 860–1930: from Peonage to Pawnshop, from Kongsi to Cooperative*. Leiden: KITLV press, pp. 102–123.

Sutherland, H. (2010). Treacherous translators and improvident paupers: perception and practice in Dutch Makassar, eighteenth and nineteenth centuries. *Journal of the Economic and Social History of the Orient*, 53(1–2), pp. 319–356.

Tamanaha, B.Z. (1993). The folly of the social scientific concept of legal pluralism. *Journal of Law and Society*, 20, pp. 192–217.

Tamanaha, B.Z. (2008). Understanding legal pluralism: past to present, local to global. *Sydney Law Review*, 30, pp. 375–411.

Tamanaha, B.Z. (2010). *Beyond the Formalist–Realist Divide: the Role of Politics in Judging*. Princeton: Princeton University Press.

Tosun, M. (2018) '(Im)practical pluralism: legal pluralism in Batavia and its environs: from codification to practice (c. 1750–1800)' (MA Thesis) Leiden University.

Wamelen, C. van (2014). *Family Life onder de VOC*. Hilversum: Verloren.

von Benda-Beckmann, F. and von Benda-Beckmann, K. (2012). Islamic law in a plural context: the struggle over inheritance law in colonial West Sumatra. *Journal of the Economic and Social History of the Orient*, 55(4–5), pp. 771–793.

von Benda-Beckmann, K. (1981). Forum shopping and shopping forums: dispute processing in a Minangkabau village in West Sumatra. *Journal of Legal Pluralism and Unofficial Law*, 13(19), pp. 117–159.

Ward, K. (2009). *Networks of Empire: Forced migration in the Dutch East India Company*. Cambridge: Cambridge University Press.

Wellen, K. (2009). Credit among the Early Modern To Wajoq. In D. Henley and P. Boomgaard, eds., *Credit and Debt in Indonesia, 860–1930: from Peonage to Pawnshop, from Kongsi to Cooperative*. Leiden: KITLV Press, pp. 80–101.

Wellen, K.A. (2014). *The Open Door: Early Modern Wajorese Statecraft and Diaspora*. DeKalb: Northern Illinois University Press.

Worden, N. (1985). *Slavery in Dutch South Africa*. Cambridge: Cambridge University Press.

Yannakakis, Y. (2015). Beyond jurisdictions: native agency in the making of colonial legal cultures. A review essay. *Comparative Studies in Society and History*, 57(4), pp. 1070–1082.

4

FACING THE LAW IN EIGHTEENTH-CENTURY GALLE[1]

Nadeera Rupesinghe

Introduction

When served with a summons in 1780, Kalegana Bastian Naidelage Maria of Dutch-controlled Galle in southern Sri Lanka was particularly displeased. She was reported to have brazenly responded that even her dog would not appear before the judicial forum that summoned her. Maria was to be flogged for this perceived affront.[2] Although her brashness gives us a glimpse of subversion against an early colonial ruler, from at least the late seventeenth century indigenous litigants in Sri Lanka brought their lawsuits before panels of Dutch and local judges. Successive European occupations since the sixteenth century had influenced Sri Lanka's legal culture to varying degrees.

This chapter discusses the reception of a judicial forum set up by the Dutch East India Company (VOC) in 1741 in Galle. The *Landraad* (literally Land Council) was a kind of district court which had a majority of VOC officials and a minority of subordinate local headmen. Given Maria's example, to what extent was the Land Council perceived as intrusive of local affairs? Law practices may by themselves be either inclusive or exclusive, or deliberately made so by those in power. Colonial judicial bodies are known to have stimulated relatively powerless groups in society to come forward (Merry 2010, p. 1068). Supplicants, in the form of litigants, sought justice by applying to the Land Council. By extension, witnesses who bolstered case narratives were engaged in a similar pursuit and will also be dealt with in this chapter as individuals who were required to face the law.

Did ordinary men and women make representations to the plural legal order of the Land Council? Sri Lanka's rich legal history has been neglected, with a call to study the Dutch records of the Land Council in the 1960s remaining unheeded till now. The Land Council used a plurality of laws, including Roman-Dutch and Sinhalese normative systems.[3] This chapter considers questions relating to the reception of the Land Council and its civil litigation. Which social groups came to the Land Council? Representations of social hierarchies in judicial matters can be unravelled through processes of identification by local participants and officials as seen in the Land Council. Status was potentially important in supporting a case, and recording status was therefore necessary. Issues such as female agency, occupation and social background provide insights into the scope of the Land Council. The samples of litigants and witnesses analyzed in this chapter paint a picture of the everyday workings of the Land Council and the legal consciousness of colonial subjects.

The VOC's primary interest was in extracting the cinnamon on the island for international trade. By 1765, the Dutch ruled the coast, effectively landlocking the indigenous Kandyan kingdom in the mountainous interior. The Land Council of Galle was in Kumbalwella, two kilometres from Galle Fort which was a walled town of mostly European inhabitants. Its councillors heard issues in closed sessions except when they delivered sentences.

Personal jurisdiction over litigants who lived outside the Galle town but within the Galle district was potentially the most important factor in selecting the Galle Land Council. This was to some extent overridden by the location of the dispute in relation to lands registered in the *thombos*, registers with cadastral and census features maintained by the Land Council, in which case inhabitants of the town who had claims to land outside it also approached the Land Council. Naturally, witnesses would not have felt the same exigencies as litigants, but the knowledge of legal processes that they acquired through their participation and their preferred status having been chosen as witnesses are important aspects in fully understanding societal participation in the Land Council. Both litigants and witnesses faced the law in this new legal institution. The distance from the individual's residence to the council either hampered or facilitated such involvement with the council. The residence of litigants is difficult to determine, but this chapter will deal with the geographical reach of the council through an analysis of *ratione loci*, which refers to jurisdiction over a dispute location, and the residence of witnesses.

The importance of the law in the everyday lives of the elite and peasant subjects of colonial Galle cannot be overestimated. The use of the Land Council was closely connected to the *thombo*, a meticulous Dutch exercise of recording every plot of land, which shareholders could not disregard. The *thombo* was a vehicle for the company to extend its rule in the countryside. Land Council officials carried out the registration over many years from the 1740s onwards, either by visiting each village or instructing inhabitants to come to the council. The Land Council settled registration issues and lawsuits that could be referred in appeal to the *Raad van Justitie* (Council of Justice) of Galle, and thereafter to the *Raad van Justitie* of Colombo and potentially to Batavia. Yet beyond the Land Council there were no local judges such as the minority of elite headmen involved in that forum as councillors. The council observed Roman-Dutch procedural law and written processes in the Dutch language that were new to the local people.[4] The VOC would not have been able to envisage how the locals would perceive the Land Council. However, its effective acceptance by the late eighteenth century at least can be gleaned through the prominence of land litigation and the participation of women and low-caste groups.

Social formations in Galle

Coastal inhabitants survived by fishing, construction work, boat-building and agriculture. Inhabitants of the more rural hinterland survived through peasant agriculture alone. Many villages would have been self-sufficient in the production of rice, and interdependent in the provision of essential services. Most inhabitants in Galle were Sinhalese, but the larger villages seem to have been economic centres with diverse groups of people including Moors and Chettiars, traditionally associated with trade. Being a coastal region, it was naturally diverse, and was inhabited by migrants from southern India as well. Europeans mostly lived in the Fort or in proximity to it and were either part of company rule or interacted with it closely. Ethnic and caste-based divisions are clearly defined in Sri Lanka today, but it would be anachronistic to apply such clarity to eighteenth-century Galle. The total population of the district was roughly 95,000 individuals.[5]

Among the Sinhalese, the *goygama* (farmer) caste was the largest and was made up primarily of agriculturalists. In the absence of reliable census data from the eighteenth century, some of the earliest figures emerge from later British rule in the country. A census taken in 1824 of the Sinhalese caste composition of the low country reveals that 54.3 per cent were of the *goygama* caste, and three non-farmer castes together, which were controversially believed to have a ritually low status, the *karāva* (15.7 per cent), *salāgama* (7.5 per cent) and *durāva* (5.6 per cent), constituted almost 30 per cent of the low-country population (Jayawardena, 2000, p. 164; Ryan, 1953, p. 264). The *goygama* were also situated above the *hakuru* and *padu* (agricultural) castes in the social hierarchy and Nirmal Dewasiri argues that they had easier access to the better paddy lands in a village (2008, pp. 143, 167). Members of the *goygama* caste, who were mostly Buddhists but converted to Christianity under Portuguese and Dutch rule at least nominally for legal and administrative purposes, remained the most influential on the island. They are likely to have been the largest group that appealed to the Land Council. Their influence did not, however, go unchallenged. The *salāgama* group gained political power and the right to govern their affairs in Dutch times through their headmen, and *karāva* headmen were present among the councillors of the Land Council. Yet real power was vested with male *goygama* chiefs, and proximity to Galle town gave them a further advantage.

The company understood the nuances within such identities to some degree, as seen in official classifications. The Dutch knew that the *karāvas* (mostly referred to as *vissers* or fishermen by them) engaged in a variety of activities such as carpentry, construction and transportation that were important to the colonial power, apart from activities more directly related to fishing. They knew that the *salāgama* not only engaged in cinnamon peeling as their traditional occupation but also went to sea. At that time, cinnamon peeling was not their exclusive occupation, nor was fishing and carpentry handled only by the *karāvas*, as is popularly believed today.

Other identities that were in flux at the time were those of the *burgers* (citizens) and Chettiars. In Dutch times the *burgers* were, generally speaking, European settlers, but also 'respectable' families of Portuguese descent who had entered the

Dutch clan. Company officials who left the service became *vrijburgers* (free citizens) The British, who mixed with these *burgers* later, referred to them as 'Burghers'. They now form a separate ethnic group in the country and to avoid confusion, I will use the spelling *burger*, which is also the form that appears in the Land Council documents and in the *thombos*. Many *burgers* of Dutch times became tavern keepers, butchers, tailors, bakers and shopkeepers, and some even became overseas merchants (Roberts et al., 1989, p. 38). Remco Raben writes of how manumitted slaves and *karāvas* were granted *burger* status on petitions made by them (1996, p. 270). Yet another group that was ambiguous at the time were the Chettiars, traditionally known as traders of south Indian origin. Dewasiri has examined the integration of the Chettiar community with the *goygama* agricultural caste and the *karāvas* (2008, pp. 201–202). Intermarriages of Europeans and Chettiars with locals made such identities mobile and vague during early colonial rule, a feature that in fact continued well into the nineteenth century as reflected in the diverse categorizations that the British employed during that century.

The legal status of the Moors and Chettiars on Dutch territory was ambiguous. Raben writes of how they settled in Colombo from the Coromandel, encouraged by the 'gradual and partial liberalization of trade' (1996, p. 106). Temporary settlers among them, at the least, had to perform unpaid public work every three months as a kind of payment for residence. Yet those who bore such an obligation often appeared in the *thombos*. VOC regulations that were not always enforced prohibited Moor ownership of immovable property from the seventeenth century onwards, but were lifted in the mid-eighteenth century (Goonewardena, 1986). By the late eighteenth century, the Dutch had fully recognized the need for cooperation with the Moors, some of whom were also involved in the collection of paddy rents in the hinterland (Rupesinghe [writing as Seneviratne], 2010, p. 76).

In addition to the dominant peasant agriculture, Galle was a centre of a 'sizeable seaborne trade and concentrations of non-farmer social elements' (Dewasiri, 2008, p. 85). The Moors and Chettiars being essentially Tamil-speaking groups, other groups from southern India very likely also resided in Galle retaining their language and Hindu religion. Galle saw groups such as the Malays who served in the Eastern militia, slaves from further across the Indian Ocean from Madagascar to South East Asia, and manumitted slaves who were already appearing in the Land Council in defence of their rights to property. Galle was part of a wide political and economic network that was linked to the Cape, Colombo and Batavia.

That group identities were vague is without doubt. Classifications based on caste were at times used in conjunction with terms signifying occupational specializations and title-holding. In relation to occupation, there was little mutual exclusivity among castes as occupational diversity was high. While the ethnicity of groups such as the Jaffna Tamils, Moors, Chettiars and Malays received official recognition to the point of codification of their laws in some cases, John D. Rogers is right that the social identities that the Dutch used in their day-to-day administration were the 'caste-like groups' that the Portuguese had also used (2004, p. 630). More specifically, inhabitants were primarily linked to occupation and service in

Land Council documents. We must keep in mind that there was little agreement in the company bureaucracy on the criteria of a social group or on a group's name. The Dutch term *geslacht* was often used to mean caste, ethnicity, nation or lineage by VOC officials in Sri Lanka and could refer to a present-day ethnic or caste group alike. How such identifications panned out in the Land Council will be explored later in this chapter.

Litigants and witnesses

The litigiousness of the natives in Sri Lanka is a commonly held view (Tennent, 1860, p. 543), but while it may be a stereotype it is a difficult conclusion to arrive at as many different factors affect involvement in a judicial forum. The ninety-nine cases in my sample involved a total of 243 litigants. They all appeared in registers from the years 1778 and 1779, but some may have appeared before and after those years in connection with their cases.[6] These years are representative of a period of relative peace, many years after the war with Kandy that ended in 1765 and before the greater emphasis on centralization policies imposed by the next governor, Willem Jacob van de Graaff, who took up office in 1785. The examples of dispute locations used in this chapter are also from the above registers. At times the same persons reappeared in the council (occasionally on the same day) in connection with different cases and in such instances I counted them only once. Following Marie-Charlotte Le Bailly's practice, I have taken a case and not a legal issue as the point of departure, as a person involved in a process that involved two or more legal issues would otherwise be enumerated more than once (2001, p. 219). A small number (18) appeared in two cases, and a smaller number (8) in more than two.

Defining a 'litigant' is not an easy task. *Ratione personae* is the particular jurisdiction of a judicial body over plaintiffs or defendants living in a territorial area. A litigant may have appeared many times in connection with a case, ranging from a single appearance to several. Not all defendants, plaintiffs or supplicants appeared in the council at every hearing, especially in cases with collectives as parties.[7] They were, however, required to be present when the sentence was pronounced. I have not attempted to remove from the count those who were not physically present despite being mentioned as litigants; their numbers are small. Principal litigants from a collective, or husbands, procurators or other authorized persons, appeared on their behalf. I have assumed that such litigants were aware of the proceedings even tangentially and included them in the count, as also their special representatives. I have left out only the procurators, who were professional process representatives officially delegated to plead a case in the name of a principal party. Occasionally officials appeared as part of the VOC government or the native department—such as the clerk of the Inlandse Boedelkamer (a board that managed the estate of deceased natives) and in particular village officials such as *mayorāls*, who gave oral evidence. I did not include them in the count of those who came to the council as litigants or participants outside their official duties. Where the minutes mention their names, I counted everyone in collectives of litigants separately. This differs from the practice applied by Schepper et al. (1988, pp. 272–274),[8] but it was important to build an image of those involved with the Land Council in a certain period. Some litigants referred to collectively (for example, as the heirs of a certain person) with no further details were counted as one but obviously involved more than a single litigant.[9]

For this analysis of the reach of the Land Council, I have included a sample of 264 witnesses from a register of depositions.[10] They appeared in the years 1778–1781. A deposition, which in most cases involved more than one witness, almost always recorded the individual's age, occupation, village of residence and religion, thereby providing information on witness participation and the use of evidence. The recording of the (official) religious identity of the witnesses was consistent, it being practically important for the oath that had a discrete form for different groups. Other information on the witnesses included their occupation, which had a direct bearing on their credibility. Most witnesses were adults (some as old as ninety years old), while the youngest I found was fifteen years old. In some instances, they would appear in more than one case. I eliminated recurring witnesses as far as possible from the sample, although name variations and possible changes in residence made this process problematic. Not surprisingly for a society that displayed pronounced age heaping (Drixler and Kok, 2016)—in brief, the rounding off of ages to the nearest five or ten—the recorded ages from deposition to deposition of a seemingly single person often did not match. When name, occupation and village are matched, as many as twenty-one witnesses (8 per cent) appeared twice. Haputantrige Johan appeared four times and Haputantrige Michiel three times. VOC officials were not blind to the incidence of professional witnesses.

The Land Council minutes show no consistency in the recording of personal information. Where available, the data on litigants and witnesses has been used to explore issues of gender and social status. The choice of information included in the Land Council minutes and depositions reveals to us the preoccupations of an early colonial judicial council with social categories. Age, religion, title and village of residence are more readily available in witness depositions.

Caseloads and jurisdiction

What kinds of legal matters did litigants raise? To understand the nature of the issues heard in the Galle Land Council, I mapped out the administration of justice in that council through the above-mentioned sample of almost a hundred cases from the minutes of 1778–1779. A larger sample which can show change over time was beyond the scope of this study as the documents relating to a case are not filed in separate dossiers and must be compiled from many registers of minutes, depositions, interrogations, annexes and correspondence. Entries on various cases and a smaller number (13) of administrative matters were written out in these minutes as there was no separation between the spheres of justice and administrative matters dealt with by the council. The Land Council minutes are an indiscriminate collection of all the business transacted by this council. I did not follow a strict chronology, tracing as far as possible the start and end of each case, thereby in some instances effectively extending the period covered by the sample cases to both before and after 1778–1779. They include simple requests that the council settled immediately, ones where it appointed commissioners from the council to travel to a village to write a report, others where the supplicants had to provide more evidence, and further cases that became civil suits with a plaintiff and defendant. The definition of a case used here is thus any matter involving a litigant brought before the Land Council. They are not all strictly speaking cases of litigation but the incidence of any issue involving a supplicant in the council is taken as a historical event in this analysis.

Classifying cases under separate categories of law is not easy, and consequently only an overview of their nature is attempted here. The causes of litigation are too complex and ambiguous, and thus defy categorization. Litigants, procurators and councillors made no reference to laws that were recorded in the documents. At times, we only know the names of the parties who appeared. This difficulty of grouping cases by subject was the result of different factors: the style of the council records; the fact that not all cases resulted in a sentence as high procedural costs and settlements may have led to their withdrawal; and patchy records (particularly in the minutes from 19 October 1776 to 16 May 1778, just before the sample taken here and the available annexes). Although we do not know the outcome of some cases, we can assume that they were either settled or abandoned.[11]

Civil issues relating to immovable property form the bulk of the cases under the category of private law. To a certain extent this is a trivial conclusion given that dealing with land issues was the principle task assigned to the council, but other civil matters were also heard by this body.[12] Many cases involved land in some way (86 per cent), the rest being mostly debt issues, some of which were not related to land. Almost half the land matters concerned the transfer of property rights; more on this follows below. Disputes about inheritance and possessory actions to recover lands feature, as do disputes about the provision of labour services. From pre-Dutch times, different social formations performed obligatory services for the state (known as *rājakāriya*) and such obligations survived into Dutch and British times. The new colonial power assumed the administrative duties of such obligations. In return for performing various services in the roles of high- and low-level headmen, soldiers, artisans and 'coolies' among others, the sovereign awarded fixed amounts of land. In the final analysis, as disputes over the service recorded in company documents that were heard in the Land Council had to do with access to property, such cases were also connected to land.

The occurrence of service issues is especially important in understanding that inhabitants regarded the *thombo* record as critical. In 1778, the heirs of a family by the name of Kandege in the Galle district asked to be recognized as *mayorāls* instead of *naindes*, a request that the Land Council granted. Among other duties, a *mayorāl* traditionally organized the compulsory service due from a village to the ruling power. He also reported to the Land Council on land matters and provided victuals for visiting commissioners and headmen. He was entitled to approximately four acres of land in return for his services. A *nainde*, in contrast, received an acre of land in return for performing menial tasks in the village. Three local headmen supported the family's claim, asserting that it was an old custom that when there were no *mayorāls* in a village the *naindes* took over the task. Accordingly, Kandege Jantje and his two sons Apponsu and Johannes and his five nephews were entered in the new registration system as *mayorāls*.[13] In another case heard that same year, a *mayorāl* successfully requested that the Land Council register his son by his first wife in his service as such titles were hereditary. Witanachchige Bastiaan said he had married his son Jantje's mother in the customary way. Jantje's mother's brother claimed to be ignorant of his sister's marriage, although stating that Jantje was indeed her son and that he had brought up the boy when he was young. Another *mayorāl* and writer said that they were not aware of the circumstances of his birth, but that Jantje had always been known as Bastiaan's son and had already performed the *mayorāl* service for many years. Despite doubt about a recognized marriage, the council conceded to Bastiaan's request.[14] Also in my sample, another service issue was settled by the Land Council by allowing the *mayorāl* service to be rendered on a yearly rotating basis by the litigants.[15] Much earlier, in 1760, Laurens Dias who was a *vidāne* (a minor local headman) took *mayorāls* to task for registering his mother as a 'coolie'.[16] Such negotiations as described here on service identification through requests for changes in registration were important in gaining affluence as service titles were connected to land holdings.

Movable property cases were also brought before the Land Council. One case concerned the ownership of a cow resulting from a dispute about its purchase.[17] Yet another case primarily concerned debt, but included a dispute about the ownership of a distillery kettle (and garden) used for the distillation of arrack, and which Cornelis Hendeling claimed back from Pellekettie Christina who had had a son by his late son Matthijs Hendeling. Matthijs had left debts that Cornelis claimed to have settled. Christina, against whom Cornelis initiated the possessory action, argued that she had nothing to live on and wanted the case to be defended *pro deo* on her behalf, a request that was granted. Yet, she lost the case, and was required to pay Cornelis all that he had paid as settlement of his son's debts in a sentence that referred to the case as a debt matter.[18]

The Land Council frequently acted in an official capacity. It was involved in disposing of property belonging to a deceased person, an official of the Inlandse Boedelkamer appearing in the council for that purpose.[19] Another case involved an investigation into the lands belonging to a revenue farmer and their subsequent sale to recover arrears in rent payments.[20] However, no cases of revenue farming involving rent payers and farmers were heard in the sample registers, although disputes between them could be heard in the Land Council (Rupesinghe [writing as Seneviratne], 2010). In another case, Coenraad Hendeling, a sergeant who lived outside the town, was instructed to pay the *mayorāl* of Unawatuna twelve stivers as garden tax that remained in arrears for his garden named Rendewatte for the 1778–1779 accounting year, and the costs of the case. Hendeling absconded on the first and second summons served in September 1779, but did appear in November. Together with the procurator Albertus Hissink, he handed over a request that was read out in the council (unfortunately this is not available in the records).[21] Inhabitants often defaulted on tax payments (Loten, 1935, pp. 23–24). This case indicates that the taxes recorded in the *thombo* were taken seriously and that the council could summon transgressors. Yet such cases involving taxes or rents were rare, with only one each in the sample.

The emergence of a land market can already be seen at this time. The Galle Political Council expressed concern in 1748 that too many Sinhalese were transferring their lands to Moors, which they feared would lead to the Sinhalese 'losing everything'.[22] Permission for the sale of lands was frequently sought. The Land Council instructions of 1789 detail the regulations for the sale of land (Mottau, 1965, pp. 10–11).[23] The council appeared to be engaging in very ordinary business in handling simple requests to sell land, but its approval was necessary to establish that the seller's title was alienable. This is a result of an originally more widespread feudal nature of land. If entered as a *paravēni* (ancestral) plot in the *thombo*, a share could be easily sold. Before the Land Council permitted the sale of gardens, native commissioners had to investigate whether there was cinnamon on the land.[24] The need to preserve the existing cinnamon reflects the constant concern of the company regarding its supply. The investigations appear to have taken place in the presence of the village headmen and the heirs. The prospective seller had to pay the costs of the native commissioners in such an operation.[25] Outside my sample in 1783, they found that twelve cinnamon trees were growing on the land and the council permitted the sale on the condition that the buyer lets the trees grow.[26] It was also necessary for the *thombohouder* (*thombo*-keeper) to confirm ownership.[27] In one case, summons by drums were issued for claimants to come forward before the sale.[28] At times, disputes arose on whether a transaction was a sale or mortgage (*verpanding*),[29] although such instances did not occur in my sample. For example, Maria Bouman claimed that Jacob Floorman and she had not sold but rather mortgaged the land the opposing party was claiming as their own.[30] In another case, a previous 'sale' of land by Kallehe Paandige Johan to his cousin Francina's husband and cousin Matthijs was challenged by Johan's daughters Edirihami and Punchihami. They said that they did not know whether their father had sold the half-acre in question or mortgaged it.[31] The Land Council had to approve land sale deeds and deeds of gift. Once a sale was completed, the *thombo* had to be updated, and many such entries were made.[32]

Land sale matters also shed light on inheritance law, which leads to a further overlap of issues. Warnesuriepattebendige Dona Maka was a woman who appeared three times in the council during the years 1778 and 1779 (and many times afterwards) in connection with the sale of land.[33] In September 1778, she had to prove exactly how many people laid claim to the gardens she wanted to sell by appearing before the council with other family members who would corroborate her story. The Land Council gave a decision on the matter, but later that year decided that a wedding gift entitled her to sell a greater share of the estate. On both occasions, the council said that her children had to agree to the sale. When Don Johan de Silva Wijesiriwardena

Dissanayake, a former *muddaliyar* (native headman of high rank), wished to sell a piece of land, he was also asked to secure the approval of all prospective heirs.[34] These and other cases indicate enforcement of the principle of bilateral inheritance, where property is divided equally among both male and female children.

The sample cases demonstrate that the primary preoccupation of those people who came before the Land Council was land litigation. The kind of cases that did not come up can also be telling. For instance, public concerns were not raised in the council. This is not surprising considering that the Land Council held the whip hand. It could impose corporal punishments on those who breached justice by withholding information or were guilty of contempt, thereby demonstrating its policing powers. I found no cases against Land Council procedure or policy, nor any disputes over competency. Such resistance could be observed in a more understated manner, such as through plaintiffs who claimed errors in the registration that resulted in the punishment of *thombo*-keepers. Petitions were more likely to have been the avenue through which people complained directly about governing issues.[35]

In practice, how far did the jurisdiction of the Galle Land Council extend geographically? The *ratione loci* (by reason of place) I considered in the cases from 1778 to 1779 is the location of the paddy fields and gardens under dispute. There were more dispute locations (93) than the number of cases involving land (83 of 99) as some cases dealt with fields and gardens in more than one village. The geographical origin of the disputes is as follows, arranged by sub-district: Four Gravets (36), Wellaboda (11), Gangaboda (12), Walallawiti (8), Talpe (7). No cases were recorded from the Hinidum Pattu, while nineteen dispute locations remain unknown. The original residence of the litigants would be important in ascertaining how close to the centre of government they lived, but this information is not available for over 50 per cent of them. The high incidence of absentee ownership makes the residence of the litigants more important, as those who had moved towards the centre of Dutch government while retaining their rights to land in other villages may have been influenced towards initiating legal action. Such an analysis is beyond the scope of this study, but the recorded residence of witnesses gives us some indication of how accessible Kumbalwella was.

Proximity to the centre was important in determining who came to the council. Galle Fort, and the sub-district of the Four Gravets, within which Kumbalwella was the seat of the Land Council, the *thombo* office and the overseer of the Galle district, were pivotal locations that connected Galle to Colombo, the centre of Dutch administration in Sri Lanka. They were relatively more 'urban' than the surrounding hinterland. Many disputed lands were in the Four Gravets. Kumbalwella had at least ten dispute locations but is likely to have been a more populated and urban area within the Galle district. The contrast of a coastal urban area versus the rural hinterland may apply here, although distinct categories of town and countryside as seen in European studies were of little consequence in Dutch Sri Lanka. Considerable parallels between the two were more likely than dissimilarity of life patterns among the inhabitants of the coast and the hinterland. At the same time, the relationship between proximity to the Dutch government and legal action may be overrated. For instance, if witnesses could travel the distances that they did, this is very likely representative of the distance that litigants could travel as well, although litigants are likely to have been more motivated to go the extra mile. Of a total of 264 witnesses for the period 1778–1781, their residence was as follows: Four Gravets (54), Wellaboda (51), Gangaboda (49), Walallawiti (5), Talpe (61).[36] No witnesses were recorded from the Hinidum Pattu.

The company instructed the Land Council to pay due regard to the distance to Kumbalwella faced by litigants and witnesses (Mottau, 1965, p. 6). Leonard Woolf, a British civil servant who also served as a magistrate in Sri Lanka, wrote on the difficulties of travelling in the region even in the early twentieth century (1981 [1913], pp. 53–54, 60). In an eighteenth-century lawsuit, a group of eight witnesses were supposedly inconvenienced by the considerable distance. First, the case was not taken up on the stipulated day in December 1779 as the Land Council postponed the sitting until the next day. The witnesses were to be cross-examined by the opposing party, but they did not have a counter-interrogation ready. The litigant for whom they appeared pleaded that his witnesses could not remain because they lived far away and could not interrupt the performance of their services to the company. The commissioners who presided over the meeting asked the opposing party to be ready the next morning or within twenty-four hours 'because the witnesses could not be delayed longer as they lived faraway in the country'. Consequently, they were forced to stay a third day as well.[37] The next day, the council's messenger said that the errant litigant had informed him that on leaving the hearing the day before he had been attacked by piercing pains in the stomach and was still in confinement.[38] Yet despite the distance, the witnesses reappeared twenty days later to be cross-examined.[39] These witnesses were from Amugoda-Keppitiyagoda (Gangaboda Pattu), Nagoda (Gangaboda Pattu), Tiranagama (Wellaboda Pattu), Katukolihe (Wellaboda) and Majuwana (Gangaboda Pattu), which are between twelve and eighteen kilometres away from Kumbalwella (see Image 4.1). It is challenging to calculate how many days of travel such distances would have entailed as terrain difficulties are difficult to gauge. The councillors and the litigant considered this to be a considerable distance, but they still appeared in the Land Council as did other witnesses from locations further away.

The evidence suggests that there was less participation in colonial rule in the hinterlands bordering the Kandyan kingdom, where the Land Council's jurisdiction may have been contested. Apart from the Four Gravets, if we consider the sub-districts of Wellaboda, Gangaboda, Talpe and Walallawiti together, they had in total only around forty dispute locations, similar to the number of disputes from the Four Gravets. The population in these so-called hinterland areas may also have been low. It is striking that there were no cases from the Hinidum Pattu, its considerable remoteness being an obvious reason. According to the available data, Hinidum also did not produce any witnesses. The area was remote from the administrative heart of Galle and was in fact on the border of the Kandyan kingdom. This indicates that if particularly long distances were involved, litigants were not keen to make representations to the Land Council. In all six well drawn up *thombos* of the Hinidum Pattu, I found no references to council decisions on the ownership of lands added to the text. The commissioners, if they travelled to that sub-district for the registration,

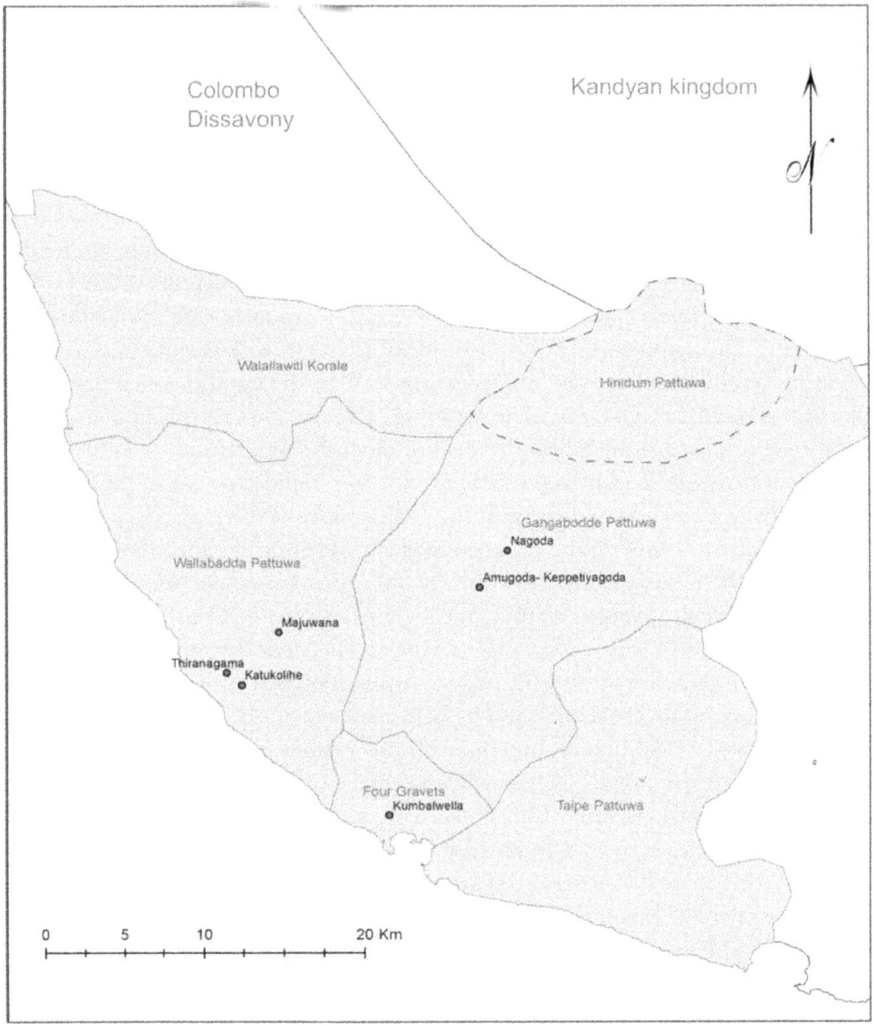

MAP 4.1 Villages in the Galle district

Villages in the Galle district (shown in grey) considered 'far' by the Land Council located in Kumbalwella, all between 12 and 18 km away. The Hinidum Pattu border shown here is tentative.

may have settled all disputes, avoiding the necessity of the full council having to hear an issue.[40] This is in contrast to other *thombos* such as Dodampe and Ganegoda of the Wellaboda Pattu (close to the coast), where disputes arose at the time of registration. These two villages had at least ten recorded issues between them from 1780 to 1781.

This analysis of *ratione loci* shows that in areas close to Galle Fort the company's new legal regime and by extension its sovereignty were not in dispute. However, in inaccessible locations that were less densely populated and closer to local powers litigation at the Land Council was rare. If the company's jurisdiction was controversial, it was still not contentious enough for people to refrain from making a long journey from the sub-districts around the seat of the council, although they were less willing to go through thick jungle and other difficult terrain further north. Colonial litigation, where it could be relatively easily accessed, led the peasant population to the Land Council in their efforts to secure justice.

In attempting to measure litigiousness through the relative frequency of lawsuits, we have no parameters by which to assess a hundred cases. Many factors including social standing, distance and costs would contribute to whether litigants engaged with a colonial judicial forum. A further complicating factor in Sri Lanka was that when the company was drawing up the *thombo* of a village, several disputes would arise from that process. Dodampe (Wellaboda) has six cases that all came up in around 1780, the year in which its *thombo* was drawn up. It is thus likely that there is a correlation between the cadastral registration of a village and land-related cases heard in the council. Some *thombos*, however, including all six Hinidum Pattu *thombos* drawn up in 1760 as mentioned above, have no references at all to disputes heard in the Land Council. Proximity to the centre, which Hinidum lacked, would have led to a predisposition towards seeking legal redress. Nonetheless, the significance of the *thombos* and the process of creating them is likely to have reached even such remote areas.

Gender: women and the law

The Dutch colonial regime affected the lives of urban and rural women in civil matters such as marriage, legitimacy of children and property through ordinances and judicial practice. The justice system was exclusively male dominated, but female litigants were not intimidated in approaching the Land Council. Land disputes were as important for men as for women. In the sample of men and women who made representations at the Land Council, 174 (73 per cent) were men and 64 (27 per cent) women.[41] The women, who were mostly Sinhalese, were connected with fifty-one cases (52 per cent of the sample cases), either singly or in groups.[42]

In Sri Lanka, there was no femme couvert. It was not possible to make the legal position of a woman in Galle subordinate to that of her husband as in seventeenth- and eighteenth-century Holland, where a married woman could not appear before the judiciary without her husband's support (Haks, 1985, p. 153; Lee, 1946, p. 65). Women 'except a mother and grandmother, and they only so long as they have not contracted a second marriage' were also prohibited from being guardians (Lee, 1946, p. 106). Some women relied on representatives to plead on their behalf in the Land Council, perhaps due to a reluctance to appear before it, but more likely for reasons of convenience. In the sample, six men represented the interests of their wives. The widow Jemoniga Jebel was represented by a former *kangān* (overseer), and another indisposed woman by her son.[43] Yet others participated actively in the Galle Land Council, including married women who went to the Land Council alone. Maria, who insulted the Land Council when she was served her summons, illustrates the agency of women in eighteenth-century Sri Lanka. Outside my sample, Kosmulage Lisa appeared without her husband, the *vidāne* of Hinatigala Willalege Janis, although she does appear to have had his active support. She was defending a gift of land that she claimed from her mother against her sisters.[44] In another case, the widow Godage Mienga appealed her case against Don Pedru Bastiaan de Silva over a property dispute from the Land Council to the Council of Justice of Galle, which refused her appeal. Displaying remarkable perseverance, she then appealed to the Council of Justice in Colombo, which, however, also rejected her request.[45] In all this, the relative independence of women at the Land Council shows a failure of the Dutch system of enclosing women under the authority of males in their role as paterfamilias. A transfer of this control over women's bodies was attempted, but not fully achieved in Sri Lanka.

Femaleness as seen in the Land Council was at times coupled with widowhood and social inferiority. In fact, twenty or almost one-third of the female litigants were widows. By the seventeenth century, widows were majors (legal personae) according to the law of Holland (Wessels, 1908, p. 428). Widows often came to the council in connection with property that belonged to their late husbands. In a case outside my sample but taken up shortly afterwards, Gamage Livina of Dodampe made claims in the Land Council to property that she believed had been unlawfully appropriated by a relative. She was the widow of a *kangān*, but came to the Land Council not in connection with her husband's property but with regard to what she believed was her legacy from her father. A cousin had had the property registered in the *thombo* under his name alone.[46] Low-caste women also made representations to the Land Council. Sepala Hakuruge Dominga of Kumbalwella was a Sinhalese woman from the ritually low-status *hakuru* caste. She wished to appeal to the Council of Justice in Galle in her case against a fellow caste member in the Land Council.[47] A former female slave also had a lawsuit heard in the Land Council: Rachel, a freed slave who lived in Kumbalwella appeared against Constantino De Costa, a Chettiar who lived in the same village.[48] In another case, the emancipated slaves Roselijn and Benjamin proceeded against a Sinhalese man whom they accused of forcibly appropriating their land.[49] Sramata, a freed slave woman, claimed a revenue farmer's property that was to be sold to recover his arrears.[50] Rikittoe Naatja, a 'coolie' woman, came to the Land Council with *thombo* extracts and requested that a garden and paddy field be registered under her name.[51] Proximity to the colonial government through residence in villages such as the Land Council seat in Kumbalwella, helped such groups to acquire greater agency in their lives.[52] Warnesuriepattebendige Dona Maka, a *karāva* woman from Galupiadde (Four Gravets) mentioned above, was unusually active in the Land Council, appearing in connection with land sale matters as both litigant and witness on several occasions. In 1781, a deposition recorded her as being 62 years old to the best of her memory, a Christian and a widow, appearing as a witness for the *thombo* copyist Josua Hopman in a debt case.[53] Female identity was differentiated by socioeconomic status, social formation and residence in a coastal urban area or rural setting.

In stark contrast to their frequency as litigants, very few women appeared as witnesses although there was no legal impediment to their testimony. Only ten from the sample, about 4 per cent, were female. They all gave affidavits from

13 July 1778 to 14 August 1781. A rare occasion when a deposition had mostly female witnesses was a case where it was necessary to prove that a woman had died in childbirth a few hours before her new-born son died. In that case, women were obviously in a better position than men to attest to the facts. Women were not considered as the best choice to verify evidence in other matters, which were mostly related to confirming ownership of land. Very few females were assigned credibility; the striking male dominance indicates a control over judicial truth held by service holders such as *lascarins*[54] who, as explained below, were frequent witnesses.

Despite their near absence as witnesses, the general belief, supported by ancient and medieval sources, is that the teachings of Buddhism were instrumental in promoting the independence of women (Andaya, 2006, pp. 32–33; Munasinghe, 2004, p. 179). Early European observers such as Robert Knox recorded female participation in agricultural work and harvest rituals that were ingrained in Kandyan society (1966 [1681], pp. 19–22). The relationship between husband and wife was presented as that of equals, the protection of the wife by her husband being assumed but not acting as a restriction on the wife (Munasinghe, 2004, pp. 147–149). Clearly, specific legal issues, such as the rights of widows, would bring women to the Land Council. Women as heirs were of special importance in inheritance law. If there was an attempt to introduce ideas of female subordination through Roman-Dutch law, they did not take hold of the female imagination in Sri Lanka in Dutch times.

Social status of local actors

To what social and socioeconomic groups did those who come to the council belong? It is necessary to categorize identity data into recognizable groups in order to facilitate referencing of the data but this can be fraught with pitfalls in practice. There are semantic problems in the process, as our understanding of caste, occupational and ethnic differences today cannot be the same as in eighteenth-century Sri Lanka. As Robert J. Morris has pointed out on the topic of occupational coding, differences of judgements and the purpose of a document or economic context could also lead to considerable variation of classification practices (1990, pp. 9–12). Any analysis of the data has to be approached with these considerations in mind.

The various documents produced by the Land Council reveal differing categories of identification. The *thombos* carry data on caste and service in separate columns, the service being important in identifying the land parcels due to them. The company at times identified persons as 'Sinhalese' in the Land Council, curiously without mentioning their caste-like identity.[55] The minutes mention the current and former service holdings such as *mayorāl, lascarin* and *vidāne* and other titles of about one-fifth of the litigants. Title demonstrated credibility and rank in society, an important factor with regard to both litigants and witnesses. The legal production of such socioeconomic identities through the land holdings attached to them was a factor that made it non-essential to articulate a 'Sinhalese' identity in the daily workings of the Land Council.

Most litigants and witnesses were Sinhalese, at 79 and 93 per cent respectively. Ethnicity was mentioned infrequently in Land Council documents and the data in Table 4.1 were mostly deduced from names.[56] If the litigants were Sinhalese, it is likely that the witnesses they produced would also be Sinhalese. Collectives of litigants rarely came from different ethnic backgrounds. There was also little diversity among witnesses, with only around 10 per cent of sixty-seven depositions evidently including a cross-section of ethnic formations. Those present at a hearing may have easily differentiated Europeans and natives by their appearance and dress. Moors were often mentioned as such, but in general hardly any mention was made of ethnic categories in the records. Mallabars, the Dutch term for Tamils, were not mentioned in the sample period.

The more privileged category of *burger*, European or Eurasian (all indicated here as European), was insignificant in terms of numbers: they comprised 5.8 per cent of litigants and 3.2 per cent of witnesses. Names such as De Silva and Perera under the 'unknown' category may refer to Europeans, but they could have also been Sinhalese or manumitted slaves. Cases involving Europeans, where they did not concern land matters outside the Fort, would have been heard in the *Civiele Raad* (Civil Council) of Galle. Yet, we see that Europeans were increasingly involved in property matters outside Galle Fort. The Land Council was a legal space that reached out to rural folk, but also had exclusive jurisdiction over land matters registered in the Galle *thombos*.

The literature has identified caste as a category through which the indigenous population could be rendered economically 'useful' to the company (Dewasiri, 2008; Rogers, 2004). Caste identities were hardly mentioned in the Land Council minutes, indicating a low interest in the council in social formation for its own sake. In some cases, it was possible to find the caste from litigants' names or occasionally from the *thombos*, which generally provides caste information. Non-*goygama* caste members also came to the Land Council. We saw above how a *hakuru* caste woman was granted leave to proceed with an appeal to the Council of Justice. *Radā* caste men, ritually associated with washing tasks, also came to the Land Council.[57] *Karāva* men and women and *salāgamas* also made representations to the Land Council. Caste, because of its associated mandatory services to the company, was a way of 'thinking about natives within the framework of productivity'

TABLE 4.1 Social formation of litigants and witnesses

Social Formation	*Litigants 1778–79*	*%*	*Witnesses 1778–81*	*%*
Sinhalese	191	79.0	246	93.0
Moor	19	7.8	5	2.0
European	14	5.8	8	3.2
Chettiar	1	0.4	1	0.4
Paravar	-	-	1	0.4
Unknown	18	7.0	3	1.0
Total	243	100	264	100

Sources: SLNA 1/6494, Depositions; SLNA 1/6511, 1/6512, 1/6520, 1/6521, Minutes.

(Benton and Ross, 2013, p. 11). Yet, even more than caste, service categories were an important inclusion in the land registers which recorded a shareholder's service rendered in return for the property holding. This record was of importance in Land Council proceedings where the rendering of a service such as *mayorāl, lascarin* or grain measurer was at stake or litigants were threatened with demotion to coolie or *nainde* status. They were all assigned fixed amounts of maintenance grants. Some services or titles were in practice seen across castes; service position or title-holding was not the exclusive prerogative of the *goygama* caste. Such positions were important for the economic activities of the colonial government. In land litigation, ethnicity and strict caste identifications were replaced by other categories of status such as title-holding and service.

Strikingly, 68 per cent of litigants were not assigned any social or occupational identity. We can assume that if they held title it would have been claimed and recorded. But the lack of status was not a setback in approaching the Land Council. 'Coolies', who performed menial labour and belonged to the subordinate ranks of the *goygama* caste, and other low-status groups came to the council and won. A dispute between two 'coolies' and *mayorāls* resulted in a judgement in favour of the former; and in another case in my sample, the conclusion of which was not found, a 'coolie' acted against the headman Sameradiwakere Jayasundara.[58] As litigants in the council, high-level local headmen may have been privileged although this was not always the case.

In contrast, there is a clear dominance among the witnesses of persons of some rank in a village. They would have been considered most capable of providing credibility to a litigant's claims. Litigants were aware of the advantages of bringing the testimony of rank and file to the council; almost 40 per cent of witnesses were (at that time or formerly) headmen from high and low ranks and persons of higher standing in the village such as *mayorāls*, schoolmasters and writers. The absence of a high-ritual birth could be remarked on—one witness was ridiculed by the opposing party for his occupation of tile-making and was asked if this was not a very low service that is disgraceful for 'honourable' *goygamas*, to which he was recorded as answering in the affirmative.[59] While some high-level headmen also appeared, *mayorāls* appeared frequently as witnesses. *Lascarins, kangāns* and former *kangāns*, who had lower-level responsibilities in a village setting, were frequently regarded favourably in terms of their ability to provide credibility, amounting to 34 per cent of the witnesses. Land Council councillors were also witnesses on occasion.[60]

Status through caste and office had a significant role in the precolonial legal and administrative orders. Officials had to be aware of a wrongdoer's caste, as persons of a higher caste and particular ranks were exempt from certain punishments. In the Kandyan kingdom, John D'Oyly wrote that corporal punishment was not inflicted on persons from noble families and other high-level title holders, and they could not be imprisoned in the 'Great Prison'. On the other hand, he said that headmen with a subordinate rank could be punished with the 'open hand' and lower-level *goygama* caste members and persons of low caste were punished with rods (D'Oyly, 1975 [1929], p. 37). The Land Council practised such corporal punishment on subordinate headmen: it found a *mayorāl* at fault in a case over a disputed land sale deed. The council directed that he be flogged after the meeting dispersed because they believed that it was quite likely that he had in fact signed the deed which he denied and moreover that he should have known what took place in his village.[61] The Land Council had to repeatedly reprimand high-level headmen for non-cooperation with the *thombo* registration, but there is no evidence that corporal punishments were meted out to them. Evidently, headmen and service holders were not a monolithic body that was equally privileged.

In cases heard before the council, almost the entire spectrum of social groups appeared as principal parties or witnesses. The dominant story is about rural inhabitants who lived in thatched houses on their lands: a paddy field with a harvest of a quarter acre of rice could be all that they had to defend. The costs of bringing an issue to the council could rise considerably but litigants could apply for *pro deo*. Non-headmen appeared on a regular basis, including persons belonging to lower-caste formations. The clergy do not appear in the sample cases, but in 1794 a Buddhist monk, traditionally not known to have private holdings of land except as part of a temple, asked for a wasteland garden and paddy field that he had cultivated in 1786 and for which he had paid the required taxes, to be registered in the *thombo* under his name.[62] As land ownership could become divided among different ethnic groups, some cases involved cross-cultural litigation, particularly with Europeans who appeared in connection with property recorded in the *thombo*. Moors appeared mostly against each other, and occasionally against a Sinhalese inhabitant. This is testimony to how indigenous people, Europeans and other groups interacted in society and its inevitable reflection in a judicial forum.

Conclusions

Under British rule, First Colonial Secretary Hugh Cleghorn, in the minute of 1799 that is now infamous for promoting the idea of a 'two-nation' theory of Sinhalese and Tamils, made a glowing report of the Land Council. He said it was 'extremely popular, and its decisions were generally respected' (Pieris, 1953, p. 134). Cleghorn may, however, have overrated the power of the *mudaliyār* and in the process contradicts his statement on the popularity of the Land Council:

> He is the only judge in the first instance of the disputes among the natives, he is a constituent member of the Land Raad, and few of the natives venture to appeal from his decision to a court where one of the judges may have been their oppressor.
>
> *Pieris 1953, p. 145*[63]

By regarding the Land Council's use of Sinhalese customary law as fact and stressing a regulation that made their presence compulsory, D. A. Kotelawele also exaggerates the role of the headmen in the Land Council, which he believes may have added to their power (1988, p. 96). If correct, although headmen were not always present at meetings (Rupesinghe, 2016), the locals would have been reluctant to appear in the council. But the evidence proves that the Land Council and the *thombo* provided a means for the Dutch government to connect directly with the inhabitants of the Galle district.

Men and women entered extensively into the colonial legal system where distance was not a serious deterrent. Witnesses from locations considered to be 'far' by the council (between 12 to 18 kilometres away) sometimes appeared on several occasions. Nonetheless, further away from the administrative heart of the south, participation in the Land Council decreased. It may not be novel that women and lower-ranking persons came to the Land Council, as they would have been accustomed to appealing to the precolonial legal system as well. The lack of title-holding was also not an eliminating factor in coming forward to face the law. Attempts to control the legal representation of women through their husbands could not be fully realized in a rural setting. Evidently, the Land Council had a wide social reach and became part of the imagination of the villagers. By investing in civil litigation, they were conscious agents in the pursuit of justice to recover or gain property. Taking an economic perspective on why people came to the Land Council, it can be said that the *thombos* fostered property litigation.

The recording of identities in the Land Council documents and *thombos* reflected the realities of colonial preoccupations that eventually led to further essentialization of such identities. In the identification of litigants, service was mentioned more frequently than ethnicity, caste, religion and gender. Service and occupational categories were preferred to strictly caste classifications: it was more important due to its legal implications in connection with land holdings to explicitly mention a *goygama* villager's *mayorāl* status than his caste. Distinctions of rank, ranging from a *lascarin* to a *mudaliyār*, were important and Dewasiri has shown how increased opportunities for land ownership by such groups under the colonial government gave rise to a new class formation (2008, pp. 141–183). Identities based on service to the company were a feature of the cultural order that emerged at the end of the eighteenth century. This focus reveals the economic interests of the VOC in the task of essentializing identities. The Land Council represented a colonial legal system that both responded to and reshaped cultural categories of identity. The purpose of the *thombos*, to record the taxation on property holdings which in turn were closely related to service categories, ensured that occupations were recorded correctly. Peasants were keen to rectify mistakes on this front. The public registry of the *thombo* was crucially linked to inheritance of land and citizens invested in the Land Council to protect all-important land rights.

Kalegane Bastiaan Nainde Maria's provocative fragment of resistance mentioned at the start of this chapter was short-lived; she had no choice but to subsequently appear in connection with her case in that very forum that ordered that she be flogged for her 'impertinent expression'. She was most probably punished on 1 April 1780 after the council adjourned for the day (we have no confirmation of the flogging itself). Coercive force would have been a determining factor in judicial participation, which in turn was a necessary evil to retain land rights. By the mid-eighteenth century, inhabitants were acquainted with the Land Council and its land registration, and used this knowledge in settling disputes. Litigants had to understand procedures and best practices of strategy. For litigants with plural identities, the Land Council was a location of identification and a site for navigating a changing legal landscape.

Notes

1 Based on a chapter of my PhD thesis, this study has benefited from advice from many individuals, including my supervisors Alicia Schrikker and Nira Wickramasinghe and the two anonymous reviewers. I thank Suranjan Fernando for the map accompanying this chapter.
2 SLNA 1/6513, Galle Land Council minutes, fol. 29r, 1 Apr 1780. I have abbreviated references to the Sri Lanka National Archives as SLNA.
3 T. Nadaraja argued that the cases of the Land Council should be studied to answer the vexed question of whether the VOC used Sinhalese laws (1972, pp. 14–16). The question has been explored in the author's PhD thesis (Rupesinghe 2016).
4 Although important in order to make sense of the use of a judicial forum, due to constraints of space this chapter will not address procedural law or the backgrounds and roles of the mixed body of councillors. See author's PhD thesis for this (Rupesinghe 2016).
5 This estimate is based on the *thombos* (Belt, Kok and Mandemakers, 2011, p. 484).
6 SLNA 1/6511, Galle Land Council minutes, 1778; SLNA 1/6512, Galle Land Council minutes, 1779. Some entries, for unknown reasons, were found only in the draft minutes (SLNA 1/6520, Drafts of Galle Land Council minutes, 1778 to 1779 and SLNA 1/6521, Drafts of Galle Land Council minutes, 1779 to 1780). The sample of depositions mentioned below is from a similar period.
7 I have not separated the litigants according to whether they were plaintiffs or defendants as this cannot always be identified correctly.
8 In a collective of litigants, only the first-mentioned person's details were recorded by them.
9 In The Netherlands as well parties were at times referred to as the children or heirs (or wife, widow etc.) of a certain person and not individually named (Schepper et al., 1988, p. 271).
10 SLNA 1/6494, Galle Land Council depositions, 1778 to 1781. The Land Council recorded some witnesses in the minutes, but they were not included in the sample.
11 I have closely followed Le Bailly's solutions for the same problems that she faced in analyzing the fifteenth-century Hof van Holland cases (Le Bailly, 2001, pp. 28–29).
12 Later, preliminary hearings of criminal cases were carried out by the Land Council. See two registers of inquiries by Land Council commissioners in cases of theft and other offences dated between 1784 and 1795, SLNA 1/6532–3, Notes of inquiries by Galle Land Council commissioners in cases of theft and other offences, 1784 to 1795.
13 SLNA 1/6511, Galle Land Council minutes, fol. 37r, 11 Jul 1778.
14 Ibid., fol. 41r, 25 Jul 1778.
15 Ibid., fol. 77r, 31 Oct 1778; 84r, 28 Nov 1778.
16 SLNA 1/6498, Galle Land Council minutes, fol. 14r, 3 May 1760.
17 Like many others, this case has interesting interrogations that focus on trying to prove the irreligiosity of the opposing parties' witnesses in order to disprove their testimonies (SLNA 1/6511, fol. 30r, 31r, 9 Jul 1778; 43r, 8 Aug 1778; 49r, 15 Aug 1778; 53r, 12 Sept 1778; 65r, 10 Oct 1778; SLNA 1/6512, fol. 14v, 6 Mar 1779; 20r, 27 Mar 1779; SLNA 1/6534, Galle Land Council interrogations, fol. 2r–10v, 11r–15v, 9 Jul 1778).
18 Such cases of women coming forward were not rare as is further explained below (SLNA 1/6494, fol. 4r, 17 Jul 1778; 43r–44r, 14 Apr 1779; SLNA 1/6511, fol. 8r, 6 Jun 1778; 89v, 28 Nov 1778; SLNA 1/6512, fol. 18r, 27 Mar 1779; 23r, 24 Apr 1779; 84r, 20 Nov 1779; 87r–v, 27 Nov 1779; SLNA 1/6514, Galle Land Council minutes, fol. 33r, 24 Feb 1781).
19 These cases were usually uneventful (SLNA 1/6511, fol. 71r, 10 Oct 1778; SLNA 1/6512, fol. 11r, 20 Feb 1779; 66v, 11 Sept 1779; 80v, 20 Nov 1779; 91r, 27 Nov 1779; SLNA 1/6521, Drafts of Galle Land Council minutes, fol. 35v, 11 Dec 1779).

20 SLNA 1/6511, fol. 4r, 23 May 1778; 11r, 6 Jun 1778; 29v, 27 Jun 1778; 40v, 25 Jul 1778; 47r, 8 Aug 1778.
21 It possibly held something that was unacceptable to the council, because when Hendeling is ordered to pay the garden tax according to the *thombo*, Hissink is also advised to abstain from 'such thoughtless expressions' (SLNA 1/6512, fol. 64r, 11 Sept 1779; 68r, 25 Sept 1779; 76v, 20 Nov 1779).
22 SLNA 1/104, Governor in Council minutes, 19 Apr 1748. The Governor in Council decided that Moors and heathens would only be allowed to possess those lands that they had planted, cultivated or legally inherited, but not purchased grounds unless with special consent. It is not clear if this order was enforced. In one case, a Moorman was accused of raising the land price unreasonably (SLNA 1/6517, Galle Land Council minutes, fol. 131v, 13 Dec 1794).
23 Land sales without the permission of the Land Council were prohibited (SLNA 1/98, Governor in Council minutes, fol. 271v–272r, 11 Jul 1746). A new law was passed in 1784 that all transfers of land, whether by last will or otherwise, must be submitted to the Land Council (SLNA 1/188, Governor in Council minutes, 9 Feb 1784).
24 SLNA 1/6512, fol. 76v, 20 Nov 1779. It was said to be the practice in Colombo as well. Two commissioned local officials submitted a report after a visit in 1783 (SLNA 1/6527, Annexes to Galle Land Council minutes, fol. 9r, 7 Feb 1783).
25 SLNA 1/6511, fol. 83v, 31 Oct 1778; SLNA 1/6521, fol. 35v, 11 Dec 1779.
26 SLNA 1/6524, fol. 64v, 30 Aug 1783.
27 SLNA 1/6523, fol. 64r, 27 Apr 1782.
28 SLNA 7/2354, Miscellaneous documents of the Galle Land Council with conditions of auction sales, notices etc., p. 29, 25 Jul 1778.
29 The translation of the Dutch word *verpanding* is mortgage, that does not represent the more informal agreements entered into by southern villagers by which they posed their lands as collateral in order to borrow money. At times, the words *huur* (rent/lease) and *verpand* were used interchangeably (SLNA 1/6504, fol. 18r, 18 Feb 1769; 29r, 18 Mar 1769).
30 SLNA 1/6513, Galle Land Council minutes, fol. 47r, 20 May 1780.
31 Ibid., fol. 60r, 24 Jun 1780.
32 One *thombo* was updated regarding a sale of land years later on 22 Apr 1785 although the Land Council proof was dated 23 Feb 1752 (SLNA 1/7557A, Unawatuna (Talpe) Thombo, 1748, p. 13).
33 SLNA 1/6511, fol. 52v, 29 Aug 1778; 62r, 26 Sept 1778; SLNA 1/6512, fol. 88r, 27 Nov 1779; SLNA 1/6520, fol. 45r, Nov 1778.
34 SLNA 1/6511, fol. 57r–v, 12 Sept 1778.
35 I thank Dr. Lodewijk Wagenaar for providing me with access to a transcription of some registers of petitions, which, however, do not reveal issues about the Land Council.
36 An 'unknown' figure of 44 includes villages that are located in two sub-districts thereby making it impossible to know to which part of the village the witness belonged without accurately locating him or her in the *thombo*. Fifteen of them were from Hinatigala, which is in both the Talpe Pattu and Four Gravets.
37 SLNA 1/6512, fol. 94v, 1 Dec 1779.
38 Ibid., fol. 95r, 2 Dec 1779.
39 SLNA 1/6521, fol. 37v, 22 Dec 1779.
40 It is not known if residents of the Hinidum Pattu travelled to the Land Council for the registration or whether commissioners went to that remote area. Given that they were all drawn up in the year 1760, and it would have been difficult to mobilize so many inhabitants to travel several miles, the latter is more likely. The Land Council minutes from 1760 have no references to the Hinidum villages. In contrast, there were cases from Mapalagama (Gangaboda Pattu), a *thombo* that was also drawn up in 1760 (SLNA 1/7501, 1760).
41 Five groups of litigants, referred to as heirs, children and/or grandchildren without any indication of their gender, have not been included in these figures.
42 Forty-nine of the sixty-four women were Sinhalese, three were Moors and one a European. The ethnicity of eleven women could not be identified: six had the name de

Silva which is ambiguous and two were recorded as the wives of their husbands who represented them in the Land Council.

43 SLNA 1/6512, fol. 89r, 27 Nov 1779; SLNA 1/6514, fol. 2r, 6 Jan 1781.

44 SLNA 1/6513, fol. 137r, 4 Nov 1780; SLNA 1/6526, Annexes to Galle Landraad Minutes, fol. 158r–159r, *Thombo* extract dated 23 Feb 1770; 160r, gift deed dated 28 Apr 1770.

45 SLNA 1/165, Governor in Council minutes, 24 Nov 1772.

46 The case is described in more detail in the writer's thesis (SLNA 1/6494, Galle Land Council depositions, fol. 84r, 20 Sept 1780; 85r, 5 Oct 1780; SLNA 1/6513, fol. 92r, 26 Aug 1780; 102r, 9 Sept 1780; 132v, 4 Nov 1780; 132v, 4 Nov 1780; SLNA 1/6514, fol. 7r, 6 Jan 1781; 20v, 27 Jan 1781; SLNA 1/7428A, Dodampe (Wellaboda) Thombo, p. 32).

47 SLNA 1/6516, fol. 4r–v, 28 Jun 1793. A case from 1793 also involved *hakuru* caste persons including a female, SLNA 1/6515, fol. 371r, 10 May 1793.

48 SLNA 1/6501, fol. 117r–v, 4 Oct 1766; 119r, 20 Dec 1766; SLNA 1/6502, fol. 4v, 7 Feb 1767.

49 SLNA 1/6525, fol. 201r–v, 30 Sept 1786.

50 SLNA 1/6511, fol. 40v, 25 Jul 1778.

51 SLNA 1/6515, fol. 290, 17 Apr 1790.

52 Dewasiri points out that the *hakuru* caste showed a tendency to concentrate around the colonial centre (2008, p. 210).

53 SLNA 1/6494, Galle Land Council depositions, fol. 95r, 16 Feb 1781.

54 Indigenous soldiers who also served as guards and messengers.

55 Dewasiri has also noticed this phenomenon in some *thombos* (2008, p. 200).

56 Sinhalese names consist usually of the *vāsagama* or *gē-nama* (sometimes omitted), which is the lineage or ancestral name, usually given to a family in the low-country according to the service or *rājakāriya* (duty due to the king) the family performed in the past or continued to perform.

57 SLNA 1/6511, fol. 30r–31r, 9 Jul 1778.

58 Ibid., fol. 5v–6v, 30 May 1778; 11r, 6 Jun 1778; 12v, 6 Jun 1778.

59 SLNA 1/6534, Galle Land Council interrogations, fol. 38r, 18 Dec 1778.

60 For example, the local councillor Adriaan de Silva Jayetilleke Seresinghe was a witness (SLNA 1/6494, fol. 14r, 18 Oct 1782).

61 SLNA 1/6513, fol. 104r, 9 Sept 1780.

62 SLNA 1/6517, fol. 116r, 22 Nov 1794.

63 Cleghorn seems to have believed that the power of the *mudaliyār* was hardly ever challenged.

References

Andaya, B.W. (2006). *The Flaming Womb: Repositioning Women in Early Modern Southeast Asia*. Honolulu: University of Hawaii Press.

Belt, A. van den, Kok, J. and Mandemakers, K. (2011). Digital thombos: a new source for 18th-century Sri Lankan family history. *The History of the Family*, 16(4), pp. 481–489.

Benton, L. and Ross, R.J. (2013). Empires and legal pluralism: jurisdiction, sovereignty, and political imagination in the early modern world. In: L. Benton and R.J. Ross, eds., *Legal Pluralism and Empires, 1500–1850* (Kindle edition). NYU Press, pp. 1–18.

Dewasiri, N.R. (2008). *The Adaptable Peasant: Agrarian Society in Western Sri Lanka under Dutch Rule, 1740–1800*. Leiden: Brill.

D'Oyly, J. (1975 [1929]). *A Sketch of the Constitution of the Kandyan Kingdom* (L.J.B. Turner, ed.) (Vol. 24). Dehiwala: Tisara Prakasakayo.

Drixler, F.F. and Kok, J. (2016). A lost family-planning regime in eighteenth-century Ceylon. *Population Studies: a Journal of Demography*, 70(1), pp. 93–114.

Goonewardena, K.W. (1986). Muslims under Dutch rule up to the mid-eighteenth century. In: M.A.M. Shukri, ed., *Muslims of Sri Lanka: Avenues to Antiquity*. Beruwala: Jamiah Naleemia Inst., pp. 189–210.

Haks, D. (1985). *Huwelijk en Gezin in Holland in de 17de en 18de eeuw*. 2nd edition. Utrecht: HES.

Jayawardena, K. (2000). *Nobodies to Somebodies: the Rise of the Colonial Bourgeoisie in Sri Lanka*. London: Zed Books.

Knox, R. (1966 [1681]). *An Historical Relation of Ceylon*. Kohuwala: Tisara Prakasakayo.

Kotelawele, D.A. (1988). Some aspects of social change in the south west of Sri Lanka c. 1700–1833. *Social Science Review*, 4, pp. 53–100.

Le Bailly, M.-C. (2001). *Recht voor de Raad. Rechtspraak voor het Hof van Holland, Zeeland en West-Friesland in het Midden van de Vijftiende Eeuw*. Haarlem and Hilversum: Historische Vereniging Holland & Uitgeverij Verloren.

Lee, R.W. (1946). *An Introduction to Roman-Dutch Law*. 4th edition. Oxford: Clarendon Press.

Loten, J.G. (1935). *Memoir of Joan Gideon Loten, Governor of Ceylon delivered to his successor Jan Schreuder 1757* (E. Reimers, Trans.). Colombo: Ceylon Govt. Press.

Merry, S.E. (2010). Colonial law and its uncertainties. *Law and History Review*, 28(4), pp. 1067–1071.

Morris, R.J. (1990). Occupational coding: principles and examples. *Historical Social Research*, 15(1), pp. 3–29.

Mottau, S.A.W. (Trans.). (1965). Instructions for the respective 'Landraden' of this government (extract from the Dutch Political Council minutes of 25th June 1789). *Journal of the Dutch Burger Union of Ceylon*, 55(1–4).

Munasinghe, I. (2004). *Sri Lankan Woman in Antiquity (Sixth century B.C. to Fifteenth Century A.C.)* (S.B. Herath, Trans.). Colombo: Author Publication.

Nadaraja, T. (1972). *The Legal System of Ceylon in its Historical Setting*. Leiden: Brill.

Pieris, R. (1953). Administration of justice and revenue on the island of Ceylon under the Dutch government (The Cleghorn Minute). *Journal of the Ceylon Branch of the Royal Asiatic Society*, 3 pt. 2, pp. 125–152.

Raben, R. (1996). *Batavia and Colombo: the Ethnic and Spatial Order of Two Colonial Cities 1600–1800* (PhD Thesis). Leiden: Leiden University.

Roberts, M., Raheem, I. and Colin-Thomé, P. (1989). *People Inbetween: the Burghers and the Middle Class in the Transformations within Sri Lanka, 1790s–1960s*. Ratmalana: Sarvodaya Book Pub. Services.

Rogers, J.D. (2004). Early British rule and social classification in Lanka. *Modern Asian Studies*, 38(3), pp. 625–647.

Rupesinghe, N. (2016). *Negotiating Custom: Colonial Lawmaking in the Galle Landraad* (PhD Thesis). Leiden: Leiden University.

Rupesinghe (writing as Seneviratne), N. (2010). *Strange Cooperation: Revenue Farmers in Eighteenth-Century Sri Lanka* (MPhil Dissertation). Leiden: Leiden University.

Ryan, B.F. (1953). *Caste in Modern Ceylon: the Sinhalese System in Transition*. New Brunswick: Rutgers University Press.

Schepper, H. de, Lombarts, R.W.G., Dolezalek, G. and Broers, E.J.M.F.C. (1988). Prolegomena voor onderzoek van rechtspraak en bestuur in de oude Nederlanden. In: J. Koster van Dijk and A. Wijffels, eds., *Miscellanea Forensia Historica: ter gelegenheid van het afscheid van prof. mr. J. Th. de Smidt*. Amsterdam: Werkgroep Grote Raad van Mechelen, pp. 263–294.

Tennent, J.E. (1860). *Ceylon: an Account of the Island* (Vol. 2). Longman: Green.

Wessels, J.W. (1908). *History of the Roman-Dutch Law*. Grahamstown, Cape Colony: African Book Co.

Woolf, L. (1981 [1913]). *The Village in the Jungle*. Oxford, Chennai: Oxford University Press.

5

LEGAL PLURALISM IN THE CITIES OF THE EARLY MODERN KINGDOM OF POLAND

The jurisdictional conflicts and uses of justice by Armenian merchants

Alexandr Osipian

Introduction

In comparison with many absolutist monarchies, the early modern Polish-Lithuanian Commonwealth escaped processes of centralization and unification of the judicial system. Every social estate and ethno-confessional community in the country was allowed its own body of law and court system. The multi-confessional and multi-ethnic environment of Polish cities and, therefore, the great variety of jurisdictions have stimulated legal pluralism.

Legal pluralism is ordinarily understood as the existence of multiple legal systems within one population and/or geographic area, a phenomenon that has drawn scholarly attention since as early as the nineteenth century, concomitant with the rise of colonial empires that stimulated interest in the heterogeneity of legal practices employed by colonizers and the colonized (Maine, 1861, 1883). The Great Reforms of the 1860s in the Russian Empire also stimulated fieldwork on customary law among the emancipated Russian peasants as well as among the indigenous peoples of the Caucasus, Siberia, and Central Asia (Samokvasov, 1876; Kovalevskiy, 1886). In this context, legal pluralism was often depicted as a dichotomy between customary law and national law. The former was conventionally defined as a non-state, non-written tradition or as a set of oral rules while the latter was implicitly understood as rational and codified. Both were perceived as stable categories within a hierarchically structured legal order.

This view has shifted since the 1970s. Law is no longer perceived as doctrine but rather as a social and cultural process. In particular, legal anthropologists working in colonial and postcolonial settings have contributed to this revisionism, and then applied it to the examination of legal change in societies labelled as 'complex' and 'modern' (Gilissen, 1971; Hooker, 1975). In the 1990s, legal pluralism became associated with an emphasis on the instability of the legal order and a 'constructionist' understanding of multi-centric legal systems as contingent products of conflict (Tamanaha, 1993). The idea of the semi-autonomous social field (Griffiths, 1986) led to the notion that there is no a priori state monopoly on the creation of legal norms and practices; subordinate groups are free to develop alternative mechanisms (Merry, 1988). The role of human agency is also perceived as significant (Starr and Collier, 1989). Historians gradually recognized that not only overseas colonies but also early modern European states maintained a marked degree of legal pluralism. European polities were 'composite' states, consisting of jurisdictions with dissimilar constitutions and a multiplicity of legitimate governing institutions (Elliott, 1992). Relatedly, the study of normative orders was replaced by a focus on patterns of jurisdictional conflicts (Benton, 2002; Benton and Ross, 2013).

In this article, the concept of legal pluralism will be applied to early modern Poland-Lithuania, and more specifically to the way Armenian courts were used by ordinary people. This will help researchers in this field to reconsider many outdated stereotypes. For instance, many scholars have considered Armenian (Jewish, Karaite, etc.) judicial autonomy as an exceptional privilege and an expression of the incomparable Polish religious tolerance – an attitude shaped in the nineteenth and early twentieth centuries when 'legal centralism' was seen as the norm. However, in legal anthropology a situation of legal pluralism is considered as 'the omnipresent, normal situation in human society' while legal centralism is treated as 'a myth, an ideal, a claim, an illusion' (Griffiths, 1986, pp. 4, 39). The change in perspective from 'above' to 'below' reveals 'that the "law" which is actually effective on the "ground floor" of society is the result of enormously complex and usually in practice unpredictable patterns of competition, interaction, negotiation, isolationism, and the like' (Griffiths, 1986, p. 39).

The issue of Armenian law in pre-modern Poland has a rich historiography. Relations in the triangle between king, city magistrates, and Armenian society were already examined in early works (Bischoff, 1864; Gromnicki, 1889; Łoziński, 1902; Balzer, 1909; Brünneck, 1914; Matwijowski, 1939; Oleś, 1966, 1966/7). These were mostly based on research of royal privileges and decrees issued to resolve the conflicts between city magistrates who had adopted Magdeburg law (who represented the dominant Catholic 'nation') on the one hand, and Armenian communities on the other. The very functioning of oriental/Armenian law in Poland/Ukraine has therefore received a fair amount of attention. However, historians have largely disregarded individual uses of justice. Such disregard also characterizes the work of historians of the past few decades. For instance, the Ukrainian historian Yaroslav Dashkevitch interpreted the jurisdictional conflicts between the city magistrates and Armenian communities in the context of such topoi as 'Polish Catholic expansion', 'assimilation' and 'denationalization' in which 'national' was understood in primordial terms (Dashkevitch, 1965, 1967, 1969, 1976). The accounts of the Polish scholars Mirosława Zakrzewska-Dubasowa (1960, 1965, 1980) and Artur Korobowicz (1964, 1989) on Armenian court practices in the private town of Zamość also largely omitted the individual strategies employed by Armenian litigants. The Polish historian Krzysztof Stopka recently (2000, 2010a, 2010b) examined the reduction and decline of Armenian judicial autonomy. He explained this reduction largely through cultural categories – such as the attractiveness of Polish high culture and the readiness of local Armenians to adopt it (Stopka, 2004, 2009, 2010c). The judicial expansion of the city magistrate is considered as the only explanation for the decline in the competence of the Armenian court in Lviv according to the recent works of Ukrainian historian Myron Kapral (2003a, 2003b, 2004, 2009) and the German historian Jürgen Heyde (2015). In short, historiography has thus far considered the Armenian urban 'nations' as homogeneous and coherent communities opposing the jurisdictional interventions of the city magistrates in order to protect their national or religious identity and/or economic interests.

This article will particularly take issue with the dominant view that the actions and rhetoric of Armenian elders/jurymen reflected the unanimous position of all community members. By bringing the perspective of the uses of justice 'from below' into the analysis, jurisdictional variety will be perceived rather in terms of individual *choice* and *option*, rather than *competition*. This chapter notably aims to uncover the agency of less powerful actors, such as ordinary merchants and their wives, factors, apprentices, maidservants, etc., who used legal pluralism in their own interests, and not necessarily in the interest of their 'nation'. The issue of legal pluralism – neglected by previous scholars – can help to explain strategies not only of competing elites, but also of less powerful litigants.

The analysis is underpinned by archival research on three towns with Armenian communities: the royal cities of Lviv and Kamianets-Podilskyi, and the private town of Zamość. They largely represent three models of possible relations between Armenian and Magdeburg jurisdictions. In Lviv, the city magistrate made deliberate efforts to maximally reduce the judicial autonomy of the non-Catholic nations. In Kamianets-Podilskyi, where the city magistrate provided necessary judicial support to the non-Catholic nations, there was a more balanced co-existence. In Zamość, all townspeople – regardless of their confessional affiliation – were granted equal economic rights by the owner of this private town. The source base of the chapter mainly consists of Armenian and Magdeburg court records and royal decrees, as well as some pamphlets, travelogues and commercial letters. The analysis is chronologically delimited to the sixteenth and seventeenth centuries, as this period was characterized by religious, socio-economic and cultural changes relevant to the place of Armenian law in the Polish kingdom. The Reformation and Counter-Reformation then led to a reconsideration of inter-religious relations, which in turn had an effect on the legal system. Socio-economic changes during the sixteenth century had an impact on social relations within cities, including the undermining of the social hierarchy. The printing press made juridical literature available to everyone willing to pay for it.

The chapter is divided into three sections. The first deals with the emergence of the pluralistic legal regime during the Middle Ages. Jurisdictional conflicts that emerged from this pluralism, notably between Armenian and Magdeburg law courts, are discussed in section two. The third section then discusses the flexibility of the forms of dispute settlement practised by judges and litigants and the uses of justice by ordinary people.

Multiple jurisdictions in the cities of the late medieval and early modern Kingdom of Poland

The remarkable complexity of the early modern Polish legal system was informed by at least three historic changes that can be traced back to the late Middle Ages. First, between the fourteenth and sixteenth centuries, territorial expansion resulted in the legal autonomy of Prussia, Courland and Livonia as well as in the maintenance of Ruthenian law applied by the Orthodox Ruthenians in the eastern provinces – the region of present-day Ukraine. Second, the suburbs of royal cities became domains of noblemen, bishops, monasteries and the royal governor, independent of the city magistrate and generally known as *jurydyka*. The residents of these domains/*jurydykas* were under the jurisdiction of the Polish or terrestrial law (*prawo ziemskie*) – if they were subjects of a nobleman or governor – or under the jurisdiction of Church law – if they were subjects of a bishop or monastery. Third, bodies of foreign law were imported during the thirteenth and fourteenth centuries concomitant with the influx of the foreign settlers, including Armenians, Germans, Jews, Karaites and Vlachs. These groups were granted legal autonomy by the Polish kings and later by the aristocrats in their domains. Since the invited German Catholic settlers invested hugely in the economic and legal transformation of urban life in late medieval Poland, German law (*Jus Theutonicum*) or Magdeburg law (*Magdeburger Recht, Jus Majdeburgensis*) became the dominant legal model in royal and private cities alike. Municipal law in Poland was thus mostly based on the code of law of the city of Magdeburg in Saxony that had been compiled in 1188, and the 'Saxon Mirror' (*Sachsenspiegel, Speculum Saxonum*) that had been composed between 1220 and 1235 by Eike von Repkow, a juryman (*Schöffen*) in Saxony (Bily, Carls and Gönczi, 2011).

Initially, Magdeburg law was granted to German settlers in order to protect them from the alleged excesses and corrupt practices of local authorities. Their judicial autonomy was to guarantee them comfortable conditions in the foreign environment and, thereby, help to attract more settlers. At the same time, the German settlers brought with them the model of the homogeneous Catholic city community with a Jewish ghetto on the outskirts. In the cities with a large Catholic burgher community, they tried to treat non-Catholics in the same way as they were accustomed to treating Jews, that is as subordinate groups excluded from the burghers' community and, therefore, from the economic and social privileges granted by the sovereign. As will be seen, however, the sovereign granted judicial autonomy to non-Catholic communities, including Armenians, in exchange for diplomatic services and loans.

In the late thirteenth and fourteenth centuries Armenian merchant communities emerged in the lands of present-day Ukraine in the cities of Lviv, Lutsk, Volodymyr, Kyiv and Kamianets-Podilskyi. From the 1340s to the 1360s, these lands were conquered and incorporated into the Kingdom of Poland and the Grand Duchy of Lithuania (these two states formed a dynastic union from 1385 and a parliamentary union from 1569). By the turn of the seventeenth century, Armenian communities in Lutsk and Volodymyr had totally vanished, and in Kyiv there were only eight families, while in Lviv and Kamianets-Podilskyi they constituted about 7 and 30 per cent of the residents respectively. At that time, numerous Armenian communities emerged in the private towns of the aristocracy. In the mid-seventeenth century, the Armenian diaspora in the Kingdom of Poland could be estimated as 7,000 persons. Armenian merchants frequented the markets of the Golden Horde, the Ottoman Empire, Persia and Crimean Khanate, and provided the Polish nobility with fashionable oriental luxury. Because of their fluency in Turkic, the language of their domestic and business conversation, Armenian merchants were in royal service as royal interpreters, diplomats or spies. For these reasons, they were protected by a sovereign and – being Monophysite Christians – granted judicial autonomy.

These communities[1] adopted a model of self-government generally known as 'German Law' – with a judge (Latin *advocatus*, German *Vogt*, Polish *wójt*) who presided at the law court ordinarily consisting of 6 to 12 jurymen (Latin *seniores, scabini*, Polish *radni, starsi, ławnicy*).[2] At the same time, Armenian courts in Poland operated in accordance with the Codex of Armenian Law (*Datastanagirk*) composed in 1184 in Greater Armenia by the religious scholar (*vardapet*) Mkhitar Gosh (*c.*1130–1213) (Mkhitar Gosh, 2000). Mkhitar's law code was based on the Bible, canon law, Armenian customary law and a number of other sources. At least one copy of the law code was dedicated to the powerful Armenian Prince Vakhtank II (1182–1214), a ruler of the Principality of Khachen (Artzakh or Karabakh), in whose domains Mkhitar had resided at that time (Pivazian, 1991, p. 200–201). In 1265, Smbat Sparapet (Sempad, Smbat Gúndestabl) (1208–1276), an older brother of King Hetoum I, composed the law code, which was based on and adapted from the earlier work of Mkhitar Gosh (Karst, 1905). The Smbat's law code was used in the Armenian Kingdom of Cilicia till its fall in 1375 (Sukiasian, 1971). Later, the Mkhitar law code was adapted to the judicial realities of stateless Armenian diasporas. Its Latin translation – *Statuta iuris armenici* – was confirmed with some changes and comments by the Polish King Sigismund I in 1519 (Kutrzeba, 1908; Brünneck, 1914; Lewicki and Kohnowa, 1957; Balzer, 1910; Kapral, 2000; Garkavets, 2002). The procedural code of the Armenian courts was codified in Polish in 1604 (Balzer, 1912).

Therefore, both Magdeburg law and Saxon Mirror were composed later than the Lawcode of Mkhitar Ghosh. Thus, *Statuta iuris armenici* could not be defined as conventional 'customary law' – non-written, unofficial and non-codified. And Armenians in Poland were neither indigenous people nor settlers similar to the English or the French in the overseas 'New England' or 'New France' respectively. In the royal cities, the Armenian communities were subordinate groups who nonetheless could directly apply to a sovereign for justice.

Although the various Armenian communities used the same court model and law code, there were differences in their jurisdiction between royal and private towns as well as among royal cities, which could be explained by the relative balance of power between the dominant Catholic community and non-Catholic ones, as will become clear in the next section.

Jurisdictional conflicts between the courts of Magdeburg law and Armenian law in the royal cities: perspectives from above and below

Lviv

The royal city of Lviv represents a case where the city council and the Armenian community repeatedly clashed over their respective jurisdictions. As will be seen, the king was an important actor in these conflicts, whose interventions were largely informed by his own fiscal or political interests. These conflicts and the way they were resolved were decisive for Armenian law and legal practice. The analysis also indicates how decisions by ordinary Armenians were an important factor in the clashes between the city court and the Armenian court. The problematic functioning and limited jurisdiction of the Armenian court often induced them to prefer the 'Magdeburg' court, which in turn aggravated the position of the Armenian court.

After the Polish conquest of Lviv in 1349, local German townspeople (*cives catholici*) became the dominant community, converting Lviv to Lemberg. They constituted the city community (*civitas*) granted the Magdeburg law by the Polish King Casimir III in 1356. All members of the city magistrate were Catholics. The rights of other urban nations – Armenians, Jews, Tatars, Saracens and Ruthenians – for their separate law courts were guaranteed and confirmed by the king (Kapral, 1998, pp. 27–28). In accordance with a royal privilege of 1356, non-Catholic inhabitants had the right to choose between their national and the city Magdeburg law court. The jurisdiction of the Armenian court headed by an Armenian *wójt* was, however, rather limited. All cases between Armenians and noblemen were judged in the governor's court (*jus castrensis*) in accordance with Polish law (*jus Polonicum*) (Balzer, 1909, pp. 69–74). Many cases between Armenian defendants and Catholic, Orthodox and Jewish plaintiffs were heard in the city court in accordance with 'Magdeburg' law (Balzer, 1909, pp. 74–76). Cases were even judged in the city court when both litigants were Armenians. Apart from the Armenian civil and criminal court, there was the Armenian consistory court, presided over by the Armenian archbishop and consisting of an archpriest, the clergymen, and the elders of the Armenian civil court. It judged cases of blasphemy and sacrilege, of marriage within forbidden degrees (*khas ev chekhas*) and marriage settlements (*krorenk*), of last will and inheritance, all in accordance with Armenian canon law (Schütz, 1971). It had jurisdiction over all Armenian communities in the kingdom. As will be seen, the parallel existence of these two Armenian courts created opportunities for local and foreign Armenians to avoid some restrictive regulations imposed by the royal and city authorities.

According to Oswald Balzer, Armenians preferred the city court in many cases because the Armenian court had too narrow a jurisdiction – they judged cases between Armenians only – and because the very legal status of the Armenian judge (*wójt*) was ambiguous since this office was absent in the privilege of 1356 (Balzer, 1909, pp. 77–81). Some Armenians tried to become full members of the German/Magdeburg community, because their economic rights were restricted and because they were burdened with taxes from which the Catholic burghers were exempted. However, only a few among them succeeded, since the city magistrate reserved such privileged status for Catholics.[3] Only very few Armenians were granted the full Magdeburg status by royal decrees for services and loans they had provided to the king (Balzer, 1909, pp. 69–74). However, the Magdeburg jurisdiction continued to attract Armenians. In the sixteenth century, the loss of members resulted in growing fiscal pressure on the diminishing Armenian nation. In response to its complaints, Sigismund II prohibited the Armenians of Lviv from transferring jurisdictions on 23 May 1561 and obliged them to pay taxes together with the whole Armenian community. Moreover, the king invalidated all the privileges on the jurisdictional transfer (*exemptionis literae*) issued by himself and his predecessors along with those that were to be issued by his successors in the future (Kapral, 2000, p. 275). Royal fiscal interests were thus of primary importance in protecting Armenian jurisdiction.

The king's real objective in protecting Armenian judicial autonomy had also been revealed in the 1460s. The royal governor (*capitaneus, starosta*) Andrzej Odrowąż at that time tried to reduce the judicial autonomy of the city of Lviv. In 1460, however, King Casimir IV re-confirmed to Lviv the privilege granted in 1356 (Balzer, 1909, pp. 107–108, 117). Then, Andrzej Odrowąż regained the king's grace and supported his protégé – Armenian *wójt* Cristin – at the Diet (*Sejm*) session in 1462. There, Cristin asked Casimir IV to allow his Armenian subjects German law in Lviv, and to grant Armenians the same rights as Catholic burghers. However, the king feared losing revenues if he did so. He preferred to confirm the office of Armenian *wójt*. In his decree, the king ordered the city magistrate and burghers to bring their disputes with Armenians before Armenian courts. He also confirmed that Armenians who had already been granted full citizenship nonetheless had to pay all the taxes together with the Armenian community (Kapral, 2000, pp. 140–141). When Andrzej Odrowąż died in 1465, the city magistrate readily annulled the concessions that had been made to the Armenian community. In accordance with the royal decree of 1469, the office of Armenian *wójt* in Lviv was abolished and the Armenian court sessions were henceforth to be presided over by the city *wójt*, that is, by a Catholic (Balzer, 1909, p. 137). In accordance with the royal decrees of 1476 and of 1510, the jurisdiction of the Armenian courts was further reduced: the cases of manslaughter, bloody and bruised wounds, larceny and Armenian real estate (so-called 'four articles'), henceforth fell under the jurisdiction of the city jury, which had to try these cases according to Magdeburg law (Kapral, 2000, pp. 147–149, 169–172).

However, the Armenian consistory court largely retained its jurisdiction. In the sixteenth century, it made a significant impact on the shaping of Armenian law in Poland through a particular jurisdictional conflict with the city court. In 1518, a widowed Armenian merchant, Ivaschko Tichnowicz, was detained for cohabitation with his Catholic maidservant. The city court qualified the cohabitation as a sacrilege and sentenced both defendants to death. The two defendants were executed on the day of the verdict. Armenians complained to the king that their jurisdiction had been violated by the city court. To be sure, Ivaschko Tichnowicz had been subject to the jurisdiction of Magdeburg law (*Armeni iure civili Maideburgensi*) (Kapral, 2000, p. 186). In 1427, Ivaschko's progenitor – Tissko, son of Armenian merchant Missir – and his descendants had been granted Magdeburg law by King Władysław II (Bischoff, 1864, pp. 14–15) for his diplomatic services. However, Ivaschko had also been a member of the Armenian Church that judged cases such as the one involving himself. On 21 October 1518, the king decided that in the case of Ivaschko the city court had indeed violated Armenian jurisdiction (*illegittime processisse*), and consequently imposed a fine of 200 marcs on the court (Kapral, 2000, p. 186). Most importantly, the judicial collision provoked by the case of Ivaschko made Sigismund I order the Armenian elders of Lviv to translate their law code to Latin and confirmed it with some comments under the title *Statuta iuris armenici* on 5 March 1519 (Kapral, 2000, p. 189–190). Ivaschko's case demonstrates how fierce inter-communal rivalry could be at a time when the Reformation had only just made its first appearance in Germany. While Ivaschko's execution was admittedly rather exceptional, the social tensions it reveals were decidedly not unusual (Zubrzycki, 1844; Łoziński, 1904; Charewiczowa, 1925; Kapral, 2003a).

New jurisdictional conflicts emerged in the late sixteenth century. In 1563, the Armenian community complained to the king about infringements of their jurisdiction by the city court. They in particular objected to the city magistrate's interventions in the Armenian jurisdiction beyond the four articles. They were incensed by the fact that some Armenians had been arrested and detained in the municipal gaol behind the backs of Armenian elders. Specifically, the detention and gaoling of the Armenian juryman Thoman Steczkowicz had prompted the Armenian elders to file a complaint with the king. The city court had accused Steczkowicz of defying three requests by the city burgomaster not to make a planned commercial trip to the trade fair in the Moldavian town of Khotyn and not to participate in allegedly suspicious assemblies that were typically held in the night time in the absence of the city *wójt* and outside the city hall. The city council claimed that these assemblies and the commercial trip to Khotyn were suspicious in the context of the Ottoman menace. In all probability, however, the 'night assemblies' involved meetings of the Armenian consistory court. From an Armenian point of view, the detention of Thoman Steczkowicz was unlawful since it had been ordered in the absence of Armenian elders. It thus contradicted the 'Ivaschko decree' of 1518 (Kapral, 2000, pp. 278–80). Relatedly, the Armenian elders complained that the city magistrate refused to provide the constables and officials the Armenian court needed to administer justice, including the detaining of defendants. The city magistrate prohibited Armenians from holding their assemblies and electing six more elders in order to substitute any of the existing six who might be absent (Kapral, 2000, p. 278). In short, according to the Armenian elders, the city council interpreted regulations too broadly, and under its pretext used those regulations to subpoena and gaol Armenians, at the same time prohibiting them from appealing to the jurisdiction of the Armenian elders (Kapral, 2000, p. 278).

In response to the complaints by the Armenian elders, the king rejected the detention of Thoman Steckowicz. He also issued numerous decrees to clarify how the contestable cases should be processed within the four articles. The king confirmed to Armenians their right to hold assemblies in their private chamber built in the style of a city hall, and to elect twelve elders in accordance with Armenian law. Sigismund II also ordered the burgomaster and councillors to provide the Armenian elders with court officials in response to every demand 'to detain Armenians themselves as well as their servants and maidservants who do not belong to the Roman Church' (Kapral, 2000, pp. 282–283). All in all, however, the problematic functioning of the Armenian court, which was partly owing to actions by the city council, probably caused many Armenians to have an ambivalent attitude towards the Armenian court, thereby encouraging them to bring their cases before the Magdeburg court.

Yet another jurisdictional conflict sheds light on the question of why Armenian elders so readily and fearlessly opposed the city magistrate. In 1625, in execution of an order of the city council, two Armenians from Lviv applied to the royal assessorial court (*sąd asesorski, sąd zadworny*) in Krakow to consider their civil case. A 'council of twenty men' – in all probability the Armenian consistory court – considered this appeal to be an attempt to avoid Armenian jurisdiction; they put the applicants under an interdict and excommunicated them from the Church and nation (Łoziński, 1902, p. 291). The applicants then appealed to the city council, who summoned two regents who had presided over the council of twenty men to the city hall, where they were sent to gaol, in spite of their claims to be courtiers (*sługa rękodajny*) of certain Polish aristocrats. The burgomaster declared that the illegal council of twenty men had violated the jurisdictions of the magistrate and of the king, by excommunicating these individuals in the civil case. The city court sentenced the regents to a month in jail, three years' exile from the city and payment of a fine of two marcs of gold. The Armenian elders applied to the king, who repealed the sentence. Even so, the two Armenian regents were only freed from jail after a second royal verdict (Łoziński, 1902, pp. 291–293).

In the mid-seventeenth century, lastly, two royal decrees granted equal rights with Catholic burghers to Armenians who adopted the religious union with Roman Church. In the next decade, the most prominent Armenians in Lviv were ennobled by King Jan Casimir (1648–1668) and left the Armenian nation. By the late seventeenth century, the Armenian court had lost most of its judicial functions. It was finally abolished in 1784 by the Austrian authorities, after Lviv had become part of the Habsburg province of Galizien in 1772.

Kamianets-Podilskyi.

The royal city of Kamianets-Podilskyi represents a royal town with a certain modus vivendi between its Catholic-Polish and its Armenian communities. It was granted German law in 1374 when it belonged to the Grand Duchy of Lithuania. In 1432, the city was incorporated into the Kingdom of Poland. There were three autonomous communities from the fifteenth century onwards: Catholic, Armenian and Ruthenian-Orthodox, all of which had their own courts and city halls. However, there was only one burgomaster and city council, namely the Catholic-Polish one. The jurisdiction of the communities' (nations') law courts included both civil and criminal cases. In 1460, Casimir IV granted Armenians the right to elect their *wójt* (Stopka, 2010a, p. 98). The competence of the Armenian law court comprised cases in which both litigants were Armenians, or where an Armenian was the defendant (Stopka, 2010a, pp. 98–99). In the mid-sixteenth century, the city magistrate tried to extend its jurisdiction over the Armenian community. In 1550, Sigismund II subsequently ordered that in cases where an Armenian violated the rights of the city or a burgher of the Magdeburg nation, he had to be detained by the Armenian *wójt*. He then had to be judged before a court composed of the Magdeburg *wójt* as well as the Armenian *wójt*. If they could not reach a compromise, the case had to be referred to the royal court (Stopka, 2010a, p. 100).

The Armenian *wójt* and elders defended the jurisdiction of their court, and invited the king to intervene. In 1574, for instance, a Catholic man seized an Armenian committing adultery with his wife. Both adulterers were sentenced to death by the Magdeburg court and executed. However, the Armenian community applied to the king, because the Armenian *wójt* had been absent at the trial. In 1576, King Stefan Batory then ordered that in cases of adultery, justice had to be administered in Magdeburg and Armenian courts consecutively. When in 1575 Zanu, an Armenian, appealed to the Magdeburg court against the decision of the Armenian court, he was detained and fined (Stopka, 2010a, p. 101).

As a judicial infrastructure, the Armenian court in Kamianets-Podilskyi had at its disposal the city hall and the gaol in its basement, while it hired the officers of justice – or at least some of them – from the Magdeburg court. For instance, in 1577 the Armenian court employed Stas, the Magdeburg court bailiff, as marshal for a yearly salary of 14 florins (Garkavets, 2002, Vol. 1, p. 872). The absence of numerous jurisdictional conflicts suggests that in Kamianets-Podilskyi a kind of modus vivendi was found. The Armenian court functioned there till 1791 when this particular municipal legal system was abolished by the Polish Diet.

Zamość

Zamość represents a third type of town with an Armenian community, notably a private town where the Armenian community enjoyed a fair amount of autonomy, yet in actual practice cooperated successfully with the Polish city government.

When the chancellor of Poland Jan Zamoyski founded the town of Zamość (1580) in his private domains, he invited Catholics, Armenians, Greeks, Scots and Sephardic Jews to settle there. Zamoyski granted the Armenian community the privilege of establishing an Armenian court on 9 January 1589 (Zakrzewska-Dubasowa, 1965, pp. 266–272). In their records, the Armenians of Zamość emphasized their model of self-government and a justice system they had adopted from the Armenian community of Kamianets-Podilskyi. Nonetheless, since Zamość was a private town, the Armenians had to appeal not to the royal court or royal governor but to the appeal court (*Trybunał Zamojski*) or court of the town owner (Korobowicz, 1964; Zakrzewska-Dubasowa, 1980). The same model was employed in other Armenian communities founded in private towns during the seventeenth century.

In contrast to the royal cities of Lviv and Kamianets-Podilskyi, Zamość demonstrated a remarkable absence of jurisdictional conflicts. The Armenian court in Zamość administered justice in cases between Armenians as well as when an individual – a nobleman, a Jew, an Armenian from another town or country – had filed a lawsuit against an Armenian of Zamość. In the latter case, a temporary change of jurisdiction was practised. In 1637, for instance, a nobleman, Stefan Nowosielecki, acknowledged the recovery of debt from an Armenian called Gabriel Ariewowicz. In accordance with the legal formula written down in the court records, Nowosielecki 'left for the mean time his proper terrestrial law and jurisdiction, and incorporated himself – so far as necessary for the current act – to the present jurisdiction of Armenian law'.[4]

In accordance with the Armenian law code of 1519, article 120, the Armenian law court was supposed to consist of twelve elders, but the presence of at least four elders and the *wójt* sufficed to issue a verdict (Kapral, 2000, p. 217). In accordance with 'The procedural code of Armenian court and law' (1604) two elders and the *wójt* were enough for cases below ten marcs (Balzer, 1912, p. 28). Yet bringing together even this reduced number of jurymen appeared to be a complicated task. As merchants, involved in the long-distance trade, they annually spent several months on commercial travels. In 1681, the Armenian court recognized that 'because of their commerce the merchants who are the jurymen cannot be present at the court sessions'.[5] A flexible solution was found that reflected not only the level of friendly co-existence of Armenian and Magdeburg courts in the city but also the open-mindedness of provincial interpreters of law. It was decided that:

> in an urgent criminal case or case with a foreigner involved [*sprawa gościnna*], if no one of the Armenian jurymen would be present, then – for the completeness of the criminal process – the jurymen of Polish nation have to be adopted as many as necessary according to the law with no derogation of the privileges of the Armenian nation of Zamość.[6]

In reality, however, the court sessions were irregular; sometimes there were no proceedings for several months (Zakrzewska-Dubasowa, 1960, p. 78). One can suppose that along with such eventualities as commercial trips by jurymen, the outbreak of epidemics and wars, another reason could be the inability to pay a salary to a court scribe, an office that was ordinarily occupied by a Pole.

As a consequence, the competence of the Armenian court in Zamość was reduced in actual practice. In the seventeenth century, only two criminal cases were recorded. Conceivably, all other criminal cases were judged by the city court. Even in these two cases, a composed court was assembled to administer justice, notably in 1681 and in 1689. In 1681, for instance, when a local Armenian, Eljasz Kistesterowicz, killed his wife, Helena, the crime was considered by the 'Criminal court of *wójt* and jurymen of the privileged Armenian law in Zamość'.[7] Actually, a composed court was assembled which included the Armenian *wójt*, the city burgomaster, four Armenian jurymen, the scribe of the city court, the municipal interrogator (*instygator*) and the prosecutor (*delator*). The accused was detained in the city gaol. It appears that the Armenian court totally lacked the judicial infrastructure necessary for a criminal process. Justice was administered in accordance with a mixture of Polish, Magdeburg and Armenian law. The accused was provided with a '*defensor*' in accordance with Polish law, a function performed by a Polish nobleman. Although this 'red-handed' criminal case should have been considered in one day in accordance with Magdeburg law, the process of Eljasz Kistesterowicz continued for a week. In accordance with Magdeburg law, the witnesses were examined with a written list of questions (*interrogatoria*), and the accused was also subjected to torture since he was also suspected of sorcery. Eljasz Kistesterowicz was sentenced to death in accordance with article 60 of *Statuta iuris armenici*.[8]

The Armenian community in Zamość was much smaller than that in Lviv or Kamianets-Podilskyi. According to the record of the head tax levied in Zamość in 1678, there were ninety Armenian taxpayers in the city and suburbs (Zakrzewska-Dubasowa, 1965, p. 56). In such a small community the *wójt* and jurymen were relatives of many members. As a result, litigants sometimes questioned the impartiality of the judgments (Zakrzewska-Dubasowa, 1980, p. 28). As Zakrzewska-Dubasowa pointed out, this was probably the main reason for a majority of appeals against a judgment (Zakrzewska-Dubasowa, 1960, p. 79). Armenian jurymen gradually introduced some norms of Magdeburg law and terrestrial law to the court sentences. In Zamość, Armenians were granted the same rights as other townspeople. Armenians also occupied some offices in the city Magdeburg magistracy. Thus, the evident ineffectiveness of the Armenian court and the apparent absence of segregation in Zamość led to the successful integration of local Armenians to the Magdeburg community. The Armenian court in Zamość was abolished in 1738 (Zakrzewska-Dubasowa, 1960, p. 80).

Functions and jurisdiction of Armenian law courts

This section explores the actual functioning of the Armenian law courts that were described above. It discusses a number of court cases that exemplify the way both Armenians and non-Armenians used these courts. First, however, the case load of the court of Kamianets-Podilskyi is discussed in a more general way. For this court, a book of records has been preserved that shows which cases were heard in the years 1559–1567, under *wójt* Yurko and *wójt* Ghuriegh (Grunin, 1967). The number of records and, incidentally, the number of elders who attended sessions varied in the course of a year and depended on two factors. First, the regular fairs and long-distance commercial trips sometimes hampered the convening of court sessions. For instance, the most popular fair in Lviv began on St. Agnes day – 21 January – and continued for three weeks. In 1560 *wójt* Yurko was absent between 16 January and 17 March. As a result, only three court sessions presided over by Yurko's deputies were held in two months. In 1561 he was again absent in January and February. This time, the nine sessions were held by his deputy Serghiy, who was assisted by two to four elders instead of twelve. The actual number of elders at any session never exceeded nine, and on average they numbered three to five per session. As a consequence, many cases were postponed 'till arrival of all elders from Lviv' (Grunin, 1967, pp. 267–268). Secondly, epidemics were a reason why the records were interrupted. For instance, the city population was affected by plague in July 1566. Every day, about 8–10 Armenians and 60 Poles and Ruthenians fell victim to the epidemic and the city was isolated for quarantine (Ališan, 1896, p. 36). Table 5.1 shows how records were only made in January to June.

The records include not only civil and criminal cases but also statements, contracts and testaments. Most records related to debt cases. Secondly, there were cases based on quarrels and scuffles. A third group constituted sale and purchase contracts and partnership agreements. In addition, the Armenian court was the first instance to which the local, non-resident and foreign Armenians applied to be granted citizenship. After paying a sum of money depending on his wealth status, an applicant was entered in the 'Album of the Fraternity of our Armenian Nation of Lviv'.[9] The court then appointed two elders to recommend an applicant to the city council. Thus, the Armenian court assumed responsibility for the recommended applicant, confirming that he was a wealthy, lawful and peaceful person, and not a foreign spy (in the case of a foreign Armenian applicant). Those Armenians ennobled by the king and the Diet – mostly for their diplomatic services – were de-registered

TABLE 5.1 Number of records made in the book of records of the Armenian court in Kamianets-Podilskyi in 1559–1567

Year	*May–December 1559*	*1560*	*1561*	*1562*	*1563*	*1564–1565*	*January–June 1566*	*1567*
Number of records	33	60	32	65	38	16	36	10
Name of *wójt*	Yurko	Yurko	Yurko	Ghuriegh	Ghuriegh	Ghuriegh	Ghuriegh	Kharbet

from Armenian 'city nation' and from the elders.[10] Henceforth, they were under the jurisdiction of the noble court (*sąd ziemski*) and were not expected to pay taxes and tributes together with their former nation.

Access to justice: masters and servants, women and their trustees

Armenian communities emerged as merchant communities. Merchants – principals and agents/factors – and their affairs therefore predominated in the court records. However, other groups also appeared before the Armenian courts. In late medieval and early modern Poland, a plaintiff as a rule applied to the court of a defender's jurisdiction (*actor sequitur forum rei*). Therefore, numerous apprentices, cart-drivers and household servants, who were often Catholics employed by Armenian merchants, who had a conflict with their (former) employer, took legal recourse to the Armenian court. The same applies for non-Armenian merchants who had dealings with Armenian counterparts. When suing a former Armenian master, a Catholic maidservant, for instance, appeared before the court along with her new master or landlord, as did maidservant Nastia in 1560, accompanied by the city *wójt* of Kamianets-Podilskyi. She claimed she had been beaten by her Armenian master and demonstrated the signs of it. Her claim was recorded in the Armenian court records (Grunin, 1967, p. 256).

On Friday 6 November 1579, a certain noble, Zakrowski, along with Anna, a former maidservant of an Armenian man called Nurses, appeared before Holub, the Armenian *wójt* of Kamianets-Podilskyi. They summoned Anna's former master. Anna said that she had been employed until Easter but had left her master after certain disputes, the nature of which is not detailed in the sources. She asked Nurses to return her belongings. When Nurses after some hesitation complied, Anna claimed one of her shirts was missing. Nurses, however, replied that he had given her a pinafore and tape, and she would get her shirt back after returning these two items. The *wójt* ordered Nurses to give back all the belongings of his former maidservant. If he wanted to get back his pinafore and tape, he had to start a separate case. Nurses appealed the case, which was to be heard the following Wednesday and involve all jurymen (Garkavets, 2002, Vol. 1, p. 877). Thus, one can assume that Anna's leaving of her service was sudden and emotional, probably as result of a quarrel, and she went back to her village and asked her landlord to represent her in court in order to get back her belongings.

It can be deduced that litigations between Armenian masters and their non-Armenian maidservants were different from cases where both sides were of the same religion. Some Armenian merchants cohabited with their local maidservants, which was considered a crime. In 1499 Alexander, the grand duke of Lithuania, in his charter to the city of Kyiv confirmed the size of the fines for cohabitation of outsiders with local women. Revealingly, the fine for Christians was established as a twelfth of the amount of that for 'Turkish, Tatar, and Armenian merchants' (Akty, 1846, p. 194). It is possible that the vague description of the quarrel between Nurses and his maid concealed an unhappy cohabitation. It may thus have involved a religious conflict. Because of economic competition between Armenian merchants and Catholic patricians, the latter made deliberate efforts to reduce the access of the former to the local labour force. One can assume that the fear of being executed made Armenian merchants more cautious in their relations with their servants.

Factors and apprentices also waged cases against their masters even if they were foreign subjects. On Monday 27 July 1635, Armenian Agopša of Suceava, who was a Moldavian subject, appeared before the Armenian *wójt* and four elders in Kamianets-Podilskyi as a plaintiff against Širin, widow of the late local Armenian Khačadur. Agopša declared that he had served Khačadur for seven years, and the latter had promised to compensate him by finding him a bride, paying for his wedding and giving him start-up capital. Moreover, Agopša had been promised the return of a loan of 40 thalers. Širin failed to pay the debts of her late husband, which prompted the prosecution by Agopša. He concluded his protestation to the court with the statement: 'And I am reserving for myself the right in proper time and in proper place to sue her [Širin] concerning all this' (Garkavets, 2002, Vol. 1, p. 929). This probably meant that Agopša reserved for himself the right to choose a court of another jurisdiction.

Women did thus appear before the court, but not in the same way as men did. In accordance with article 123 of *Statuta iuris armenici* (1519), Armenian women sued in Armenian civil and consistory courts through the agency of a trustee (*opiekun*) – a husband or a close male relative (Kapral, 2000, p. 217). For instance, on 19 July 1594 in the Armenian court in Kamianets-Podilskyi:

> appeared Magda, the wife of Marko, and appointed her son Khačko as her trustee, delivering to him all rights to win and lose any lawsuit, to take oath, to collect debts, to recognize the recovery of a debt, assuming an obligation to be grateful for his agency.
>
> *(Garkavets, 2002, vol. 1, p. 887)*

There is some evidence that a husband had priority over other trustees.[11] In the case of litigation against a close relative, a woman might choose a law officer as her trustee. For instance, on 11 January 1641, Katruša Lamanka appeared in the Armenian court and recognized a debt to her son Aswadur. She appointed Vasyl Filipovič, a bailiff (*urad*), as her trustee (Garkavets, 2002, Vol. 1, p. 932). On the other hand, in cases where both parties were women they might act without male trustees (Garkavets 2002, Vol. 1, p. 896). In accordance with article 29 of the procedural code of the Armenian courts of 1604, a husband and a wife could equally act as trustee for each other (Balzer 1912, p. 38). Moreover, a wife might be a sponsor of her husband (Garkavets, 2002, Vol. 1, p. 890).

Arbitration: fairs and beyond

Commercial controversies between merchants were often arbitrated at fairs by their business partners without going to court. For instance, in 1599 at the fair in Lublin there was a controversy over a bill of exchange (*membran*) between the Armenian merchant Murath Melenki of Zamość, an issuer, and the endorsees – Norbek Popowicz and Murath Kierymowicz of Lviv. Murath Melenki declared that there was a mistake in their calculations. A new register was written down in the presence of another three Armenian merchants, but arbitration was postponed because of Norbek Popowicz's illness. Then (after the death of Murath Kierymowicz), all these merchants sat together in Lviv in the house of Bochdan Donowakowicz and, in the presence of the city court secretary, made the calculations and proposed an agreement to Murath Melenki. The latter, however, refused to comply and ultimately filed a lawsuit at the Armenian civil court in Lviv the following year.[12]

Sometimes Armenians chose non-Armenians as their arbitrators. An arbitrator had to be man of substance who enjoyed credibility both within and outside the Armenian community. Bazyli Rudomicz, who lived in the mid-seventeenth century, is a good example. Born in a Ruthenian family, he converted to Roman Catholicism. He was a Professor of Civil Law and Provost of the Academy of Zamość, a member of the city council and *wójt*, a member of the Tribunal of Zamość and of the castle court (*jus castrensis*). Rudomicz maintained friendships with some Armenian merchants and priests, frequently banqueting with them as he recorded in his diary. Rudomicz also noted in his diary that on 23 December 1658 he had been asked by wealthy Armenian merchants Balejowicz and Tutulowicz to act as arbitrator in their controversy over an inheritance. Interestingly, Rudomicz's friendships with many litigants were not perceived as an obstacle for his arbitration duties. Probably, it was impossible for a man of substance in a small town to be equally distant from all potential litigants. Presents were also not perceived by the contemporaries as an obstacle for impartial administration of justice. For instance, on 18 July 1663 Rudomicz noted in his diary that the Armenian priest Jan Kistostorowicz gave him a cap made of beaver fur as a gift. The next day, Rudomicz acted as an arbitrator in the litigation between a certain Krassowski and the brother of the aforementioned Jan Kistostorowicz (Rudomicz, 2002, Vol.1, p. 311).

Extra-territorial justice: the caravan trade

Polish Armenians regularly organized so-called caravans for their long-distance trade with the Middle East. The *caravanbashi* – the headman of a caravan – usually represented the caravan in negotiations with local authorities and gangs of robbers. He also carried out the functions of a judge. The election of a *caravanbashi*, his power and functions are, for instance, mentioned in a lawsuit between a defendant *caravanbashi*, Owanisowicz, and a plaintiff, Iwaszko Sepherowicz, a merchant of the same caravan, that was adjudicated by the Armenian civil court in Lviv on 25 February 1642. According to the court records:

> the litigant Owanisowicz was chosen by the company of merchants, travelling to the Turkish land, as the head of this caravan, as a *caravanbashi*, thereby voluntarily giving [him] legal and supervisory power over them during their travels, all will obey his orders, since in accordance with the ancient merchant custom a *caravanbashi*

is authorized to adjudicate the disputes that emerge during the travel and to punish the recalcitrant.[13]

The Ottoman sultans granted such extra-territorial jurisdiction to the Polish Armenian caravans in the Ottoman domains. The sultan's charters were kept in the Armenian courts in Lviv and Kamianets-Podilskyi. Before a caravan trip to the Ottoman Empire, a *caravanbashi* went to the Armenian court and asked for these so-called 'Turkish privileges'. Probably, the privileges were confirmed by every subsequent sultan in exchange for a special payment.[14] The young Dutch humanist Georg van der Does (Dousa), who travelled with an Armenian caravan from Lviv to Constantinople in 1597, described a case in which an Armenian merchant was arrested in Ottoman domains by a Muslim judge (*qadi*). The detainee made a statement that, in accordance with the privilege given by the Ottoman sultan, an Armenian merchant could not be condemned by any Muslim judge but only by his *caravanbashi*. The *qadi* therefore called the Armenian *caravanbashi* who showed him the privileges granted by the Ottoman sultan (Dousa, 1599, pp. 29–30).

The uses of justice by foreign Armenian merchants

In the late fourteenth and early fifteenth centuries, Lviv was the main centre of Polish trade with the Golden Horde and Eastern Mediterranean. According to the royal decree of 1444, foreign merchants – actually all non-Catholics (*Greci, Armeni, Saraceni, Iudei, Bessermeni*) – were subject to the jurisdiction of the city jury of Lviv. The decree prohibited foreign and local merchants from bringing their mutual disputes before the courts of the 'Polish Law' exercised by the royal officials (Kapral, 2000, pp. 90–92). Henceforth, the decree provoked jurisdictional conflict. As can be seen from the royal decrees of 1469 and 1476, the Armenian court of Lviv also adjudicated cases of foreign Armenians. The decrees clarified that fines in the litigations between the local Armenians (*Armeni domestici*) had to be paid to the Armenian community, while in the litigations between the foreign Armenians (*Armeni forensi*) and anybody else fines had to be paid to the city judge (*advocatus*) (Kapral, 2000, pp. 146, 148). On the other hand, the foreign Armenians sometimes used another possible option, notably the Armenian consistory court.

On 23 September 1628 in the city of Tabriz in Persia, Armenian merchant Khodja Mahmat Gülipeks authorized another Armenian merchant, Khodja Farukh from Julfa, to act as his attorney on his travels to Europe.[15] If Farukh were to meet Gülipeks' commercial agents (*vakil*), he was authorized to take from them all the entrusted commodities. It seems likely that Gülipeks had lost contact with his agents and suspected them of being dishonest. Farukh also received a letter of support from Movses, the Patriarch of all the Armenians (1629–1632), addressed to the Armenian bishop of Lviv – Nigol Torosowicz. Patriarch Movses asked bishop Nigol to help Farukh obtain commodities from three Armenian merchants who were Persian subjects. On 20 July 1630, on arrival in Lviv, Farukh appeared before the local Armenian consistory court and submitted both letters, which were then registered in the court records, while Farukh obtained a Polish translation authenticated with the bishop's seal (Tryjarski, 2010, pp. 219–220). From then on, if the agents were detected anywhere in the Polish-Lithuanian Commonwealth, Farukh could demand the royal or municipal authorities to apprehend them. Thus, once again, the Armenian consistory court, having no jurisdiction over the business cases of foreign Armenians, was actually turned into their legal representative and appropriated the legal functions – translation and apostille or legalization of documents – that had never actually been granted by the Polish king.

Conclusions

The Armenian court system in the early modern Kingdom of Poland was a unique phenomenon, unknown in contemporary Armenia – divided between the Ottoman Empire and Safavid Persia – and in Armenian diasporas elsewhere. Armenian merchant communities in Western Europe, the Middle East, and South and Eastern Asia never gained the same level of judicial autonomy. The kings of Poland invited numerous German settlers – particularly after the devastating Mongol invasion of the 1240s – to develop cities in their domains and granted the colonists judicial autonomy and independence from intervention by royal officials. All the other diaspora communities were granted judicial autonomy. At the same time, Armenians as well as other non-Catholic communities were attached to the Magdeburg law system, though with some variations from city to city. The existence of multiple jurisdictions within one city periodically resulted in jurisdictional conflicts arbitrated by the king.

The king was a guarantor of the legal rights of diasporic nations in the same way that he was a guarantor of the rights and liberties of the nobility, the clergy and other estates, of vassal principalities, religious communities, artisan guilds and other corporations. The king was not interested in imposing a uniform official national law. On the contrary, his main task – as understood by contemporaries – was to defend the rights of all his loyal subjects, to maintain a balance that was to maintain existing legal pluralism and its hierarchy. Starting from 1574, every newly elected king had to take an oath to follow the *Pacta conventa* that he concluded with the nobility. He also confirmed the rights and privileges of all estates, nations and corporations that had been granted by his predecessors.

Analysis of the jurisdictional conflicts reveals not only the relations between dominant and subordinate nations in the city but also a division inside the Armenian nation, which consisted of two subgroups: the elders – wealthy merchants who were lifelong holders of a juryman office – and the 'ordinary' members of the community. In the royal cities of Lviv and Kamianets-Podilskyi, the Magdeburg jurisdiction was attractive for many Armenians because of tax exemptions, greater economic opportunities and the legality of verdicts issued by the Magdeburg law court. Moreover, the Armenian court was not as effective as its Magdeburg counterpart: first, the sessions of the Armenian court were not held for many weeks because of the absence of jurymen who were on commercial trips; second, the fairness of the court was in question since the elders were close relatives of each other and of many community members; and finally, the criminal and real estate cases were removed from Armenian court competence. Thus, some Armenian litigants preferred to bring their legal claims to a court they considered more beneficial. At the same time, Armenian elders tried to maintain Armenian judicial autonomy not only to control their co-believers but also because it provided them with social prestige and with opportunities to represent the whole nation at the royal court. On the other hand, in the private city of Zamość both subgroups – the elders and the commoners – frequently applied to the city court of Magdeburg law. As in many other private cities, there was less discriminating segregation as non-Catholics enjoyed the same rights as Catholic burghers. Therefore, over time Armenians from Zamość lost the reason to maintain their separate court, which was abolished in 1738.

An autonomous Armenian court was important for foreign Armenian merchants coming to Poland and for newcomers who settled there with no knowledge of Magdeburg law. Because from 1444 foreign merchants in Lviv could apply only to the city court, the foreign Armenian merchants sometimes employed the Armenian consistory court as a mediator in their relations with the city authorities.

Long-distance and cross-cultural trade made Armenian merchants particularly flexible and sensitive to the different judicial systems they operated in and which they readily adopted. They also developed a high level of self-organization, electing a *caravanbashi*, a 'jury of twenty men' and arbitrators at fairs. The role of human agency was thus particularly strong.

Armenian communities in Poland established a particular judicial institution – the extra-territorial adjudicative power of Armenian *caravanbashi* – which was used by non-Armenian travellers who joined the caravans going to or from the Ottoman domains. The legal status of a *caravanbashi* was defined and confirmed by a particular article in the treaty between the sultan and the king. The limits of his judicial competence in the Ottoman domains was defined in the so-called 'Turkish privileges' issued by the sultan. On the other hand, his administration of justice was probably based on the merchants' customary law. Nothing is known about its codification.

The division between 'dominant' and 'subordinate' was complicated in the case of Armenian merchant communities and could not be reduced to the relations between the Catholic and Armenian nations. Catholic cart-drivers and maidservants were subordinates of their Armenian masters. The Catholic merchants and cart-drivers, as well as other fellow travellers, were under the jurisdiction of Armenian *caravanbashi* during their trips to the Ottoman domains. On the other hand, Catholic servants were not treated in the Armenian civil court in the same way as in the city court, that is, as aggrieved 'subordinates'. The precedent of Ivaschko's execution in 1518 and of the Catholic archbishop's intervention in the relations between Armenian merchants and their Catholic cart-drivers in 1512 made Armenian elders more cautious and attentive to duty.

Notes

1 Except for Kyiv, where Armenians along with Greek Orthodox Ruthenians and Polish Catholics constituted the united city community, though there was a separate Armenian Church court.
2 Since Turkic – defined as 'Tatar' or 'Khpchakh' (Qipchaq that is: Cuman) – was mainly the colloquial language of these Armenians, in the Armenian court records in Lviv and Kamianets-Podilskyi the jurymen were called *aga* (elder), *antičkan* and/or *töräči* (from törä – 'law court'), though in seventeenth-century Polish the terms *starsi* (elders) or *przysięgli* (jurymen) prevailed. An Armenian traveller, Simeon of Poland (of Zamość), in 1620s in his travelogue used the Armenian word *tanuter* (տանուտէր) – 'elder/headman/paterfamilias' (Simeon of Poland, 2007).
3 Though, Armenian Catholics were full citizens of the 'German nation'.
4 Wojewódzki Archiwum Państwowe w Lublinie. Księgi prawa ormiańskiego. Acta Armenica Zamosciana, file 1, fol. 97v.
5 Wojewódzki Archiwum Państwowe w Lublinie. Księgi prawa ormiańskiego. Acta Armenica Zamosciana, file 6, fol. 58.
6 Ibid.
7 Wojewódzki Archiwum Państwowe w Lublinie. Księgi prawa ormiańskiego. Acta Armenica Zamosciana, file 6, fol. 14.
8 Wojewódzki Archiwum Państwowe w Lublinie. Księgi prawa ormiańskiego. Acta Armenica Zamosciana, file 6, fol. 14–35.
9 Dzieje Ormian lwowskich od roku 1649 aż do r. 1713. *Dział Rękopisów Biblioteki Zakładu Narodowego im. Ossolińskich we Wrocławiu* [The Manuscript Department of the Ossoliński National Institute Library in Wrocław], file 1646 II, p. 75.
10 Dzieje Ormian lwowskich, file 1646 II, pp. 50, 71.
11 Central State Historical Archive of Ukraine in Lviv, fond 52 (City Magistrate of Lviv), holding 1, file 136, fol. 421–423.
12 Central State Historical Archive of Ukraine in Lviv, fond 52 (City Magistrate of Lviv), holding 2, file 517, pp.14–15.
13 Central State Historical Archive of Ukraine in Lviv, fond 52 (City Magistrate of Lviv), holding 2, file 526, p. 718.
14 In the calculations of the public expenses made by the Armenian civil court in Lviv from 1614 to 1647 there is a note that 'For the Turkish privileges were given out 1348 [Polish] zlotys.' Dzieje Ormian lwowskich, file 1646 II, p. 151.
15 Julfa or New Julfa (*Nor Jugha*) was an autonomous Armenian suburb of the Persian capital Ispahan. Founded in 1605, New Julfa became the hub of Iran's silk trade and the centre of an Armenian commercial network stretching from Amsterdam to the Philippines.

References

Akty, otnosyashchiesya k istorii Zapadnoy Rossii, sobrannye i izdannye Arkheograficheskoy komissiey. Saint Petersburg: Arkheografichaeskaya komissiya, 1846, vol. 1 (years 1340–1506).

Ališan, Ġ., ed. (1896). *Kamenic': Taregirk' hayoc' Lehastani ew Rumenioy hawastč'eay yawelowacovk'*. Venice: Mkhitarean Miabanutin.

Balzer, O. (1909). *Sądownictwo ormiańskie w średniowiecznym Lwowie*. Lviv: Towarzystwo dla Popierania Nauki Polskiej.

Balzer, O., ed. (1910). *Statut ormiański w zatwierdzeniu Zygmunta I z roku 1519*. Lwów: Towarzystwo dla Popierania Nauki Polskiej.

Balzer, O., ed. (1912). *Porządek sadów i spraw prawa ormiańskiego z r. 1604*. Lviv: Towarzystwo dla Popierania Nauki Polskiej.

Benton, L. (2002). *Law and Colonial Cultures: Legal Regimes in World History, 1400–1900*. New York: Cambridge University Press.

Benton, L. and Ross, R.J. (2013). Empires and legal pluralism: jurisdiction, sovereignty, and political imagination in the early modern world, in: L. Benton and R.J. Ross, eds., *Legal Pluralism and Empires, 1500–1850*. New York: NYU Press, pp. 1–17.

Bily, I., Carls, W. and Gönczi, K., eds. (2011). *Sächsisch-magdeburgisches Recht in Polen. Untersuchungen zur Geschichte des Rechts und seiner Sprache*. Berlin: de Gruyter.

Bischoff, F., ed. (1864). *Urkunden zur Geschichte der Armenier in Lemberg*. Vienna: K.K. Hof- und Staatsdruckerei.

Charewiczowa, Ł. (1925). *Ograniczenia gospodarcze nacyj schizmatyckich i Żydów we Lwowie XV i XVI wieku*. Lviv: z drukarni zakładu narodowego imienia Ossolińskich.

Dashkevitch, Ya.R. (1965). Kipchak Acts of the Armenian law court at Kamenetz Podolsk (1559–1567) as a cultural and historical monument. *Ural-Altaische Jahrbücher*, 36 (3–4), pp. 292–310.

Dashkevitch, Ya.R. (1967). Armianskaya koloniya v Kamentse-Podolske v 50–60-kh godakh XVI veka. In: T. Grunin, ed., *Dokumenty na polovetskom yazyke XVI v. (Sudebnye akty Kamenets-Podols koy armianskoy obshchiny)*. Moscow: Nauka, pp. 65–96.

Dashkevitch, Ya.R. (1969). Armianskoe samoupravlenie vo Lvove v 60–80 gg. XVII v. (Protokoly armianskogo soveta stareyshin kak istoricheskiy istochnik). *Banber Matenadarani*, 9, pp. 213–240.

Dashkevitch, Ya.R. (1976). Ustav armianskoy obshchiny v Kamentse-Podolskom 1616 g. *Rocznik Orientalistyczny*, 38, pp. 103–109.

Dousa, G. (1599). *De itinere suo Constantinopolitano, Epistola*. Leiden: Ex Officina Plantiniana, Apud Christophorum Raphlelengium, Academiae Lugduno-Batavae Typographum.

Elliott, J.H. (1992). A Europe of composite monarchies. *Past and Present*, 137, pp. 48–71.

Garkavets, A., ed. (2002). *Kypchakskoe pismennoye nasledie* (2 volumes). Almaty: Desht-i-Kypchak.

Gilissen, J. (1971). Le pluralisme juridique: essai de syntèse. In: J. Gilissen, ed., *Le pluralisme juridique*. Brussels: Editions de l'Universite de Bruxelles.

Griffiths, J. (1986). What is legal pluralism? *Journal of Legal Pluralism*, 24, pp. 1–55.

Hooker, M.B. (1975). *Legal Pluralism: an Introduction to Colonial and Neo-Colonial Laws*. New York: Clarendon Press.

Gromnicki, T. (1889). *Ormjanie w Polsce: ich historja, prawa i przywileje*. Warsaw: Drukarnia Franciszka Czerwińskiego.

Grunin, T., ed. (1967). *Dokumenty na polovetskom yazyke XVI v. (Sudebnye akty Kamenets-Podolskoy armianskoy obshchiny)*. Moscow: Nauka.

Heyde, J. (2015). Polityka Rady miejskiej Lwowa wobec Żydów i Ormian w XV/XVI wieku. Heterogeniczność etniczno-religijna w mieście jako wyzwanie ustrojowe. *Kwartalnik Historii Kultury Materialnej*, 63(2), pp. 283–292.

Kapral, M., ed. (1998). *Pryvilei mista Lvova (XIV-XVIII st.)* Lviv: MGKO 'Dokumentalna skarbnytsya Lvova'.

Kapral, M., ed. (2000). *Pryvilei natsionalnykh hromad mista Lvova (XIV–XVIII st.)*. Lviv: Piramida.

Kapral, M. (2003a). *Natsionalni hromady Lvova XVI-XVIII st. (sotsialno-pravovi vzaiemyny)*. Lviv: Piramida.

Kapral, M. (2003b). Pravovoe ustroistvo armianskoy obshchiny Lvova v XIV–XVIII vekakh: obzor dokumentov. In: A.N. Garkavets and G. Sapargaliev, eds., *Kypchaksko-pol'skaya versiya Armianskogo Sudebnika Mkhitara Gosha i Armiano-kypchakskiy Protsessual'nyi kodeks. Lvov, Kamenets-Podol'skiy, 1519–1594*. Almaty: Desht-i-Kypchak, Baur, pp. 741–754.

Kapral, M. (2004). Legal regulation and national (ethnic) differentiation in Lviv, 1350–1600. In: Th. Wünsch and A. Janeczek, eds., *On the frontier of Latin Europe: integration and segregation in Red Ruthenia, 1350–1600*. Warsaw: Institute of Archaeology and Ethnology of the Polish Academy of Sciences.

Kapral, M. (2009). L'viv and its ethnic groups in the second half of the sixteenth century. In: A. Bues, ed., *Martin Gruneweg (1562–after 1615) – a European Way of Life*. Wiesbaden: Harrassowitz Verlag, pp. 79–110.

Karst, J. (1905). *Sempadscher Kodex aus dem 13. Jahrhundert in Verbindung mit dem Grossarmenischen Rechtsbuch des Mechitar Gosch aus dem 12. Jahrhundert*. Strasbourg: K. Trubner.

Korobowicz, A. (1964). Sąd ormiański w Zamościu i postępowanie przed nim w świetle ksiąg sądowych. *Annales Universitates M. Curie-Skłodowska*. Vol.11. section G Lublin, pp. 195–212.

Korobowicz, A. (1989). Elementy rodzime i obce w sądownictwie ormiańskim w Zamościu. In: J. Kłoczowski, ed., *Dzieje Lubelszczyzny*. Vol. 6, Warsaw: Państwowe Wydawnictwo Naukowe, pp. 339–351.

Kovalevskiy, M. (1886). *Sovremennyi obychay i drevniy zakon. Obychnoe pravo osetin v istoriko-sravnitel'nom osveshchenii*. 2 vols. Saint Petersburg.

Kutrzeba, S. (1908). Datastanagirk Mechitara Gosza i statut ormianski z r. 1519. *Kwartalnik Historyczny*, 22, pp. 658–679.

Lewicki, M. and Kohnowa, R. (1957). La version turque-kiptchak du 'Code des lois des Arméniens polonais' d'après le ms. No 1916 de la Bibliothèque Ossolineum. *Rocznik Orientalistyczny*, 21, pp. 153–300.

Łoziński, W. (1902). *Patrycjat i mieszczaństwo lwowskie w XVI i XVII wieku*. Lviv: H. Altenberg.

Łoziński, W. (1904). *Prawem i lewem: obyczaje na Czerwonej Rusi w pierwszej połowie XVII wieku*. Lviv: H. Altenberg.

Maine, H. (1861). *Ancient Law, Its Connection with the Early History of Society, and Its Relation to Modern Ideas*. London: John Murray.

Maine, H. (1883). *Dissertations on Early Law and Custom: Chiefly Selected from Lectures Delivered at Oxford*. London: John Murray.

Matwijowski, L. (1939). *Prawo ormiańskie w dawnej Polsce*. Lviv: Skł. Gł. Księg. 'Książka' Aleksander Mazzucato.

Merry, S.E. (1988). Legal Pluralism. *Law & Society Review*, 22, pp. 869–896.

Mkhitar Gosh, M. (2000). *The Lawcode*, translated from Old Armenian by Robert W. Thomson. New Jersey: Rodopi.

Oleś, M. (1966). *The Armenian Law in the Polish Kingdom (1356–1519): a juridical and historical study*. Rome: Edizioni Hosianum.

Oleś, M (1966/67). Casimir the Great and The Armenian privileges, 1333–1370, *Études Slaves et Est-Européennes / Slavic and East-European Studies*, Vol. 11, No. 3/4, pp. 67–90.

Pivazian, E.A. (1991). Eshche raz o Mkhitare Goshe. In: Muradian P.M., ed., *K osveshcheniyu problem istorii i kul'tury Kavkazskoy Albanii i vostochnykh provintsiy Armenii*. Yerevan: Izdatel'stvo Yerevanskogo gos. universiteta, pp. 195–207.

Rudomicz, B. (2002). *Efemeros czyli diariusz prywatny pisany w Zamościu w latach 1656–1672*, Part 1 (2 parts). Wł. Froch, trans., M.L. Klementowski, ed. Lublin: Wydawnictwo Uniwersytetu Marii Curie-Skłodowskiej.

Samokvasov, D.Ya., ed. (1876). *Sbornik obychnogo prava sibirskikh inorodtsev*. Warsaw: Tipografiya Ivana Noskovskogo.

Schütz, E. (1971). Armeno-kiptschakische Ehekontrakte und Testamente aus dem XVI. Jahrhundert. *Acta Orientalia Academiae Scientiarum Hungaricae*, 24, pp. 265–300.

Simeon of Poland (2007). *The Travel Accounts of Simeon of Poland*, trans. by George A. Bournoutian. Costa Mesa: Mazda Publishers.

Starr, J. and Fishburne Collier, J. (1989). Introduction: dialogues in legal anthropology. In: J. Starr and J. Fishburne Collier, eds., *History and Power in the Study of Law: New Directions in Legal Anthropology*. Ithaca: Cornell University Press, pp. 1–28.

Stopka, K. (2000). *Ormianie w Polsce dawnej i dzisiejszej*. Kraków: Księgarnia Akademicka.

Stopka, K. (2004). Migracje a przemiany tożsamości ormiańskiej w średniowiecznej Europie Wschodniej. In: M. Salamon and J. Strzelczyk, eds., *Wędrówka i etnogeneza w starożytności i średniowieczu*. Kraków: Towarzystwo Wydawnicze Historia Iagellonica, pp. 355–365.

Stopka, K. (2009). 'Nasza polska nacja'. Kształtowanie się patriotyzmu polskiego wśród Ormian w okresie staropolskim. In: A. Nowak and A.A. Zięba, eds., *Formuły patriotyzmu w Europie Wschodniej i Środkowej od nowożytności do współczesności*. Kraków: Polska Akademia Umiejętności, pp. 37–54.

Stopka, K. (2010a). Interakcje etniczne w mieście staropolskim. Kamieniec Podolski w ujęciu źródeł ormiańskich od XV do połowy XVII wieku. *Prace Komisji Wschodnioeuropejskiej Polskiej Akademii Umiejętności*, 11, pp. 85–124.

Stopka, K. (2010b). Ormianie. In: M. Kopczyński, and W. Tygielski, ed., *Pod wspólnym niebem. Narody dawnej Rzeczypospolitej*. Warsaw: Bellona i Muzeum Historii Polski, pp. 115–133.

Stopka, K. (2010c). The religious culture of Polish Armenians (Church-public structures and relations). *Acta Poloniae Historica*, 101, pp. 163–205.

Sukiasian, A.G., ed. (1971). *Sudebnik Smbata Sparapeta (Gundstablia) 1265 g*. Yerevan: Yerevanskiy universitet.

Tamanaha, B. (1993). The folly of the 'social scientific' concept of legal pluralism. *Journal of Law & Society*, 20 (2), pp. 192–217.

Tryjarski, E., ed. (2010). *Zapisy sądu duchownego Ormian miasta Lwowa za lata 1625–1630 w języku ormiańsko-kipczackim*. Kraków: Polska Akademia Umiejętności; Ormiańskie Towarzystwo Kulturalne, pp. 219–220.

Von Brünneck, W. (1914). Zur Geschichte des Magdeburger Rechts und der Statuten der Armenier in Lemberg. *Zeitschrift der Savigny-Stiftung für Rechtsgeschichte. Germanistische Abteilung*, 35, pp. 1–40.

Zakrzewska-Dubasowa, M. (1960). Organizacja gminy ormiańskiej w Zamosciu w XVI-XVII wieku. *Rocznik Lubelski*, 3, pp. 63–82.

Zakrzewska-Dubasowa, M. (1965). *Ormianie Zamojscy i ich rola w wymianie handlowej i kulturalnej między Polską a Wschodem*. Lublin: Uniwersytet Marii Curie-Skłodowskiej.

Zakrzewska-Dubasowa, M. (1980). Ormiańska Temida. *Palestra*, 24 (7), pp. 19–37.

Zubrzycki, D. (1844). *Kronika miasta Lwowa*. Lviv: Nakładem autora.

6

THE USE AND ABUSE OF LEGAL SERVICES IN NINETEENTH-CENTURY RUSSIA[1]

Elizaveta Blagodeteleva

Introduction

In the middle of the nineteenth century, the Russian Empire underwent a radical transformation, with the abolition of serfdom in 1861 shaking up the whole social order of the *ancien régime* and prompting rapid and profound changes in local government, the administration of justice and military conscription. However, it was the renovation of the judicial system that stood out the most. The judicial reform of 1864 introduced the nation to public adversarial trials, the jury and the Bar, and therefore became an almost universal symbol of common liberal aspirations and was widely regarded as a blueprint for the future peaceful evolution from an autocracy to a liberal rule-of-law state. But, despite the newly acquired veneer of the modern judicial institutions, the autocratic government continued to exercise virtually unlimited administrative power, while any attempt at political liberalization became stifled by the volatile nature of the regime.[2]

Moreover, political and cultural elites were far from recognizing the fact that new judicial institutions might function efficiently in the country, where the population predominantly consisted of the uneducated lower classes. Public figures of all political stripes never failed to question the agency of the lower-class people in the solemn realm of law. It was a truly striking similarity between otherwise antagonistic political factions, which was rooted in the shared sense of the deep cultural divide between the Westernized elites and the traditional majority of the population. Conservatives and radicals, both of whom were openly hostile to the idea of the rule of law, celebrated the rural population of Russia for its alleged indifference to legal disputes. Meanwhile, liberal proponents of the rule-of-law state severely criticized popular attitudes towards justice, while denigrating those courts where the peasantry and the urban lower classes prevailed, for not adhering to the letter and spirit of statute law.

An acute sense of disjunction between the legal cultures of the upper and lower classes provides an inextricable context for a study of courts and litigation in nineteenth-century Russia. It also makes the Russian Empire a fairly instructive case within the growing body of research on court usage and popular legal culture in modern Europe as it offers an example of how the judicial system, which was constantly questioned by the political and cultural elites, might have worked for the people. Since, in recent decades, both social and legal historians have taken an increasing interest in the relationship between ordinary people, political elites, and the law, they have successfully shattered the long-standing assumption that the majority of the population took little advantage of the evolving legal institutions of early modern and modern Europe. This new strand of research, which originated with the seminal works of Richard Kagan and Christopher Brooks (Kagan, 1981; Brooks, 1986, 1998), has brought into the spotlight popular litigiousness, considered as 'a function of a worldview that placed greater emphasis on individual rights than on individual responsibilities' (Kagan, 1981, p. xix). Multiple in-depth studies have recast the highly fragmented jurisdictions of early modern courts, uneven treatment on the basis of social status and the professionalization of legal practice in a more favourable light, compared to the previous historical and legal research on these matters.[3]

The studies of the Russian Empire have also benefited from this line of research. By exploring popular legal attitudes and practices, the studies challenged the conventional views of the rural and urban lower classes as inherently ignorant and contemptuous of the law (Farnsworth, 1986; Neuberger, 1994; Popkins, 1999, 2000; Burbank, 2004, 2006). For example, in her ground-breaking study of lower-level courts, Jane Burbank provides good evidence that by the beginning of the twentieth century, recourse to legal action was fairly common among the rural population. Not only did peasants make ample use of the lowest-level courts, they also truly appreciated the fact that court decisions were based on statute law. The author argues that although the estate status of peasants still affected their choice of courts, this legal particularity was an asset rather than a liability for peasant litigants, as they came to communicate with the law on their own terms (Burbank, 2004, pp. 247–248).

What is glaringly missing from the picture all the studies paint is the immediate interaction between the general public and the legal profession. Since they concentrate on an almost self-contained milieu of the lowest-level courts, where professional lawyers were absent, these studies depict laypeople as passively accepting the authority of legal experts and never questioning the institutions these experts designed. The lack of research on the relationship between the general public and the legal profession partially stems from the fact that the studies of lawyers in nineteenth-century Russia predominantly focus on the effects that professionalization and specialization of knowledge had on social mobility and patterns of political engagement, so they have paid little attention to the role lawyers played as intermediaries between the general public and the law (Burbank, 1995; Levin-Stankevich, 1996; Pomeranz, 1999; Troit͡skiĭ, 2000). It is noteworthy that the

Russian case is hardly an exception in this respect since major accounts of the legal profession in nineteenth-century Western Europe have also been written without a thorough examination of the popular demand for professional legal help (Karpik and Scott, 1999; Pue and Sugarman, 2003; Burrage, 2006; Ledford, 2006).

This chapter strives to fill the gap by exploring the use of legal services along with the ways laypeople and legal practitioners interpreted their relationship and mutual responsibilities. It suggests that the communication with lawyers constituted an important element of the popular experience of law in the metropolitan areas of the Russian Empire during the second half of the nineteenth century. Since, unlike judges and litigants, lawyers and clients were essentially on an equal footing, their relationship was a matter of negotiation and, therefore, a perfect arena where competing interpretations of law and the opportunities it provided for the people might have clashed fiercely. For this reason, complaints lodged against legal practitioners by the members of various social groups seem to be a good proxy for assessing how wide the social divide between the legal culture of educated society and the lower classes actually was.

The chapter first outlines the general organization of the court system and legal practice in the central provinces of the Empire in the second half of the nineteenth century; it then assesses the proportion of different social groups among those who sought legal help, and, finally, takes a closer look at the most common grievances and claims raised by laypeople complaining about the professional misconduct of their attorneys. The chapter focuses on the middle level of the imperial court system (district courts), where litigants were most likely to encounter professional lawyers. The study draws upon the records kept in the Central State archive of the city of Moscow (T͡SGA g. Moskvy), which contains information on the second largest metropolitan area in the country. The scope of primary sources is narrowed down to the records spanning the period between 1884 and 1903 and concerning exclusively civil cases as they prove more useful for exploring how ordinary people assessed the quality of the legal advice they were given.

Judicial organization

The renovated judicial system offered two major avenues for those seeking justice (see Figure 6.1). The Justices of the Peace constituted the judicial branch of local self-government, aiming at satisfying the popular demand for swift and affordable justice. They resided both in urban and rural areas and were in charge of prosecuting petty crimes and resolving civil disputes worth up to 500 rubles.[4] If dissatisfied, a litigant (or an offender in the case of criminal charges) could appeal against a verdict to any justice at the Provincial Conventions of the Justices of the Peace and then at the Senate, the highest court of the land (Gosudarstvennai͡a Kant͡seli͡arii͡a, 1867, p. 31). In 1889, appointed town and county judges superseded the Justices of the Peace throughout the Empire, with the exception of two capital cities, St. Petersburg and Moscow.

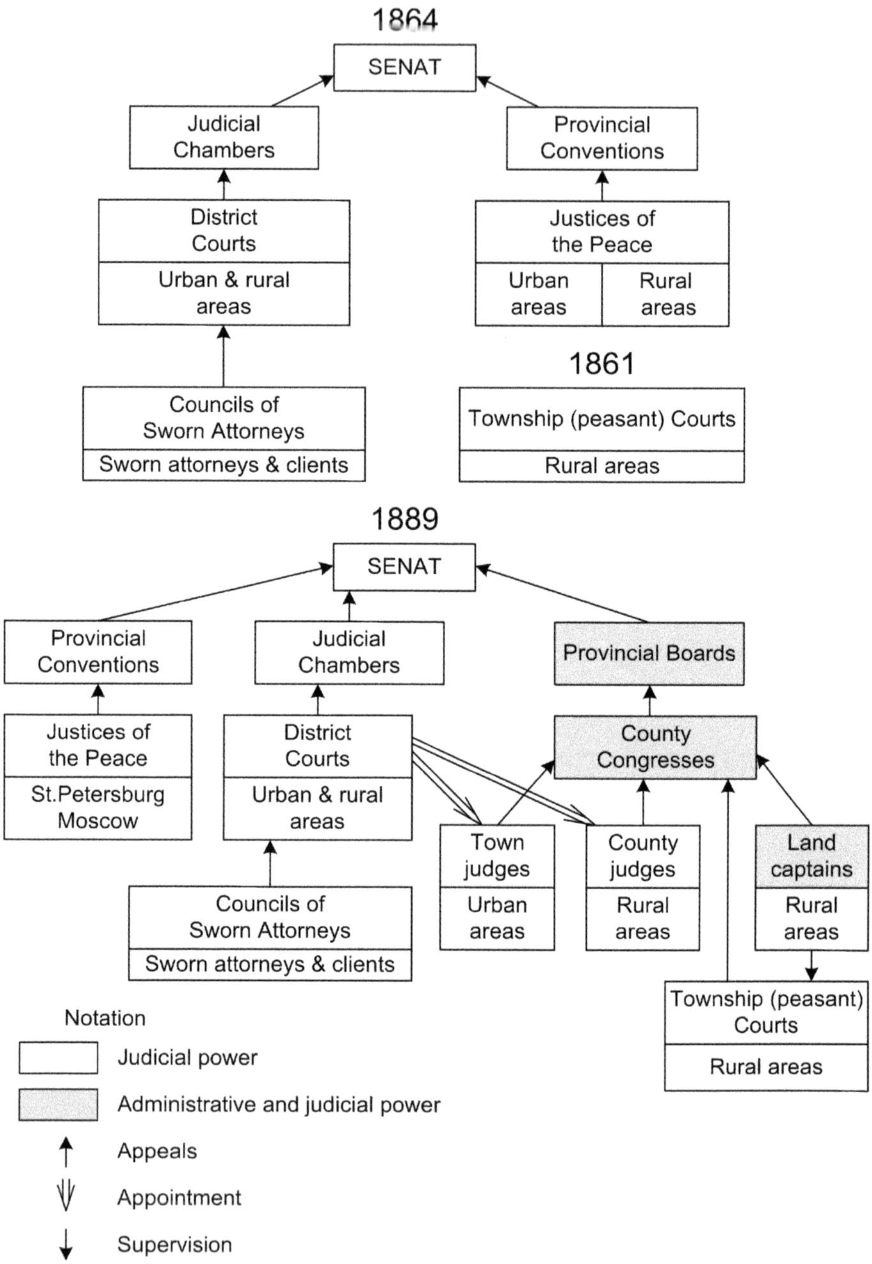

FIGURE 6.1 The structure of the courts in the Russian empire after 1864 and after 1889

Another way of taking legal action was by filing a lawsuit in a district court where lifetime-appointed judges and elected jurors of all classes tried and adjudicated civil and criminal cases that exceeded the jurisdiction of the Justices of the Peace. District courts resided in the largest provincial towns and seemed well beyond the reach of the rural population. Their decisions, if appealed, could be overturned by a higher court, called a judicial chamber, which sat in the principal city of a judicial district and had the right to supervise all district courts within a given area. One could further appeal against the rulings of a judicial chamber and bring the case in question to the Senate (Gosudarstvennaia͡ Kant͡selia͡rii͡a, 1867, p. 77).

There also remained separate courts for the peasantry and ethnic and religious minorities with judges elected from local communities and limited options for appeal. Unlike the Justices of the Peace and district courts, which crossed the traditional social boundaries, these judicial settings remained within the confines of the legally delineated estates, although their existence did not deny the rural and non-Christian population the right to seek justice elsewhere. In 1889, when crown officials, so-called land captains, were put in charge of supervising township courts, and county congresses, government bodies with both administrative and judicial powers, started accepting appeals against their rulings, township courts became reasonably efficient judicial institutions, which served a peasant majority of the population well (Polnoe sobranie zakonov Rossiĭskoĭ imperii, 1881–1913).

Apart from township courts, where parties would appear in person, all judicial settings allowed various forms of legal representation. There were two officially recognized groups of legal practitioners, namely sworn attorneys and private attorneys, who acted on behalf of individuals, communities and organizations, although ordinary people retained the right to plead their own cases and were eligible to appear in court on behalf of a third party three times a year. According to the Judicial Statutes of 1864, sworn attorneys were supposed to represent laypeople in courts throughout the Empire and had a right to unite in local associations, which entitled them to a great deal of self-regulation. Their governing bodies, otherwise called the councils of sworn attorneys, were to control admission, supervise legal practice and bring disciplinary proceedings against those practitioners who were suspected of malpractice. Since the Statutes required any sworn attorney to hold a law degree and complete a five-year apprenticeship before setting up his own practice, these regulations inevitably left some legal practitioners in limbo (Gosudarstvennaia͡ Kant͡selia͡rii͡a, 1867, p. 218).

The additional regulations of 1874 introduced another option for those who were unable to meet the established criteria but were still willing to practise. Private attorneys thus appeared to be another group of licensed legal practitioners whose practice, however, was confined to a particular court where they purchased an annual work permit. Private attorneys had no professional organizations and were subject to the supervision of the courts (Polnoe sobranie zakonov Rossiĭskoĭ imperii, 1825–1881). Although the difference between these two groups of practitioners was striking in terms of admission, the bulk of sworn attorneys also had to practise under the supervision of the courts like their less accomplished counterparts since only three professional associations were established before 1874 – in St. Petersburg, Moscow and Kharkov – and a further four would not appear until 1904 (Gessen, 1914, p. 442). On top of that, the nebulous milieu of unlicensed practitioners, called 'the street Bar', significantly affected the administration of justice by swamping various courts with written claims that laypeople presented as if they were of their own authorship.

The social composition of clients

Unfortunately, there is no good source that allows a thorough assessment of the demand for legal counselling in general and the market share of each group of practitioners in particular. Since retaining a lawyer was not obligatory for the parties in civil litigation, neither the Ministry of Justice nor the courts went to the trouble of registering this on a regular basis. Moreover, an accurate reconstruction of the collective portrait of those seeking professional legal advice is further complicated by the lack of primary sources on the social composition of litigants. Despite the fact that the Ministry of Justice closely monitored the volume of civil litigation at the level of district courts, it hardly paid any attention to the parties involved, which was in stark contrast to its painstaking efforts to profile criminal defendants. Nevertheless, it is still feasible to infer some information on the social composition of litigants and their use of legal services from the combination of the general court statistics, the rolls of civil cases and the registers of complaints filed against sworn attorneys.

This study initially started with three registers of complaints filed at the Moscow council of sworn attorneys between 1884 and 1903 (Nastol'nyĭ reestr Soveta, 1883, 1893, 1901). Dissatisfied with their attorneys or suspicious of fraud and trickery, clients brought their grievances to the council or to the Moscow district court, which was in charge of supervising private attorneys, depending on the professional status of an alleged wrongdoer. However, the court records of disciplinary proceedings against private attorneys were utterly rudimentary and sketchy, consequently the registers of complaints kept by the council appeared to be the only consistent source of information on the matter. The registers contained the names and the social background of complainants, the duration of ensuing disciplinary proceedings and the eventual disciplinary outcomes. Unfortunately, no specifics pertaining to initial complaints were recorded in these kinds of documents. To fill the gap, the contents of twenty disciplinary proceedings, which include the written claims of complainants, replies submitted by sworn attorneys in self-defence and the decisions of the council, were explored.

This data was then supplemented with the information on the social status of litigants obtained from the rolls of civil cases from the Moscow district court. Since collecting the data from every roll deposited at the court archive throughout a couple of decades presented a particularly intractable problem, only two rolls were chosen for analysis. The first one was kept by the court secretariat and contained the records of civil actions set in motion by sworn attorneys in 1877 (Alfavit grazhdanskikh del, 1877). This is the only source known to the author that specifically registers the cases involving professional lawyers. The second roll was compiled by one of the court's civil divisions, of which there were two at the time, and listed a number of cases, starting in 1879 and 1880 and ending before July 1887

(Opis'parkhivnykh del, 1879–1892, 1879). It is worth pointing out that none of the rolls represents the total volume of civil litigation in a given year. Nevertheless, provided that all cases were randomly distributed throughout the court's civil divisions, these rolls are useful shortcuts to the whole picture. The general estimates of the volume of civil litigation along with the numbers of registered legal practitioners are derived from the annual reports of the Ministry of Justice for the years 1868, 1884, 1893, 1897 and 1903 (Ministerstvo I͡Ustit͡sii, 1871, 1887, 1894, 1899, 1904). Unfortunately, the ministry put the publication temporarily on hold between 1871 and 1887, so the data for these years is not readily available.

According to the ministerial reports, the volume of civil litigation in the Moscow judicial chamber rose dramatically during the first two decades after the implementation of the judicial reform in 1866, as shown in Table 6.1. Although a noticeable increase in the caseload coincided with the territorial expansion of the chamber, which led to an increase in the number of district courts from 10 to 15, there was also a genuine rise in litigation. At the Moscow district court alone, the caseload went up by more than 50 per cent, although the relative share of the court in the total number of cases commenced in the judicial chamber dropped from 33 to 22 per cent. From the mid-1880s through to the late 1890s, despite the moderate growth of the population residing within the jurisdiction of the chamber, the volume of civil litigation contracted. The Moscow district court, however affected, suffered a lesser setback than any other court in the region, while handling an ever-increasing proportion of civil cases. The concentration of civil litigation in the metropolitan area continued to grow at the turn of the century when the combined business of all district courts was increasing by 5 per cent a year. In 1903, the Moscow district court handled almost 28 per cent of the cases, the monetary value of which exceeded the combined value of the other 72 per cent.

The development of Moscow sworn attorneys followed a slightly different pattern. Between 1868 and 1884, the growth of the professional association corresponded to the changes in the caseload of the courts, although it continued uninterruptedly yet at a much slower pace, when the rise of civil litigation came to a standstill in the mid-1880s and 1890s. Once the business of the district courts showed signs of rapid recovery, the numbers of sworn attorneys almost doubled, going up from 645 to 1200 between 1897 and 1903. Moreover, the concentration of the legal practice far outstripped the concentration of civil litigation since 82 per cent of the Bar practised in Moscow by 1903. Under these circumstances, private attorneys, considerably smaller in numbers both in 1897 and 1903, seemed unlikely rivals to their more privileged counterparts. However, being far less concentrated in the metropolitan area, they were more readily available at provincial district courts where the paucity of sworn attorneys was becoming increasingly apparent as the volume of civil litigation rose considerably at the turn of the century.

Although the number of complaints issued against sworn attorneys never surpassed 3 per cent of the total number of cases initiated in the Moscow district court, the business of the council generally mirrored the changes in the volume of

TABLE 6.1 The Moscow judicial chamber, 1868–1903

Year	*1868*	*1884*	*1893*	*1897*	*1903*
Number of district courts	10	15	13	14	14
Population, in hundreds of thousands					
in all districts		163.0		185.2	
in Moscow district		21.8		24.3	
Caseload, civil litigation only					
in all district courts	13,097	29,560	28,847	27,077	35,182
in the central district court in Moscow	4,347	6,537	7,196	6,968	9,699
Caseload in the central district court, %	33.2	22.1	24.9	25.7	27.6
Increase in caseload, %					
in all district courts		125.7	−2.4	−6.1	29.9
in the central district court in Moscow		50.4	10.1	−3.2	39.2
Increase in caseload, % per year					
in all district courts		7.9	−0.3	−1.5	5.0
in the central district court in Moscow		3.1	1.1	−0.8	6.5
Total value of civil cases, in hundred thousand rubles					
in all district courts		231.9	188.5		375.2
in the central district court in Moscow	64				193.1
Number of sworn attorneys and their trainees					
in all district courts	45*	445	493	645	1,200
in the central district court in Moscow				513	979
Increase in numbers of sworn attorneys and their trainees, %		n/a	10.8	30.8	86.0
Increase in numbers of sworn attorneys and their trainees, % per year			1.2	7.7	14.3
Number of sworn attorneys and trainees in the central court in Moscow, %				79.5	81.6
Number of private attorneys					
in all district courts				349	374
in the central district court in Moscow				95	99
Number of private attorneys in the central court in Moscow, %				27.2	26.5

* Sworn attorneys only
Sources: Ministerstvo ÎUstitsii, 1871, 1887, 1894, 1899, 1904; Nos, 1891

civil litigation. As can be seen in Table 6.2, the business of the council rose by 27 per cent up to the early 1890s, then went down by 11 per cent until the end of the century, and then skyrocketed with the numbers of complaints almost doubling between 1899 and 1903. Nevertheless, this dramatic increase in the caseload did not seem to affect the efficiency of the disciplinary proceedings. Although in the early 1900s it admittedly took the council longer to process an average case, it still managed to complete three-quarters of its investigations within the first five

TABLE 6.2 Disciplinary proceedings in the Moscow Council of Sworn Attorneys, 1884–1903

Year		*1884–88*	*1889–93*	*1894–98*	*1899–03*	*Total*
Total number of proceedings		531	672	600	1,146	2,949
Duration of disciplinary proceedings, in week						
Average		3.4	4.4	3.9	5.5	
Median		2	3	2	3	
Min		0	0	0	0	
Max		59	74	61	170	
Quartiles	25	1	1	1	2	
	50	2	3	2	3	
	75	4	5	4	5	

Sources: Nastol′nyĭ reestr Soveta, 1883, 1893, 1901

weeks, which did not differ markedly from the business of earlier decades. What was particularly noteworthy about the changes in the caseload between 1884 and 1903 was that the share of individuals demanding accountability from sworn attorneys climbed from 77 to 91 per cent, while the proportion of complaints filed by courts and state agencies significantly declined, going down from 21 to 9 per cent.[5] The only institution that stepped up the pressure was the council itself since it was twice as likely to open an investigation of its own volition in the early 1900s as it had been during the 1880s and 1890s.

The social composition of those taking legal action at the Moscow district court in 1879 and 1880 is shown in Table 6.3. The data from the roll is split into two sets with the first set representing all cases, including lawsuits, inheritance claims, probates and the registration of property rights, and the second one focusing on civil actions. The reason for considering civil actions separately is twofold. Firstly, certain legal expertise was required to prepare and file a lawsuit properly; hence plaintiffs seemed to be more likely to seek legal advice compared to those claiming an inheritance or having their wills or property rights confirmed. Secondly, court clerks went about registering civil actions more carefully than other proceedings and, as a result, the data on lawsuits has considerably fewer missing observations. In both sets of data, entrepreneurs appear the most litigious group with almost 26 per cent of cases, and 30 per cent of civil actions started in 1879 and 1880. The upper classes, including the landed gentry and the families of military officers and civil servants, come second with 17 and 19 per cent respectively. The share of the petty bourgeoisie matches that of the upper classes in the overall number of cases, although it goes down to 16 per cent if only lawsuits are taken into consideration. The participation rate of the peasantry reaches 11 per cent of all cases and 12 per cent of lawsuits. Women comprise about 40 per cent of the litigants among the upper classes and the petty bourgeoisie. In contrast, the numbers of female members of entrepreneurial and peasant families only slightly exceed 20 per cent.

The proportion of females declines if the scope of cases is narrowed down to lawsuits with the notable exception of peasant women, whose share rises from 21 to 26 per cent.

Since there is no information on whether those listed in the roll of 1879–1880 all employed the services of professional lawyers, it is important that the register of 1877, which contains civil cases involving sworn attorneys, corroborates these findings. As Table 6.3 shows, the proportion of entrepreneurs and the upper classes among the litigants enlisting the services of sworn attorneys far surpasses the most generous estimates based on the roll of 1879–1880, with entrepreneurs comprising more than 39 per cent and the upper classes about 29 per cent of the total number of litigants. The share of the petty bourgeoisie and peasantry, on the contrary, lags behind with 13 and 8 per cent respectively. Furthermore, low-class women are considerably underrepresented as their share plunges from 40 to 23 per cent in the case of the petty bourgeoisie and from 21 to 11 per cent in the case of the peasantry. The proportion of privileged women declines only slightly, by 4 per cent among the upper classes and 5 per cent among entrepreneurs.

This provides good evidence of a considerable disparity in access to legal services, which might have only been further exacerbated by the growing concentration

TABLE 6.3 The social composition of litigants in the Moscow district court, 1877, 1879–1880

	*Roll, 1879–1880, all cases**			*Roll, 1879–1880, lawsuits*			*Register of cases with sworn attorneys, 1,877*		
	Count	*%*	*Female in group, %*	*Count*	*%*	*Female in group, %*	*Count*	*%*	*Female in group, %*
Upper classes	127	17.1	40.9	53	19.3	30.2	261	28.6	37.1
Clergy	3	0.4	66.7	0	0.0	0.0	0	0.0	0.0
Entrepreneurs	190	25.6	20.9	81	29.5	18.3	360	39.5	16.1
Petty bourgeoisie	127	17.1	40.2	43	15.6	37.2	121	13.3	23.1
Peasants**	82	11.0	21.3	34	12.4	25.9	75	8.2	10.7
Menial workers ***	15	2.0	26.7	8	2.9	12.5	0	0.0	0.0
Professionals	15	2.0	6.7	7	2.5	0.0	23	2.5	26.1
Foreigners	9	1.2	33.3	5	1.8	20.0	19	2.1	26.3
State agencies	10	1.3	0.0	9	3.3	0.0	3	0.3	0.0
Total	578	77.8	30.6	240	87.3	25.5	862	94.5	23.2
Missing (non-identified)	165	22.2	.	35	12.7	.	49	5.4	.
Total (missing data included)	743	100	23.0	275	100	20.4	911	100	21.4

* all cases include lawsuits, inheritance claims, probates and the registration of property rights

** communities included

*** clerks, non-ranked military personnel, soldiers, manual workers

Sources: Alfavit grazhdanskikh del, s uchastiem prisi͡azhnykh poverennykh, 1877; Opis′ arkhivnykh del. 1879–1892, 1879

of civil litigation in the ensuing decades. Given that the initial design of the district courts, with their seats in the largest urban centres and the cut-off value of a case amounting to 500 rubles, structurally disadvantaged the lower classes, it is not surprising that such privileged groups as the landed gentry, military officers, civil servants and entrepreneurs proved to be the most efficient users of these judicial settings. Compared to their numbers in the general population, as recorded by the first Imperial Census of 1897 (see Table 6.4), these groups were largely overrepresented both among the litigants at the Moscow district court and among the clients of sworn attorneys. The peasantry, which constituted 78 per cent of the population in Moscow province and 64 per cent in the city of Moscow in 1897, on the contrary, was the most disadvantaged group in terms of access to legal counselling at this level of the judicial system. Meanwhile, the petty bourgeoisie, the populous lower urban class, seemed to have fairly good opportunities for enlisting the help of professional lawyers as their share in the general population did not differ markedly from their participation rate either in civil litigation or the usage of services provided by sworn attorneys. This points to the fact that close proximity to the seat of a district court might have been enough to offset the negative impact of lower social status.

However, the social profile of those lodging complaints against sworn attorneys makes this picture much more nuanced. According to the council's registers, in the late 1880s, the upper classes comprised almost a third of those bringing their grievances before the Moscow council of sworn attorneys, while entrepreneurs accounted for only 13 per cent (see Table 6.5). Meanwhile, the petty bourgeoisie constituted the second largest group with 16 per cent of complaints, and the peasantry came a close third with 14 per cent. Professionals also appeared much more prominent among the complainants than litigants; however, three-quarters of this group were represented by sworn and private attorneys who enlisted the aid of the council to resolve professional conflicts. Between 1884 and 1903, the social composition of complainants underwent a drastic transformation with the proportion

TABLE 6.4 The social composition of the population of Moscow province and the city of Moscow according to the First Imperial Census, 1897

	Moscow province, 1897		*Moscow, 1897*	
	%	*Female in group, %*	*%*	*Female in group, %*
Upper classes	3.2	53.8	6.6	53.7
Clergy	1.1	54.8	1.1	57.1
Entrepreneurs	2.1	48.9	4.0	48.5
Petty bourgeoisie	13.9	53.0	22.0	52.9
Peasants	77.9	49.0	63.7	37.6
Others	1.3	39.4	1.3	37.9
Foreigners	0.6	52.2	1.3	52.5
Total	100.0	49.8	100.0	43.0

Sources: Troĭnit͡skiĭ, 1905

TABLE 6.5 The social composition of complainants in the Moscow Council of Sworn Attorneys, 1884–1903

	1884–88			*1889–93*			*1894–98*			*1899–03*		
	Count	*%*	*Female, %**	*Count*	*%*	*Female, %**	*Count*	*%*	*Female, %**	*Count*	*%*	*Female, %**
Upper classes	123	32.3	32.5	91	16.7	38.9	77	15.4	36.4	112	11.4	44.6
Clergy	2	0.5	50.0	5	0.9	0.0	6	1.2	0.0	8	0.8	50
Entrepreneurs	49	12.9	27.3	47	8.6	14.6	63	12.6	26.9	116	11.8	20.2
Petty bourgeoisie	62	16.3	29.0	81	14.9	35.0	92	18.4	32.6	174	17.6	26.4
Peasants**	53	13.9	23.1	90	16.5	18.8	114	22.8	26.8	272	27.6	23.6
Menial workers***	14	3.7	7.1	25	4.6	20.0	21	4.2	28.6	30	3.0	13.8
Professionals	41	10.8	4.9	51	9.4	13.7	43	8.6	9.3	77	7.8	7.8
Foreigners	1	0.3	0.0	9	1.7	11.1	6	1.2	33.3	18	1.8	33.3
Non-identified	36	9.4	29.0	145	26.7	32.3	79	15.8	19.2	179	18.2	24.3
Total	381	100	25.7	544	100	27.2	501	100	26.6	986	100	25.2

* Female in group, %
** Communities excluded
*** Clerks, non-ranked military personnel, soldiers, manual workers
Sources: Nastol'nyĭ reestr Soveta, 1883, 1893, 1901

of the upper classes plummeting to 11 per cent and the share of peasants doubling to reach nearly 28 per cent. The role of rural communities as clients, though not prominent in the previous decades, completely vanished at the turn of the century as their share among the peasant complainants dropped from 11 per cent in the early 1890s to a modest 3 per cent ten years later. The share of the petty bourgeoisie and entrepreneurs decreased noticeably in the early 1890s, but then recovered, hovering at about 18 and 12 per cent respectively. The share of professionals fell to 8 per cent by 1903, as did the proportion of lawyers, which declined to 65 per cent of all professionals. Unlike the social composition, the gender distribution of complainants hardly showed any easily discernible pattern. In general, men appeared three times more likely to complain about the professional misconduct of their attorneys than women. However, apart from the upper classes, where a decline in the overall share of the group went hand in hand with the rising rate of female participation, the proportion of women fluctuated wildly in all social groups under consideration.

The dramatic change in the share of the upper-class and peasant complainants between 1884 and 1903 might indicate either a shift in the general social composition of clients and, correspondingly, litigants, or a radical transformation of strategies that people from those social groups adopted while dealing with legal practitioners, although this could signify a combination of both. The relatively stable proportion of entrepreneurs and petty bourgeoisie suggests that sworn attorneys successfully met their demand for legal services very early in the period, and since then neither the demand nor the attitudes of those groups towards legal practitioners changed in any meaningful way. Hence, although entrepreneurs tend to be the most litigious social group, they hardly favoured resolving conflicts with their lawyers through the council. The upper classes, on the contrary, did not shy away from lodging complaints against sworn attorneys, yet they, especially upper-class males, were becoming increasingly reluctant to resort to the procedure over the years. Meanwhile, the petty bourgeoisie was rather consistent, enlisting the help of the council in calling practitioners to account, and the peasantry seemed to be adopting this strategy throughout the last decades of the nineteenth century. However, it is still likely that the growing numbers of peasant complainants reflected an actual rise in the use of legal services among the rural population, and more and more peasants were hiring sworn attorneys. Moreover, they were doing so for the protection of their individual rights and property rather than in defence of communal interests.

Complaints and claims against legal professionals

Before taking a closer look at particular grievances and claims laid before the Moscow council, it is worth sketching out how the relationship between a client and a sworn attorney began and evolved. It usually started with a layperson giving power of attorney and both parties signing an agreement that stipulated mutual obligations and fees. Depending on the situation, sworn attorneys charged a fixed amount of money or a contingency fee, which was to be paid out of the settlement sum or damages awarded, as a percentage of that amount, if the suit in question succeeded. Clients were then expected to provide all documents available to justify and support their legal claims as well as a specific amount of money to cover litigation costs and, partially, fees. Sometimes, however, sworn attorneys took legal action at their own expense, deferring reimbursement until the case was settled. The duties of legal practitioners were rather diverse and included negotiating an amicable settlement, filing proceedings and taking other formal steps in court such as, for example, claiming an inheritance. They supervised police officers sequestrating the property of a defeated party, pawned real estate and settled outstanding debts, handled bills of exchange and withdrew sums recovered from an opponent on their clients' behalf.

Being deeply involved in the financial and litigation matters of their clients, sworn attorneys often found themselves a target of complaints, most of which, however, were supposedly written by a scrivener, a private or even sworn attorney, and this is where caution is in order. At first sight, it is tempting to think of it as if the malicious third party deceived and dragged clients into squabbles with their attorneys. However, although the likely involvement of professional clerks and lawyers definitely sheds some light on striking similarities in the wording of complaints, it does not explain why clients decided to complain in the first place, what prompted them to put forward those particular grievances and claims they strove to articulate in those documents. So, it seems genuinely unwise to deny laypeople an initiative in bringing up the disputes against their actual or former legal representatives since suspicion and feelings of discontent must have appeared before any written words came out.

Accusations against sworn attorneys basically boiled down to the following: (1) a practitioner allegedly did not take any legal action on behalf of his client; (2) he did not respond to the client inquiring about the state of affairs; (3) he wilfully withheld money or/and documents which he was supposed to hand over; (4) he pocketed the money.[6] In fact, these accusations covered a broad range of alleged misconduct and underpinned rather different claims. For example, two peasant communities, which had hired sworn attorneys for the resolution of land disputes with a landlord and another rural community, complained about them not providing obligatory financial support for the court personnel coming and surveying the land in question and, therefore, delaying the end of the lawsuit, which had already caused significant financial losses. However, in the first case, a peasant who represented his community before the council reported that he had given a practitioner all the required documents and money to cover litigation costs and claimed them back as the lawyer failed to fulfil his duties (Vishni͡akov M.S., 1899). In the second case, the community had not provided a sworn attorney with a single penny, so he had been taking legal action at his own expense for almost a decade. Having already spent a sizable amount of money (up to 500 rubles), he was unable to walk away from the suit before receiving reimbursement and had to tolerate recurring attempts by his clients to intervene and force him into action, which apparently became worse as internal conflicts arose inside the community (Dolinskiĭ N.Ė., 1899).

When peasants as private individuals applied for the help of sworn attorneys also as private individuals, they often entrusted practitioners with recovering damages for an unauthorized use of land. In two rather similar cases, involving a peasant and a petty bourgeois, since legal proceedings did not go as smoothly as expected, clients filed complaints asking sworn attorneys to give back the documents and sums each of them had been provided to pay litigation costs. Although both clients blamed the delay on their lawyers, the first case became stuck because the peasant seemed to evade presenting the crucial document justifying his property rights and the second suit was suspended according to the wishes of the petty bourgeois who insisted on filing criminal charges against the adversary – a demand which his lawyer found himself unable to satisfy since there were not sufficient grounds for this kind of action. Nonetheless, both sworn attorneys reluctantly agreed to return the sums which they had not spent taking legal actions, so they neither earned anything nor lost their own money (Vishni͡akov M.S., 1893; Gogolev I.S., 1897).

However, when it came to upper-class clients (the landed gentry, high-ranking military officers and civil servants and members of their families), the same situation played out slightly differently. Although these sorts of complainants also castigated sworn attorneys for procrastination, they did not hesitate to point out that professional misconduct not only harmed their financial interests but concealed deliberate attempts to deceive and pocket their money. High-status complainants also paid far more attention to the way practitioners communicated than ordinary people did. Both males and females saw late and no responses to their letters and the fact that a sworn attorney might be unavailable at convenient hours as an affront to their dignity and this, of course, added insult to injury (Plevako F.N., 1887, 1892). Besides, noblewomen often insisted that a practitioner had sworn the case in question was a success and then reneged on his word, thereby proving the initial criminal intent (Paradizov S.A., 1881, 1892; Plevako F.N., 1892). Clients pertaining to the upper classes never failed to stress how much this disgraceful behaviour diminished the public profile of the legal profession and frequently called for the disbarment of an alleged perpetrator (Paradizov S.A., 1881, 1892; Plevako F.N., 1892). As for sworn attorneys, they tended to act more aggressively in these cases, compared to the disputes where the lower classes were involved. Practitioners argued in response that as soon as they took legal action and provided they committed no errors that could have led to the delays or incorrect court rulings, they felt free to charge their wealthy clients for services rendered and retain sums they had provided. Furthermore, sworn attorneys even occasionally sued (or threatened to sue) high-status clients for either fees or defamation of character (Paradizov S.A., 1892; Plevako F.N., 1887, 1889; SHmakov A.S., 1890).

Sometimes clients strove to obtain a full refund of their eventual financial losses at the expense of sworn attorneys. They clamoured for the reimbursement of the money they might have earned provided disputed or already recovered assets had been in their possession. For example, an illiterate peasant woman complained about the lawyer who had claimed her inheritance amounting to 200 rubles in cash and retained it for several months (Vishni͡akov M.S., 1893). She believed the council should force him not only to hand over that sum of money but also to pay interest on it for the months of delay and, in addition, cover the costs of her 209-mile trip to his office in Moscow and foot the bill for her correspondence with the council. Likewise, a wealthy nobleman claimed some 3,800 rubles along with interest from a sworn attorney who had recovered this money on his behalf as civil damages and failed to deliver it (Paradizov S.A., 1892). With regard to landed estate, the poorer clients, such as a petty bourgeois or a poor middle-ranking military officer, demanded that sworn attorneys should reimburse the revenue or capital gain that had been lost as a result of their procrastination (Plevako F.N., 1887; Protas'ev S.A., 1883). The council, however, consistently dismissed such claims as disputes that were outside its jurisdiction.

Women were more likely to conspire against their lawyers, allying themselves with former adversaries and members of 'the street Bar'. Low-class females seemed very susceptible to the lure of scriveners who apparently volunteered to write repetitive complaints to the council and, occasionally, did not even try to conceal their vested interest, as in the case of a peasant woman whose passionate claim to obtain a refund of the money she had spent on correspondence came with a bill issued by a scrivener (Vishni͡akov M.S., 1895; Dolinskiĭ N.Ė., 1895, 1898). Females with considerable personal wealth were more prone to the influence of relatives and business partners. For example, after inheriting a fortune from her husband, a peasant woman hired a sworn attorney to manage legal and financial matters related to the inheritance and guardianship of her children. Although she seemed generally satisfied with the practitioner who did a decent job putting her rather complicated affairs in order, she filed a complaint requiring him to provide an additional report for one of the state agencies following the advice of her new (petty bourgeois) co-guardian and, therefore, stretching the terms of the initial agreement (Vishni͡akov M.S., 1899). Another striking example was the complaint by a noblewoman involved in a decade-long family fight over inheritance. First, she sought legal protection against her malicious brother-in-law who attempted to obtain a share of the inheritance through sham purchases. However, as soon as her lawyer failed to secure the victory at a district court, she secretly negotiated an amicable settlement with her adversary, denying the sworn attorney his well-earned fees. When the practitioner sued her on account of this, she falsely accused him of seeking the fees for the second time. Although the court ruled in favour of the lawyer, the quarrel continued in the council where a number of sworn attorneys who were also familiar with the initial dispute over the inheritance testified that the client's brother-in-law was the actual mastermind, who took revenge on the practitioner for threatening him with criminal charges (SHmakov A.S., 1890).

Conclusions

As all the cases discussed above show, the great cultural divide that many contemporaries eagerly proclaim does not seem so wide when it comes to the use of legal services. Laypeople from various social backgrounds commonly aspired to share the financial burden of civil litigation with their attorneys. While acknowledging the right of a lawyer to charge a contingency fee if the case succeeded, they felt entitled to the reimbursement of legal costs and, occasionally, total financial losses if a practitioner failed to ensure a desirable outcome. Those who tried to recover damages from sworn attorneys apparently saw disciplinary proceedings as a free alternative to a lawsuit, though the council efficiently blocked such attempts. Conversely, the way sworn attorneys responded to the complainants was deeply affected by their social status. They tended to be more amenable to the claims of low-class complainants and, in fact, offered some financial support to destitute clients on a charitable basis. Meanwhile, lawyers tenaciously opposed the upper-class complainants whose demands they found unjustifiable, right up to the point when a lawyer and his former client had to meet in court. Unlike social class, gender seemed to have a significant effect on the way laypeople complained about legal practitioners since women appeared much more malleable to the influence of a third party who was at times unwilling to put the case to rest if there was the slightest chance of gaining additional profit or benefit.

Although much remains to be learned about court usage and the utilization of legal services in nineteenth-century Russia, these findings, however preliminary, reveal a picture that seems to be rather consistent with an understanding of a layperson as an efficient and reasonably knowledgeable litigant that has recently emerged from the studies of popular litigiousness in modern Europe. Despite the fact that the rule of law never came into existence in the Russian Empire, this did not impede the broad application of the law to resolving day-to-day disputes among various groups of the imperial population. Although social status affected the choice of courts, the disparity in access to the different levels of the judicial system did not inevitably mirror delineated estates. Every social group included individuals who efficiently attended to their legal affairs, while some of them casually enlisted the help of professional lawyers. Routine communication with legal practitioners constituted the shared experience that united people of various social backgrounds, from a wealthy nobleman to a poor peasant woman. The cultural differences between the upper and lower classes that were a perennial concern for the educated Russian elites were not very pronounced as various social groups showed surprisingly similar attitudes when it came to their dealings with legal practitioners. From this perspective, the great cultural divide appeared predominantly conditional upon the circumstances of day-to-day communication, rather than an essential and inescapable inevitability.

Notes

1 Support from the Basic Research Programme of the National Research University Higher School of Economics is gratefully acknowledged.
2 For an in-depth discussion of the relationship between the Russian autocratic government and the rule of law, please see an illuminating article by Laura Engelstein (Engelstein, 1993).
3 Griet Vermeesch provides a comprehensive overview of the recent developments in this area of historical research in her work 'Reflections on the relative accessibility of law courts in early modern Europe' (Vermeesch, 2015).

4 According to the estimates obtained by the research project 'Historical monetary and financial statistics for Sweden', 500 Russian rubles was the equivalent of 49.5 British pounds in 1884 and of 52.3 pounds in 1903 (Edvinsson, 2016).
5 Missing data accounts for 2 per cent of the cases between 1884 and 1888.
6 Out of twenty disciplinary proceedings, the content of which were explored in their entirety, fourteen contained complaints about sworn attorneys taking no action, seven included the accusation of pocketing sums of money and four the allegation of withholding money, while another four specifically mentioned the refusal of sworn attorneys to communicate with their clients.

References

Archive materials

Alfavit grazhdanskikh del, s uchastiem prisi͡azhnykh poverennykh. (1877). [Docket] T͡SGA g. Moskvy, Fond 142 Moskovskiĭ Okruzhnoĭ Sud. Opis' 16: Kant͡seli͡arii͡a Predsedateli͡a. Delo 24. Moscow.

Dolinskiĭ N.Ė. (1895). [Disciplinary Proceedings] T͡SGA g. Moskvy, Fond 1697 Sovet prisi͡azhnykh poverennykh okruga Moskovskoĭ sudebnoĭ palaty. Opis' 1. Delo 322. Moscow.

Dolinskiĭ N.Ė. (1898). [Disciplinary Proceedings] T͡SGA g. Moskvy, Fond 1697 Sovet prisi͡azhnykh poverennykh okruga Moskovskoĭ sudebnoĭ palaty. Opis' 1. Delo 323. Moscow.

Dolinskiĭ N.Ė. (1899). [Disciplinary Proceedings] T͡SGA g. Moskvy, Fond 1697 Sovet prisi͡azhnykh poverennykh okruga Moskovskoĭ sudebnoĭ palaty. Opis' 1. Delo 325. Moscow.

Gogolev I.S. (1897). [Disciplinary Proceedings] T͡SGA g. Moskvy, Fond 1697 Sovet prisi͡azhnykh poverennykh okruga Moskovskoĭ sudebnoĭ palaty. Opis' 1. Delo 228. Moscow.

Nastol'nyĭ reestr Soveta. (1883). [Docket] T͡SGA g. Moskvy, Fond 1697 Sovet prisi͡azhnykh poverennykh okruga Moskovskoĭ sudebnoĭ palaty. Opis' 1. Delo 9. Moscow.

Nastol'nyĭ reestr Soveta. (1893). [Docket] T͡SGA g. Moskvy, Fond 1697 Sovet prisi͡azhnykh poverennykh okruga Moskovskoĭ sudebnoĭ palaty. Opis' 1. Delo 14. Moscow.

Nastol'nyĭ reestr Soveta. (1901). [Docket] T͡SGA g. Moskvy, Fond 1697 Sovet prisi͡azhnykh poverennykh okruga Moskovskoĭ sudebnoĭ palaty. Opis' 1. Delo 985. Moscow.

Opis' arkhivnykh del. 1879–1892 (1879). [Docket] T͡SGA g. Moskvy, Fond 142 Moskovskiĭ Okruzhnoĭ Sud. Opis' 4: Chetvertoe Otdelenie (grazhdanskoe). Delo 102. Moscow.

Paradizov S.A. (1881). [Disciplinary Proceedings] T͡SGA g. Moskvy, Fond 1697 Sovet prisi͡azhnykh poverennykh okruga Moskovskoĭ sudebnoĭ palaty. Opis' 1. Delo 595. Moscow.

Paradizov S.A. (1892). [Disciplinary Proceedings] T͡SGA g. Moskvy, Fond 1697 Sovet prisi͡azhnykh poverennykh okruga Moskovskoĭ sudebnoĭ palaty. Opis' 1. Delo 603. Moscow.

Plevako F.N. (1887). [Disciplinary Proceedings] T͡SGA g. Moskvy, Fond 1697 Sovet prisi͡azhnykh poverennykh okruga Moskovskoĭ sudebnoĭ palaty. Opis' 1. Delo 623. Moscow.

Plevako F.N. (1887). [Disciplinary Proceedings] T͡SGA g. Moskvy, Fond 1697 Sovet prisi͡azhnykh poverennykh okruga Moskovskoĭ sudebnoĭ palaty. Opis' 1. Delo 624. Moscow.

Plevako F.N. (1889). [Disciplinary Proceedings] T͡SGA g. Moskvy, Fond 1697 Sovet prisi͡azhnykh poverennykh okruga Moskovskoĭ sudebnoĭ palaty. Opis' 1. Delo 629. Moscow.
Plevako F.N. (1892). [Disciplinary Proceedings] T͡SGA g. Moskvy, Fond 1697 Sovet prisi͡azhnykh poverennykh okruga Moskovskoĭ sudebnoĭ palaty. Opis' 1. Delo 633. Moscow.
Protas′ev S.A. (1883). [Disciplinary Proceedings] T͡SGA g. Moskvy, Fond 1697 Sovet prisi͡azhnykh poverennykh okruga Moskovskoĭ sudebnoĭ palaty. Opis' 1. Delo 656. Moscow.
SHmakov A.S. (1890). [Disciplinary Proceedings] T͡SGA g. Moskvy, Fond 1697 Sovet prisi͡azhnykh poverennykh okruga Moskovskoĭ sudebnoĭ palaty. Opis' 1. Delo 973. Moscow.
Vishni͡akov M.S. (1893). [Disciplinary Proceedings] T͡SGA g. Moskvy, Fond 1697 Sovet prisi͡azhnykh poverennykh okruga Moskovskoĭ sudebnoĭ palaty. Opis' 1. Delo 173. Moscow.
Vishni͡akov M.S. (1895). [Disciplinary Proceedings] T͡SGA g. Moskvy, Fond 1697 Sovet prisi͡azhnykh poverennykh okruga Moskovskoĭ sudebnoĭ palaty. Opis' 1. Delo 175. Moscow.
Vishni͡akov M.S. (1899). [Disciplinary Proceedings] T͡SGA g. Moskvy, Fond 1697 Sovet prisi͡azhnykh poverennykh okruga Moskovskoĭ sudebnoĭ palaty. Opis' 1. Delo 180. Moscow.

Secondary literature

Brooks, C. (1986). *Pettyfoggers and Vipers of the Commonwealth*. Cambridge: Cambridge University Press.
Brooks, C. (1998). *Lawyers, litigation and English society since 1450*. London: Hambledon.
Burbank, J. (1995). Discipline and Punish in the Moscow Bar Association. *Russian Review*, 54(1), pp. 44–64.
Burbank, J. (2004). *Russian peasants go to court*. Bloomington, IN: Indiana University Press.
Burbank, J. (2006). Mercy, punishment, and law: the qualities of justice at township courts. *Kritika: Explorations in Russian and Eurasian History*, 7(1), pp. 23–60.
Burrage, M. (2006). *Revolution and the Making of the Contemporary Legal Profession*. Oxford: Oxford University Press.
Edvinsson, R. (2016). *Historical Currency Converter*. Stockholm: Stockholm University. Available at: www.historicalstatistics.org/Currencyconverter.html [Accessed 23 September 2017].
Engelstein, L. (1993). Combined underdevelopment: discipline and the law in Imperial and Soviet Russia. *The American Historical Review*, 98(2), pp. 338–353.
Farnsworth, B. (1986). The litigious daughter-in-law: family relations in rural Russia in the second half of the nineteenth century. *Slavic Review*, 45(01), pp. 49–64.
Gessen, I. (1914). Istorii͡a russkoĭ advokatury. Tom 1: Advokatura, obshchesto, gosudarstvo (1864–1914). Moscow: Izdanie Sovetov prisi͡azhnykh poverennykh.
Gosudarstvennai͡a Kant͡seli͡arii͡a (1867). Sudebnye ustavy 20 noi͡abri͡a 1864 goda, s izlozheniem razsuzhdeniĭ, na koikh oni osnovany: izdannye Gosudarstvennoi͡u Kant͡seli͡ariei͡u. Vtoroe izdanie.. St. Petersburg: Tipografii͡a Vtorogo Otdelenii͡a Sobstvennoĭ E.I.V. Kant͡seli͡arii.
Kagan, R. (1981). *Lawsuits and litigants in Castile, 1500–1700*. Chapel Hill: The University of North Carolina Press.
Karpik, L. and Scott, N. (1999). *French lawyers: a study in collective action, 1274 to 1994*. Oxford: Clarendon.

Ledford, K. (2006). *From General Estate to Special Interest: German Lawyers 1878–1933*. Cambridge: Cambridge University Press.

Levin-Stankevich, B. (1996). The transfer of legal technology and culture: law professionals in Tsarist Russia. In: H. Balzer, ed., *Russia's Missing Middle Class: the Professions in Russian History*. Armonk, NY: M.E. Sharpe, pp. 223–250.

Ministerstvo I͡Ustit͡sii (1871). *Otchet Ministerstva I͡Ustit͡sii za 1869 god*. St. Petersburg: Tipografii͡a Pravitel'stvui͡ushchego Senata, pp.66–67.

Ministerstvo I͡Ustit͡sii (1887). *Sbornik statisticheskikh Svedeniĭ Ministerstva I͡Ustit͡sii za 1884 i 1885 god*. St. Petersburg: Tipografii͡a Pravitel'stvui͡ushchego Senata, pp.3, 8–12, 62–63.

Ministerstvo I͡Ustit͡sii (1894). *Sbornik statisticheskikh Svedeniĭ Ministerstva I͡Ustit͡sii za 1893 god*. St. Petersburg: Tipografii͡a Pravitel'stvui͡ushchego Senata, pp.2–3, 16, 18, 22, 64–65.

Ministerstvo I͡Ustit͡sii (1899). *Sbornik statisticheskikh Svedeniĭ Ministerstva I͡Ustit͡sii za 1897 god*. St. Petersburg: Tipografii͡a Pravitel'stvui͡ushchego Senata, pp.2–3, 16, 18, 23, 80–83.

Ministerstvo I͡Ustit͡sii (1904). *Sbornik statisticheskikh Svedeniĭ Ministerstva I͡Ustit͡sii za 1903 god*. St. Petersburg: Tipografii͡a Pravitel'stvui͡ushchego Senata, pp.2–3, 16, 18, 23, 80–83.

Neuberger, J. (1994). Popular legal cultures: the St. Petersburg Mirovoi Sud. In: B. Eklof, J. Bushnell and L.G. Zakharova, eds., *Russia's Great Reforms, 1855–1881*. Bloomington and Indianapolis: Indiana University Press, 1994, pp. 231–246.

Nos, N. ed., (1891). Dvadt͡satipi͡atiletie Moskovskikh Prisi͡azhnykh Poverennykh: Sbornik mater'i͡alov, otnosi͡ashchikhsi͡a do sosloviia prisi͡azhnykh poverennykh okruga Moskovskoĭ sudebnoĭ palaty s 23 apreli͡a 1866 goda po 23 apreli͡a 1891 goda. Moscow: Tipografii͡a I.A. Mamontova i Ko.

Polnoe sobranie zakonov Rossiĭskoĭ imperii. 1825–1881. 2nd edn., no 53573.

Polnoe sobranie zakonov Rossiĭskoĭ imperii. 1881–1913. 3rd edn., no 6196.

Pomeranz, W. (1999). 'Profession or estate'? The case of the Russian pre-revolutionary 'advokatura'. *The Slavonic and East European Review*, 77(2), pp. 240–268.

Popkins, G. (1999). Popular development of procedure in a dual legal system. *The Journal of Legal Pluralism and Unofficial Law*, 31(43), pp. 57–87.

Popkins, G. (2000). Code versus custom? Norms and tactics in peasant volost court appeals, 1889–1917. *Russian Review*, 59(3), pp. 408–424.

Pue, W. and Sugarman, D. eds., (2003). *Lawyers and Vampires: Cultural Histories of Legal Professions*. Portland, OR: Hart.

Troĭnit͡skiĭ, N. ed., (1905). Pervai͡a Vseobshchai͡a perepis' naselenii͡a Rossiĭskoĭ imperii 1897 g. T. 1. Obshchiĭ svod po Imperii rezul'tatov razrabotki dannykh Pervoĭ Vseobshcheĭ perepisi naselenii͡a, proizvedennoĭ 28 i͡anvari͡a 1897 goda. St. Petersburg: izdanie T͡Sentral'nogo statisticheskogo komiteta Ministerstva vnutrennikh del.

Troit͡skiĭ, N. (2000). Advokatura v Rossii i politicheskie prot͡sessy, 1866–1904. Tula: Avtograf.

Vermeesch, G. (2015). Reflections on the relative accessibility of law courts in early modern Europe. *Crime, Histoire & Sociétés*, 19(2), pp. 53–76.

7

SKIPPING COURT

Civil disputes in sixteenth-century Rouen

Katherine Godwin

Introduction

> As the legal proceeding was left stalled before the *vicomté* of Rouen or his lieutenant in the court session at the *sergent*'s hall of Pavilly, between Pierre Delamare residing in the parish of Sainte Austreberte near the said Pavilly on the one side and Jean Delamare his brother residing in the parish of Saint Nigaise of Rouen on the other—wherein Pierre Delamare wanted to prevent Jean Delamare his brother from taking possession and enjoying the benefits of a piece of land gifted to Jean by their mother Marion, widow of Romain Delamare their father, by formal letters of title drawn up on the fourth of July 1497 before Charles Monfault, commissioned lieutenant of the Bailli of Rouen, which the said Pierre Delamare contested that his mother had no right to leave to Jean—after several days of proceedings before the court and seeing that the proceeding was shaping up to be a long one, and to be avoided etc.; in order to preserve peace and brotherly love between them, their friends brought them together to come to an agreement. . . in order to avoid continuation of the legal proceeding. . . [they come to an agreement in which Pierre pays 50 sous per year to Jean for use and hereditary possession of the land on the condition that Pierre can let the land to one or two parties agreeable to both of them]. . . and in leaving the meeting, the parties agree to go without further session in court by which they agree to vacate the court and to do what pertains to them and to hold to their agreement. . . Robert Langloys and Jaques Alain bearing witness.[1]

The account of family strife and legal dispute narrated above is hardly exceptional and in that regard it will serve as a useful center-point for this study. The dispute between brothers Pierre and Jean Delamare represents common discontent and disagreement over inheritance and transfer of property, especially when a woman was involved, in the early sixteenth century in Rouen (and elsewhere). That the dispute moved in and out of a court and ended in a settlement formalized before a notary is also not extraordinary and yet is of great interest. This case represents the agency of people in resolving civil disputes as well as the importance of notaries over the courts in this process. The notaries bore witness to a resolution that the courts only played a tangential role in influencing. Although going to court and appealing to its legal authorities may have been an option, it was not necessarily the most common or definitive option for resolving a dispute.

This chapter will show that the courts' role in resolving civil disputes stands disproportionate to its representation in scholarship on the legal system. Overemphasis of the importance of the courts and their legal authorities and over-analysis of court records risk distorting practice, misunderstanding the processes of resolving disputes, and misunderstanding the role of the courts in the legal system and society on a larger scale. Much has been made of the relationship of civil disputes and the courts to state formation in scholarship on the legal system,[2] but this study, although not openly challenging this work, does seek to add nuance to it and to advocate for broadening the standard set of sources utilized when studying the legal system.

Drawing on Julie Hardwick's work on litigation and daily life for the seventeenth century, this paper is, additionally, part of a larger discussion about the new insights that civil litigation can provide on crucial questions about legal culture, daily life, and family in France before the Wars of Religion (Hardwick 2009). Focusing on civil cases serves to balance a distortion in current scholarship in the early sixteenth century which has privileged criminal records. This chapter will explore the insights provided by civil litigation into the daily life and dispute resolution practices of greater Rouen in the early sixteenth century. In so doing, it will suggest ways in which the history of daily life and the legal system in the sixteenth century in France might be understood differently if we shift our attention from criminal punishment to civil disputes.

Civil law in France, especially in the sixteenth century, remains an understudied area of society because many of the sources are voluminous, largely unindexed, and deal with seemingly mundane issues of life, but it is important to understand how this aspect of the legal system functioned in order to understand the system as a whole. People were much more likely to be drawn into civil cases than criminal ones. If we privilege the criminal system, we arrive at a skewed understanding of daily life and of the courts—an institution that has been attributed such importance.

That being said, scholarship on the subject is increasing, and each study offers a new and important way of understanding the behaviors observed on the civil side of the legal system. Daniel Smail provides an intellectual history of civil law procedure in late medieval Marseille framed by the issues of consumption and emotion. The ideas of consumption and emotion help illuminate the motives and value of litigating and the legal system more generally. Drawing on this approach, Julie Hardwick uses civil litigation cases to reconstruct economies of daily life in seventeenth-century French families and communities. The framework of economy and community underscores the relationships that influenced the behavior of the subjects and anchors the observed behaviors within a larger set of dynamics. Zoe Schneider frames her study on lower courts, including the civil ones, in late seventeenth- and early eighteenth-century Normandy using local governance and focusing on officials and their relationships both within their communities and with the monarchy. Shifting the angle of analysis to focus on the officials and the idea of governance helps to challenge the divide between civil and criminal law and the disruptive potential of both proceedings. Finally, for my purpose here—and I do not claim that this is a definitive list—Hervé Piant offers a social history of justice and infrajustice from the perspective of the lower courts and presents justice as a social activity. In so doing, he uses the framework of sociability. Sociability and infrajustice add to the discussion of motives and community and of social networks and legal culture that we find in Smail and Hardwick's studies and further shifts the focus away from the courts (Smail 2003; Hardwick 2009; Schneider 2008; Piant 2006).[3]

Drawing on my research in civil archives for this period, court and notarial records suggest that the courts' role in resolving civil disputes was small. I will show alternative routes to resolving civil disputes, enabled by the complex legal pluralism of sixteenth-century Rouen, by combining a quantitative analysis of settlements out of court and defaults with a close reading of several important case studies. My quantitative inquiry will analyze the characteristics of plaintiffs and defendants in civil litigation (including their occupation, gender, position within the family, relationship to other parties to the law suit) as well as the object of the litigation, the monetary value at stake and the outcome. This data, read alongside particularly representative and interesting case studies, will enable reconstruction of some of the social fabric of daily life and the processes of conflict, negotiation, and arbitration at its heart. Analysis of legal activity outside of court enriches our understanding of the role of the courts in society and the decisions that brought people into which court, if any.

My analysis thus relies on an accumulation of data drawn from mundane civil cases. The challenge of relying on quantitative methods lies in defining the data set and finding a representative sampling. For very practical reasons—the volume of available sources and the limited space in which to discuss them—I will focus my analysis here in time and space and will limit consideration of legal activity to the court of Elbeuf in the year 1510 read alongside notarial records from Rouen from the year 1500. I chose these years specifically because they offer a manageable set of records and allow me to pinpoint my analysis. More importantly, 1510 is one of several years for which records survive in meaningful quantities for multiple jurisdictions.

Sixteenth-century Rouen is particularly interesting for a study of legal pluralism because it was a port city and a center of commerce, administration, religious activity, and law (Benedict 1981; Brunelle 1991). It was also surrounded by centers of agriculture and the cloth industry. Because of its different administrative and commercial capacities, it drew in people from the surrounding areas and had multiple jurisdictions to meet the needs of these people. And because so much of the business conducted in the city involved people and property residing outside of the city, it makes more sense to consider the influences of the surrounding area on the city and vice versa and to discuss the legal pluralism and legal culture of greater Rouen rather than trying to limit discussion to the city itself, which would be very difficult and misleading.

In terms of the surrounding area, Elbeuf is of particular interest and relevance to a study on Rouen because it was in close geographical proximity to the city of Rouen but was a center of cloth production in its own right. Elbeuf had a set of seigneurial courts that had the capacity to exercise haute justice including a *bailliage* and a *vicomté* (lowest court in the legal system of the region), which, after the sixteenth century, were referred to interchangeably and were imperfectly consolidated in stages through the Old Regime. This *bailliage* had the privilege of appealing directly to the Parlement of Rouen. This study will focus on the records from the *vicomté* which has an extensive surviving record set, better than Rouen's *vicomté*. And in terms of the bigger picture of legal pluralism and legal culture, the people of Elbeuf contributed to the overall legal culture of Rouen, which, as a major administrative and legal center, drew people in from outside its walls to conduct legal business, and their legal activities linked into the legal system and legal pluralism of greater Rouen. Analyzing cases from Elbeuf provides insight not only into the process of civil litigation as people moved through the courts but also various influences on the legal culture of Rouen.

The challenge of using the law, broadly conceived, as a category of analysis, discrete concept, and subject of study is that the law, with its institutions, officials, and records, intersects with and is interwoven into many other categories and subjects like business and family affairs. The law is a useful lens of comparison, but it is not so useful to try to examine it detached from these categories because they offer meaning to its creation, practice, and impact.[4] The social practices and implications and impact of the law on the community more broadly must always be understood as context to the conversation on the law in this chapter. If I use the law as shorthand, it is not meant to be the end but rather the beginning, conceptually. The law is a comparative concept even within fairly narrowly defined geographical and temporal parameters because it intersects with so many other strata and conceptual categories. Even if one legal system is under discussion, the inherent pluralism within that system, especially in sixteenth-century France, wears away at its coherency. Legal pluralism is inherent to the legal system not only of France more broadly but of Normandy, even Rouen, more specifically.[5] Speaking of the law as the law or the legal system as the legal system will always be fraught with the risk of oversimplifying the narrative; however, it would be a mistake not to meet this risk head on to further our understanding of life in this time and place.

Overview of the legal system

A preliminary sketch of the structures—the law codes and institutions—of the legal system will reveal how the system worked on paper—that is, in theory and in writing. Although not exhaustive or comprehensive, this overview illustrates the most obvious options with which people had to work and guiding principles behind the legal system. Before beginning, it is important to acknowledge a significant problem with reconstructing the legal system more broadly and with studying legal pluralism more specifically—namely, how one studies legal pluralism when surviving records do not represent all institutions or options for legal action by people and when we may not even know of all options. It is an attempt at reconstruction without all of the pieces or knowing how many pieces there are. Furthermore, significant discrepancies existed between theory and practice; nevertheless, mapping the idealized structures of the legal system to the best of our ability helps anchor our understanding of what was theoretically possible as well as underscoring the significance of the divergent practices uncovered by the sources. The overview that follows will cover different sources of the law in sixteenth-century Rouen before moving to a discussion of the most commonly used institutions and jurisdictions and ending with a brief discussion of privileges and the role of notaries in the legal system. Given the chapter's focus on civil law, this overview focuses more on the courts charged with enforcing civil law rather than criminal (with the acknowledgement that civil and criminal could overlap in jurisdictions and the unfolding of cases).[6]

There were many complementary and competing sources of the law in sixteenth-century Rouen. The most well-known, and arguably the most influential, source of law in Rouen, as in much of northern France, was customary law, which was rooted in a much older oral tradition. The customary law tradition prevalent in the North of France set it apart from the South, where Roman law was the primary structuring source well before and well beyond the sixteenth century. The South of France, as a *pays de droit écrit*, had a legal system and legal culture distinctive from that of the North, a *pays de coutume*. While the Corpus Juris Civilis shaped legal activity in the South, the Ancienne Coutume de Normandie shaped legal activity in Rouen (De Gruchy 1881).

It should be noted that Norman law, like much of French law, did not organize itself neatly into categories like criminal and civil law—or even public versus private law according to the modern French legal code—in the sense that the laws were codified into these categories. However, in terms of procedure, especially in the highest courts, a division was made between criminal procedure and civil procedure so that different chambers of the Parlement heard one type of case or another. It is therefore following the procedural distinction, largely for ease of discussion, that I use the terms criminal and civil in talking about the law. Although capacious as a category, for the purposes of this study, I would break down civil law, roughly, into family law, property law, and business law. Of these subcategories, property law, including personal and lineage property, intersects with the other two (Diefendorf 1995).

Although I will not go into too much detail about specific laws, it is important to delve into property law a bit since it was so important in civil law and so central to many disputes. Property—acquiring it, exploiting it, selling it, and transferring it—was at the center of livelihood, family relations, social mobility, and personal honor, as Julie Hardwick, Barbara Diefendorf, Robert Harding, Jonathan Dewald and many others have shown (Hardwick 2009; Diefendorf 1983; Harding 1978; Dewald 1980). It was at the center of major life cycle moments—marriage and death. It was carefully guarded and hotly contested. Moreover, Norman law was (in)famously strict in governing inheritance and the transfer of property. The restrictions placed on women in the inheritance, management, and alienation of property were especially rigid among its neighbors in other regions of France and Europe more broadly (Schneider 2000; Lemonnier-Lesage 2005; Hardwick 1997). The stakes for those involved in civil disputes were thus high, and one could argue that these cases could be just as much a matter of life and death as criminal cases. This is especially so if we consider that it was not unusual for murderers to receive a civic death—to have their goods seized and to be exiled. The importance of a civic death underscores the significance of civil disputes and the stakes involved.

Adding great complexity to customary law was the more localized seigneurial (customary) law with the institutions and jurisdictions to match. Lords of higher rank had the privilege of governing—making laws and rendering judgments—within their territory, and the lord's rank and status determined the weight of the laws and authority of the jurisdictions therein. These laws were often based on customs, practices, and interpretations of the more overarching Norman custom within that territory. The lord could hold fixed or itinerant court (the latter being more common) and could claim jurisdiction over cases alongside other jurisdictions in the area. Appeals from seigneurial courts and where in the system of royal courts the case would enter was determined by the status and privilege of the seigneurial court and of the litigants. Thus, where someone lived could determine which regulations they were subject to and which jurisdictions they had a right to turn to. The same applied to the location of fixed property. The seigneurial laws made less difference to those residing within the city of Rouen itself, though in its own right within the Duchy of Normandy (Ancienne Coutume), because of municipal privileges granted by the monarchy, but people residing in the city owned property outside of the walls, and the city drew in a lot of people from the surrounding area to enter into legal agreements or disagreements, and the seigneurial laws could make a difference there.

At the top of the hierarchy, though not necessarily the most immediately influential within the geographical or social community, in the legal system more globally was the monarchy which issued royal ordinances and statutes. The monarchy issued laws that ruled and affected the entire kingdom, but it could also pass laws with a more specific target. Although the monarchy did not seem to issue laws systematically—repeatedly, yes, but not systematically in the sense of putting together an overarching code—it did issue a lot of them. Even though the laws could apply to the entire kingdom, the biggest impact could be more localized, depending on the existing customary law in place.

One of the most important ways the monarchy shaped the legal system was through the judicial system, through the rendering of decisions in disputes and interpreting laws or even favoring competing laws or jurisdictions. It also in theory enforced these decisions, though there are a lot of questions about how effectively it did so and how to measure this. Although the monarchy reserved the right to grant pardons at the top of the system and to pass additional laws to clarify interpretations of laws, it generally delegated adjudication to a hierarchy of courts and officials (Zemon Davis 1987). The lowest level of courts was the *vicomté*—which held sessions (itinerant or fixed, though fixed became more common especially within the city) at which people could present themselves and their cases. Acting as an appellate court for the *vicomté* of Rouen and other *vicomtés* of the surrounding area was the *bailliage*—known as the *sénéchaussée* in other parts of France. The highest court of appeals, which heard cases from the *bailliages* of the region—the most predominant royal *bailliages* in Normandy were Alençon, Caen, Caux, Cotentin, Evreux, and Rouen but which in closer proximity to Rouen also included Aumale (with a seigneurial *bailliage* too), Cany, Caudebec, Dieppe, Longueville, Montivilliers, Neufchatel, and Le Havre among others—was the Parlement, which became a permanent institution in 1499 and was known as the Exchequer until 1515. Parallel to the Parlement was the Cour des Aides which rendered final judgments concerning taxes. These courts all had their sets of officials—judges, lawyers, and sergents (agents who did most of the out-of-court business)—and interpreted and enforced relevant laws—not only royal statutes, but customary law and corporate statutes too. These courts, especially at the lower levels, also competed in jurisdiction and authority with other *vicomtés* and specialized courts within the breakdown of royal courts and with courts external to it, such as seigneurial or ecclesiastical courts. To the extent that laws and institutions could be controversial, the controversy (in the sense of conflict or open disagreement), or even the unpopularity, could inform decisions with regards to taking legal action. Overlapping jurisdictions enabled these decisions. Which court had the right to hear which cases or overrule other jurisdictions was a matter of great contention among legal authorities not only out of concerns for authority but due to competition over revenue. It is indeed difficult to clearly explain a system that was so lacking in clarity.

On a smaller scale, but no less important for the local legal system, municipal rules and regulations also played an important role. Local officials were tasked with keeping public order in their municipalities, and if they failed to do so, they were held accountable to the monarchy (Benedict 1981; Schneider 2008). These local laws attended to the specific needs of the city. Being a resident of the city brought with it special status and privilege, and being of a certain social status (bourgeois) even more so, including the ability to participate in city governance. Therefore, municipal rules and privileges could shape existing options and offer new ones.

In direct competition with secular law—customary or Roman, civil or criminal—was ecclesiastical law deriving from the Christian tradition. Rouen was no exception. Although predominantly rooted in canon law and the Catholic Church's tradition, bureaucracy, and institutions, the reform movements of the fifteenth and sixteenth centuries and the particularities of the Gallican Church undermined whatever coherence there may have been of ecclesiastical law in France (Baumgartner 1994;

Tallon 1997; Wanegffelen 1997, 1999, Parsons 2004). Even though the period under consideration predates the large-scale reform movements of the sixteenth century, it is nevertheless worth pointing out that Rouen, at different periods of the sixteenth century, alternated between being a Catholic and Protestant stronghold (Benedict 1981). The seeds of these diverse viewpoints among the population existed in the period under consideration and earlier (as there were many reform movements prior to the sixteenth century) and may have stemmed from the different draws of the city as a major port, center of legal activity, and the rest. This may have weakened ecclesiastical law and jurisdictions in the face of secular institutions once the instability of the Wars of Religion faded and the monarchy made strides toward consolidating its power and authority, but early in the sixteenth century incoherence and competing and overlapping jurisdictions created opportunity for those seeking to resolve disputes.

Rouen, partly due to and partly resulting from its status as an administrative, legal, and religious center, had a strong ecclesiastical presence in the sixteenth century. Regarding the Catholic Church, it was the home of an archdiocese and several large monasteries and convents, residing within or just outside of the city itself. Members of the clergy, both secular and regular, played different roles in the larger legal system in Rouen as elsewhere, depending on the circumstances. They could act as judges hearing cases and rendering judgment; as legal counsel advising different parties of their options or drawing up legal documents that may or may not have had to withstand challenges in the courts; as plaintiffs bringing suit (or criminal charges) against other clerics or non-clerics for thefts, embezzlement, trespassing, damage to property, or dispute over ownership of property; and of course, as defendants in the same sorts of cases.

The size and compartmentalization of the (Catholic) Church allowed for internal rivalries and disputes that fed into its courts but also shaped the opportunities for lay people both in resolving disputes with members of the clergy and with other lay people. The most notable of such divisions (and rivalries) for the purposes of this study was the separation of the clergy into secular and regular clerics, which was further divided into cloistered (monks) and mendicant (friars) categories. The archdiocese represented the highest authority for the secular clergy in the city and surrounding area. For the regular clergy, there were numerous groups, but the monastery of St. Ouen and the convent of Dominicaines have the richest sets of surviving records for the period under consideration. St. Ouen was large, old, and wealthy (it owned extensive property in the area) and had the privilege—the option—of bypassing lower jurisdictions to appeal directly to the Parlement to resolve disputes that fell outside of ecclesiastical purview.[7]

Increasing institutional complexity—in size, number, and competition—was not limited to religious institutions in the sixteenth century. There existed an uneasy relationship between canon law and secular law in the larger legal system. Although secular law in this period coexisted and supported ecclesiastical law for the most part, there were important points of contention, which flared up during disputes and which could influence certain decisions in the ensuing efforts to resolve them, such as who to turn to in order to have a judgment rendered, to solve or to stall, or even to advise. One such contested area was marriage. Canon law and secular law defined the age of majority at vastly different ages, which could make a difference controlling the entire process of marriage. On the one hand, marriage was a sacrament, but on the other hand, it was an important node of social alliance and networking and of property transmission and inheritance. It was as much a legal and social act as a religious one. The increasing prominence of the bureaucratic class, the *robins* (*noblesse de robe*), exacerbated these tensions as parental control and prerogative became much more important, expanding in power and authority, especially as the sixteenth century passed (Diefendorf 1996, 1983; Descimon 1996; Hanley 1989).

Adding nuance to these laws and jurisdictions were privileges, which acted as exceptions and made the system much more complicated and full of contradictions and overlapping jurisdictions. Privileges could be large or small, could grant immunity from certain regulations or jurisdictions, and could grant expedited access. They could redefine the boundaries of jurisdictions. They could apply to individuals, groups, offices, and institutions. We have already seen that the monastery of St. Ouen had the privilege of having its cases heard directly before the sovereign court of Parlement. The monarchy was the most important source of privilege, but it is unclear whether granting privileges enhanced or undermined the authority of those granting, receiving, mediating, or executing such privileges. If we take the privilege of St. Ouen before the Parlement as an example, does this privilege lend authority to St. Ouen, the Parlement, the monarchy, or a combination of these? Privileges were both exceptions to and part of the legal system. In other words, privileges made a messy system even messier.

Guilds and other corporations, like universities, enjoyed special privileges within a city like Rouen and created statutes to govern the activities of their members. Rouen was an important city in terms of the scale of its corporations. The wool and cloth industries were especially influential in the city and surrounding area. Guilds not only created some of their own regulations (others came from the city and the monarchy), they also negotiated (and sometimes hotly contested) boundaries of production with other guilds. The cloth and clothing guilds are but one example with tailors, seamstresses, *lingères*, cloth-makers, hat-makers, and others all guarding their rights to production. The guilds also had a quasi-policing force, in the sense that their privileges gave them the right to regulate and police the trade, a function performed by their elected officials (Crowston 2001; Kaplan 1996; Hafter 2007).

Finally, with regards to this overview, another important node of the legal system which will receive a lot of attention in this study is notaries. Notaries were key players in the civil legal system. More like tradesmen than like lawyers in the royal courts, these legal officials went through specialized training. They received their offices by appointment, and their activities and numbers were regulated by the monarchy.[8] Though not exclusively—priests and even legal officials doing double duty in smaller jurisdictions drew up contracts—they were charged with drawing up and formalizing legally binding contracts, agreements, wills, and even settlements of disputes, among many other things. These legal documents, which could be sold to other notaries, were designed, in theory, to minimize disputes between people and to give clear direction to the transfer of property. In order to make such documents as sound as possible the notaries had to navigate and reconcile as many of the different laws relevant to the interested parties as possible.

Civil disputes

Now that we have laid some groundwork for how the legal system worked in theory, we can turn to an examination of how people used the resources available to them. What follows will be a detailed analysis of activity in the *vicomté* of Elbeuf and before the notaries of Rouen. It will show that court cases were either very short or quite long and drawn out as well as the importance of documentation and preparation. It will also show that the court did not have a strong presence in the resolution of disputes among people and that, rather, notaries played a much larger role in the process as a whole, both on the side of prevention and of resolution of disputes.

The first striking aspect of the set of records under consideration is what is absent—civil cases before the *vicomté* by far outnumber the criminal. In fact, it appears that the *vicomté* in Elbeuf did not hear any criminal cases in the year 1510.[9] This absence could be the result either of disappearance of records or, more likely, overlapping jurisdictions common in this period—meaning that criminal cases were likely heard elsewhere even though they technically could have been heard here. In any case, this absence is a striking example of the pervasiveness of civil cases over criminal ones.

Alongside the absence of criminal cases heard before the court is the near absence of women. Of the 109 appearances before the judge recorded, only seven involve women, one of which involves two men appearing with their wives in an inheritance dispute. Another man and wife appear together seeking an appointment, and a husband represents his wife. The four remaining appearances by women involved two widows, one of whom appeared three times—once in May and twice in September—to contest a *decret d'héritages*.[10] But even in their relative scarcity, the cases involving women offer a small representative slice of larger patterns.

The next striking aspect of this set of records is the number and length of ongoing litigation. Although the cases involving multiple parties in multiple appearances offer us little satisfaction when it comes to details or narrative, they nonetheless provide important information about the process of civil litigation. Even within the span of one year, it is clear that cases heard by the court were most often either very short, with only one appearance in court, or a long, drawn-out process. The length of time most often resulted from parties trying to put all of the supporting materials together for their case and to find people to testify on their behalf. But even the cases with only one appearance were mostly postponed for the purpose of preparation. In this regard, the courts seemed quite indulgent to the litigants. (It should be noted that the scribe did not appear to be automatically noting ongoing cases at every session because there were sessions in which nothing was recorded for a case that was still clearly ongoing.) Of course, delaying the process could also be part of the litigation strategy if one party was trying to obstruct or discourage the activity of the other (Smail 2003). Accusations of deliberately delaying the process were not unheard of (Smail 2003; Benedict 1981). It is also possible that the court deliberately lengthened the procedure because it could collect a fee with each appearance or, alternatively, it wanted to encourage settlements out of court.[11] Given the evidence as a whole, although possible, these latter intentions by the court seem risky and therefore less plausible. Postponing a case did not force people to return to the court (and generate more revenue) because they could reach a settlement without the court, which may or may not serve the interest of public order, for which the court officials were responsible. Settlements would undermine potential revenue and could also undermine the court's power and authority more globally by denying it a role in the resolution of the dispute. It is more likely that procedure before the court was more strict in its requirements to render a decision and offer resolution, forcing parties to regroup and possibly reconsider.

Of the 109 appearances before the *vicomté* of Elbeuf, there are only 40 distinct cases, which deflates the presence of the court. The remaining appearances are part of ongoing cases in which the same parties reappear either in the same manner as before or with a switch in who is complaining against whom. It is in some cases a long process of moves and countermoves. Moreover, a number of people were involved in several different cases. While it is risky to assume that people bearing the same name were the same person, certain people stand out nonetheless. For instance, Jacques Dufay, *escuier* of Bois Guillaume (now a suburb of Rouen), must have fallen on hard times by 1510. He was called into court 14 different times by four different people, of whom Jean Carre stands out. Carre called Dufay to court eight different times before the court finally ruled in his favor.[12] It is also interesting that this case was heard in Elbeuf, rather than Rouen, considering that Bois Guillaume is closer geographically to Rouen than Elbeuf and is not contiguous with Elbeuf. It is possible that there was a piece of land situated in the jurisdiction of Elbeuf under contention. The repetition of cases suggests complexity in the unfolding of, and rendering a decision in, those cases.

To put these multiple appearances in greater perspective, the *vicomté* was only in session on 14 different days in 1510. This means that some people, like Jean Carre, were there every consecutive session while their case was ongoing. It also suggests that people may have needed to turn elsewhere if resolution was more time-sensitive, which would account for some of the defaults noted in the records. Whether the court was in session less often because it did not need to be in session more often—i.e. because there were no cases—is unclear. Because of the nature of the surviving record set, I have not been able to verify the average frequency of court sessions from year to year. While there is not an exact correspondence between the number of appearances and the number of people involved on either side of a case, more people, more often than not, meant more appearances and suggests that more people meant more complexity to the unfolding of cases.

Other than the case involving the husbands representing their wives mentioned previously, four others stand out, and they are the only ones that involve multiple appearances. This case and the ones that follow offer an important glimpse into civil litigation procedure—the back and forth, the length, the importance of documentation etc. They also suggest that the court's role in settling disputes is rather small.

Of particular interest is the case between the children of Jean Ausoult, who was deceased at the time of the proceeding, and the *éliseurs* of the *prévôté* of Thuit Signol.[13] The details of the case and what brought them into court can only be guessed at (though there appears to be an underlying tax dispute), but the parties involved appeared eight different times before the court. There is a suggestion of underlying family tension. The representatives of each party—Pierre Tallon as *tuteur* for the children and Robert Tallon for the *éliseurs*—share the same family name, and on two separate occasions Nicolas Ausoult, father of Robert Tallon, and Jean Tallon, son of Robert Tallon, both make appearances. In one session Robert Tallon, summoned by Jean Tallon, suggests that he and the *éliseurs* were contracted to provide documents needed for another trial but that the children submitted the information in such a disorganized way, including submitting more at the last session, that it has been impossible to produce them, which is why he has not paid the required damages and fees. The children blamed him for the delay of the trial, and he turns the blame back on them. In the session immediately following, Nicolas Ausoult promises '26 *feuilles tant écrits que non écrits*' from the children to be delivered to his son, Robert Tallon, and the *éliseurs*.[14] Again, the exact details are unclear, but it appears that there are several layers of court cases wrapped up in theses appearances.

This case is also an example of the importance of documentation and of giving parties the opportunity to look over the opposition's materials in civil procedure. The dispute between the children of Jean Ausoult and the *éliseurs* of Thuit Signol over documents is not unique. Nor is the activity of the *procureurs*. Documentation is critical in civil procedure before the court. The court does not seem to presume literacy on the part of the litigants, as the numerous postponements suggest. The postponement would allow finer scrutiny of the letter, declaration etc. and, more practically, the opportunity to find someone to read it. People presumably used this to their full advantage. That this led to accusations of delaying the process deliberately is hardly surprising.

An even more striking case of multiple parties making multiple appearances is the case of Jean Regnault versus Jean Leribert the elder, *fermier de monsieur Jacques, monsieur de la rivière Seine*. Leribert hired Michel Deleslardiere to be his *procureur*. The case may have ended in the courts, but it did not start there. Leribert was not shy about taking matters into his own hands. He took it upon himself to collect a debt—48s 9d—which he claimed Regnault owed him, executing a seizure of some of his goods personally. This seizure prompted Regnault to follow up in court with a formal declaration of his opposition. In the meantime, Regnault had called two brothers, Jean and Guillaume Leblanc, listed as *garçons*, to testify on his behalf. Guillaume refused. Jean did not refuse but made things difficult for Regnault nonetheless.[15]

Regnault called Jean and Guillaume Leblanc to testify as to what Leribert had done to him. The *sergent* Guillaume Bourdet reported that he had summoned Jean Leblanc *en garranti* and collected the paperwork of Regnault and Leribert for Michel Leflameng, the *procureur* representing the Leblancs, who was in the process of preparing four reports and a declaration. Regnault, in another appearance, in the presence of Leribert's *procureur*, insisted that Guillaume Leblanc should testify, seeking a *garanti* to this effect from Leflamang, who refused because Leribert had not appeared in court. Leribert, it was noted, had not shown up to court because he was a *fermier*.[16] The case was adjourned to summon Leribert to the next session. In the next session, Leribert, in response to a request from Jean and Guillaume Leblanc, who would otherwise refuse to testify on Regnault's behalf, produced a letter to prove that he was a *fermier*, and the case was adjourned to give the Leblancs time to look at it. Finally, after the fourth summons, Jean Leblanc appeared in court as a guarantor for Regnault. The case was adjourned, with the court holding on to the disputed property. After a few more sessions, we see a Vincent Regnault appear in court with a Francois Leflameng as *procureur* to defend a declaration and *clameur de marché de bourse* made against him by Jean Leribert. Although it is unclear whether this case is related to the other, it is clear that Leribert is a busy man in court. Several more sessions, all of which are postponed, take us to the end of the year.[17]

The cases discussed above show the fluidity of the jurisdiction itself and the relatively passive role the court is playing in these cases. Moreover, the court often seems to be standing in more as an arbiter than as a judging force. Of the 109 appearances, 85 are explicitly postponed, while 12 list the opposing parties only. In fact, the court only renders seven final decisions in the whole year. The remaining appearances are listed as defaults, but this does not imply a final decision, as even more cases are postponed in spite of a default. There are 22 defaults recorded, only two of which prompt a final decision.[18] The court is either indulgent to people's inability to be present in court, or it has little power to bring them in, or a little of both. Of course, this is an accusatory system, and in civil matters it is usually in the party's interest to show up, so it is not surprising that the court is not sending out agents to haul people in. The court also assessed a fine for a default. What is surprising is how often the summonses are ignored and the lack of (immediate) repercussions beyond the fine.

These cases suggest a great deal of agency on the part of litigants. But they are not simply taking their cases to court. They are in many cases initiating legal action outside of the court. Of the 109 appearances, 35 began with a *clameur de marché de bourse* and three began with one party seizing the goods of another. Only in a handful of cases was a *sergent* called to record the activity.[19] These people are inviting the court into their disputes. The agency of the litigants is far more striking than the agency of the court officials. We are left with an impression of the civil system that is fluid. The court is not central to resolving civil disputes, and people can influence the length of the case and the court's role, if any, in deciding its outcome.

In terms of women and gender, it appears that women are only directly involved in the courts in a limited capacity. They are either widows representing themselves, or they are represented by their husbands or male kin. To understand their roles in civil disputes in this period, we are forced to infer based on indirect evidence. The cases involving female guilds, like the *lingères*, in Rouen, are an important exception to this trend, but delving into this set of records is beyond the scope of this paper, especially since these records are quite sparse. The scarcity of women in the courts is I think due to strictures in Norman custom governing the management of property (Schneider 2000; Lemonnier-Lesage 2005; Hardwick 1997).

If we factor in the number of cases left hanging, then it is tempting to view the court as peripheral to civil disputes. It is not at all unlikely that some of these cases are settled out of court. Notarial records drive this point home. There are records of people settling out of court, even though they had taken action in court. They then formalize this settlement before a notary. Here we can recall the case that opened this chapter. Two brothers fighting over inheritance begin a heated court battle in the *plés de la sergenterie de Pavilly* (outside of the city) before the *vicomté* of Rouen or his lieutenant (in an itinerant session), but in the interest of 'peace and brotherly love' (and quite probably cost), they resolve the matter out of court and draw up a formal document to this effect in front of a notary in Rouen.[20] This act of settlement and the desire to avoid court was so common that the notary had a formula for drawing it up which was so well understood that he abbreviated it ('etc.'). This also underscores the importance of notarial records for understanding legal practices. Notarial records offer information about civil disputes and legal maneuvering outside of the courts. Whether it is a formalization of settlement or arbitration or even a well-crafted contract or will—which among other reasons, is designed to prevent disputes—documents like these complete the picture the court records paint, not only in terms of biographical information but also in terms of procedure.

Delving further into notarial records from this period, we find that Rouen was an important center of legal business as with many other activities. The city, of course, bore witness to the activities of its lively and diverse residents but also hosted those dwelling in the surrounding area who made the trip to the city to conduct their affairs, legal or otherwise. Legal business was often conducted between residents of the city and those of the surrounding area. It was indeed rare for the parties to a contract, suit, or case before court to be exclusively from the city of Rouen. Looking at notarial records from Rouen (a sampling of 210 out of about 1820), we find roughly 70 percent of the records involving residents outside of the city limits of this period (the city has since enveloped some of these places or attached them as suburbs). Even more of these records involved land outside of the city.[21] Even if the parties resided in the city, records will indicate that an individual came from an outlying area. For instance, we find a transaction from Antoine Bonjon the *cordonnier* who is a native of the parish of St. Amand Laillier près Moulins en Bourbonnois at the time of the transaction residing in the parish of St. Laurent of Rouen with his cousin.[22] This is why when thinking about the city of Rouen, we are rather thinking about greater Rouen.

For all of the contracts we have, a number of them contain evidence of prior court proceedings. These records take the form of settlement agreements outside of court, meaning the parties negotiated and reached an agreement outside of court and cancelled their suit. The parties may notify the court, or they may simply not return to the next session to resume proceedings. It is unclear, failing records that may or may not have been kept regarding cancellations or appointments to appear before court, whether the parties would have needed to notify the court and whether they bothered. Records survive of decisions—even if the decision was to postpone a final ruling—but little remains of the more mundane practices. This is why notarial records are so important read alongside civil court records to understand practice of civil disputes. Of the notarial records under examination, nearly 15 percent were either a formalization of a settlement out of court or a follow-up to a sentence, which contains a summary of court proceedings. This means that a significant percentage of notarial records contains information about activity in the courts. Many of these proceedings were in courts for which records no longer survive both outside of the city of Rouen and within the city itself such as the *vicomté*. For example, we have a follow-up to a sentence rendered by the *assises de Pontautou* before the notaries of Rouen.[23] This suggests a fluidity of legal practice. Parties could appear before a court for a decision and then come to their own agreement afterwards. This also suggests that enforcement may have been a challenge for the litigants and that to some degree, coming to an agreement outside of the court may have been a matter of practicality in reaching closure. Litigants could appear before one jurisdiction then continue on their own and formalize the decision within another jurisdiction. Presumably the notarial records in Rouen were meant to stand up in multiple jurisdictions or within a scenario of overlapping jurisdictions because many contracts involve property and parties residing outside of the city. In the end, notarial records were the formalization of negotiations, some of which were tense and involved a legal dispute, between two parties or among several. What is clear is that going to court was simply one step—one optional step—in resolving a civil dispute and that to understand more completely the practices of resolving civil disputes, whether it involved litigation or not, it is necessary to look beyond the courts and their records.

Over a third of the notarial records mention a woman as being either directly or indirectly involved in the contract or agreement. The woman might be making a contract in her own right, if she were a widow or accompanied by her husband, or she could be the mother who left property to her children or even a sister making a partial claim of inheritance. Women also entered marriage contracts, received dowries via contract, and had male relatives looking out for them and buying land on their behalf.

Roughly a quarter of the notarial records make no mention of the occupation or social status of the parties, though they might be guessed by the value of property involved. Of the records which do mention an occupation, just over 20 percent mention one or more clergymen. Nearly half mention a 'bourgeois' or a specific tradesman, and about 15 percent mention a legal official. These groups are the most common and are, of course, entering into contracts with members across groups in varying combinations. We also see the occasional nobleman and laborer and others. This breakdown suggests that these records are not consistently representing the lowest socioeconomic strata (possibly due to notarial fees and other costs), which is admittedly the largest segment of the population, but they do represent negotiations between other strata.

Additionally, notarial records contain explicit or implicit references to wanting to avoid proceedings in court. One such case is that of a settlement such as the one at the opening of this chapter.[24] The settlement is agreed to and formalized before the notaries to avoid further proceedings. There is even more to suggest that one of the main functions of notarial contracts was to avoid litigation. More than 40 percent of the cases make reference to a prior agreement, overwhelmingly documented before notaries, to give legitimacy of ownership and right to enter into an agreement with the property in question. There is another intriguing case of a man taking in a widow of two husbands and the agreement between this man and this woman not to make any claim or have any claim to the other's property:

> Jeanne, widow of the late Pierre Desforges and before that of the late Guillebert Lechevalier, residing in the parish of St. Jean of Rouen with and in the house of Henry Duparc, on the one hand, and the said Henry Duparc, on the other, both parties being present freely consent and agree that whatever dwelling or residence that they have made together in the past and that they will make together in the future does not happen to the prejudice or damage of the other and that for this reason they cannot claim any common share of goods in acquisition. Confessing otherwise, that by friendship and courtesy the said Duparc had placed and welcomed the said widow with him in his hôtel for no other reason than to help her and see to her needs as a gesture etc. Robin Langloys and Robert Poree bearing witness.[25]

In essence, this agreement is designed to prevent any claim akin to that resulting from a common law marriage resulting from their cohabitation.

Notarial records also exhibit re-negotiations. Such is the case where parties had negotiated and entered into a contract which had not been fulfilled. The fulfilling of that contract does not lead to a dispute in the traditional sense but rather to re-negotiation formalized before a notary. In one case in particular, involving residents from Rouen and the surrounding area, representatives of parties of a contract made in 1470 formalize an agreement about an outstanding debt of 8 mynes of wheat out of an original 20. Here the son and heir of Jean Ango, of the same name, comes to terms with Simon Haset, representing the party of Colin Devos who owed the 8 mynes to Jean Lemachon, the original party to the contract with Jean Ango the elder. In this record, Jean Ango the younger formally acknowledges receipt and fulfillment of the principal and arrears. No mention is made of a court or legal professional aside from notaries. Disputing in or outside of court is therefore best understood as one end of a spectrum of negotiation.[26]

In addition to inheritance, debt was a major matter of contention in civil disputes. People often entered into debt through contracts and agreed to pay it off in installments. What is more interesting about many of the cases where debts go unpaid is not the open legal disputes which come of them but rather the re-negotiation of the debt and agreement to pay it off, even among heirs of the parties to a previous contract. Collecting debts made under contract that had not been fulfilled represent another 'shade' of the spectrum of disputing. The formalization of the re-negotiation of the debt was not a contract that reveals an open dispute, especially not heard before a court (though it could have been as a breach of contract, presumably), but it reveals an acknowledged problem and attempts to resolve it and come to another agreement.[27]

Conclusion

We must remember that even though people may have had access to various courts and legal authorities, not all (perhaps not even most) chose to take advantage of this access. My research suggests that the courts' roles in resolving disputes was relatively small in relation to the courts' representation in scholarship. By privileging courts and court records, we risk capturing a small piece of practice, over-emphasizing the importance of the courts and legal authorities, and even of misunderstanding the courts, how they functioned, and their role in society more broadly. Moreover, this activity outside of court does not have to imply that the court is less authoritative or powerful, but it does suggest that the role of the court in resolving civil disputes is limited. Appearing (or not) before a court is only one, non-definitive option in pursuing a dispute. Both Dan Smail and Julie Hardwick have emphasized the importance of having options in litigation and how the decision to go to court led to the growth of the legal system and of the state (Smail 2003; Hardwick 2009). But the cases I have studied raise the question of the extent to which utilizing this option lends authority, power, and legitimacy to the court when it is frequently not involved in the resolution. This is not to say that the relationship is not there, but rather, that the relationship is not so easily determined (Ross and Stern 2013).

Notes

1 Archives de Seine Maritime (hereafter ADSM), 2E1 228. 2 January 1500. The brothers negotiated a *rente*, which was a type of loan.
2 Ross and Stern have notably cautioned against the teleology of state formation, yet state formation seems to dominate the discussion of legal pluralism nonetheless (Ross and Stern 2013). See also: Hardwick 2009; Smail 2003.

3 Michael Breen has recently published an excellent essay on recent historiography on law and social history in early modern France. Although praising the above works, he argued that:

> the current tendency to focus on litigants' agendas and strategies, and the ways in which they 'consumed' justice and manipulated the law in pursuit of their own ends, can sometimes come perilously close to removing the law and those who administered it from the equation altogether. Or at the very least, it reduces them to little more than mere accessories.
>
> (Breen 2016, p. 44)

Taking his point very seriously, I would nonetheless argue that the legal system as a whole in this period is more fluid in terms of institutions (like courts) and practice both on the part of litigants and legal officials than it is often given credit for. Breen has even alluded to the legal professions as an important new direction of study as the 'growing differentiation between practitioners' 'may have originally been more distinct in theory than in practice' (p. 53). Shifting attention away from the courts helps us to better understand their role within a larger system of practice and helps bring into focus the parts played by legal professionals, the options that people had in resolving disputes, and the decisions that people made in pursuing different options. In that sense, arguing that the courts' role in resolving disputes was small is not to remove them from the equation but to change them from constant to variable within the equation (Breen 2016).

4 For a more detailed discussion of the relationship between legal history and social, political, and cultural history in the historiography of early modern France, see: Breen 2016.

5 Broadly speaking, the question of whether it is appropriate to refer to a legal 'system' has been raised recently, and it is an interesting question with much promise for fruitful debate among scholars, especially, but not exclusively, when studying a customary 'system'. C.W. Brooks has argued that a 'legal system' did not exist in sixteenth-century England for instance. Michael Breen in particular has suggested that it may be better to think of France as having two (at least) legal systems to reconcile apparent contradictions of discourse and practice. As intriguing as this line of questions is, I would encourage caution. Even if the emergence, evolution, and practice of the institutions and laws was not systematic in the purest sense, the connections and influences between overlapping, contradictory, contested institutions, laws, and divergent practices outweigh the dis-connects and differences. In short, a pluralistic system is still a system, as apparently inefficient, disorganized, and contradictory as it may be. For more on this discussion, please see: Brooks 1986 and Breen 2016.

6 For more on the legal system and institutions in France, see: Olivier-Martin 2010; Barbiche 1999; Zeller 1948.

7 This is clearly a very simple breakdown of ecclesiastical laws and institutions influencing the legal system in the city, and of course, it does not go into great detail on reform movements (interests for reform) either internal or external. Although this study ends its analysis before the Wars of Religion began in France, it is nevertheless important to be cognizant of such movements. Unfortunately for this study, source material on reform movements, especially in relationship to legal practice, are sparse and difficult to work with. It is worth recalling that, in theory, reform movements, could strengthen or undermine the authority and integrity of ecclesiastical laws and institutions.

8 For more on notaries, see: Le Clech 1993; Hardwick 1997, 1998; Dolan 1998); Collins 2016.

9 ADSM, 52BP 11.

10 ADSM, 52BP 11.

11 This interpretation has been suggested by Michael Breen—the courts prolonged cases to encourage settlements as a way of promoting discreet resolution and public order. I would not deny it as possible, but it raises other questions about the shape and effectiveness of the order and the authority of the courts (Breen 2016).

12 ADSM, 52BP 11.

13 An *éliseur* was a tax collector. Eventually, cases heard before the *prévôté* of Le Thuit Signol appealed to the *bailliage ducal d'Elbeuf*.

14 ADSM, 52BP 11.
15 ADSM, 52BP 11.
16 In addition to the agricultural sense, *fermier* was (based on readings of cases from other years) the term for a customs officer or tax collector, but the sense is not explicit here. Nonetheless, based on the context, I would favor the tax collector interpretation.
17 ADSM, 52BP 11.
18 ADSM, 52BP 11.
19 ADSM, 52BP 11.
20 ADSM, 2E1 228. 2 January 1500.
21 ADSM, 2E1 228 and 229.
22 ADSM, 2E1 228. 2 January 1500.
23 ADSM, 2E1 228. 3 January 1500.
24 ADSM, 2E1 228. 2 January 1500.
25 ADSM, 2E1 228. 3 January 1500.
26 ADSM, 2E1 228. 3 January 1500.
27 ADSM, 2E1 228. 3 January 1500.

References

Barbiche, B. (1999). *Les insitutions de la monarchie française à l'époque moderne, XVIe–XVIIIe siècle*. Paris: Presses Universitaires de France.

Baumgartner, F.J. (1994). Louis XII's Gallican Crisis of 1510–1513. In: A.E. Bakos, ed., *Politics, Ideology and the Law in Early Modern Europe: Essays in Honor of J.H.M. Salmon*. Rochester, NY: University of Rochester Press, pp. 55–72.

Benedict, P. (1981). *Rouen during the Wars of Religion*. New York: Cambridge University Press.

Breen, M.P. (2016). Law and social history in early modern France. In B.B. Diefendorf, ed., *Social Relations, Politics, and Power in Early Modern France: Robert Descimon and the Historian's Craft*. Kirksville, MO: Truman State University Press, pp. 42–60.

Brooks, C.W. (1986). *Pettyfoggers and Vipers of the Commonwealth: the 'Lower Branch' of the Legal Profession in Early Modern England*. Cambridge: Cambridge University Press.

Brunelle, G.K. (1991). *The New World Merchants of Rouen, 1559–1630*. Kirksville, MO: Sixteenth Century Journal Publishers, Inc.

Collins, J.B. (2016). The notary as rural power broker: Maître Coujard and Pierre Collenot, Syndic of Alligny. In B.B. Diefendorf, ed., *Social Relations, Politics, and Power in Early Modern France: Robert Descimon and the Historian's Craft*. Kirksville, MO: Truman State University Press, pp. 107–133.

Crowston, C.H. (2001). *Fabricating Women: the Seamstresses of Old Regime France, 1675–1791*. Durham: Duke University Press.

De Gruchy, W.L., ed. (1881). *L'Ancienne Coutume de Normandie*. Jersey: Charles Le Feuvre.

Descimon, R. (1996). The birth of the Nobility of the Robe: dignity versus privilege in the Parlement of Paris, 1500–1700. In: M. Wolfe, ed., *Changing Identities in Early Modern France*. Durham: Duke University Press, pp. 95–123.

Dewald, J. (1980). *The Formation of a Provincial Nobility: the Magistrates of the Parlement of Rouen, 1499–1610*. Princeton, NJ: Princeton University Press.

Diefendorf, B.B. (1983). *Paris City Councillors in the Sixteenth Century: the Politics of Patrimony*. Princeton: Princeton University Press.

Diefendorf, B.B. (1995). Women and property in ancient régime France: theory and practice in Dauphiné and Paris. In: J. Brewer and S. Staves, eds., *Early Modern Conceptions of Property*. London: Routledge, pp. 170–193.

Diefendorf, B.B. (1996). Give us back our children: patriarchal authority and parental consent to religious vocations in early counter-reformation France. *The Journal of Modern History*, 68(2), pp. 265–307.

Dolan, C. (1998). *Le Notaire, La Famille et La Ville: Aix-En-Provence à La Fin Du XVIe Siècle*, Histoire Notariale. Toulouse: Presses universitaires du Mirail.

Hafter, D.M. (2007). *Women at Work in Preindustrial France*. University Park, PA: Pennsylvania State University.

Hanley, S. (1989). Engendering the state: family formation and state building in early modern France. *French Historical Studies*, 16(1), pp. 4–27.

Harding, R.R. (1978). *Anatomy of a Power Elite: the Provincial Governors of Early Modern France*. New Haven: Yale University Press.

Hardwick, J. (1997). Women 'working' the law: gender, authority, and legal process in early modern France. *Journal of Women's History*, 9(3), pp. 28–49.

Hardwick, J. (1998). *The Practice of Patriarchy: Gender and the Politics of Household Authority in Early Modern France*. University Park, PA: Pennsylvania State University Press.

Hardwick, J. (2009). *Family Business: Litigation and the Political Economies of Daily Life in Early Modern France*. Oxford: Oxford Univ. Press.

Kaplan, S.L. (1996). *The Bakers of Paris and the Bread Question, 1700–1775*. Durham: Duke University Press.

Le Clech, S. (1993). *Chancellerie et Culture Au XVIe Siècle: Les Notaires Et Secrétaires Du Roi De 1515 à 1547*. Toulouse: Presses universitaires du Mirail.

Lemonnier-Lesage, V. (2005). *Le statut de la femme mariée dans la Normandie coutumière: droit et pratiques dans la généralité de Rouen*. Clermont-Ferrand: Presses Univ. de la Faculté de Droit de Clermont-Ferrand.

Olivier-Martin, F. (2010). *Histoire du droit français des origins à la Révolution*, 3rd edition. Paris: CNRS Éditions.

Parsons, J. (2004). *The Church in the Republic: Gallicanism and Political Ideology in Renaissance France*. Washington DC: Catholic University of America Press.

Piant, H. (2006). *Une justice ordinaire: justice civil et criminelle dans la prévôté royale de Vaucouleurs sous l'ancien régime* Rennes: Presses universitaires de Rennes.

Ross, R.J. and Stern, P.J. (2013). Reconstructing early modern notions of legal pluralism. In L. Benton and R.J. Ross, eds., *Legal Pluralism and Empires, 1500–1850*. New York: New York University Press, pp. 109–41.

Schneider, Z. (2000). Women before the bench: female litigants in early modern Normandy. *French Historical Studies*, 23(1), pp. 1–32.

Schneider, Z.A. (2008). *The King's Bench: Bailiwick Magistrates and Local Governance in Normandy, 1670–1740*. Rochester, NY: University of Rochester Press.

Smail, D.L. (2003). *The Consumption of Justice: Emotions, Publicity, and Legal Culture in Marseille, 1264–1423*. Ithaca: Cornell University Press.

Tallon, A. (1997). *La France et le Concile de Trente (1518–1563)*. Paris: École française de Rome.

Wanegffelen, T. (1997). *Ni Rome Ni Genève: des fidèles entre deux chaires en France au XVIe siècle*. Paris: Honoré Champion.

Wanegffelen, T. (1999). *Une Difficile Fidélité: Catholiques malgré le concile en France, XVIe–XVIIe siècles*. Paris: Presses Universitaires de France.

Zeller, G. (1948). *Les institutions de la France au XVIe siècle*. Paris : Presses Universitaires de France.

Zemon Davis, N. (1987). *Fiction in the Archives: Pardon Tales and their Tellers in Sixteenth-Century France*. Stanford, CA: Stanford University Press.

8

IN HOPE OF AGREEMENT: NORM AND PRACTICE IN THE USE OF INSTITUTES FOR DISPUTE SETTLEMENT IN LATE-SEVENTEENTH-CENTURY LEIDEN

Aries van Meeteren and Griet Vermeesch

Introduction

When examining social control and social relations, historians have in recent decades broadened their attention from criminal to civil courts. This is a welcome shift, since civil courts on various institutional levels heard a mass of litigations during the early modern era, in which parties were juxtaposed to each other on issues they had brought before the court themselves. Initially, historians often examined criminal courts as a means by which elites tried to impose preferred forms of behaviour on lower social groups. They paid a great deal of attention to regulations, but also turned their attention to the history of crime, typically by performing quantitative analyses of perpetrators, victims, transgressions and verdicts. Their interest was mostly confined to governmental control (Soman, 1980; Spierenburg, 2004). The 1970s, however, also witnessed a broadening of research agendas to encompass extra-judicial institutions of social control, including the Church (Spierz, 1985; Schilling, 2004). A new understanding gradually surfaced, notably that mechanisms of social control did not necessarily aim at disciplining and punishing transgressors of elite-imposed norms, but were often intended to reconcile the parties concerned and maintain social peace. Historiographic attention for governmental control thus increasingly gave way to analysis of the conflict-settling objectives of a wide range of institutions, recently including civil courts (Roodenburg, 2004; Deceulaer, 1996).

In the past decade or so, this research has been raised to a new level by developing new perceptions of the position of judicial institutions in processes of conflict settlement. Historians nowadays increasingly go beyond the mere analysis of those institutions of conflict settlement and the ways such institutions intervened in the interpersonal business of ordinary people (King, 2004; Shaw, 2006; Hardwick, 2009). They notably examine how ordinary people used such institutions for their own purposes, and thereby impacted their functioning. Parties chose, for instance, whether or not to take their conflict to court, after a wide range of extra-judicial forms of mediation had been tried. They more often than not withdrew their case to seek reconciliation outside court, using the court merely to gain leverage over the counterparty, rather than using it to achieve a verdict (Garnot, 1996; Brachtendorf, 2003; Roodenburg, 2004; Blaufarb, 2010). These new insights have been most clearly articulated in the work of Martin Dinges, who has described how inhabitants of eighteenth-century Paris used the filing of complaints with the police as complementary to other, more daily mechanisms of social control, including gossip, slander and brawls. Mutual agreements accomplished without the interference of officials were the norm. Only when such agreements proved hard to achieve did parties invite police commissioners into the conflict. They did so in order to prevail over the counterparty rather than to obtain decisive intervention, and more often than not they withdrew their complaint before a verdict was reached. The services of police commissioners, in other words, were used instrumentally by the inhabitants of Paris. Dinges denoted this instrumental use of institutions with the concept of 'uses of justice', a translation of the German *Justiznutzung*. He restricted this concept to criminal justice, and viewed criminal courts as the last resort people took recourse to (Dinges, 2000; Dinges, 2004).

Recently, the notion of 'uses of justice' has inspired new research on the history of civil and criminal justice in the Low Countries as well. By taking into account the diverse institutions of conflict settlement that people invited into their interpersonal conflicts, existing interpretations of the extent to which women committed crimes for instance has been thoroughly revised. Whereas the allegedly low participation of women in violence is traditionally perceived as mirroring their limited participation in public life, Manon van der Heijden has asserted that female crime rates were much higher when prosecution by lower courts is taken into account (Heijden, 2013, 2016; Van der Heijden and Pluskota, 2015). Illegitimate motherhood and all the conflicts that pertain to discussions over paternity and transgression of morality have also been examined. Studies have been made of the extent to which single mothers used the broad range of judicial resources as a means to pressurise fathers to assume paternal care, and the extent to which they conversely became subject to criminal prosecution. Revealingly, criminal procedures were similarly actively used by single mothers in their bargaining over paternity. In short, analyses of the uses ordinary people made of justice reveals the ways they actively used state and communal infrastructures to improve their prospects. This kind of research allows for valuable contributions to history written from below (Kamp and Schmidt, 2018; Vermeesch, 2016). However, we also need to be cautious not to assume too readily that all sections of the early modern urban populace found their way to the courts to the same degree. Informal conflict settlement is most likely to have predominated, particularly for lower social groups (Vermeesch, 2015). In short, current historiography emphasises the need to further broaden research to include lower and informal instances of conflict settlement.

This article builds on these insights, by attesting the extent to which the instrumental use of courts was indeed prevalent in the early modern context, notably in the Dutch town of Leiden in the late seventeenth century. The overall question that underlies the research presented in this article is to what extent institutions of conflict settlement were in command of the cases they treated, and – on the other hand – to what extent parties were rather able to hold sway over the way they used such institutions. Here, the concept of 'uses of justice' is developed somewhat differently from the way it was defined by Martin Dinges. First, the concept is not solely applied to criminal courts, but to a wider range of institutions of conflict settlement that were first and foremost directed at reconciling rather than punishing parties. Second, the 'uses of justice' will be rather labelled as 'instrumental use of institutions for conflict settlement' to emphasise the strategic ways parties invited a wide range of institutions into their conflicts, not as a last resort, but as one of the many ways conflicts could be settled. Relatedly, the phenomenon of forum shopping will receive more attention, i.e. the way parties switched between institutions of conflict settlement so as to stage manage the terms in which the conflict was negotiated (von Benda-Beckham, 1984, p. 37; Mather and Yngvesson, 1980–1, p. 783–818). The innovative aspect of the research presented in this article is the bringing together of various institutions of conflict settlement in one examination, and allowing the users of those institutions to take centre stage.

This article is divided into two parts. First, the norm will be elaborated, i.e. the way the Leiden city authorities intended the wide range of institutions of conflict settlement to relieve the Court of Aldermen from the ever-increasing case load during the long sixteenth century and thereafter. The first section thus comprises a discussion of the institutions of conflict settlement that have left source materials in the Leiden city archives. The second section will subsequently discuss indications in those source materials for the actual ways the diverse institutes of conflict settlement were used. It will explain the type of case matter that came before these forums, the volume of the case load and which social groups took recourse to these institutions. Most importantly, it will assess whether these institutions were used in the ways intended by the city government. The overall purpose of the article is thus to contribute to a better understanding of the ways users of justice shaped the institutions of conflict settlement in early modern Leiden.

The city of Leiden is a useful case for closer analysis. During the seventeenth century, its Golden Age, Leiden was the Dutch Republic's second wealthiest city (after Amsterdam), thriving on its blossoming textile industry, which employed the large majority of the city's then 60,000 inhabitants. As will become apparent below, Leiden accommodated a wide range of institutions – judicial, infra-judicial and extra-judicial – of conflict settlement where inhabitants could file complaints. The archival resources produced by these institutions have often been well preserved. Moreover, there is a rich research tradition on the social and institutional history of the city that was instrumental in conducting the research that underpins this article. The core of the research consists of a database of over 7,000 conflicts that were waged in the period from 1664 to 1668. These years have been chosen because the city of Leiden then accommodated the highest number of inhabitants, about 60,000, who lived in about 9,000 houses. Crammed together in often expensively rented houses, and confronted with exceptionally high food prices, the inhabitants generated a maximum of conflicts during these years. A time limit of five years made the time-intensive archival research and cross-linking of sources achievable.[1]

Norm – forums for dispute settlement in early modern Leiden

From the late sixteenth century until the last quarter of the seventeenth century, Leiden witnessed a demographic and economic boom that increased the incidence of interpersonal conflicts. In the late sixteenth century, the demographic boom was triggered by a stream of immigrants seeking refuge from the war-stricken Southern Low Countries. When the Leiden textile industry began to expand from the late 1570s onwards, immigrants from the nearby countryside and from farther abroad also flocked to the city (Davids, 1985, pp. 141–142). City dwellers lived in increasingly cramped conditions and engaged in a rising number of economic interactions. The consequent upsurge of conflicts made contemporaries fear the manageability of the urban law court of Leiden, the Court of Aldermen (*vierschaar*). Paralleling evolutions elsewhere in Europe, an enormous increase in petty lawsuits was brought before the urban court from the second half of the sixteenth century, demanding ever more time and energy from the city governors, who also had to cope with other new demands of a rapidly growing and changing city.[2]

Legal recourse to the Court of Aldermen was relatively time consuming, both for the litigants and for the aldermen and burgomasters who staffed it. Plaintiffs and defendants needed to hire legal spokesmen to navigate complex legal procedures and to help them translate their grievances into juridical claims. Recourse to the *vierschaar* typically required at least a few months. Although 79 per cent of the cases were concluded within three months, this still required more time and effort than many parties considered convenient. 12 per cent of the cases needed four to six months in order to be concluded, and almost 10 per cent took longer than half a year.[3] The court operated on the basis of the so-called role procedure in which the contesting parties were treated as equals. Legal spokesmen, called *procureurs*, represented the parties and exchanged judicial documents according to a fixed protocol so as to defend their client. Law cases were registered sequentially in the roll register, as well as all judicial deeds relevant to the case (Blok, 1884, pp. IX–X). The aldermen sat three days a week to hear the cases. In 1646, it was promulgated that henceforth, to keep court business manageable, all cases relating to a sum below 50 guilders were to be kept on the 'small roll' (*kleine rol*), while other cases were reserved for the 'big roll' (*grote rol*). By 1660 the division between 'small' and 'big' cases had shifted to 200 guilders.[4] The big cases in particular proved time consuming due to the many judicial steps that had to be taken by plaintiff and defendant regarding fixed time periods.[5] The cost of such cases is hard to estimate, as it depended entirely on the size of the claim and the duration of the procedures. The legal spokesmen were, for instance, paid for each sheet of paper they wrote and for each appearance at court. As can be expected, the longer the case took, the greater the cost. An important stumbling block for using the court must have been that it was hard to foresee the duration and thus the cost of a case.

To reduce the ever-growing case load that typically related to small claims and did not truly necessitate the extensive procedural protocol of a fully fledged civil law case, and also to help inhabitants to settle disputes more cheaply and speedily, the city government decided to install a number of additional forums for conflict resolution, presented in Figure 1 below. The figure also shows a number of non-governmental institutions that were encouraged to engage in conflict settlement. In 1583, a separate Commission for Neighbourly Disputes, typically relating to boundary partitions, was installed, and staffed by two aldermen who had to attempt to reconcile disputes before recourse to the Court of Aldermen was permitted.[6]

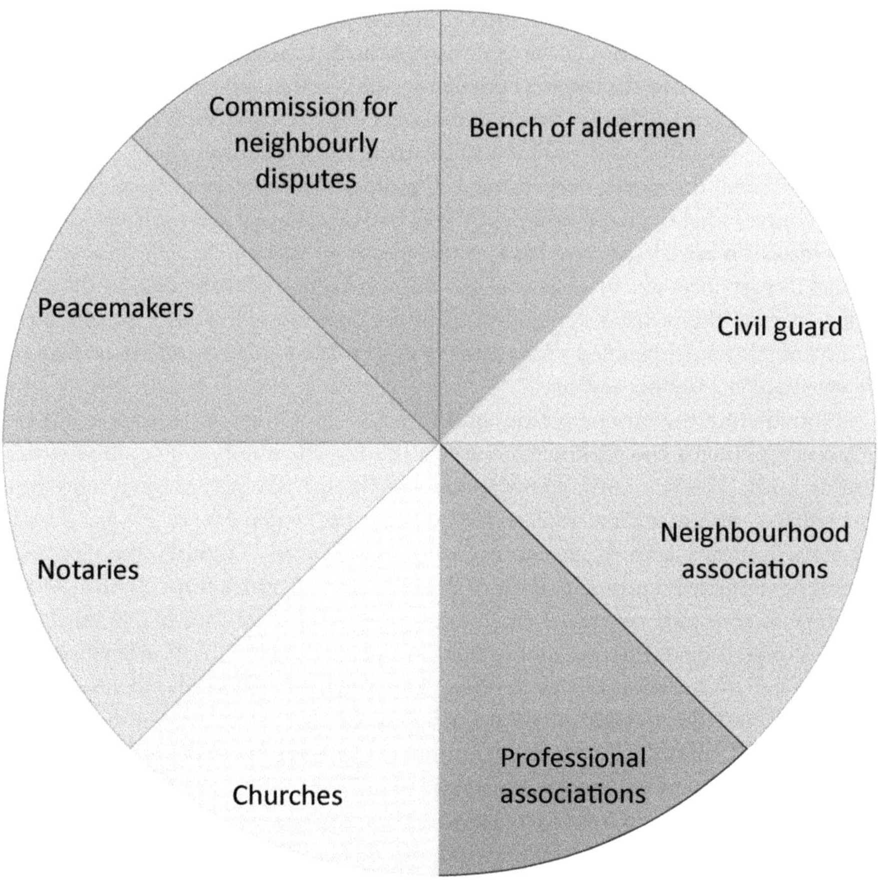

FIGURE 8.1 Forums for dispute settlement in early modern Leiden

The commission consisted of aldermen-masters (*schepenmeesters*), a duo of aldermen that were replaced every three months, who could be invited by quarrelling neighbours to come to hear their differing accounts on the spot. They then tried to reconcile the parties, or to appoint mediators to help resolve the disagreement. The *vierschaar* was only to be taken recourse to if the aldermen-masters failed to achieve an agreement between the quarrelling parties.[7]

In 1598, the Peacemaker Court was installed, operated by two aldermen and one of the four burgomasters.[8] Until then, interpersonal conflicts had been handled by the Court of Aldermen, no matter how small the claim. Henceforth, litigants first had to take their case to the peacemakers, who, first and foremost, endeavoured to reconcile the parties and thus avoid a formal lawsuit. Whatever the nature and size of their claim, a plaintiff was allowed to file a case with the Court of Aldermen only if the peacemakers were unable to negotiate a settlement. The peacemakers proved highly successful in attracting cases and swiftly handling them. Based on the length of a working day during the seventeenth century (six hours) and the average number of cases it treated on such day (36), it may be estimated that the peacemakers only needed ten minutes to handle a case. The number of days each week that the peacemakers heard cases was gradually extended to three. And while the court initially functioned as a conciliator only, in the mid-seventeenth century it gradually obtained adjudicating competences. By the eighteenth century, it was adjudicating cases that involved sums of less than 100 guilders. For conflicts relating to house rents, the threshold became 120 guilders.[9] As will be elaborated below, these courts – that operated in the grey area between formal and informal justice – substantially relieved the case load of the Court of Aldermen. The Peacemaker Court in particular was intensely sought after by Leiden's inhabitants. In the years 1664 to 1668 the peacemakers heard no fewer than some 23,600 cases, while the Court of Aldermen handled about 1,600 cases. In 1664, they heard on average no fewer than 54 cases per session.[10]

Nonetheless, the number of disputes heard at the Court of Aldermen and the Peacemaker Court was without a doubt dwarfed by the number of conflicts settled out of court. This was outspokenly encouraged by the city government, who took measures to stimulate extra-judicial forms of dispute settlement. In 1593, a decade after the installation of the Commission for Neighbourly Disputes, the city government stipulated a reorganisation of neighbourhood associations (Walle, 2005). In the late sixteenth century, Leiden comprised around seventy neighbourhoods each of which encompassed on average 36 houses.[11] These associations had thus far operated autonomously, yet the new directive for neighbourhood associations predetermined the delegation of quite a few governmental responsibilities and enhanced the control of the city government over these associations. Henceforth, the 'neighbourhood supervisors' who traditionally headed neighbourhood associations were to be chosen by the city government from among three candidates who had been put forward through elections by the inhabitants of each neighbourhood. The supervisors were also given new powers that mostly related to conflict settlement, which became a key responsibility. If neighbours failed to settle their differences and took legal recourse to one of the urban courts, the supervisor was to fine them a sum of 2 guilders (corresponding to almost two days' wages for skilled labour) or a ham. If matrimonial quarrels upset the neighbourhood, husband and wife were to be fined as well.[12] The active intervention in conflicts among neighbours was but one way to stimulate communal cohesion. Neighbourhoods continued to set up communal meals for neighbours, and continued the age-old practice of communal burials, in which all neighbours were expected to attend the burial of their fellow residents. These regulations remained in place until the end of the eighteenth century, and were extended occasionally, illustrating the continued reliance of the city government on the neighbourhood's abilities to settle conflicts. For instance, in 1667 neighbourhood supervisors were granted the right to adjudicate instead of only arbitrate disputes.[13] The neighbourhood supervisors were thus expected to act as gatekeepers for the urban courts, and to be pivotal figures in the assortment of forums for conflict settlement in early modern Leiden. Quite a few contemporaries admired the way conflicts were thus settled informally and locally. In 1660, the Leiden educationalist J.N. de Parival, for instance, noted that the neighbourhood associations were invaluable for Dutch cities, contributing to communal life, and more particularly for settling disputes among neighbours (De Parival, 1660, pp. 29, 31–32).

The civil guard (*schutterijen*) must be considered a forum for dispute settlement as well. It consisted of financially independent Leiden citizens and constituted a vital instrument of pride and distinctiveness for the local higher-middle classes. The civil guard brought together citizens of diverse backgrounds and trades and symbolised urban harmony and unity (Knevel, 1994). In 1599, the civil guard had around 700 members, and keeping track with urban growth, reached a membership of more than 1,700 men by the mid-seventeenth century.[14] They were prominently present when eminent guests came to the city, for instance William of Orange in 1575, the Earl of Leicester in 1587 and Maria de Medici in 1638 (Knevel, 1994, pp. 200–202, 274–275, 285). The importance of city guards in Leiden and in other Dutch cities was especially pronounced at the most eventful moments in the history of the Dutch Republic, when factions strived fiercely for governmental seats and aggressively mobilised middling groups by means of the civil guard. In times of peace, however, the civil guard could be a source of tension as well, for instance when prolonged guard duties and over-consumption of alcohol led members to misconduct, as was the case on the night of 4 July 1658, when some randomly used their weapons.[15] The board of the dean – a function assumed by one of the burgomasters and eight captains of the civil guard – was therefore vested with the powers of a lower urban court so as to intervene in interpersonal conflicts between members of the civil guard, to counteract disorder and to ensure compliance with regulations, among others on the guard duties of members.[16] Again, this relieved the Court of Aldermen from a heavier case load.

Professional associations also heard disputes. In Dutch cities, close to half of the population were members of a guild, which shows the importance of dispute settlement by these bodies. They comprised another array of non-governmental forums for dispute settlement that were actively encouraged by the city government, who conferred far-reaching prerogatives on craft guilds to arbitrate and adjudicate conflicts that related to their trade and their guild membership (Dekker, 1985). The heads of the glaziers' guild met for instance once every two weeks and received 1 guilder for every dispute brought before them, to be paid by the party who was found guilty. Members who failed to turn up after being summonsed by the guild council were fined. The primary aim of the heads of the guild was to try to reconcile the two parties, yet if they failed they were entitled to impose an agreement. Members of the trade guild were the main users of these non-governmental courts for dispute settlement, although clients could use these courts as well, for instance if they disagreed about the invoice they were supposed to pay.[17]

A fourth group of non-governmental bodies for dispute settlement in seventeenth-century Leiden were the Church councils who oversaw their congregants. Since the beginning of the Dutch Revolt in the late sixteenth century, the Dutch Reformed Church had become the so-called 'public church' in the Dutch Republic, though other confessions, notably Roman Catholicism, were tolerated if not practised in public. According to a survey from the early nineteenth century, 22.6 per cent of Leiden's population in the mid-eighteenth century was of the Roman Catholic faith, and 72.7 per cent was of the Dutch Reformed confession. Furthermore, so-called Old Catholics, Walloon Reformed, Remonstrant Reformed and Lutheran churches also existed in early modern Leiden (Tjalsma, 1985, p. 37). These churches all had their own councils who oversaw the harmonious co-existence of the members, and who imposed disciplinary sanctions to encourage congregants to maintain the peace. To be sure, the 'members' (*lidmaten*) of the Dutch Reformed Church constituted a minority among the wider community of Dutch Reformed practitioners. Members in the strict sense participated in the common Holy Communion, which echoed their union with Christ's body and denoted their belonging to the confined community of believers. Apart from the smaller group of strict members, there was a much larger group of so-called 'worshippers' (*liefhebbers*) who had rather loose ties to the local church, using it for celebrating life events such as baptism, marriage and burial, yet being less subject to Church discipline. The discipline meted out by the Dutch Reformed Church board, including the settlement of interpersonal conflicts, mostly regarded members in the strictest sense. If such members had infringed certain moralities, they could be temporarily excluded from the common Holy Communion until they improved their behaviour, settled their differences and showed remorse (Roodenburg, 1990). The Church courts represented the forum that was least encouraged by the city government as a means of assisting in the settlement of conflicts among Leiden inhabitants. To avoid conflicts among the various confessional communities who inhabited the city of Leiden, the Reformed Church board was discouraged and even prohibited from using disciplinary measures against non-members (Overvoorde, 1912; Koppenol, 1998).[18]

Lastly, notaries played a key role in the settlement of conflicts among citizens. They basically earned a living by writing documents for co-citizens just as other literate men did, yet notarial documents had relatively more legal value because notaries had been formally admitted by the Court of Holland, a High Court, and because their writings were organised along a standard pattern, including a well-defined date and location, a clear-cut identification of the parties involved and the signatures of witnesses (Leeuwen, 1664, part 20, art. 15–9). The wide range of notarial documents also encompassed semi-procedural documents. For instance, in so-called 'attestations' (*attestaties*) one party who was in conflict with another formally had his or her account of the events registered as well as the accounts of witnesses. Another semi-procedural document was the so-called 'insinuation' (*insinuatie*), which helped to formally remind someone of a mutual agreement, more often than not regarding financial charges. If such an insinuation remained unanswered it could be followed by a 'protest-action' (*protestactie*), which formally protested the non-compliance with a mutual agreement (Gehlen, 1986). These documents did not necessarily serve as full evidence in the court case that possibly followed the conflict, yet when the party then swore an oath on such a document, it helpfully became an element of proof. Semi-procedural documents that had been drafted shortly after the events especially bore credibility in a court case (Pitlo, 1948). Notarial archives thus contain a treasure trove of documents created in the context of conflicts that often never reached the stage of a formal court case. They show, in particular, the ways litigants used formal judicial infrastructures as part of a wider range of forums for dispute settlement, as will be further evidenced below.

Practice – instrumental use of forums for dispute settlement

All in all, the city government made several efforts to institute infra-judicial institutions and encourage extra-judicial institutions to serve as shifters to handle some of the rising number of conflicts that surfaced in sixteenth- and seventeenth-century Leiden. They envisioned a certain order in which inhabitants first and foremost applied to neighbourhood supervisors to intervene in their conflicts before turning to the Commission for Neighbourly Disputes or the peacemakers. Recourse to the *vierschaar* was only permitted when the Commission for Neighbourly Disputes or the peacemakers had failed to help the parties settle their differences. The mediation activities of notaries, the professional associations and the civil guard were also supported by the city government, and had to be addressed before taking legal recourse to the Court of Aldermen.

In this section, the functioning of this pyramid of conflict settlement is examined in actual practice. This is not an easy task, since the diverse institutions for conflict settlement have left uneven archival resources. It is hardly surprising that the more formal the method of conflict settlement, the more archival traces it has left. Notably the numerous interventions in the context of professional associations, neighbourhood associations and civil guards have largely remained under-registered, since these institutions operated chiefly orally and informally. The archival resources produced by the Peacemaker Court and the Court of Aldermen, conversely, contain numerous cases. In 1664 alone, the peacemakers heard no fewer than 4,193 cases, and the *vierschaar* 1,572 cases in the course of the years 1664–1668. It is tempting to consider these formal institutions of conflict settlement as more substantial. Almost certainly, however, this goes against historic reality. An overview of the numbers of cases that were included in the database for each forum is presented in Table 8.1.

The source materials that are preserved in the Leiden city archives do, however, make it possible to examine to a certain extent whether the judicial, infra-judicial and extra-judicial channels of dispute settlement cooperated in the ways intended by the late-sixteenth-century urban government. Let us start with the types of case matter brought by Leiden inhabitants to the diverse institutes. Whereas the neighbourhood supervisors mostly assisted the settlement of conflicts relating to defamation, boundary partitioning and familial conflicts, professional associations unsurprisingly settled differences that ensued from the breaking of guild rules or from debt cases between clients and guildsmen. As for the latter, there are important differences between guilds. For instance, the board of the glaziers' guild mostly handled conflicts related to the infringement of guild regulations, and to a lesser extent conflicts related to debts.[19] The board of the barber-surgeons' guild, on the other hand, was mainly occupied with settling debt cases.[20] Less material conflicts, for instance regarding defamation, did not surface in the archival sources of trade guilds. Apparently, guild members preferred other forums for such disputes, notably the notaries or the Peacemaker Court. The civil guard was mostly occupied with prosecuting the infringement of regulations, and handled only a limited number of conflicts relating to defamation or the use of violence.[21] The Church boards mostly dealt with cases regarding familial disturbances and misconduct among members. To be sure, in the eighteenth century, the Church boards also heard conflicts among non-members, for instance regarding paternity. They then summonsed

TABLE 8.1 Overview of number of cases examined

Judicial forum	*Period*	*Number of cases*	*Yearly average*
Peacemakers	1664	4,193	4,193
Court of Aldermen (civil)	1664–1668	1572	314
Notaries (4)	1664–1668	575	115
Professional associations (5)	1664–1668	405	81
Church councils (3)	1664–1668	254	51
Civil guard	1664–1668	93	19
Court of Aldermen (criminal)	1664–1668	109	22
Commission Neighbourly Disputes	1664–1668	47	9
Total		7,248	4,804

Sources: ORA, inv. nrs. 3, 2H, 2I, 4, 44F-G, 48G; Oud Notarieel Archief, inv. nrs. 774–782, 904, 908, 964–8, 1044–8; Gildenarchief, inv. nrs. 12, 23 and 29, 314, 390, 382, 523–4; Kerkeraadsarchieven Nederduits Gereformeerde Kerk, inv. nr. F1808; Archief Waalse Kerk, inv. nr. 44; Archief Doopsgezinde Gemeente, inv. nr. 1; Archief Schutterij, inv. nr. 8.

women and men involved in the birth of bastard babies, and were instrumental in inciting formal recourse at the Court of Aldermen over paternity. The Church board notably used the withholding of baptism rituals as a means of making women and men who had conceived illegitimate babies promise to improve their ways (Vermeesch, 2016). The case matter handled by these forums was not necessarily fixed throughout the early modern period. As suggested before, however, many conflicts handled by these extra-judicial institutes may have remained unregistered.

The nature of the well-documented cases handled by notaries, the Peacemaker Court and the Court of Aldermen is less problematic to imagine. As will be explained further below, 709 acts of a semi-processual nature of the four most active notaries of the city of Leiden have been selected for this research, which related to 575 single conflicts. These acts predominantly comprised 615 attestations, relating to 480 issues over the years 1664–1668. Certainly, not all these issues will have amounted to a conflict, as attestations could also be drafted to impede the possible development of a conflict. For instance, a pupil of a guilds master could ask a notary to draft an attestation that included testimonies proving that he had fulfilled his contract in terms of the number of years he had served. No judicial conflict would then arise, but the attestation may have been crucial in averting a potential conflict. From the 480 conflicts that surfaced in the 615 attestations, 26 per cent related to personal misconduct, 6 per cent concerned familial disputes and 34 per cent involved contracts and agreements.[22] The latter category of conflicts dominated the business of the Peacemaker Court and the Court of Aldermen, as can be seen in Table 8.2 below.

The Peacemaker Court was rarely used for settling familial disputes. This type of conflict mostly related to disputes between husband and wife, or relating to paternity. They were mainly dealt with by Church boards and notaries. The latter could provide services that proved convenient when the disputes escalated to a fully fledged case at the Court of Aldermen. The peacemakers' summary way of dealing with conflicts was considered unfit for familial disputes, which were habitually too complex. If extra-judicial bodies failed to achieve an agreement between the quarrelling parties, the Court of Aldermen was the proper body for helping to resolve the differences. Disagreements relating to 'personal misconduct' mostly

TABLE 8.2 Case matter at Peacemaker Court and Court of Aldermen

Category	*Peacemaker Court (1664)*		*Court of Aldermen (1664–1668)*	
	Total	*percentage*	*Total*	*Percentage*
Personal misconduct	270	13	31	2
Familial disputes	7	<1	62	4
Contracts and agreements	1939	87	1461	94
	2216	100	1554	100

Sources: ORA, inv. nr. 44 F, G; 47 2H, 2I.

involved conflicts over defamation. The peacemakers handled no fewer than 168 such conflicts in 1664, which amounted to many more than those that could be traced in the registers of neighbourhood supervisors or in the notarial attestations. This is noteworthy, because the city government had intended defamation to be settled by extra-judicial bodies, for instance by the Church boards, the notaries or the neighbourhood supervisors. This is already an indication that Leiden inhabitants made other choices in the institutions they picked for taking recourse to than was intended by the city government. The peacemakers proved rather successful in having injuring words withdrawn by the defendant. In over 60 per cent of cases they ordered the defendant to beg the plaintiff for forgiveness.

Both the Peacemaker Court and the Court of Aldermen were first and foremost used for mediating and adjudicating disputes about contracts and agreements. At the Peacemaker Court, over 70 per cent of these disputes related to debts, and another 23 per cent related to rented property. Interpersonal debts were ubiquitous in the early modern context. The general scarcity of currency meant that most people used credit for their daily purchases. Others borrowed money through obligations or other instruments of credit and many of these loans were extended through oral agreements. Summonsing debtors before the peacemakers proved an efficient way of reclaiming the borrowed money. In practice, defaulters only seldom denied their debt since failure to pay often stemmed from inability to pay rather than unwillingness to do so. In 30 per cent of cases, the peacemakers instructed payment of the debt in instalments, and in 14 per cent a postponement of payment was imposed. Only 28 per cent of the debtors were ordered to pay right away. The large majority of the group of creditors who took recourse to the Peacemaker Court were retailers who had extended credit and risked becoming unable to meet their own financial obligations. The conflicts about rented property also suggest creditors only took legal recourse regarding debts when they were about to get into difficulty themselves. While the rent was usually paid weekly, landlords on average only took recourse to the peacemakers after seven months of defaulting. The Court of Aldermen dealt with debts and contracts that amounted to sums much larger than the ones heard by the peacemakers. The registers of the Court of Aldermen show how chains of interdependent credit permeated the city of Leiden. Of the 885 creditors who were traced in judicial archives, 16 per cent surfaced elsewhere as debtors. The grain merchant Hendrick Roelantsz. van der Does, for instance, filed nineteen cases against debtors in the years 1664–1668, mostly against bakers, and was summonsed twelve times regarding debts by his own suppliers. Two-thirds of the putative debts amounted to sums above 100 guilders, and more than a quarter involved sums larger than 500 guilders.

To what extent, then, did litigants respect the hierarchy of forums that were designated by the city government? For instance, did they indeed address the Peacemaker Court before taking recourse at the Court of Aldermen? Almost 40 per cent of the debt cases that came before the Court of Aldermen had actually first appeared before the peacemakers. However, according to the relevant regulations, this should have been the case for all debt disputes, no matter how high the sum under contention. Although the massive case load of the Peacemaker Court attests to its attractiveness among the Leiden population, the fact that 60 per cent of debt cases at the Court of Aldermen had not passed through the peacemakers is revealing for the limited extent to which it fulfilled its role as buffer. Over a hundred creditors skipped the Peacemaker Court, in spite of regulations on court use, and unswervingly took recourse at the Court of Aldermen that was in effect a court of first instance. In cases that had dutifully been addressed to the peacemakers, an average of 24 days elapsed between the peacemaker session and that of the Court of Aldermen. Most of these debts proved hard to mediate; they amounted to sums higher that the limit of competence of the peacemakers, and necessitated firmer intervention by the aldermen. The peacemakers therefore straightforwardly redirected such cases to the Court of Aldermen. However, it appears that the majority of cases redirected by the peacemakers did not surface in the registers of the Court of Aldermen after all. This is a strong indication that the expensive, complicated and time-consuming procedures of the Court of Aldermen deterred quite a few litigants. Although it is impossible to assess the outcome of these withdrawn cases, the imminent start of a court case may often have sufficed to reach an out-of-court settlement.

The Peacemaker Court and the Court of Aldermen also attracted a considerable case load that was intended to be dealt with by the Commission for Neighbourly Disputes. In 1583, it had been specifically stipulated that the peacemakers were not to interfere in neighbourly disputes. Nonetheless, they handled a similar number of such conflicts in 1664 as the Commission for Neighbourly Disputes, respectively sixteen and fifteen cases. The Court of Aldermen handled nine such cases in 1664 in the first instance. The Peacemaker Court was ostensibly the most popular forum among the urban courts, conceivably because it was markedly inexpensive and sat several times a week. Moreover, the peacemakers did not visit the location of the conflict, and were particularly functional for conflicts that were not overly complex, or for conflicts that needed the appointment of arbitrators who could intervene extra-judicially. The Commission for Neighbourly Disputes was rather called to intervene in conflicts that involved serious local unrest.[23] All things considered, it appears that inhabitants made their own choices regarding the institutions they took recourse to for dispute settlement, disregarding the intentions of the city government.

There are additional indications for seventeenth-century court use in Leiden that deviated from the norms imposed by the late-sixteenth-century city government. As was explained above, the neighbourhood supervisors had been intended to become pivotal figures in forum use and gatekeepers who were to relieve the burden of the urban courts as much as possible by settling petty conflicts mainly locally, in the neighbourhoods. They were also expected to avoid the escalation of conflicts into broader and more threatening disturbances. Although quite a few contemporaries expressed their confidence about the way neighbourhood supervisors effectively intervened in interpersonal conflicts, this emerges much less clearly from the sources that have been preserved. To be sure, source materials are scarce and all the evidence is by necessity indirect. There are no registers of verdicts, and accounts only contain the amounts of fines received and never mention the reason for claiming them. Moreover, conflicts that were successfully mediated potentially left disproportionally few traces in the preserved registers. It appears that the above-mentioned accounts of contemporaries are the only straightforward indications for the success of conflict settlement by neighbourhood associations, yet those sources are not unambiguous. Authors such as the above-mentioned De Parival, for instance, did not target a detailed and nuanced report on the operation of neighbourhood associations, but included this in a glorification of the county of Holland (De Parival, 1660).

The activities of neighbourhood supervisors appear most clearly in the attestations drawn up by notaries, which indicate that they were often less present in dispute settlement among neighbours than might have been expected. One attestation by notary Leonardt Jansz. van Overmeer, dating from 1661, particularly sheds light on the duties performed by a neighbourhood supervisor called Frans Arentz. van Overzee. In 1665, grave marital problems arose between Michiel Willemsz. and Jannetje Andriesz. Michiel had been widowed twice before marrying Jannetje. They were an unhappy couple. He was often drunk, earned little and repeatedly mistreated his wife. Five years into the marriage, the problems had escalated. When Michiel threatened Jannetje with a knife, the neighbours intervened. After many attempts to calm Michiel, the neighbours appealed to neighbourhood supervisor Van Overzee at night, when the situation in the household had again worsened. However, Van Overzee was asleep, and could not be woken (he was possibly ill), so his wife accompanied the neighbours to Michiel's house. Years later, the couple came before the Court of Aldermen, because Jannetje sought a formal separation.[24] This attestation is informative in several ways. First, the role of the wife of the supervisor is revealing. Neighbourhood supervisors were busy men, who could not be approached for every petty conflict that arose in their neighbourhood. Van Overzee, for instance, was also a steward of the urban finances. The wives of neighbourhood supervisors often performed their duties in the realm of conflict settlement. Second, the attestation especially shows how neighbours self-reliantly assumed intervention in conflicts, and in some instances, after many years and efforts, only approached their neighbourhood supervisor as a last resort. This is also underpinned by testimonies in other attestations.[25]

However, inhabitants often even bypassed supervisors when conflicts became critical, and directly addressed the Peacemaker Court, the notaries or other forums for dispute settlement. Quite a few attestations regarding defamation were drafted by notaries on the same day the conflict emerged, indicating that no neighbourhood supervisor was asked to intervene. This can also be seen from the story of Louwijsge Salomonsdr, whose husband threw her out of her house during a quarrel in 1668, and challenged her to call the neighbourhood supervisor. She, however, responded by re-entering the house and slapping him in the face. In this instance, there was no intervention by the neighbourhood supervisor.[26] Another indication of the reduced role of neighbourhood supervisors in conflict settlement is the limited number of fines they claimed, as appears from their account books. In theory, a wide range of fines could be imposed for fights on the street or at home, for defamation, and for bypassing the neighbourhood supervisor when initiating a formal lawsuit. If the supervisors had performed their duties as the city government had intended them to, their account books would have been well filled with fines collected among neighbours. The account book of the 'Billenburg' neighbourhood, with a population of some 700 people, however, contains no more than 56 fines over a period of twenty years.[27] Lastly, the fact that neighbourhood supervisors were hardly ever called by the Court of Aldermen as witnesses when hearing cases is revealing of their reduced involvement in dispute settlement.

All in all, rather than being pivotal figures, neighbourhood supervisors appear to have been just one among many forums for dispute settlement in early modern Leiden. There are several reasons for the fact that practice did not comply with the prescribed norm. First, neighbourhood supervisors had been intended to represent the city government among inhabitants in the neighbourhoods. In actual fact, such supervisors demonstrated divided loyalties as horizontal ties in the neighbourhood interfered with vertical ties with the city government. Habitually imposing fines would most certainly not have benefitted their position in their communities. Second, neighbourhoods were often too large for supervisors to be able to follow up all kinds of clashes and disagreements. By the late seventeenth century, the city had grown immensely, as had the number of houses and inhabitants in the respective neighbourhoods. As early as the early seventeenth century some supervisors complained of the inability to organise communal meals and funerals in view of the large numbers of inhabitants, let alone intervene in the many conflicts that arose from the close proximity in which numerous 'conditions and humours' co-habited.[28] Thirdly, it may be the case that quite a few inhabitants experienced difficulties in overcoming the large social distances between themselves and their neighbourhood supervisors. Intended as being the local representatives of the city government, the supervisors typically belonged to the city's wealthier middling groups.[29] Some wealth was required so that the more prosperous neighbours would acknowledge the authority of the supervisor. Less-moneyed neighbours may well have experienced some hurdles in addressing the supervisor.

If neighbourhood supervisors were not very successful in their role of gatekeeper, notaries appear to have been more effective in diverting conflict matter away from the urban benches. The database underlying this research includes the 709 acts of semi-processual nature – relating to 575 cases – that were drafted by four notaries of the city of Leiden who were active during the period from 1664 to 1668. At the time, there were no fewer than thirty notaries in Leiden, yet not all of them were equally active or have passed on records. The four notaries whose registers have been explored have been randomly selected from among the most active ones. Attestations appear to have been the most frequent type of act (i.e. among those of a semi-processual nature). No fewer than 615 of the 709 acts were formally registered statements by witnesses who had been asked by one party – who was in conflict with another – to testify before the notary. Almost 60 per cent of the witnesses were neighbours of the individual who had initiated the drafting of an attestation, 9 per cent were colleagues and only 2 per cent were members of the individual's family.[30] The notary played more than a passive role in this kind of dispute settlement. He turned witness accounts into authoritatively utilisable acts. He also interrogated the witnesses without the presence of the parties involved in the conflict so as to obtain a sensible account. Registering the truth was not necessarily the purpose, although straightforward lies must have been rare as well. Rather, notaries asked questions and selected answers in such a way that those facts that were most beneficial to the client were recorded. The client, after all, had paid the notary as a strategy to prevail in the conflict (Roodenburg, 1992; Zemon Davis, 1987).

It is of interest to assess to what extent the conflicts that prompted the drafting of attestations resurfaced in the urban courts. Cross-linkage of cases between the notarial archives on the one hand and the records of the Court of Aldermen on the other shows that attestations were predominantly used to warn counterparties and were particularly targeted at keeping the conflict matter outside the formal law courts. They appear to have been successful in doing so. No more than 4.5 per cent of inhabitants who had asked a notary to draft an attestation in the final event took legal recourse at the Court of Aldermen. An attestation appears to have been a firm signal to the counterparty that a litigant was willing to go to court and defend his claims. Similarly, counterparties sometimes invited a notary to register a counter-statement. This type of dispute settlement had the marked advantage of limiting the costs and speeding up the procedure. In legal processes before the Court of Aldermen, witness accounts were characteristically scheduled in the later stages of judicial proceedings, when much time and money had already been spent. The threat of such arduous procedures was an effective way of gaining victory over the counterparty. In all probability, the use of notaries was the only means of formal dispute settlement that lower-middling groups could afford. Although it is impossible to estimate the number of conflicts that were successfully settled owing to the notaries' services, it seems that they were worthy alternatives for formal legal recourse given the limited number of attestations that were actually used in lawsuits.

To what extent did Leiden inhabitants bypass prescribed forums, that is, use a range of alternative institutions for conflict settlement? Considering the records for the diverse judicial forums as a whole, the indication is that forum hopping occurred only to a limited extent. To be sure, only a limited number of notaries have been included in the research and various forums under-registered their conflict-settling activities. For the year 1664, the database contains 121 cases that were conducted before more than one forum. Unsurprisingly, the most common combination of forums is the Peacemaker Court and the Court of Aldermen, with 80 per cent of the 121 cases. Defamation was the only case matter that made parties invite notaries before addressing the peacemakers. This is striking, as attestations were first and foremost drafted with the intention of using them in a formal lawsuit before the Court of Aldermen. It may well be that these inhabitants preferred the peacemakers because of their promptness and their low cost.

Another question of interest to the users of justice relates to the gender balance. Table 8.3 shows the percentages respectively of men and women active as plaintiffs before the Peacemaker Court, the Court of Aldermen and the notaries, for each kind of dispute. Men dominated court business, as they dominated the most voluminous type of conflict, i.e. disputes over conflicts and agreements. However, women played a larger role in dispute settlement than the regulations would allow for. Again, there appears to be a discrepancy between the prescribed norm and practice. Formally, women could only take legal recourse with the assistance of their father, husband or another male guardian. However, quite a few women single-handedly initiated a case at the Peacemaker Court as well as asking notaries to draft an attestation. Notably, conflicts regarding familial disputes were started, above average, by women. Conflicts on agreements and contracts were predominantly waged by men. Such disputes involved entire households, yet they were understandably waged by the head of household, who was by default a man. The women involved in such disputes were more often than not widows.

A final element regarding the uses of justice in early modern Leiden that needs to be discussed relates to the social profile of users. The relative use of judicial, infra-judicial and extra-judicial forums for dispute settlement in all probability differed among the various wealth groups. As appears from Table 8.4, the Leiden urban courts were mostly used by middling groups of independent guildsmen, tradesmen and shopkeepers. It should, however, be mentioned that the professions of only 40 per cent of all plaintiffs and defendants could be extracted from the sources. Moreover, the occupation of 30 per cent of the plaintiffs was given as 'legal spokesman' (*procureur*); such a person acted as a rule on behalf of an otherwise unidentified party. The occupational structure that emerges from the tax register of 1674 is included in the table, to enable comparison to the (taxable) Leiden population as a whole.

Wage-dependent individuals and their families predominated in early modern Leiden, but seemed to remain largely absent from the Leiden courts. It is possible that the city's many textile workers disproportionally failed to mention their profession when appearing in the judicial and notarial records. Research into the clientele of the Leiden Peacemaker Court in mid-eighteenth-century Leiden, however, confirms its relatively elitist nature. This was achieved by cross-linking the names of a sample of plaintiffs and defendants during the years 1750–1754 and

TABLE 8.3 Percentages of male and female plaintiffs

	Personal misconduct		*Familial disputes*		*Contracts and agreements*	
	Men	*Women*	*Men*	*Women*	*Men*	*Women*
Peacemaker Court	52	48	57	43	83	17
Court of Aldermen	93	7	52	48	86	14
Notaries	76	24	39	61	77	23

TABLE 8.4 Occupations of plaintiffs (N = 2706) and defendants (N = 1149) in Leiden, 1664–1668, in percentages

Occupational sector	*Plaintiffs*	*Defendants*	*Tax register 1674*
Liberal professions	36	11	7
Trade and traffic	21	22	30
Manufacturing	19	38	33
Textile	12	18	19
Government	5	1	2
Services	1	3	4
Agriculture	<1	1	2
Other	6	6	3
Total	100	100	100

a census of 1749 comprising socioeconomic data for the entire Leiden population. The lower 60 per cent of the population filed just 14 per cent of the complaints. The poorest 20 per cent of the city's inhabitants rarely appeared in court, either as plaintiffs or as defendants. There were slightly more plaintiffs and defendants among the second and third quintiles, yet their participation in the business of the Peacemaker Court was limited, especially as plaintiffs. Households from the fourth and fifth quintiles appear to have been the foremost users of the Peacemaker Court. These households were mostly headed by the guildsmen, manufacturers and shopkeepers who also surface in Table 8.4 (Vermeesch, 2015). These people performed a key role in the Leiden economy and were particularly vulnerable to defaulting clients. Hence the marked popularity of the Peacemaker Court to swiftly deal with debts. These people also scrupulously protected their reputations, and did not hesitate to mobilise notaries and peacemakers to counteract insults. Yet representatives of this group were also particularly cautious about pursuing their counterparty too aggressively, and were therefore often prepared to settle out of court. In short, they made choices that best fitted their personal interests, and thus helped shape judicial infrastructures in early modern Leiden.

Conclusions

In this article, norms and practices in dispute settlement in early modern Leiden have been discussed for a wide range of judicial, infra-judicial and extra-judicial forums. A total of 7,248 conflicts have been examined for the years 1664–1668, that were waged before neighbourhood supervisors, guilds, the civil guard, professional associations, notaries, peacemakers, the Commission for Neighbourly Disputes and the Court of Aldermen. The most time-consuming and expensive route for dispute settlement was undoubtedly to be experienced at the Court of Aldermen. The late-sixteenth-century city government sought ways to divert conflicts away from the urban court by encouraging extra-judicial dispute settlement and by installing a number of infra-judicial institutions. They, for instance, planned for neighbourhood supervisors to act as pivotal figures in the settlement of disputes on the spot. They also demanded that parties should first appear before the Peacemaker Court before taking formal legal recourse at the Court of Aldermen. An analysis of the way this wide range of forums for dispute settlement functioned in actual practice revealed that the Leiden inhabitants often made their own choices regarding the forums they addressed. In more than one sense, the neighbourhood supervisors' agendas for instance did not allow for intervening in all disputes among their neighbours. Contrary to the regulations, the majority of parties who took legal recourse at the Court of Aldermen simply bypassed the Peacemaker Court before doing so. And quite a few parties who had been redirected by the peacemakers to the Court of Aldermen eventually sought settlement of their dispute out of court.

The extent to which conflicts never reached the urban courts is most clearly revealed by the registers of the notaries. They were active in drafting witness accounts regarding conflicts or potential conflicts, which often sufficed to settle disputes without formal recourse. Although these so-called attestations were drafted to be used in formal procedures at the Court of Aldermen if the counterparty was unwilling to yield, more than 95 per cent of these acts were never used in court. This denotes the sheer immensity of the volume of conflicts that never made an appearance in the court records. To this may be added the finding that only particular sections of the Leiden population surfaced in the records of the diverse institutions for dispute settlement. Notably economically independent families who belonged to the middling groups appear to have used judicial infrastructures. The masses of wage-dependent inhabitants active in the local textile manufactures hardly found their way to the Peacemaker Court or the notaries, let alone the Court of Aldermen. The fact that many conflicts did not appear before the urban courts does not, however, refute their importance for the Leiden community. For many inhabitants who found themselves in conflict with a fellow citizen, the threat of being summonsed before these institutions was reason enough to be prepared to come to an agreement. Conceivably, judicial institutions did not necessarily have to be used by all inhabitants involved in disputes in order to be useful.

Notes

1 The research underlying this article is extensively discussed in the monograph written by Aries van Meeteren (2006).
2 Regionaal Archief Leiden (henceforth RAL), Bibliotheek Leiden en Omgeving, 16804, Vredemakerskeur, 1598.
3 RAL, Old Judicial Archives (henceforth ORA), inv. nr. 44 F, G.
4 RAL, Stadsarchief 1572–1816 (henceforth SAII), inv. nr 12, pp. 268–9.
5 RAL, SAII, inv. nr. 12, p. 269vv, art 14.
6 RAL, Bibliotheek Leiden en Omgeving, 15271pf, Maanen, Leidse keurboeken van 1583, 1657 en 1658.
7 RAL, SAII, inv. nr. 9, p. 94.
8 RAL, Bibliotheek Leiden en Omgeving, 16804, Vredemakerskeur, 1598.
9 RAL, Bibliotheek Leiden en Omgeving, 16807pf, art. 13, 16808-10pl; Algemene bibliotheek Regionaal Archief Leiden, 1051f, Groot Placaet-boeck IV, p. 477, art. 14.

10 RAL, ORA, inv. nr. 47 2H–2K.
11 RAL, SAII, inv. nr. 1220, p. 8.
12 RAL, SAII, inv. nr. 16, p. 58v (4-3-1593), inv. nr. 1220, art. 1.
13 RAL, SAII, inv. nr. 1220, p. 35a.
14 RAL, SAII, inv. nr. 16, p. 176v (1-4-1599), Archief Schutterij, inv. nr. 164.
15 RAL, SAII, inv. nr. 189, (4-7-1658).
16 RAL, SAII, inv. nr. 15, p. 50v.
17 RAL, Gildenarchieven, inv. nr. 504.
18 RAL, SAII, inv. nr. 3417 (30-5-1586).
19 RAL, Gildenarchieven, inv. nrs. 523–4.
20 RAL, Gildenarchieven, inv. nrs. 314, 382, 390.
21 RAL, AS, inv. nr. 8.
22 RAL, Old Notarial Archives, inv. nr. 774–782, 904–908, 964–968, 1044–1048.
23 RAL, ORA, inv.nr. 48G; inv. nr. 27 2H, 2I.
24 RAL, ONA, inv. nr. 965, nr. 15 (28-1-1665), 17 (30–1-1665) en 29 (28–2-1665); SAII, inv. nr. 24, p. 50.
25 See for instance RAL, ONA, inv. nr. 776, nr. 251 (13-7-1665); inv. nr. 777; nr. 371 (23–4-1665).
26 RAL, ONA, inv. nr. 782, nr. 510 (10-12-1668).
27 RAL, SAII, inv. nr. 6960.
28 RAL, SAII, inv. nr. 1216, p. 23–24; inv. nr. 1221, 3b.
29 RAL, SAII, inv. nr. 1217.
30 RAL, ONA, inv. nr. 1044–1048.

References

Blaufarb, R. (2010). Conflict and compromise: *Communauté* and *Seigneurie* in early modern Provence. *The Journal of Modern History*, 82, pp. 519–545.

Blok, P.J. (1884). *Leidsche rechtsbronnen in de Middeleeuwen*. Den Haag: Martinus Nijhoff.

Brachtendorf, R. (2003). *Konflikte, Devianz, Kriminalität: Justiznutzung und Strafpraxis on Kurtrier im 18. Jahrhundert am Beispiel des Amts Cochem*. Marburg: Tectum Verlag.

Davids, C.A. (1985). De migratiebeweging in Leiden in de achttiende eeuw. In: H.A. Diederiks, D.J. Noordam and H.D. Tjalsma, eds. *Armoede en sociale spanning. Sociaal-historische studies over Leiden in de achttiende eeuw*. Hilversum: Verloren, pp. 137–156.

De Parival, J. (1660). *De vermaeckelijckheden van Hollandt. Een werck deses lands Lof uijtbasuijnend met een tractaet van de regeeringe end' een kort begrijp van 't gene aenmerckenswaerigst voorgevallen is tot en met jaar 1655*. Amsterdam: Samuel Imbrechts.

Deceulaer, H. (1996). Guilds and litigation: conflict settlement in Antwerp (1585–1796). In: M. Boone and M. Prak, eds., *Individual, corporate, and judicial status in European cities (late Middle Ages and early modern period)*. Leuven, Apeldoorn: Garant, pp. 171–206.

Dekker, R.M. (1985). Arbeidsconflicten in de Leidse textielindustrie. In: Herman A. Diederiks, D.J. Noordam and H.D. Tjalsma, eds. *Armoede en sociale spanning. Sociaal-historische studies over Leiden in de achttiende eeuw*. Hilversum: Verloren, pp. 69–86.

Dinges, M. (2000). Justiznutzung als sozialle Kontrolle in der Frühen Neuzeit. In: A. Blauert and G. Schwerthoff, eds., *Kriminalutätsgeschichte: Beiträge zur Sozial- und Kultur geschichte der Vormoderne*, Konstanz: UVK Universitätsverlag, pp. 503–544.

Dinges, M. (2004). The uses of justice as a form of social control in early modern Europe. In: H. Roodenburg and P. Spierenburg, eds., *Social control in Europe 1500–1800*, Columbus: Ohio State University Press, pp. 159–175.

Garnot, B. (1996). *L'infrajudiciaire du Moyen Age à l'époque contemporaine. Actes du colloque de Dijon 5–6 Octobre 1995*. Dijon: Editions Universitaires de Dijon.

Gehlen, A. Fl. (1986). *Notariële akten uit de 17de en 18de eeuw. Handleiding voor gebruikers.* Zutphen: Walburg Pers.

Hardwick, J. (2009). *Family business. Litigation and the political economies of daily life in early modern France.* Oxford: Oxford University Press.

Heijden, M. van der (2013). Women, violence and urban justice in Holland c. 1600–1838. *Crime, History and Societies*, 17, pp. 71–100.

Heijden, M. van der (2016). *Women and crime in early modern Holland.* Leiden, Boston: Brill.

Heijden, M. van der and Pluskota, M. (2015). Leniency versus toughening? The prosecution of male and female violence in 19th-century Holland. *Journal of Social History*, 49, pp. 149–167.

Kamp, J. and Schmidt, A. (2018). 'Getting justice': a comparative perspective on illegitimacy and the use of justice in Holland and Germany, 1600–1800. *Journal of Social History*, 51, pp. 672–692.

King, P. (2004). Summary courts and social relations in eighteenth-century England. *Past and Present*, 183, pp. 125–172.

Knevel, P. (1994). *Burgers in het geweer. De schutterijen in Holland, 1550–1700.* Hilversum: Verloren.

Koppenol, J. (1998). *Leids heelal. Het loterijspel (1596) van Jan van Hout.* Hilversum: Verloren.

Leeuwen, S. van. (1664). *Het Rooms-Hollands-Regt waarin de roomse wetten met het huydendaegse Neerlands regt, in alles dat tot de dagelijkse onderhouding kan dienen, met een bijsondere kortheijt, so wel inde vaste regts-stoffen als in de manier van regts-vordering over een gebragt werden.* Leiden, Rotterdam: Hackens.

Mather, L. and Yngvesson, B. (1980–1). Language, audience and the transformation of disputes. *Law and Society Review*, 15, pp. 775–821.

Meeteren, A. van (2006). *Op hoop van akkoord. Instrumenteel forumgebruik bij geschilbeslechting in Leiden in de zeventiende eeuw.* Hilversum: Verloren.

Overvoorde, J.C. (1912). Advies van burgemeesters en gerecht van Leiden aan de Staten van Holland over de acta van de in 1578 te Dordrecht gehouden synode. *Nederlands archief voor kerkgeschiedenis*, 9, pp. 117–149.

Pitlo, A. (1948). *De zeventiende en achtiende eeuwsche notarisboeken en wat zij ons omtrent het oude notariaat leren.* Haarlem: Tjeenk Willink.

Roodenburg, H.W. (1990). *Onder censuur. De kerkelijke tucht in de gereformeerde gemeente van Amsterdam 1578–1700.* Hilversum: Verloren.

Roodenburg, H.W. (1992). De notaris en de erehandel. Beledigingen voor het Amsterdamse notariaat 1700–1710. *Volkskundig Bulletin*, 18, pp. 367–388.

Roodenburg, H.W. (2004). Social control viewed from below: new perspectives. In: H.W. Roodenburg and P.C. Spierenburg, eds., *Social Control in Europe, Volume 1, 1500–1800.* Colombus: Ohio State University Press, pp. 145–158.

Schilling, H. (2004). Discipline: the state and the churches in early modern Europe. In: H.W. Roodenburg and P.C. Spierenburg, eds., *Social Control in Europe, Volume 1, 1500–1800.* Colombus: Ohio State University Press, pp. 25–36.

Shaw, J.E. (2006). *The justice of Venice: authorities and liberties in the urban economy, 1550–1700.* Oxford: Oxford University Press.

Soman, A. (1980). Deviance and criminal justice in Western Europe. *Criminal Justice History*, 1, pp. 1–24.

Spierenburg, P.C. (2004). Social control and history: an introduction. In: H.W. Roodenburg and P.C. Spierenburg, eds., *Social Control in Europe, Volume 1, 1500–1800.* Colombus: Ohio State University Press, pp. 1–22.

Spierz, M.G. (1985). Die Ausübung der Zucht in der IJsselstadt Deventer in den Jahren 1592–1619 im Vergleich zu den Untersuchungen im Languedoc und in der Kurpfalz. *Rheinische Vierteljahrsblätter*, 49, pp. 139–172.

Tjalsma, H.D. (1985). Een karakterisering van Leiden in 1749. In: H.A. Diederiks, D.J. Noordam and H.D. Tjalsma, eds., *Armoede en sociale spanning. Sociaal-historische studies over Leiden in de achttiende eeuw*. Hilversum: Verloren, pp. 17–44.

Vermeesch, G. (2015). The clientele of an eighteenth-century law court: an analysis of plaintiffs and defendants at a small claims court in the Dutch city of Leiden, 1750–1754. *Social History*, 40, pp. 208–229.

Vermeesch, G. (2016). The legal agency of single mothers: lawsuits over illegitimate children and the uses of legal aid to the poor in the Dutch town of Leiden (1750–1810). *Journal of Social History*, 50, pp. 51–73.

von Benda-Beckham, C.E. (1984). *The broken stairways to consensus; village justice and state courts in Minangkabau*. Dordrecht: Foris Publications.

Walle, K. (2005). *Buurthouden. De geschiedenis van burengebruiken en buurtorganisaties in Leiden (14e–19e eeuw)*. Leiden: Ginkgo.

Zemon Davis, N. (1987). *Fiction in the Archives: Pardon Tales and Their Tellers in Sixteenth-Century France*. Cambridge: Cambridge University Press.

9

JUSTICE AND THE CONFINES OF THE LAW IN EARLY MODERN SPAIN[1]

Tomás A. Mantecón

Introduction

On the subject of justice, the research material seems clear. Justice is about understanding behaviours that society has declared intolerable, along with the institutions and people employed to monitor these behaviours, both before and after these behaviours have been identified as criminal. Similarly, it is crucial to know how these crime control instruments are used, and to assess their effectiveness. The problems of daily coexistence test the limits of the law, and it is a permanent challenge in our societies to continually define the law, in order to make it fit for a dynamic and changing daily life. It is therefore logical that the debate should include areas outside the law. This category allows for the identification of areas in which the law ought to express itself unequivocally to explain how even today it is possible to put a price on the head of an international criminal or to fail to abide by the terms of international laws on the treatment of prisoners of war, and more generally the so-called dirty war against organised crime, or breaches of international agreements affecting human rights. Every society has existed with areas of social control both within and outside the law, and has projected them onto every facet of life, from daily life to international relations.

This chapter will not cover areas outside the law, but those that during the Old Regime fell within the limits of the law, although in many cases only just inside it, that is, in settings where official, institutional justice intermingled with its more informal facets. These settings involved the deployment of methods that were no less powerfully aimed at reducing conflict to socially tolerable levels. I will focus on the social uses of justice in building or rebuilding public peace. Many of these areas of justice have been defined as infrajustice.

The debate on this topic has its roots in the historiography of the final decades of the twentieth century and is still far from being closed. In this chapter, the topic is analysed from the perspective of judicial practice. Particular attention will be paid to the ways justice responded to its own logic, and to the challenges thrown up by society. Such an approach to legal history substantially corrects older institutional approaches that, as is now understood, painted a rather distorted image of the process of historical change that put the onus on developments undertaken unilaterally by the elites under the Old Regime. Purely institutional analyses after all involved a teleological reading of the development of modern liberal systems, which were supposedly the result of the triumph of a legal revolution. In other words, justice purportedly became an instrument for the gradual monopolisation of the exercise of discipline and legitimate violence, including a progressive development of the definition of illegal or delinquent behaviours, of judicial institutions and of judicial administration (Gatrell, Lenman and Parker, 1980). Taking the angle of judicial practice, and assessing the actual place of formal law courts in conflict settlement, however, helps us assess the real complexity of historical change, which must have been debated far more extensively among rulers, institutions and those who were governed. Infrajustice involves those settings where such interactions took place.

This chapter will examine infrajustice in early modern Spain. First, international historiography on this concept will be discussed to develop a definition of the concept. Then, the case of Spain will be discussed, and the concept will be further clarified by a number of concrete examples, drawn from some microhistorical studies. A third section will examine the mediators that were central to infrajudicial practice. The chapter will end by suggesting a hypothesis on the relative scale of infrajustice, and how it evolved during the early modern period in Spain. The chapter is based on an analysis of existing historiography, combined with archival research on the case of Cantabria, a northern Spanish region. This will help us define the nature of justice in pre-industrial Spanish society.

Infrajustice: definition of a concept

In 1982, Alfred Soman (Soman, 1980, pp. 3–28; Soman, 1982, pp. 369–376) sensed the problems involved in explaining the complex relationship between rulers and those who were governed, or simply between people of all social groups and the justice system. He stimulated historians of crime to study infrajudicial matters, and proposed that notarial procedures should be consulted, in which documents pertaining to mediation and compensation between litigating parties in civil and criminal cases were registered, in addition to many different kinds of agreements. Soman's preoccupations were shared by other historians. Cynthia Herrup (1987) for instance understood – for seventeenth-century England – the so-called 'common peace' as the result of judicial and infrajudicial actions or forces. David Sabean (1984) studied six historical episodes experienced by residents of Württemberg during the early modern period, and analysed how many conflicts remained outside the courts and were unknown to judges. Such conflicts nevertheless created social control in the community, embodied by individuals and social groups, and by the conjunction of residents brought together by shared principles and interests, or by dominion and its expression through patronage.

Present-day historians are well aware of the fact that not all conflicts came before the courts, and that many were settled with no judicial intervention. Benoît Garnot has, however, warned that the term 'infrajustice' should not be used too lightly (Garnot, 2000, pp. 103–120). By not clearly specifying the aims of infrajustice every time it is referred to, there is a risk of resorting to it as a kind of panacea, given that by including so many things, this category might in no way improve the explanation of any kind of reality and might instead become a form of 'historiographic illusion'. This is a risk that must be avoided. Garnot helpfully offers a specific lexicon to define 'infrajustice', i.e. forms of public and semi-public mediation. He also offers additional concepts, notably 'extrajustice', i.e. proceedings that are complementary to official proceedings, and 'parajustice', strictly private and informal practices that take place out of court.

The term infrajustice thus refers to a phenomenon both specific and hybrid. It refers to the interaction between legal practice and the social uses of justice, or to justice in action, which is to say, the expression of the dialogue between society on the one hand and institutions for responding to situations of conflict and crime, and for rebuilding peace, on the other (Mantecón, 2011, pp. 333–367). This debate has focused as much on the institutional sphere, the courts, as on extrajudicial settings. Both developed a range of formalities. These formalities are a magnificent expression of the historical interaction between positive law, jurisprudence, customs and practices, judicial decisions, and the rationality and culture of the judges and of those who participate in everyday conflict settlement: parties, experts and mediators or arbitrators.

Infrajustice operated in every area of life, but particularly in the more peripheral areas. Sometimes it encouraged mediation and arbitration. At other times its manifestations caused conflicts between increasingly formalised official justice, and the more custom-based, non-systematic forms of justice. The latter largely escaped institutional and governmental control, but were supported by tradition and custom. However, authorities and institutions aimed to channel within the official justice system all the facets of mediation, arbitration, sentencing and sanctions that were deemed legitimate. All this involved the extrajudicial (combined and complementary to official and popular or customary justice) and parajudicial areas (entirely private and outside the law). A particular concern of these authorities and institutions was to preserve practices aimed at controlling social deviance, whether these amounted to a crime or not. In this way, infrajustice operated not only to manage social control but also to define tolerable and intolerable behaviours in each community.

The history of crime and criminal justice has worked for several decades to draw up an elaborate framework on the modalities of crime and its judicial control in modern Europe. Huge efforts have been deployed since the end of the 1960s, and the results today are tangible. Gatrell, Lenman and Parker (1980) attempted to demonstrate the uneven rates of adoption of penal law in European society from 1500, driving forwards global developments that they defined as a 'legal revolution' that shadowed the process of state formation. The contributions to that publication, along with those contained in another similar work subsequently edited by John Bossy (1983) titled *Disputes and Settlements, Law and Human Relations in the West*, were instrumental in revealing the wide contrasts that existed between different parts of Europe. Some regions boasted a large weight of custom-based social control measures that preserved the manifestations of traditional private justice, while others witnessed the penetration of penal law. There, urban and institutional developments enabled governments to mediate and arbitrate ever more effectively in disputes between their subjects, and to channel their efforts into achieving public peace. This dialogue between contrasting yet complementary official and customary forms of justice continued throughout the early modern period, and even into the present time, expressing itself in different ways. During the Old Regime, public or common peace combined the official and extra-official spheres, formal and informal, with the aim of restoring peace and order.

The stronger the infrajustice, the weaker the superposition of official justice to monopolise social control from above (official rulers and institutions). Sometimes, however, this phenomenon had another cause and explanation. The relative strength of infrajustice could also be the result of the success of social forces at adapting traditional forms of mediation and arbitration practices to the changing social context. Whatever the reason, it affected the process of modernisation of justice. In the end, historical change was not just the result of the monopolisation of justice and discipline by professionals, institutions and rulers. Although much work remains to be done, the sustained dialogue during the early modern period between official or hegemonic justice and infrajustice, customary or subordinate justice, has appeared in ever sharper focus in historical research during the last forty years, proving its historical relevance for understanding the process of state formation. This brings us to the case of early modern Spain.

The case of early modern Spain

In the period under consideration, urban magistrates (*corregidores*), usually helped by local judges (*alcaldes ordinarios; alcaldes mayores*), typically performed a key role at the lower levels of the Spanish royal judicial system. Appeals subsequently had to be filed at superior courts called audiences or chancelleries. Apart from these courts, there was a range of specialised tribunals in specific fields such as financial and military affairs, heresy, the control of communication roads and even protocol. Both civil and criminal cases proceeded following the patterns of the inquisitorial procedure, which meant that for every lawsuit it was the judge who had to settle the conflict and rebuild peace. This same procedure was also applied in other jurisdictional spheres, including in ecclesiastical courts. As a result, judges played a vital role in every judicial step. This was particularly important in lower, local courts, where judges typically did not have a law degree, but rather were local citizens who had been nominated by a *corregidor* or by the nearest high court, audience or chancellery. Instead of strictly applying the law, these local judges received instructions from the highest courts to implement justice as prudent fathers. Although the law was thus not strictly applied, this kind of justice was considered to be equivalent to formal justice. Especially in these local arenas, customary traditions had an impact on judicial proceedings, and helped to define the historical evolution of justice. The latter thus incorporated not only official and formalised law but also informal and unofficial rules that had been legitimated by tradition, local customs and social practices. These infrajudicial forms of dispute settlement that operated in the confines of the law in seventeenth- and eighteenth-century Spain are the focus of this chapter.

Awareness of the infrajudicial forms of dispute settlement at local level helps historians reconsider the established views on the alleged disfunctioning of the Spanish judicial system during the early modern period. Even though more cracks appear every day in the obsolete model, it is still a widely accepted conviction about justice in early modern Spain that it was profuse, clogged with bureaucrats lacking professionalism, hampered by slow procedures and lengthy processes, and affected by the influence of power groups, interests and social factions. In addition, it is habitually considered as a weakness that local judges, who were after all the main guardians of the integrity of the law, in actual practice failed to apply themselves to carrying out the law as strictly as they ought to have done. They allegedly showed a lack of rigour in procedure, and often deserted their duties or delegated them to under-qualified officials and civil servants (Pike, 1976, pp. 689–704; Weisser, 1980, pp. 76–96).

The result of this combination of unfortunate events would be that civil and criminal judges left many cases unsentenced. This aspect was allegedly particularly significant at the lowest strata of legal administration, where the vast majority of civil and criminal cases withered away without sentence. This pattern was even more marked in rural and slightly urbanised areas than in the more intensely urban regions. In striking contrast to this apparently lax form of justice was another, particularly harsh one. It related to criminal justice that was used with uncommon cruelty to mutilate, torture and execute many of the condemned. Scenes were orchestrated involving complicated and theatrical protocols, displaying the greater rigour of legal discipline. This theatrical way of sentencing criminals is commonly viewed as a way to overcome judicial ineffectiveness. The harshest punishments not only repaid the criminal's debt to society, but also instilled social fear that was expected to inhibit crime. In established historiography, therefore, both faces of justice conferred considerable weakness upon the legal system.

The narrative then goes that this preliberal (primitive) and ineffective form of justice was replaced by a more 'modern' justice that established itself as the first dissipated. Thus, a long process of 'modernisation' involved welcome and continuous progress in imposing official, legal or institutional justice on other extra-official judicial uses and practices. Simultaneously, a process of legitimisation of the institutional monopoly on lawful violence purportedly progressed, concomitant with the rise of modern states. This process would have been accompanied by a stepping up of the process of defining offending behaviour, and a refinement of the administrative machinery, within the progress of the creation of modern states.

In Spain, conflicts articulated through the so called '*pendencias*' or quarrels, for instance, gradually disappeared (Mantecón 2007, pp. 151–184). These included struggles between family members, factions and clienteles, as well as clashes that were the product of male youth culture, gang fights in urban areas, expressions of defiance of authority, or the disciplinary control exerted by groups of workers over what they felt were permissible or not permissible behaviours in working-class society (Mantecón 2006, pp. 159–194 and Mantecón 2008, pp. 165–189). Resorting to these extreme forms of discipline became increasingly unusual in European societies as the seventeenth century progressed, even though these practices and other variations on private justice, such as those that enabled seventeenth- and eighteenth-century Languedoc peasants to seek solutions to civil or criminal conflicts outside the courts, hinted at the existence of a wide area of justice outside the legal system (Castan 1974; Castan 1976, pp. 331–361; Castan 1977; Castan 1980).

Many historians have studied Old Regime Spanish justice with the paradigm of 'primitive' as opposed to 'modern' justice in mind. This archetype acts even today as a reference point in many studies (see, for instance, Martínez Dhier 2008, pp. 425–464). In this author's view, this dual image only partly matches reality, since it fails to explain the complexity of the uses, nature and impacts of justice in past societies. Research into the fields and manifestations of infrajustice has shown the superficiality of the arguments upon which this paradigm rests. Practices designed to encourage agreements to help overcome a conflict (mediation), as well as those that relied on decisions fostered by people or institutions with acknowledged authority not only to mediate but also to deliver a solution that could enable a conflict to be resolved (arbitration), were central to the uses of justice in pre-industrial societies.

Microhistory has increased the depth of knowledge about the variety of conflict-settling practices comprised by infrajustice. Tommaso Astarita (1999) has, for instance, researched the spousal murder of a man named Antonio Cuzzucli, who was poisoned by his adulterous wife Domenica Orlanda in the Italian region of Calabria in the middle of the seventeenth century. Astarita concluded that the judicial process reinforced village-based structures of power and authority dominated by clan loyalties. This may explain why no one was apparently punished for the crime. Benoît Garnot's study on another conjugal murder in the early eighteenth century that ended the life of a certain Mr Boiveau, a farmer from Dijon, along with research that I carried out myself into the circumstances of the death of Antonia Isabel Sánchez in the Cantabrian valley of Alfoz de Lloredo, both reveal the strong presence of the community in the resolution of conflicts (Garnot, 1993; Mantecón, 1998). Notions and values such as 'scandal' or 'common knowledge' and 'custom' appeared to help implement other instruments than those used by formal law courts. All of these factors together operated both before and after the committing of the crime, showing how communal regulations and actions operated to overcome conflict. Before the crime was perpetrated, gossip, recriminations, counter-claims, neighbourhood councils, parish priests and men of standing within the community all attempted to help avoid the tragic outcome.

Later, after the crime had occurred and the legal process had begun, these same instruments and others continued to intervene, impacting the course and conclusion of the criminal case, influencing justice through testimonies, opinions and views of neighbours, the claims of the accused, and the skill or incompetence of legal guardians, prosecutors and judges.

The legal outcome of the Boiveau case studied by Garnot was the execution of Mme Boiveau, the instigator of the death of her husband. She remained dignified in the eyes of her neighbours, because she accepted, in a resigned and repentant way, the punishment process and the capital punishment she ultimately received. The sentence of capital punishment handed down to this woman and her acceptance of it had a redemptive effect, as though this were the suffering of a martyr. This was the aim sought by official justice, but in this case, the whole social system that knew of the crime and punishment also participated. The dignified acceptance of the punishment was a point of convergence between justice and infrajustice that influenced the different phases of the conflict and its final resolution.

In the other two examples cited, this meeting point was not arrived at in the sentence, but in the forces and tensions that the judge attempted to relieve. In the Calabrian case, a maid named Anna de Amico was found guilty of obtaining the poison for Domenica Orlando and spent fifteen years in a Naples prison. Domingo Garcia, instigator of the death of his wife Antonia Isabel Sánchez in the Cantabrian valley of Alfoz de Lloredo in the early summer of 1799, had a worse fate. This man lost his farmhouse in Cantabria and grocery store in Seville. Furthermore, during the court case (1799–1804), he forfeited his life to the harshness of prison in the town of Comillas. Between his detention and his death, harassment by various agents of the local reeve and loss of favour of his village chieftain and of his neighbourhood council (Udías) ultimately undermined his mental and physical health. In all of this, the impact of infrajustice was felt. Whilst it was 'common knowledge' that the husband had had something to do with the death of his spouse, it was the same 'common knowledge' allied with legal action, and pressure from the local chieftain and his relatives, that ended up undermining his health and morale, factors that ended the life of this capricious husband.

Infrajustice either acted as an alternative to or complemented official justice. In the first case, the judge and court never even came to hear of the conflict and it was resolved informally, in keeping with existing local patterns and customs. In the second case, the conflict reached the court. There, the parties set out their positions and tried to find common ground, in order to reach an agreement away from the court. In this scenario, the legal case ended without a sentence and the parties managed to reach extrajudicial understandings that were formalised only occasionally in the shape of agreements, pacts, transactions or notarised compositions. At other times, mediation between parties and agreements left no written traces, and the historian can only conclude that conciliation was achieved from indirect testimonials, such as phrases or comments mentioned in notarial or legal documents by parties or their families. Previous agreements were used as points of reference when new problems arose or to back up entitlements. These were perhaps achieved by means of compositions that were never formalised in writing, but were rather maintained by the good faith of the parties and by the testimony of intermediaries ('good men'), often neighbours of a certain standing and moral authority within the rural community or urban district.

At this level of mediation and conciliation, restoring peace between the parties was not the only consideration. The 'common peace' was tested at every conflict and its settlement. The social environment, with the intervention of particular mediators who took on the task of bringing the parties' positions closer together, played a decisive role on the path to mediation and negotiation between the parties. People's values, prejudices, customs and traditions, as well as their different interests, all came to the surface. All these factors contributed to defining what was acceptable or condemnable in this environment. These values helped to define archetypes of good and bad neighbourliness that affected daily life and explained the structure of actions aimed at maintaining public peace as an expression of common good.

Agents of infrajustice, guardians of public peace

Infrajustice often acted in parallel with and complementary to the judicial process, encouraging parties to reach agreements and to negotiate the appropriate compensation amongst themselves (extrajustice), at times via intermediaries who themselves lived in the relevant society, 'good men' or worthies, 'conflict negotiators', 'persons of good standing', 'good Christians', friends and family. These, along with more professional agents such as parish clerics, abbots, the judges themselves, mayors and deputies, attempted to bring the parties' positions together to reach agreements or compositions to overcome the conflict. Council procurators also regularly intervened. There is, however, a great deal of work still required to explain the true scope and effects of the actions of these intermediaries.[2]

The role played by local and first-instance judges was crucial to boosting the effectiveness of infrajudicial mediations and arbitrations, especially when other informal settings failed one after the other. These local judicial officials remained steeped in a culture of mediation that was socially constructed in their environment. They took part in mediation, and their interventions likewise gave it a certain level of dynamism. In nearly every case, interventions by these officials helped foster a climate in which infrajustice operated. The parties and mediators continued intervening informally even when the case was being handled by the courts. Sometimes because of this, cases were suspended following an extrajudicial pact between the parties. At other times these local judges took a paternalistic approach to their role, and after hearing the parties' submissions, issued conciliatory decisions with which they terminated cases with no major sentence apart from advice, admonishments and payment of legal costs.

The arbitrators active in infrajustice included parish priests. In fact, mediating conflicts between parishioners was an important aspect of the work of parish priests.[3] In order to perform their duties properly, they had to have moral standing within their communities. However, not all parish priests could rely on such standing to the same extent. In the early eighteenth century, roughly half of all secular clerics in rural areas such as the Cantabrian area of Cornisa had some kind of moral 'disqualification' in the eyes of their bishops. According to these bishops, more than a quarter of the priests were then cohabiting. Figures were similar in southern Spain, including in urban areas.[4] Generally, the neighbours and potential 'clients' of parish priests were less sensitive to such moral failings. Such neighbours could rather single out other inadequacies as disturbing. For instance, some local clerics attracted negative comments from their neighbours, generally on the grounds of their functioning as a transmission mechanism for local potentates, usurping authority, taking advantage of their role as clerics to carry out excesses, abusing their rights and collecting debts contracted with them by neighbours or from parish institutions. The fact that some clerics lived as laymen, which in the eyes of the prelates was synonymous of 'moral failing', did not however always attract criticism from neighbours.

Social permissiveness regarding the transgressing of Christian morals nevertheless had its limits. When these were overstepped, neighbours could end up expressing their disapproval very intensely. This is what happened in the Cantabrian parish of Ruiloba towards the end of the Old Regime. In this parish, there was a succession of notorious clerics plagued by loose morals, from the end of the eighteenth century until the middle of the nineteenth century. Ultimately, the neighbourhood lost patience. The priest who served the church in 1789 was a card player and frequented the local taverns both day and night. It was said at times that 'he had deserted the people by accompanying and courting ladies' and that 'there was little point in him preaching because instead of bringing peace, he fell out with neighbours'.[5] The priest's moral admonishments and mediations must have been of little use to his parishioners.

Years later, in 1819, in the same parish, another priest named José Diéz was considered by his neighbours to be a 'shameless priest' who 'gave a sad and shameful example of a most relaxed cohabiting with his female servants, which altered and changed according to the whim of the maddest obscenity'.[6] That year, with a priest of such poor reputation, the admonishments from another parish priest named Bernardo Rojo to a prostitute called Isabel Valdés that she should change her lifestyle and stop being a bad example for other young people, cannot have been of much use.[7] The moral weaknesses of the priest limited his ability to mediate in conflicts. Another priest who served this parish later also suffered from diminished authority in mediating conflicts between parishioners. In 1842, pamphlets were left in public areas of the town and songs were sung denouncing the dissolute life of the priest.[8] In 1844, a criminal case initiated by parishioners against the licentious parish priest was concluded by a pact between the parties. In this case, the outcome was not so grave as that which had literally happened in 1704 to the priest of Vejorís de Toranzo, who died after having been thrown in the river, where he was found dead. The culprits or circumstances of the crime were never ascertained. Thus, the arbitration role performed by the parish priest was afforded him by parishioners, but with some limitations, depending on the moral authority he had managed to carve out in the neighbourhood.

Local communities also fostered forms of arbitration supported by council institutions and religious communities. All the fraternities within the Vera Cruz or Third Order vocations (linked to the mendicant religious Franciscans) contained in their rules and statutes procedures for arbitrating conflicts, avoiding courts and achieving:

> the increase and preservation of material possessions, not wasting them on useless litigation, when it is so easy to avoid them through the intervention of individuals of such proper intentions and with the ability to obtain for the injured party a resolution that is not only Christian but also honourable and equal.[9]

Every conflict had to be brought to the fraternity in secret. If a case had already been initiated, the appellant had to 'relax the case that they had set in motion' in the court. Not to do so meant expulsion from the fraternity and being excluded by the neighbourhood mutualism.

Fraternities conducted arbitration of both civil matters and criminal cases. The litigating parties were bound to accept the decision of the fraternity, since its members acted as one. Their duty to accept such decisions was independent of the gravity of the matter and the nature of the conflict. Arbitration restored the standing within the community of each litigious party. The fraternity guaranteed the pacts and agreements achieved during mediation by two 'guardian' community members, one secular and one religious, who were nominated every year and employed to 'check how the brothers [of the community] were living', and to observe 'whether they were causing any scandal, be it cohabitation, drunkenness, blasphemy, perjury, theft, or any other vice from which a scandal might arise'. They had to be 'subject to all virtue, judgment, prudence and diligence' and be 'leaders in dignity' which is to say, to be what was considered 'good men'.[10] Their authority in mediation and arbitration stemmed from this reputation within the local community.

Every time a conflict arose between members of the fraternity, the guardians attempted to ensure that the parties reached a satisfactory agreement. Out of necessity, this was communicated to the abbot of the community and if there was a refusal to accept mediation, the guardians could call a general meeting of the fraternity, which usually came down to calling a meeting of the entire neighbourhood in a rural community, or of the entire parish in an urban district. The bulk of the community acted as the social setting through which to exert pressure on the parties to achieve 'compositions' and attempt to overcome their differences. The guardians of the communities appear in notarised compositions as 'good men' and 'diligent persons', nominated by the parties as intermediaries. All these intermediaries sought to achieve negotiated and consensual solutions, carrying out negotiation and arbitration tasks similar to those that in both urban and rural environments in other European and American areas were performed by so-called 'neighbourhood courts'.[11]

Gossip by neighbours and admonishments by parish priests played a similar preventative role against crime. Scandal thus became the demarcation between behaviours that were tolerated and those that were not. This would have to be an extreme level of gossip, given the ineffectiveness of previous gossip in controlling scandalous conduct, which is to say behaviour that disturbed the public peace and showed itself to be deviant or reprehensible by also being a bad example to the community. At that time, gossip played a complex social control role, enabling disciplinary admonishments to be expressed in order to bring behaviour back within a tolerable range. However, gossip did not always perform these functions or adopt these meanings; it might also simply provide a warning of hidden problems within the community, or remain cemented around social prejudices, passions and enmities that in some cases had been latent for a long time. At times, what was achieved was not the resolution of the conflict but its intensification.

The legal revolution and the culture of mediation

A statistical examination of indicators for the respective evolutions of judicial and infrajudicial actions uncovers changes in these phenomena in the long term. Assessing the volume of business of formal law courts is the most straightforward undertaking. Assessing the volume of infrajustice and changes in that volume is markedly more challenging.

Richard Kagan has studied the uneven evolution of numbers of first- and second-instance cases in the courts of Castile during the sixteenth and seventeenth centuries (Kagan, 1981, pp. 77–127, 165–209, 210–235). He revealed a striking drop in the number of civil cases brought before the appeals courts during the second half of the seventeenth century. Kagan hypothesised that this decrease may have been part of a process of devolution of powers from the higher to the lower courts. This was a development that was accompanied by other phenomena (that have also been noted in other parts of Europe) such as the growing professionalisation of law officials. Kagan's analysis stopped there, but a projection of these figures leads to conjecture about the possible evolution of litigation patterns during the eighteenth century, which may result in an approximation of a timeline of the process of modernisation defined in Spain as a legal revolution.

Kagan's thesis is a significant stimulus for reflection on the topic, and it raises some interesting questions. Thus far, it has not been demonstrated that in Spain from the sixteenth to eighteenth centuries first-instance courts truly increased their activities both in absolute and relative terms. Regional studies have shown that activities, litigiousness, and civil and criminal cases rose markedly during the Age of Enlightenment in lower courts. However, the population size grew extraordinarily as well. In fact, this growth occurred much faster than the rise in the number of cases brought before the judges. In other words, the rise in the number of cases at lower courts might have been affected by demographic growth.

Data on court use in a rural society under the Old Regime thus helps to test whether or not a legal devolution occurred from higher to lower courts from the second half of the seventeenth century. Evidence on Cantabria, a region in the north of Spain, contributes some evidence of general processes. In this region, the annual growth rate of first-instance civil and criminal cases rose rapidly during the seventeenth century and even more sharply in the eighteenth century. At first sight, therefore, Richard Kagan's hypothesis is confirmed. However, there are some other significant nuances that must be considered in order to avoid excessive simplification in explaining the phenomenon. Firstly, a distinction must be made among legal actions between the growth in civil cases on the one hand, and criminal cases on the other hand, since the rise in activities could be unevenly distributed. Secondly, we must consider whether the demographic curve affected the number of legal cases. Basic errors can thus be avoided, such as deducing that 'criminality' (the number of criminal cases in relation to population size) or 'litigiousness' (the number of civil and criminal cases brought before courts in relation to population size) increased or decreased at particular times, when the one sure thing is that the population underwent variations, affecting the volume of cases in the courts.

In Cantabria, the population showed a slow but steady growth rate for most of the seventeenth and eighteenth centuries, and an intense growth rate in the second half of the eighteenth century. However, even though there were more cases annually in the eighteenth century than in the seventeenth century, comparing this data with annual increases in population gives a different reading. Figure 9.1 shows how the annual proportional rise in cases tended to drop markedly in relative terms. The relative fall seems to have been slightly more marked for criminal cases than for civil cases in the last part of the eighteenth century, possibly indicating a decline in criminality, as well as a general drop in litigiousness. In lower provincial courts in this region of Spain, the number of cases per 100,000 inhabitants declined from the start of the seventeenth century, a trend that continued into the eighteenth century. Even though judges were given an increasingly larger number of cases to judge in absolute terms, the evolution of these numbers was markedly lower than population growth. In other words, although there were more people and they brought more issues to court, these were proportionally less frequent in relation to judge-led mediation and arbitration, which grew through the seventeenth and eighteenth centuries. This secular trend gathered pace during the second half of this period. It does appear from this that the seventeenth-century process of devolution of powers from the higher to the lower courts was not the only factor in play.

It may have been the case that the relative levels of interpersonal conflict decreased, under the influence of secular sociocultural changes. On the other hand, it merits consideration that a rather more overarching process may have occurred, notably a devolution of powers from formal law courts to wider social spheres, or from justice to infrajustice, i.e. informal justice, mediation and unformalised arbitration outside institutions. The uneven trajectory of the total number of court cases in relation to the entirety of criminal cases, and among these cases of interpersonal violence, contributes a valuable body of comparative information. The decline in criminal cases seems to have been more muted than the reduction in civil cases, although both trends allow for conjecturing a decline in cases and

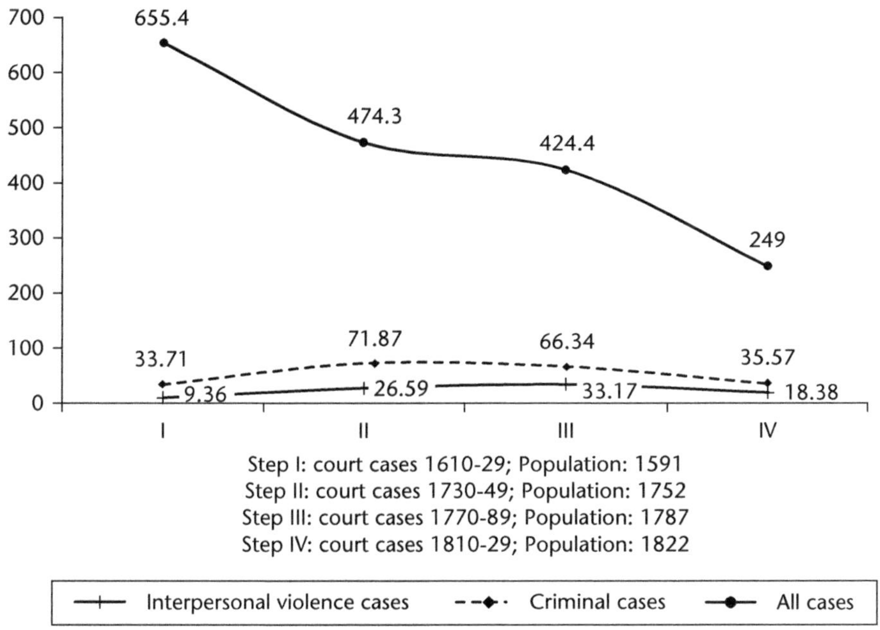

FIGURE 9.1 Evolution in civil and criminal cases brought before the courts in Cantabria 1591–1830 (court cases per 100,000 people)

Source: AHPC, *Alfoz de Lloredo* (legs. 78–94), *Reocín* (legs. 119–132) and *Cayón* (legs. 74–85). Population data for Lanza (1990).

perhaps an advance of informal practices for mediation and arbitration, a field in which both family and neighbourly links as well as the converging of cultures on the basis of shared customs played a decisive role as actors in negotiations. Elsewhere, I have suggested a statistical approach to assess a number of indicators of the extent of infrajustice, including the membership of confraternities, which – as we have seen – offered many mediating services. Analysis of the many variables that are needed to map both the scope of interaction, negotiation, mediation and arbitration of conflicts and the evolution of these forms of conflict regulation are, however, beyond the scope of this article (Mantecón, 2016).

To be sure, the Cantabrian case that is reflected in Figure 9.1 displays some peculiarities within early modern Europe. The strong presence of informal justice or infrajustice was palpable, as it was in most rural areas of Europe which, like this northern Spanish region, remained on the periphery of the major decision-making centres at the time. Many cases, both civil and criminal, nevertheless, came before the judges in that region during the seventeenth and eighteenth centuries. Maybe because of this, this region registered rates of cases very similar to rural parts of the most urbanised area of Europe in the seventeenth and eighteenth centuries. In Holland, notably, fifty cases a year per 100,000 residents were registered during this period (Lenman and Parker, 1980, pp. 11–48).

Taking into account the very low levels of urbanisation in Cantabria at that time, this litigiousness can be explained by the huge fragmentation of the judicial territorial system, in which first-instance courts operated in very local settings, every tiny valley becoming a jurisdiction, a judicial area for a peasant community. Using the legal system in these circumstances was not expensive, and furthermore the judge was a member of the community, who operated in a similar way to the justices of the peace that would appear later. These local judges (mayors and deputies) encouraged mediation for all cases, whether civil or criminal. Where appropriate – although not necessarily in all cases – they provided arbitration in the shape of resolutions that subsequently became the substance of the sentences handed down by the urban chief magistrates if necessary. These last could request the legal support of lawyers and jurists from upper courts for help in deciding the sentence for the most difficult cases.

This type of setting for judicial intervention, as well as the substantial role played by mayors and deputies, coupled with the fact that sentencing appeals had to be referred to distant higher courts, made the activities of these courts more attractive. More than three-quarters of both civil and criminal cases treated by these judges were resolved without a sentence being passed. This reflects the wide scope of infrajustice. In this way, in this Spanish region, society used legal courts more frequently than was usual in other rural and Spanish areas, but they also made their mark on justice and developed a pattern that had common features with other rural environments and peasant societies in western Europe.[12]

Conclusions

The complex framework of infrajustice is represented by a wide range of phenomena, including preventative measures by parish priests in the exercise of their daily parish duties, admonishments by scandalised neighbours, popular flyers and rhymes, gossip, subduing through threats and violence, mediation and arbitration delivered by community 'guardians' or 'good men', by 'conflict managers', family members, friends and local authorities. These expressed informalised justice that remained overlaid by legal considerations, but that was taken into account by the judges handling each case. Conflicts frequently ended without sentence, due to the role played by infrajudicial mediation and arbitration. Traces of such mediation often were a legal decision or a notarised composition between the parties. From conciliatory resolutions to condemnatory sentences, judges applied a rationale that combined both justice and infrajustice, possibly because they had similar objectives. Infrajustice similarly was justice.

In any event, Spanish justice under the Old Regime comprised both types of intervention, in diverse combinations, and presupposed a specific hybrid social use of the law and of the institutions. At the same time, from this point of view, the law was recognised as the instrument to achieve balancing daily tensions that threatened the community, and, by extension, the monarchy. It is the hybrid nature of justice that prevents us talking of a monopoly of justice, or of legalised types of discipline or violence, in the societies of the Old Regime – or even of a secular trend. What was evident was a dialogue between legal mechanisms and the social usage of them, or –which is the same thing – between official or formalised justice and informal justice or infrajustice. The latter had a central and growing importance throughout the Old Regime in bringing some kind of balance, albeit a tense one, to daily life. This chapter has argued that there was not just one simple devolution of legal powers from higher to lower courts, but rather a progressive advance of infrajustice, mediation and arbitration. This process did not weaken justice, but rather showed a dimension of it that was increasingly adopted by society.

In any event, these types and uses of justice competed with others that affected justice in many different ways. Power groups and social factions focused around the construction of asymmetrical personal dependency links, neighbourhood communities themselves, all had a disciplinary effect on the behaviour of individuals. These interventions were not always receptive to notions of admonishment and education in reducing levels of conflict. They could also express themselves in ways that provoked and reinforced conflict. Therein lay the risk. As the eighteenth century progressed, in peasant societies of the Iberian Peninsula, the so-called *pendencias* gradually disappeared. These were assaults carried out by armed members of a family group or a client group, expressing their right to revenge or their own particular perception of what was or was not fair.

Whether with or without violence, infrajustice referred to a world of mediation, and, at times, arbitration that was located almost always within the law. It used both court practices and recommendations from the highest tribunals, lawyers and legal tradition, as well as customs and social uses of justice. Documentary evidence is clear in this respect. Justice was of a complex nature in Spain under the Old Regime; it is neither easy nor appropriate to separate the aims of justice and infrajustice, since they were part of the same whole. The limits between some types of justice and areas outside the law and rules were very subtle, but the people making use of legal culture, custom and whatever resources were made available to them by the law, knew these limits. This was true as much for the most professional actors, i.e. agents, officials, experts, judges and scribes, as for common people. Infrajustice had a decisive weight in traditional societies under the Old Regime, as it does to this day, albeit under different guises and conditions from the type that operates in everyday life, up to the fields of diplomacy and international relations. Having occupied historians of crime over the last few decades, research on this topic will give rise to much discussion over the coming years.

Notes

1 This research was sponsored by the project HAR2015-64014-C3-R (Spanish Research National Funds and European FEDER Funds Programme).

2 Raquel Iglesias (2004, pp. 349–374; 2007) has provided examples from notarial documents. On the matter of the intervention in these mediations of religious confraternities, see: Mantecón, 1990, pp. 106–130, 145–152 and 199. Undurraga (2012, pp. 226–238) has

offered examples of mediation in honour disputes in Chilean society in the eighteenth century. In Leiden the Peacemaker Court dealt with many of these affairs (Vermeesch, 2015).

3 Still in 1837, the bishop of Santander Gutiérrez Valdés (1837, p.15) reiterated this important task in a pastoral letter to his diocesan priests. Three European and American examples from the Old Regime about Spain (Mantecón, 1995), Germany (Sabean, 1984, pp.144–173) and Argentina (Barral, 2016) are sufficient to outline the types and effects of mediation by parish priests.

4 This was reflected in the pastoral visit conducted by Bishop Fernández Navarrete in 1708–1709 (Mantecón, 1997, pp. 111–119). Research by Candau Chacón (1993; 1994) offers comparative information about Seville.

5 AHPC (Archivo Histórico Provincial de Cantabria), *Alfoz de Lloredo*, file 88, doc. 26, ff. 2–4.

6 AHPC, *Alfoz de Lloredo*, file 93, doc. 34, ff. 37–38 and file 94, doc. 24.

7 Isabel Valdés by then already had quite a history in prostitution. When the area was invaded by the French army she was compelled to move to Santander, where, before emigrating to Asturias and thence to Andalucia, returning in 1819 to Ruiloba, she was spotted in 1809 in the company of other wenches from Ruiloba, all of them 'rolling around like pumpkins' among the French soldiers. AHPC, *Alfoz de Lloredo*, file 93, doc. 34, f. 8.

8 On this topic, collecting the texts of leaflets and songs sheds light on the complex relationship between priests and their parishioners; see: Mantecón, 1997, pp. 350–352.

9 ADS (Archivo Diocesano de Santander), *Libro de Cofradía de Vera Cruz* (Riaño), sig. 1590, ff. 14–15. I have highlighted the peaceful dimension of religious fraternities, the types of mediation and their logic in: Mantecón, 1990, pp. 106–122.

10 ADS, *Libro de Tercera Orden Franciscana* (Liérganes), sig. 1529, ff. 12–13 and also ACS (Archivo Catedralico de Santander), *Libro de la cofradía de La Consolación*, files A-93, ff. 44–44. In 1788 the Brotherhood of the Christian Militia, founded in Santander as an arch-fraternity grouping together several pre-existing ones, also took on their approaches and identified themselves as secret arbitration 'guardians'. BMMP (Biblioteca Municipal Menéndez Pelayo), sig. 02890.

11 Robert von Friedeburg and Carl Hoffmann have provided Central European examples for this type of mediation in their contributions to the collected work published by Roodenburg and Spierenburg on *Social control in Europe* (2004, pp. 247–266, 309–328). On Latin America, see: Undurraga, 2010, pp. 35–71. An example for the Dutch city of Leiden is discussed elsewhere in this volume. See also: Hunt, 1992, p. 23.

12 Dubert (1992, pp. 330–331, 354–355) has observed a 'reluctance to litigate during the harsher years' in Galicia. This did not happen in Cantabria. The greater remoteness and cost of justice in Galicia than in Cantabria, along with the greater receptiveness of local courts to local Cantabrian culture, might be the reasons for these differences. Iglesias (2004, pp. 349–374) also alludes to reticence to resort to justice in the province of Santiago in the eighteenth century.

References

Astarita, T. (1999). *Village justice: community, family and popular culture in early modern Italy*. Baltimore: Johns Hopkins University Press.

Barral, M.E. (2016). *Curas con los pies en la tierra. Una historia de la Iglesia en la Argentina contada desde abajo*. Buenos Aires: Penguin Random House Grupo Editorial Argentina.

Candau Chacón, M.L. (1993). *Los delitos y las penas en el mundo eclesiástico sevillano del siglo XVIII*. Sevilla: Universidad de Sevilla.

Candau Chacón, M.L. (1994). *El clero rural de Sevilla en el siglo XVIII*. Sevilla: Caja Rural de Sevilla. 1994.

Castan, Y. (1974). *Honnêteté et relations sociales en Languedoc, 1715–1780*. Paris: Plon.

Castan, N. (1976). La justice expéditive. *Annales (Économies, Societés, Civilisations)*, 2, pp. 331–361.

Castan, N. (1977). *Les criminels de Languedoc. Les exigences d'ordre et les voies du ressentiment dans une société prérévolutionnaire (1750–1790).* Toulouse: Association des publications de l'Université de Toulouse-Le Mirail.

Castan, N. (1980). *Justice et répression en Languedoc à l'époque des Lumières.* Paris: Flammarion.

Dubert, I. (1992). *Historia de la familia en Galicia durante la época Moderna, 1550–1830.* La Coruña: Ediciós do Castro.

Garnot, B. (1993). *Un crime conjugal au 18e siècle. L'affaire Boiveau.* Paris: Imago.

Garnot, B. (2000). Justice, infrajustice, parajustice et extrajustice dans la France d'Ancien Régime. *Crime, History and Societies*, 4, pp. 103–120.

Gatrell, V.A.C., Lenman, B. and Parker, G., eds. (1980). *Crime and the law: the social history of crime in Western Europe since 1500.* London: Europa Publications.

Gutiérrez Valdés, A. (1837). *Pastoral que dirige al clero y demás fieles de estas diócesis su gobernador eclesiástico.* Santander.

Heras, J.L. de las (1991). *La justicia penal de los Austrias en la Corona de Castilla.* Salamanca: Ediciones Universidad de Salamanca.

Herrup, C.B. (1987). *The common peace: participation and the criminal law in seventeenth-century England.* Cambridge: Cambridge University Press.

Hunt, M. (1992). Wife beating, domesticity and women's independence in eighteenth-century London. *Gender & History*, 4, pp. 10–33.

Iglesias, R. (2004). El recurso a la justicia como vía de resolución de la conflictividad criminal gallega a fines del Antiguo Régimen. Santiago de Compostela (1700–1834). *Stvdia Historica. Historia Moderna*, 26, pp. 349–374.

Iglesias, R. (2007). *Crimen, criminales y reos. La delincuencia y su represión en la antigua provincia de Santiago entre 1700–1834.* Santiago de Compostela: Nigra Trea.

Kagan, R.L. (1981). *Lawsuits and litigants in Castile, 1500–1700.* Chapel Hill: Books on Demand.

Lanza, R. (1990). La Población de Cantabria en el Antiguo Régimen (Tesis Doctoral, Apéndice 1). Universidad de Cantabria.

Lenman, B. and Parker, G. (1980). The state, the community and the criminal law in early modern Europe. In: V.A.C Gatrell, B. Lenman and G. Parker, eds., *Crime and the law: the social history of crime in Western Europe since 1500.* London: Europa Publications, pp. 11–48.

Mantecón, T.A. (1990). *Contrarreforma y religiosidad popular en Cantabria. Las cofradías religiosas.* Santander: Universidad de Cantabria.

Mantecón, T.A. (1995). La capacidad del clero secular para apaciguar las disputas entre los campesinos montañeses del siglo XVIII. In: E. Martínez and V. Suárez, eds. *Iglesia y Sociedad en el Antiguo Régimen.* Vol. I. Las Palmas: Universidad de Las Palmas de Gran Canaria, pp. 149–156.

Mantecón, T.A. (1997). *Conflictividad y disciplinamiento social en la Cantabria rural del Antiguo Régimen.* Santander: Universidad de Cantabria, 1997.

Mantecón, T.A. (1998). *La muerte de Antonia Isabel Sánchez. Tiranía y escándalo en una sociedad rural del Norte de España durante el Antiguo Régimen.* Alcalá de Henares: Centro de estudios Cervantinos.

Mantecón, T.A. (2006). Las culturas criminales portuarias en las ciudades atlánticas: Sevilla y Ámsterdam en su edad dorada. In: J.I. Fortea and J.E. Gelabert, eds. *La ciudad portuaria atlántica en la historia: siglos XVI–XIX.* Santander: Universidad de Cantabria, pp. 159–194.

Mantecón, T.A. (2007). 'Sobre linajes y peleas de perros'. Parentelas y pendencias en la Castilla Moderna. In: F. Chacón Jiménez, J. Hernández Franco and F. García González, eds., *Familia y organización social en Europa y América: siglos XV–XX*. Murcia: Universidad de Murcia, pp. 151–184.

Mantecón, T.A. (2008). 'La ley de la calle' y la justicia en la Castilla Moderna. *Manuscrits: Revista d'història moderna*, 26, pp. 165–189.

Mantecón, T.A. (2011). La acción de justicia en la España Moderna: una justicia dialogada, para procurar paz. In: P. Broggio and M.P. Paoli, eds., *Stringere la pace. Teorie e pratiche della conciliziacione nell'Europa moderna (secoli XVI–XVIII)*. Rome: Viella, pp. 333–367.

Mantecón, T.A. (2016). Justicia y fronteras del derecho en la Espana del antiguo regimen. In: E. Caselli, ed., *Justicias, agentes y jurisdicciones: la monarquia hispanica a los estados nacionales (Espana y America, siglos XVI–XIX)*. Madrid: Fondo de Cultura Economica, pp. 25–58.

Martínez Dhier, A. (2008). Un tránsito del Antiguo Régimen al estado liberal de derecho en España. *Revista de Estudios Histórico-Jurídicos*, 30, pp. 425–464.

Pike, R. (1976). Crime and punishment in XVIth century Spain. *Journal of European Economic History*, 5, pp. 689–704.

Roodenburg, H. and Spierenburg, P., eds. (2004). *Social control in Europe. Vol. 1. 1500–1800.* Columbus: The Ohio State University Press.

Sabean, D.W. (1984). *Power in the blood. Popular culture and village discourse in early modern Germany*. Cambridge: Cambridge University Press.

Shoemaker, R.B. (1991). *Prosecution and punishment: petty crime and the law in London and rural Middlesex, c. 1660–1725*. Cambridge: Cambridge University Press.

Soman, A. (1980). Deviance and criminal justice in Western Europe, 1300–1800: an essay in structure. *Criminal Justice History*, 1, pp. 3–28.

Soman, A. (1982). L'infrajustice à Paris après les archives notariales. *Histoire, Économie et Société*, 3, pp. 369–376.

Undurraga, V. (2010). 'Valentones', alcaldes de barrio y paradigmas de civilidad. Conflictos y acomodaciones en Santiago de Chile, siglo XVIII. *Revista de Historia Social y de las Mentalidades*, 14, pp. 35–71.

Undurraga, V. (2012). *Los rostros del honor. Normas culturales y estrategias de promoción social en Chile colonial, siglo XVIII.* Santiago, Chile: Editorial Universitaria.

Vermeesch, G. (2015). The social composition of plaintiffs and defendants in the Peacemaker court, Leiden, 1750–54. *Social History*, 40, pp. 208–229.

Weisser, M. (1980). Crime and punishment in early modern Spain. In: V.A.C. Gatrell, B. Lenman and G. Parker, eds. *Crime and the law: the social history of crime in Western Europe since 1500*. London: Europa Publications, pp. 76–96.

10

LO EXTRAJUDICIAL

Between court and community in the Spanish empire[1]

Bianca Premo

Introduction

In 1775, the *promotor fiscal*, or Church's attorney – a key figure in the judiciary of the Spanish viceregal capital of Mexico City – argued that women's formal cases against husbands over abuse or other marital matters were not *really* lawsuits. He conceded that, yes, the suits procedurally aligned with codified law that permitted women to file criminal charges for men's excessive physical punishment. And, certainly, women often submitted the proper written documentation to the right authorities. Still, these legal actions were different from lawsuits since women often went to judges not as magistrates but rather as 'paternal resources', and could – and often did – drop their suits.

The *promotor fiscal* referred here to a popular use of the law in the eighteenth-century Spanish empire: sometimes litigants, especially subordinates such as women, slaves and commoner natives, engaged Spanish courts in a semi-formal manner, entering a sphere of legal interaction they called *lo extrajudicial*. Their cases were intended to provoke summary verbal decisions, out-of-court settlements, face-to-face encounters or public declarations. But their initiators did not always intend for them to lead to formal trials and sentences.

The archives of the Spanish empire hold evidence of just how ample a legal space *lo extrajudicial* was: many, perhaps most, lawsuits or complaints in the civil archives of various repositories of the empire are little more than opening petitions or preliminary steps to a lawsuit that trail off with no resolution. Indeed, in one Spanish high court in Castile, 'forgotten suits' comprised the majority – 57.7 per cent – of all civil cases on record.[2] In a more ordinary colonial court such the ecclesiastical tribunal of Trujillo, on the north coast of Peru, 16 of the 21 divorce petitions that remain in the archive for the eighteenth century end with no explanation.[3]

That these suits were 'forgotten', 'dropped', or 'abandoned' make them no less worthy of historical consideration than formal, sentenced cases. Indeed, such legal fragments reveal perhaps more of ordinary people's legal practices than do full lawsuits, which tended to feature litigants who had the time, commitment and money to see cases through. On a more theoretical plane, reading half-finished suits of the Spanish empire alongside fully formed cases for what they can reveal about the actions of historical subjects outside of court forces us to abandon our own assumptions of what constitutes the legal archive.[4] While we might privilege the sentence and the disciplinary regimes of states, early modern people in the Spanish empire approached the bench more instrumentally, looking for intervention but not necessarily resolution to conflict.

Legal action in *lo extrajudicial* was frequently, though not exclusively, verbal. Yet the documents that capture it were written. This binds us to the petitions that Spanish imperial litigants did end up placing before judges. Bridging the gaps in the way justice was approached and how it was recorded – in other words, bridging the gaps in the archive – requires careful attention particularly to the early parts of the suits brought before authorities in the 1700s, a period of expanded legal activity, particularly among ordinary litigants in Mexico and Peru.[5] Early petitions in many suits, whether heard on the peninsula or in the American colonies, were submitted to court officials before procurators and attorneys were named, and petitioners often had these documents drawn up in the streets and homes of towns and cities rather than the courts themselves. It was not unusual for these petitions to be penned without any indication of who had done the legal writing, and they were written in the first person. There were a multitude of freelance writers throughout the Spanish empire, particularly cities, called '*agentes*', who knew how to follow the format of petitions laid out in legal manuals, but litigants had educated patrons, priests, friends or family members pen the early documents of the suits, or, in some rare cases, they wrote them themselves (Premo, 2017b).

The earlier writings in the suits are the most likely to reveal the world of *lo extrajudicial* not only because they sprang from the community but also because they recount the steps already taken in a conflict – other authorities to whom parties appealed, attempts at verbal reconciliation, even prior visits to the judges. The petitions in the chapters come from ecclesiastical and civil courts at three jurisdictional levels: first-instance courts, called *justicia ordinaria*; the courts of district magistrates, called *alcaldes mayores* or *corregidores*, which often presided over primarily rural inhabitants; and high courts, or *audiencias*, in larger cities. The regions examined range from the heavily indigenous districts of Oaxaca, in Southern Mexico, to the multi-ethnic coastal region surrounding the city of Trujillo, Peru, as well as viceregal capital cities including Mexico City and Lima, and rural areas of Castile, Spain.

If references to *lo extrajudicial* in the written archive demand methodological and theoretical attention to the life of law beyond the courts, they also challenge us to rethink our approach to stark divisions between the functioning of law in colonial settings such as Spanish America and those of Europe, and not only in the eighteenth century but also today. In this sense, the chapter's comparative regional frame, which includes Spain as well as Spanish America, seeks to disturb neat divisions between Western and non-Western legal cultures. Certainly, the prevalence of certain features of colonial domination – such as native servitude and African slavery – impacted the practices and application of law and recording of lives.[6] But this chapter also seeks to reveal *lo extrajudicial* as a common field that drew practices of law together, making the imperial legal system cohere.

What is more, the chapter's temporal frame, encompassing the eighteenth century, bridges the divide between the modern and early modern. This permits us to scrutinize an assumption made patent in the *promotor fiscal*'s commentary above: that formal, written action aimed at concrete legal outcomes, or sentences, is 'real' law, and that there is another kind of legal practice among marginal groups that is somehow outside or beyond it. This assumption is itself a product of hegemonic global encounters around law, and it functions to elevate the actions of privileged, often male, subjects as authentic legal history. While legal anthropologists certainly have forced us to contend with a wide range of verbal legal activities and normative orders aimed at justice among non-Western peoples, exploring *lo extrajudicial* in the eighteenth-century Spanish empire allows us to do even more.[7] It tells us that the realm of justice negotiated beyond formal procedures was not a non-Western alternative or parallel world to that of the formal courts of Spain but was instead integral to the functioning of law in a more global sense.[8]

Community justice

Historians of early modern legal culture in various regions have rightly placed a great deal of emphasis on the importance of community justice, as opposed to formal justice in tribunals, as the theatre in which most people in the past interacted with the law. For example, Tommaso Astarita, examining a rural village in Calabria, Italy, reflects on the way that trials there involved interplay between more erudite jurisprudence coming from the counter-Reformation state and community values focused on 'individual honour and reputation', and channelled along 'a network of links between local women, the respective position of insiders and outsiders in village society, the expectations placed on men and women within the family and the community, and the fluidity, vibrancy and relatively egalitarian character of community life' (Astarita, 1999, p. 3).[9] Laura Edwards's description of 'local law' in the pre-Revolutionary US south paints a similarly lively portrait of impromptu town gatherings or conflagrations. There, doubts about the causes of a villager's death or a dispute over a sale would escalate until a circuit judge might be called to the scene. Critically, that judge was not some impartial purveyor of laws but more akin to a distinguished 'neighbour' (Edwards, 2008, pp. 69–71).

These descriptions of village justice from places as far apart as southern Italy and South Carolina echo, almost verbatim, scholarly depictions of rural areas of the Spanish empire, from Cantabria to Castile to Southern Mexico, in the seventeenth and eighteenth century (Mantecón Movellán, 1997; Taylor, W.B., 1979). While rural regions far from the corridors of high courts were particularly alive with customary, semi-formal legal practices, it is important to recall that neighbourhoods and familial networks functioned as kinds of courts of first resort in cities as well (Garnot, 2009). In fact, the concept of 'infrajustice', elaborated by European historians of crime, was derived from observations not about rural villages but Paris.

Benoît Garnot warns us not to stretch the concept of 'infrajustice' out of shape by using it to encompass divergent legal actions. He distinguishes acts such as a refusal to go to court at all from binding practices of justice adjudicated by a superior entity, be it community or individual, in which the goal was to achieve agreement between parties rather than to impose sentences (Garnot, 2000; Mantecón Movellán, 2002, pp. 43–75. Also see Herzog, 2004; Stern, 1995).

Only the latter, in Garnot's estimation, qualifies as an alternative mode of justice that should be called 'infrajustice'. I would maintain that *lo extrajudicial*, as an ambit of law that contemporaries in the Spanish imperial world specifically discussed by name, qualified as such a mode of justice. It is important to recognize that the way that subjects defined it, *lo extrajudicial* was not always set in opposition to formal law in the tribunals. It was, rather, interactive with formal law. In 1732, the *Diccionario de Autoridades* defined 'extrajudicial' as 'that which is treated, convened and adjusted outside of a suit, without following the formalities of law [*derecho*]'.[10] Notably, the definition went on to discuss the process by which unwritten legal actions became notarized and formalized.

While the long process of centralization of the Iberian realms meant that the tendency over time was toward formalization and the channelling of conflict into royal courts and official ledgers – with a 1567 Castilian law expressly attempting to limit the legitimacy of contracts and accords made in writing without royal sanction – in truth, the realities of running a large empire meant that an array of semi-formal activities, including oral statements and agreements, were considered valid.[11] For example, in the native pueblo of San Vicente Lachixío in Oaxaca in the 1790s, a dying community member's last will and testament would be uttered before 'the republic', meaning the gathered members of the village council, who held local jurisdiction over civil and criminal affairs. Such testimony was considered as binding as any written document, despite the fact that, in this region as in others in Mexico, each major village had native notaries well versed in written Spanish legal genres and able to record them in native languages.[12] Even during the sweeping absolutist administrative reforms of the late 1700s, when the Spanish Bourbon monarchy left little of the legal system untouched, the crown not only continued to tolerate but even encouraged dispute settlement outside the formal processes of law to facilitate the 'friendly rectification of parties, excusing them from [formal] procedure whenever [cases] are not serious'.[13]

Although justice took place within more community-embedded, semi-formal relationships and processes than in the courts of our modern imagination, it was no less fractious. A testy villager in the Montes de Toledo named Juan Gómez Gordo, who quarrelled frequently with his wife, ran afoul of village officials one hot summer evening. The entire affair would have been settled verbally and informally had Juan not lost his temper at their intervention and stabbed the *alcalde*.

As they hauled him off to the town jail, he reminded them loudly, 'Your homes do not lack for disagreements, either'.[14] Juan's saucy response reminded the legal officials that their private lives were no less subject to scrutiny than was his, and that the community, in the end, was the true judge in the village.

Honour and reputation

Indeed, one central aspect of community justice, as it was enacted beyond the courtrooms, involved the adjudication of honour. Scholars have long been attracted to the workings of this key cultural institution in determining the course of justice – as a legitimate excuse for violence, for example, or as a feature impacting debt relations (Stern, 1995; Taylor, S., 2003). While honour certainly left its imprimatur on formal trials and litigation in the Spanish empire, it had a particularly colourful extrajudicial legal life. It was often negotiated verbally and through cultural signs, such as tipped hats and forms of address, including the use of the title 'don' or 'doña' (Taylor, S.K., 2008; Johnson and Lipsett-Rivera, 1998). Women played key roles enforcing and negotiating these norms of honour through gossip and shaming (Taylor, 2008, p. 179; Stern, 1995, pp. 142–148; Poska, 2005, pp. 105–108).

In fact, Spanish colonial inhabitants could consider courts of law as merely an extension of the community theatre of reputation. When the native woman María Oloya Pérez, from a district seat called Yanhuitlan in southern Mexico, appeared before the Spanish magistrate, her petition began not with the standard statement that she was 'complaining civil and criminally' against her husband, as a civil or criminal case might. Rather, she was 'availing myself of the laudable Justice that You distribute'. Her husband, the statement reads, 'whom I justly love and venerate, and give not the least reason to abuse my conduct and honour, has given himself over to the disgrace that is rightly named drunkenness'. When later pressed on what exactly she wanted from the judge, she stated that she wished for her husband 'to proclaim under oath whether or not she was a woman of good habits and complied with the marital bonds of matrimony to raise, feed and care for their offspring'.[15]

In this respect, María considered the Spanish colonial tribunal she approached as simply another venue, if a more public one, for seeking reputational justice. Perhaps she was inclined to envision it in this way because the court was located in the same native town where she lived, making the Spanish district magistrate a true member of the community. When women departed their homes and sought to formally use the courts to police husbands rather than to seek reputational rectification, they might have a harder time obtaining the outcome they wanted. Or, perhaps, complaining to a judge was part of the everyday negotiation of daily life in marriages and communities. Bartola Bayona, from the pueblo of Guadalupe on Peru's north coast, approached the rural district judge (*juez territorial*) several times in her conflicts with her unfaithful husband in the 1780s, to no effect. Finally, in a fit of drunken rage, her husband cut off her braids – a gendered social punishment that marked a woman as dishonourable. This symbolic violence, rather than beatings and unfaithfulness to their vows of monogamy, finally prompted Spanish colonial authorities to imprison Bartola's husband.[16]

There are some cases that indicate that the very act of formally suing or levelling charges rather than waiting until a violent act made going to court inevitable was seen as dishonourable, or at least undesirable. '*Cabiloso*', a negative term tantamount to 'litigious' that was frequently thrown around in late-eighteenth-century cases, was exclusively reserved for men.[17] The term could be used against a wide variety of figures, including native elites, Spaniards living in native regions, husbands, and anyone else who was considered a 'friend of discord', or '*pleitista*' ('a suer'). But even if men were expected to refrain from entering court in a rash manner, appealing to a judge formally could be seen as particularly indecorous for women, particularly those from rural areas.

As women's petitions recounted extensive prehistories of enlisting families, neighbours and priests into their disputes with husbands, they indicated that turning to law proper was not their first choice since it exposed them publicly. Indeed, silent suffering over a long period of an unhappy marriage could strengthen a woman's side of a marital dispute. Doña María Casela's petition to an ecclesiastical judge for divorce narrated a ten-year history of trying to hide her troubled marriage from her parents until her husband physically abused her, at which point it was no longer possible 'to silence this act'. She then turned to her godfather and, in succession, other relatives who intervened on her behalf. 'Many were the extrajudicial reprimands undertaken by my relatives and his', as well as by an unnamed 'person of respect'. In the end, her petition narrates, none of this quasi-judicial castigation worked. Meanwhile, she gave him repeated notice that divorce was on the table. 'I had to admonish him multiple times that if he did not act in a different manner, I would appear before this Tribunal.'[18]

Certainly, a well-worn archetype of the long-suffering wife scripted the stories of extrajudicial appeals in such petitions (García, 2006; Delgado, 2009, pp. 101–103). But if insisting on a lawsuit proper could be construed as a masculine act, one Doña Melchora Oyos decided to embrace it. She left her children in a pueblo close to Chota, Peru, traveling to the city of Trujillo to bring a civil suit against her husband, borrowing 200 pesos from a priest in order to do so. Her husband, Pedro Alvarez, complained that, in suing him, she had abandoned their five children, including one aged only four, and he nakedly argued that her civil suit was of 'little legality because of her sex'. She, for her part, turned the gendered contradiction of suing him to her advantage: 'In sixteen years of marriage, he has not given me a single thing', her argument reads, and 'I have been Wife and Husband. At the cost of my work, today he wears the cape and clothes that serve to make him decent. . . In the mountains, the woman is the man for the work I have done, and the man is the woman in living an ostentatious life'.[19] If her husband had intended to argue that her official lawsuit before the city judge was inappropriate for a woman, she cleverly used that very fact as evidence of his neglect.

Few were as bold as the masculinized mountain-woman Melchora, but she, along with Doña María Casela, reveal that threats of going to court were useful weapons in the negotiation of reputation, and that honour had a decidedly legal edge.

Likewise, honour was frequently implicated in law. Which is to say that individuals who were fighting with their neighbours understood their exchanges as 'judicial' even when no judge or even mediating authority had been roped in. Consider the conflict that occurred in 1781 between two renters of a house and garden in Lima. Don José Taramona had signed a contract renting the house, but the current occupant refused to leave.

> Although various times I have extrajudicially summoned [*requerido*] the renter who is occupying the [house] against the owners' will and my own, not only did he excuse himself to me from moving, but did so lacking the boundaries of good upbringing, so that it was necessary for me to avail myself of judicial means.[20]

It is telling that Don José chose such legally loaded language to describe his interactions with the renter, positioning himself as the executor of a binding contract, and blaming the intransigent occupant's 'lack of good upbringing' for the fact they had ended up in court. But ending up in court was not only a failure for Don José and his extrajudicial efforts to police the dispute. It also dragged the defendant down. This made the threat of having a dispute aired before a judge – rather than the suit itself or its sentence – enough to make an opponent pre-emptively buckle. In eighteenth-century Spanish America, the petitions enslaved men and women of African descent increasingly brought during the century against their masters for excessive physical punishment (*sevicia*) seemed intended in many cases not to prompt a formal ruling but to force the owner to consider selling the slave to another owner, perhaps one more amenable to permitting self-purchase arrangements.[21]

On, off and in between the court record

Spouses, too, tentatively filed suits, never intending for them to be sentenced. We have already encountered this in the case of the native woman María Oloya, who envisioned the court as a public theatre for her husband to proclaim her good honour. But even suits with ostensibly clearer aims were geared toward extrajudicial solutions. One husband, Don Pedro Crosco, openly admitted that he filed for divorce to shock his wife into reconciling with him, an intention the ecclesiastical judge supported.[22] But this kind of instrumental use of the courts was riskier for unmarried couples. When court cases would reveal sinful or criminal behaviour, such as in the case of a gentleman from Lima who was sued by his lover over child support for his illegitimate child, privacy became paramount. The don agreed to a quiet monthly payment of 6 pesos in order to avoid her 'stripping my reputation with legal appeals'.[23]

Indeed, although civil and Church courts served as theatres for negotiating honour, not every inhabitant, or even every community, in the Spanish empire was keen to put their reputation on the stage. Or on the page. In Church courts, there was an established tendency to leave the names of women accused of sexual impropriety off the papers of proceedings, where they were abstractly morally chastised but not necessarily formally prosecuted. Such was the case of a woman involved in an eight-year love affair with Don Manuel Fernández Gago, city magistrate of Colmenar de Arroyo, a village of only a couple hundred inhabitants in central Spain. The unnamed women and the judge had been living together unmarried for years. The parish priest reported having repeatedly attempted to rectify this scandalous union '*en lo extrajudicial*', but with no success. The Church's attorney for the archbishopric of Toledo became involved after his court notary had run into Fernández at a religious festival in a nearby town, where Fernández confided in him 'as a friend' and asked if he knew how to obtain medicine to produce an abortion, since his lover was pregnant. The news led the notary first to his own confessor then finally to his boss, who initiated a case against the couple. Villagers' testimony indicated that the matter set a bad example that could circulate through the village and spread beyond it. But they were cleverly vague, insinuating that the written prosecution, not the extra-sacramental pairing itself, was the dangerous part of the affair.[24]

The admission of gossip and extrajudicial information that underlay this case was not at all unusual. Community judges often reported initiating criminal suits '*de oficio*' because 'it had become notorious' in the village or town that a moral infraction was occurring.[25] Other times, even appeals-level judges would settle cases based on information that they expressly stated they gathered off the record. The magistrate known as the Fiel del Juzgado in the city of Toledo, who held civil and criminal jurisdiction over eleven pueblos in the mountainous region south east of the city known as the Montes de Toledo, often legally traded in such information. When a 21-year-old maiden named Josefa Morena, who had long been rumoured to be having an affair with a married man in the town of Sonseca, fled her village with him on a stolen horse, she was arrested and brought to the imperial city of Toledo. There, the Fiel del Juzgado gathered information '*estrajudicialmente*' to prove that the black horse used in her escape had been stolen from a poor man in a neighbouring village, as well as to amass information indicating that Josefa's parents had been too quick to believe the rumours. He arranged her return to her pueblo, admonishing her parents to treat her 'with more tenderness and refrain from mistreatment'.[26]

Just as verbal and written information flowed back and forth in *lo extrajudicial*, legal interactions with judges easily slipped the shackles of strict jurisdictional categorization. Magistrates like the Fiel del Juzgado often engaged in what we might understand as counselling or spiritual advising rather than ruling. In turn, priests often filled the role of judge from the confessional, as did elders and native village officials, all of whom held quasi-familial intimacy with community members. All of these authority figures counselled irritable villagers or spatting spouses, often seeking to make peace without formal proceedings. Church authorities' movement into *lo extrajudicial* was to be expected in marital disputes, since ecclesiastical courts held jurisdiction over sacramental affairs. But it also pertained, often by custom, to priests' often-muscular intervention in civil legal affairs among villagers.

This was particularly true in more remote villages, including the native pueblos of Spanish America.

Of course, indigenous peoples had their own judges in the pueblos, and those judges often operated on the margins of formal Spanish law because of their tendency to conduct business in verbal transactions or in native languages and legal cultures only partially legible to Spanish authorities. But one priest who administered to a parish in San Pedro de Virú in Peru diminished native jurisdiction in order to elevate his own authority. He tried to convince the *corregidor* in the city of Trujillo that he rightly exercised actual civil jurisdiction in the community:

> Your Mercy does not live here as it is not possible (if only it were), [and] the priest is not just a bale of hay [sitting out in the countryside]. T]here being no other rational person to govern the Indians in the civil sphere, the priest offers himself to the Indians, and the [native judges] follow the parish priest in everything; and the [Indians] should not have to go to Trujillo every day, troubling Your Mercy with ridiculous things, when there are notable things that do not involve Indians [for you to oversee.] Your Mercy sometimes does hear suits, and I see to this so your orders are promptly executed, and I even let them appeal to you for ridiculous things, when they want, such as when they get drunk and fight. . .[27]

The priest obviously got himself a bit tangled in his own assertion of civil authority, having to acknowledge that indigenous peoples did make use of formal, secular jurisdiction presided over by colonial authorities, as well as having to concede that a sphere of native judicial authority also existed in the pueblo. This entanglement is telling. Despite his colonial fantasy of absolute dominion over the legal life of his parishioners, as well as reference to his role as gatekeeper for community members wishing to approach the bench of secular magistrates, distinct jurisdictional spheres blurred and overlapped in *lo extrajudicial.*

The overlap built into the early modern Spanish imperial legal system – between moral and civil, between verbal and written, between community and court – could work to the disadvantage of some potential litigants. The enslaved María Moncada, a woman identified as being from the Chala caste of West Africa, found a new owner in 1765 who would allow her to purchase her own freedom on instalment at the rate of 4 pesos a month. The new owner and María seemed to have made this arrangement before a judge but did so 'extrajudicially'. Later, her original owner died, leaving María free by testament. The extrajudicial purchase arrangement might have provided freedom for María in the short term but jeopardized her liberty in the long term.[28]

Enslaved litigants did, however, find ways to work the semi-formality of the system of self-purchase to their advantage. An enslaved *pardo* from the indigenous Mixtec town of Teposcolula named Manuel de la Trinidad approached the district magistrate in 1748, using *lo extrajudicial* to try to level the playing field with his owner. His owner and he had verbally arranged [*pactado*] that Manuel would pay him a total of 240 pesos for his freedom. That amount would be worked off with his own labour as well as that of his wife, children and some of his brothers, who pitched in to help Manuel achieve his liberty faster. In the meantime, the owner seems to have engaged in various crimes including stealing mules and kidnapping an old indigenous man. In an altercation with Manuel, the owner threatened him to 'shut up; the value of the mule is that of your entire liberty'. So Manuel decided to keep quiet, at least until the owner refused to reimburse Manuel's brothers for their work. At this point, Manuel gathered an 'extrajudicial' statement [*declaración extrajudicial*] from a local man of elite status that attested to Manuel's owner's misdeeds. The case became complicated as the judge sorted the criminal accusations from Manuel's claims to freedom but, in the end, Manuel's legal savvy in collecting his own evidence in the form of testimony was successful, and he was declared free.[29]

Manuel was lucky to find a magistrate willing to formalize his extrajudicial arrangement and accept the testimony he gathered outside of the institutions of the court. Other judges were less reliable allies for subordinates seeking formal litigation. Families or individuals could appeal multiple times only to be told that their disputes should be solved *en lo extrajudicial* – making it a space that could constrain ordinary people, prolonging their disputes. This was especially true of marriages, where ecclesiastical authorities tended to drag their feet in permitting formal divorce, seeing their primary responsibility as keeping partners married.[30] But civil officials also could turn their backs on formal cases. The criminal judge of first instance in Mexico City ignored a family's multiple reports of spousal abuse against Don Antonio Moreno, including locking his wife for days on end in a mule shed and threatening her with scissors.[31] Such official evasion devolved responsibility for settling domestic and local conflict onto individuals and the community. Particularly resourceful individuals who could or would not settle matters on their own were often left to continually seek out other authority figures besides judges, be they local priests, relatives or magistrates in other jurisdictions, to mediate their disputes.

But even these other authority figures could put off fulfilling their duties by attempting to move disputes into a more informal sphere. When a new renter objected to the amount of time it was taking to get a former occupant out of her new home, the landlord ignored the written eviction order that the new renter had had drawn up by a court official, promising to pass an 'extrajudicial message to evacuate' to the occupant.[32] Thus, in some ways, *lo extrajudicial* functioned not only to maintain the family, neighbourhood and community as the central loci of negotiating legal conflict; it also worked to preserve the status quo of imperial hierarchies by keeping people out of court and reinforcing the authority of those who already held power.

Conclusion

When the Mexico City *promotor fiscal* distinguished between real lawsuits and women's paternalistic appeals to judges, he constructed a conceptual division between law and society that privileged men as more authentic legal actors than women. When the priest of the parish in San Pedro de Virú in Peru attempted to argue that any troubles the native communities might bring to the district magistrates would be 'ridiculous things', he likewise attempted to diminish them as trivial in comparison to the legal activities of other inhabitants, namely Spaniards. In some ways, it was this conceptual division that served as a harbinger for modern legal systems, where the law was presented as a realm of state action distinct from its social milieu. In the words of Italian legal historian Paolo Grossi, in the eighteenth century, law began to be conceived as having 'its own ontological reality, to pertain to an objective order'. While in modern systems, 'justice continues to be the aim of the juridical order', he continues, 'it is an external end', separated from the ordinary person and imaged to exist at a plane accessible to a privileged few (Grossi, 2003, pp. 27, 22).

Legal historians have participated in keeping what Grossi calls this 'juridical myth of modernity' alive through our disciplinary distinctions between 'law and society', as if the law could or should be decontextualized and approached as a timeless object apart from the historical place in which it was made. As legal historians now take up the challenge of reimagining our subject not as a world apart from society but rather constitutive of it – as we turn from a 'law and. . .' to a 'law as. . .' approach – reckoning with *lo extrajudicial* might prove particularly instructive (UC Irvine Law Review, 2013, 2014, 2015.) In part this is because it reminds us that inhabitants of the early modern world approached the law as part of society, at times envisioning themselves as able to execute a 'summons' to a neighbour or to call on a judge as a father.

But this is not all it teaches us. *Lo extrajudicial* was no romantic domain of justice that was necessarily better or more egalitarian when compared to more formal systems because it was more socially embedded and communally administered. Rather, examining the space between community and court reveals that formal legal systems formed dynamically as a way to distinguish themselves from the operation of justice outside the tribunals of an expanding West. The promotor's statement speaks to a way of thinking that separates women's complaints from lawsuits, native conflicts from serious politics, unwritten from written law. Modern courts, in other words, were built not as bricks-and-mortar institutions that sealed judges off from society but rather as textual spaces that made a mythic distinction between real law and real legal subjects, and the rest.

Notes

1 The author wishes to thank the organizers and participants of three lively gatherings where this work was vetted: Karen Graubart and readers at Notre Dame History Department, and Mitra Sharafi and the scholars assembled at the 2017 Hurst Institute at the University of Wisconsin-Madison; and Damián González Escudero and the Jornada de Historiadores del Derecho at the Pontificia Universidad Católica del Perú.

2 For example, the Archivo de la Real Chancellería de Valladolid, Spain, holds 212067 abandoned cases compared to 20884 suits heard from the sixteenth to the nineteenth century.

3 This is based on my analysis of all eighteenth-century divorce and annulment suits in the Archivo Arzobispal de Trujillo (AAL), Peru.

4 Now-classic theoretical meditations on the way that the mere cataloguing of historical documents shapes our understanding of history and time include Derrida and Prenowitz (1995); Foucault (1994), and several of the contributions to Hamilton et al. (2002), especially Mbembe (2002) and Stoler (2002).

5 While beyond the scope of this chapter, it is worth noting that the number of civil disputes on file for various regions of Spanish America increases over the course of the eighteenth century while in Spain the number stabilizes or declines from earlier centuries. The trends for Spain are consonant with what has been dubbed 'the Great Litigation Decline' for eighteenth-century Europe more broadly. See Vermeesch (2015), Premo (2011b, 2017b).

6 The silences that this creates are particularly notable in the case of slave women, as explored by Fuentes (2016). However, in the case of *lo extrajudicial* in the Spanish empire, the result is often not silence but excess in the archives – an excess of materials that refer to actions outside the courts that seem fragmentary, irrelevant or unfinished, and thus that have escaped legal historians' consideration as law proper.

7 Key among these works are the classics by Nader (1997); and Merry (1999). For recent work on Latin America, see Rappaport and Cummins (2012). On the inherent 'hybridity' of early modern law, see Donlan and Heirbaut (2015). For the centrality of Spanish colonial law to understanding the global development of law, see Duve and Pihlajamäki (2015.)

8 Edwards makes the same argument for understanding 'local' legal culture in post-Revolutionary US: 'local legal practice was not some quaint, folksy exception to a formalized, rational body of state law, as is commonly assumed' (Edwards, 2008, p. 5).

9 'Peace' as a discourse and approbation of litigious or fractious neighbours can be found from Coyoacán to Cantabria to Calabria, though the terminology used to express it could be 'peace', 'order' or 'friendship'. See Astarita (1999, pp 133–136; 144), Owensby (2008, pp. 236–238) and Mantecón Movellán (1997, pp. 124–126).

10 *Diccionario de Autoridades*, tomo III (1732):

> EXTRAJUDICIAL. adj. de una term. Lo que se trata, conviene y ajusta fuera de juício, y sin arreglarse a las formalidades del derecho. Es compuesto de la preposición Extra, y del adjetivo Judicial. Latín. *Extrajudicialis.* RECOP. lib. 2. tit. 8. l. 28. Otrosi de las escritúras extrajudiciales y contratos que ante los dichos Escribanos passaren, lleven por el registro y lo que dieren signado, lo que se manda por el Arancel hecho por sus Altezas para todos los Escribanos del Reino.

> EXTRAJUDICIAL. adj. of a term. That which treats, conforms and fits outside of a suit, and without following the formalities of law. It is composed of the preposition Extra and the adjective Judicial... Furthermore, extrajudicial writings and contracts should be before Scribes, be carried in their registers and marked off by them, as mandated in the official price list of your Highnesses for all Scribes of the Kingdom.

11 *Novísima Recopilación de Castilla*, Libro X, Título, XIII, Ley VIII : 'D. Felipe II en Madrid, año 1566. Con arreglo á la ley precedente, no pueda dar fe de contrato alguno, ni acto judicial ó extrajudicial Escribano que no sea de los contenidos en ella', *Novísima Recopilación de las leyes de España*, 6 vols. (Madrid: Boletín Oficial del Estado, 1805–7).

12 'Madalena María, natural del pueblo de San Vicente Lachixío deja sus derechos a Luciano Antonio Melia, natural del mismo pueblo, de los bienes del difunto Juan Molina', Archivo del Poder Ejecuctivo del Estado de Oaxaca (APEGEO), Intendencia, Villa Alta, Leg. 1, exp. 25, 1792. For a study of such writings, see Restall, Sousa, and Terraciano (2008).

13 Instrucción a Corregidores, 15 de mayo, 1788 cáp. 2 y 3, in *Recopilación de Castilla*, Ley X, cited in *Los Códigos españoles. Concordatos y anotados*, vol. 9 (Madrid: Publicidad a carta de DM Rivadeneyra, 1850), p. 173.

14 Causa de malos tratos por oficio contra Juan Gómez Gordo, acusado de maltratar a María López su esposa, a quien escuchan llorar los alcaldes en su casa una noche, AMT (Archivo Municipal de Toledo), Navalmoral, Criminal, caja 6324, no. 3643, 1736, 1v.

15 Maria Oloya Pérez natural y vecina de Yanhuitlan... dice que Juan Montesinos, su marido, a dado en embriagarse, resultando de esto que la maltrata. Archivo Histórico Judicial de Oaxaca (AHJO), Teposcolula, Criminal, Legajo (Leg.) 42, expediente (exp.) 43, 1797, 1–1v.

16 Autos que sigue Bartola Bayona contra su marido Cipriano Dias por malos tratamientos y amancebamiento, Archivo Regional de la Libertad (ARL), Intendente, Criminal, Leg. 35, cuaderno (c.) 1347, 1788. On braids, see Socolow (1980, p. 49).

17 Da. María Josefa De Arizaga, vecina de Tehuacan contra su marido Don Fernando Monteagudo sobre malos tratamientos, Archivo General de la Nación-México (AGN-M), Civil volumen (vol.) 1500 exp. 2, 1793, 3; Traslado de los autos que D. Mateo y Martínez como apoderado del cabildo de naturales de la ciudad de Los Reyes, promovió en la corte de Madrid, sobre que se separase del cargo de procurador de los naturales a Toribio Ramos, por no ser indio entero, sino sambaigo: y sobre se le acordase a los naturales, Archivo General de la Nación del Peru (AGN-P) Derecho Indiano (DI), Leg. 23, C. 402, 1782, 29 v; Carta alegando la nulidad de elecciones de justicias en dos pueblos del partido de Comaltepec, APEGEO, Intendencia, Villa Alta, Leg. 1, exp. 3, 17, 1791, 1; Cuaderno de los autos promovidos por el subdelgado del partido de Zaña... por el cabildo de Lambayque, sobre que se remobiese y separase del cargo de protector sustituto de los naturales a D. Manuel Sararredo no obstante de que el fiscal protector general D. Jose Pareja le había prorrogado el ejercicio de dicho cargo, AGN-P DI, Leg. 25, C. 459, 1795, 22 v.

18 No me fue pocible silenciar esta acción. Fueron muchos las recombenciones extrajudiciales que se le hicieron a si por mis parientes como por los suyos, y otras personas... huve de amonestarle varias ocasciones que si no se portara de otra manera ocurriría a este Tribunal'

> Doña Ana María Casela, vecina de esta ciudad, casada con Don Vicente López de Frías, oficial de libros de los almacenes de la Dirección del Tabaco de este reino solicitando el divorcio por malos tratamientos de palabras y de hechos, AGN-M, Inquisition, vol. 1242, exp. 9, 1783, 49–73.

19 Autos seguidos Por Doña Melchora Oyos, mujer De Pedro Francisco albarez, residente en rio de Maygosbmamba jurisdicción de Chota, contra Don Pedro, sobre demanda de pensión de alimentos." In ARL Intendente, Causas Ordinarias (CO), Leg. 447, C. 316, 1796.

20 Autos Seguidos por D. José De Taramona contra Doña Francisca De Lara sobre que desocupe una vivienda." In AGN-P, Cabildo Civil (Civ.) Leg. 46, C. 831, 1781.

21 See, for example, Tomasa Rayo, negra libre con Doña Inés de la barrera sobre que se le ortogue carta de libertad, AGN-P, Real Audiencia (RA), Civ., Leg. 108, C. 914. s/f. For more on self-purchase, see de la Fuente (2007) and Premo (2011a).

22 Autos de demanda de divorcio interpuesta por don Pedro Crosco contra su eposa doña Gregoria Daza, AAT, Divorcios, 1761.

23 Autos Seguidos por Doña Juana de Luna contra Don Antonio Moreno, sobre alimentos de una hija, AGN-P RA Civ, Leg 343, C. 3100 1795, 3v.

24 De oficio contra el Alcade de Comenar dl Arroyo, Don Manuel Fernández Gago, Archivo Diocesano de Toledo, 1757.

25 See, for example, n/t, AMT, Yébenes, Criminal, caja 545, no. 20, 1722, f. 1 v.

26 Criminal Contra Pedro Venitto Vez de Sonseca sobre haverse llebado de d[ic]ha villa a una muger soltera, In AMT, Criminal, Marjaliza, caja 511, no. 18, 1728.

27 no viviendo a que VMd ni siendo posible que ojalá lo fuera y no siendo el cura bulto de paja ni aviendo otra persona rasional que govierne a los indios en lo sivil que se ofrece de indios quienes occuren a su cura de que los alcaldes la hagan en todo lo que en el curato se ofrece; que no han de ir a truxo todos los dias a quebrar la cabesa de VMd para cosas ridículas; que las cosas notables y que no son de indios a VMd se ozcura y yo cuido de esso, y de que sus ordenes tengan prompta execusión y aún en cosas de yndios y ridículas como en sus peleas que tienen quando se emborachan, dejo que occuran algunas veces y quando ellos quieren a VMd como dro.

> Expediente seguido por Juan Lorenzo Rizo, protector de los naturales del corregimiento de Truxillo, por lo tocante al común de ellos del pueblo de San Pedro De Virú, contra los alcaldes y mandones del dicho pueblo para que no apremien a los indios de su comunidad a pagar derrames gravosas, ARL, Corregimiento, CO, Leg. 224, C. 1898, 1748.

28 Autos seguidos por María Moncada, de casta chala, esclava que fue del Licenciado Don Alonso Moncada, sobre se le declare persona libre y no sujeta a servidumbre dando cumplimiento a la última voluntad de su amo como consta en una cláusula de su testamento. ARL Cab. CO, Leg. 51, C. 893, 1765.
29 Manuel de la Trinidad, pardo esclavo, sobre su libertad, AHJO Teposcolula, Criminal, Leg. 31, no. 22, 1748.
30 Among many examples, see the recounting of how the ecclesiastical judge repeatedly ignored a woman's report of abuse and forced reunion in Delito: Recurso de fuerza que interpuso Fco. De Villavendas, sobre el divorcio que entabló Don Joseph Vicente con su mujer Maria Ana Rosel; Lugar: Sta. Ma. Tlamimilolpa, AGN-M Criminal, vol. 221 exp. 6. fojas: 179–208, 1768.
31 Mariano Rodríguez, sobre el matrimonio que contrajo su hijo Manuel con María del Carmen, y malos tratamientos. Mexico, AGN- M, Bienes Nacionales, vol. 25, exp. 6, 1774.
32 Autos ejecutivos seguidos por Doña Cayetana Marín contra Doña Melchora Laines, sobre desalojo de la casa en que habita. In AGN-P, RA, Civil, 1774.

References

Astarita, T. (1999). *Village Justice: Community, Family, and Popular Culture in Early Modern Italy*. Baltimore, MD: The Johns Hopkins University Press.

Burns, K. (2010). *Into the Archive: Writing and Power in Colonial Peru*. Durham: Duke University.

de la Fuente, A. (2007). Slaves and the creation of legal rights in Cuba: *Coartación* and *Papel*. *Hispanic American Historical Review*, 87(4), pp. 659–692.

Delgado, J. (2009). 'Sin temor de Dios': women and ecclesiastical justice in eighteenth-century Toluca. *Colonial Latin American Review*, 18(1), pp. 99–121.

Derrida, J. and Prenowitz, E. (1995). Archive fever: a Freudian impression. *Diacritics*, 25(2), pp. 9–63.

Donlan, S.P. and Heirbaut, D., eds. (2015). *The law's many bodes: studies in legal hybridity and jurisdictional complexity, c. 1600–1900*. Berlin: Duncker and Humblot.

Duve, T. and Pihlajamäki, H., eds. (2015). *New Horizons in Spanish Colonial Law: Contributions to Transnational Early Modern History*. Frankfurt: Max Planck Center for European Legal History.

Edwards, L.F. (2008). *The People and Their Peace: Legal Culture and the Transformation of Inequality in the Post-Revolutionary South*. Chapel Hill: University of North Carolina Press.

Foucault, M. (1994 [1966]). The order of things, a preface. In: *An Archaeology of the Human Sciences*. New York: Vintage Books, pp. xv–xxiv.

Fuentes, M.J. (2016). *Dispossessed Lives: Enslaved Women, Violence and the Archive*, Philadelphia: University of Pennsylvania Press.

García, A.L. (2006). *El fracaso del amor: Género e individualidad en México del siglo XIX*. México DF: Colegio de México/UNAM.

Garnot, B. (2000). Justice, infrajustice, parajustice, et extra justice dans la France d'Ancien Régime. *Crime, Histoire, et Sociétés*, 4(1), pp. 103–140.

Grossi, P. (2003). *Mitología juridical de la modernidad*. Madrid: Editorial Trotta.

Hamilton, C. et al., eds. (2002). *Refiguring the Archive*. Dordrecht: Kluwer Academic Publishers.

Herzog, T. (2004). *Upholding Justice: Society, State and the Penal System in Quito (1650–1750)*. Ann Arbor: University of Michigan Press.

Johnson, L. and Lipsett-Rivera, S., eds. (1998). *The Faces of Honor: Sex, Shame and Violence in Colonial Latin America*. Albuquerque: University of New Mexico Press.

Mantecón Movellán, T.A. (1997). *Conflictividad y disciplinamiento social en la Cantabria rural del antiguo regimen*. Santander: Universidad de Cantabria/Fundación Marcelino Botín.

Mantecón Movellán, T.A. (2002). El peso de la infrajusticialidad en el control del crimen durante la Edad Moderna. *Estudis*, 28, pp. 43–75.

Mbembe, A. (2002). The power of the archive and its limits. In: C. Hamilton et al., eds. *Refiguring the Archive*. Dordrecht: Kluwer Academic Publishers, pp. 19–27.

Merry, S.E. (1999). *Colonizing Hawai'i: the Cultural Power of Law*. Princeton: Princeton University Press.

Nader, L., ed. (1997 [1969]). *Law in Culture and Society*. Los Angeles: University of California Press.

Owensby, B. (2008). *Empire of Law and Indian Justice in Colonial Mexico*. Stanford: Stanford University Press.

Poska, A.M. (2005). *Women and Authority in Early Modern Spain: the Peasants of Galicia*. New York: Oxford University Press.

Premo, B. (2011a). An equity against the law: slave rights and Creole jurisprudence in Spanish America. *Slavery & Abolition*, 32(4), pp. 495–517.

Premo, B. (2011b). Quejas ilustradas. Litigios en la historia de España e Hispanoamérica (siglo XVIII). *Memoria y Civilización: Anuario de Historia* (Navarra, Spain), 14, pp. 155–173.

Premo, B. (2017a). *The Enlightenment on Trial: Ordinary Litigants and Colonialism in the Spanish Empire*. New York: Oxford University Press.

Premo, B. (2017b). Legal writing, civil litigation, and agents in the 18th-century Spanish imperial world. *Oxford Research Encyclopedia of Latin American History*, 6 August 2017. http://latinamericanhistory.oxfordre.com/view/10.1093/acrefore/9780199366439.001.0001/acrefore-9780199366439-e-247. (Accessed 16 October 2018.)

Rappaport, J. and Cummins, T. (2012). *Beyond the Lettered City: Indigenous Literacies in the Andes*. Durham: Duke University Press.

Restall, M., Sousa, L. and Terraciano, K., eds. ([2005] 2008). *Mesoamerican Voices: Native-Language Writings from Colonial Mexico, Oaxaca, Yucatan and Guatemala*. New York: Cambridge University Press.

Stern, S.J. (1995). *The Secret History of Gender: Men, Women and Power in Colonial Mexico*. Chapel Hill: University of North Carolina Press.

Stoler, L.A. (2002). The colonial archives and arts of governance: on the content in the form. In: C. Hamilton, et al., eds. *Refiguring the Archive*. Dordrecht: Kluwer Academic Publishers, pp. 19–27.

Taylor, S. (2003). Credit, debt and honor in Castile, 1600–1650. *Journal of Early Modern History*, 7(1–2), pp. 7–27.

Taylor, S.K. (2008). *Honor and Violence in Golden Age Spain*. New Haven: Yale University Press.

Taylor, W.B. (1979). *Drinking, Homicide and Rebellion in Colonial Mexican Villages*. Stanford: Stanford University Press.

UC Irvine Law Review (2013). 'Law As. . .' Theory and method in legal history, *UC Irvine Law Review*, 1(3), pp. 239–512.

UC Irvine Law Review (2014). 'Law As . . .' II, History as interface for the interdisciplinary study of law. *UC Irvine Law Review*, 4(1), pp. 1–493.

UC Irvine Law Review (2015). 'Law As . . .' III, Glossolalia: toward a minor (historical) jurisprudence. *UC Irvine Law Review*, 5(2), pp. 519–1079.

Vermeesch, Griet (2015). The social composition of plaintiffs and defendants in the Peacemaker Court, Leiden, 1750–4. *Social History*, 40(2), pp. 208–229.

11

LEGAL PLURALISM, HYBRIDIZATION AND THE USES OF EVERYDAY CRIMINAL LAW IN QUEBEC, 1760–1867[1]

Donald Fyson

Introduction

In November 1784, a young Panawahpskek (Penobscot)[2] man, Charles Nichau Noite, was executed just outside Quebec City, for murdering two European colonists near Kamouraska, downriver, while they were on their way to Nova Scotia. But what may appear on its face as simply another instance of colonial domination of Indigenous peoples instead exhibits the sort of fluidity and interpenetration of legal orders that Lauren Benton and others have shown to be characteristic of the legal pluralism (the existence of multiple legal orders) that underlay many colonial empires (Benton, 2002; Benton and Ross, 2013). In this case, it was an encounter between two legal orders, one Indigenous, the other European, whose relationship can best be described by what Benton terms 'weak' legal pluralism: 'implicit (mutual) recognition of "other" law but no formal model for the structure of the legal order' (Benton, 2002, p. 11). Nichau Noite had been brought to Quebec City three months earlier, not by European settlers, but by a group of Wolastoqiyik (Maliseet) from the Madawaska region south-east of Quebec. After a town magistrate committed Nichau Noite to gaol to await his trial, two Wolastoqiyik leaders met with the colony's governor, Frederick Haldimand, accompanied by representatives from the Huron-Wendat nation settled just outside of Quebec City. During their exchanges, the leading Wolastoqiyik chief, François-Xavier, described Nichau Noite's actions as an outrage which had sullied and bloodied the Indigenous trails which the British had frequented since their conquest of the colony. Haldimand replied that 'following our laws and yours',[3] the guilty party must be punished by death; a clear recognition on his part of the existence of distinct European and Indigenous criminal law. François-Xavier replied that had Nichau Noite been of their own nation, they would have punished him themselves, but that since he was not, it would be better to summon Nichau Noite's own people to attend the judgment, to avoid their taking revenge for his death.

When Nichau Noite went to trial two months later, he pleaded guilty to the murders, despite being urged not to do so by his interpreter. As a result, the two judges on the bench of the colony's Court of King's Bench condemned him to death and sentenced him to hang, that being the only legal method of execution for murder under English criminal law at the time. But Indigenous leaders, including some from Nichau Noite's own group (who had come to Quebec City as requested) and others from the Six Nations Haudenosaunee (Iroquois), important military allies of the British, pleaded with Haldimand that hanging was dishonourable, asking that he be shot instead. Haldimand consulted his Executive Council, which unanimously recommended that the hanging be replaced by death by firing squad, as being 'more consonent [sic] to the Ideas of Savages'. Two of the councillors who supported this entirely extra-legal decision (at least in English criminal law) were the very judges who had just sentenced Nichau Noite to hang. Haldimand ordered the change in sentence, and Nichau Noite became the only civilian executed in Quebec under British rule not to be hanged. Many members of Indigenous groups attended the execution itself, and the two Wolastoqiyik leaders stood next to the officer in charge, apparently lending Indigenous legitimacy to a European execution and turning the ceremony into something of a hybrid affair. From Nichau Noite's perspective, though, life still ended.[4]

The Nichau Noite affair certainly illustrates the sorts of legal and political compromises that took place throughout the world during encounters between European colonizers and Indigenous peoples. However, other more mundane aspects of the case underscore another facet of the colonial encounter, this time between two different European legal norms. The Quebec City magistrate who initially committed Nichau Noite to gaol was Pierre Panet, a member of the colony's French-descended, Catholic majority. Panet had been a notary under the French régime before the British conquest, and was thus well-versed in French legal practices. He was now a Common Pleas judge and an *ex officio* justice of the peace. True to his linguistic preferences, the committal order he drew up for Nichau Noite, directed to gaoler John Hill, was written in French, and identified Nichau Noite's crime as '*avoir assasiné* [sic]', which had no clear legal equivalent in English.[5] Neither a Catholic judge nor a magistrate's order drawn up in French, using French legal terms, would have been possible in eighteenth-century England, or most of its American colonies to the south. In a newly conquered colony with an overwhelmingly French-speaking and Catholic population, they represented not so much legal pluralism, but rather the hybridization of law that accompanied empire and conquest, where the dominant colonial legal order (in this case, English criminal law) was itself fundamentally altered by contact with other legal orders (in this case, French legal traditions) and by the colonial context itself.

In legal history scholarship, Quebec[6] is indeed often presented as a prime example of legal pluralism and the hybridization of legal cultures. This is largely because of the bijuralism which resulted from the fusion of French and British legal influences in the colony's private law. Following the British conquest of 1759–1760, the existing private law of the colony, based on customary French law along with civilian and Roman influences, was forced into an often uneasy marriage with English procedural elements and other common law elements, much to the chagrin of legal nationalists in Quebec. This mix has led to a rich scholarship on the history of Quebec civil law in the century following the Conquest as a site of encounter between legal orders, the culmination being the adoption in the colony in 1866–1867 of a Civil Code and a Code of Civil Procedure that though based on French precedent, incorporated a great deal of English private law.[7]

Until recently, far less attention was paid to how criminal law and criminal justice in Quebec was also influenced by multiple legal sources and pluralistic perspectives, and how this in turn shaped how the colony's inhabitants used and were used by the criminal justice system.[8] Particularly in the period between the 1760s and the 1830s, the criminal law in Quebec was often described as a simple copy of the unreformed English criminal law received into Quebec in 1763.[9] In this view, successive colonial legislatures left the criminal law virtually unreformed for almost 80 years, due largely to legislative paralysis resulting from constant conflicts between different factions in the colony. Hence, even in the 1830s, the colony was still subject to many of the provisions of the infamous 'Bloody Code' that had been progressively softened in England itself. Following the bloody military repression of anti-colonial rebellions in 1837–1838, new political alignments opened the door to rapid modernization of the law and the state in the 1840s. However, even when more substantial criminal law reforms did occur in Quebec, they simply copied reforms already adopted in England. This colonial subordination persisted even after Canadian confederation in 1867: even when in 1869 the Canadian federal parliament adopted a series of statutes to harmonize the criminal law of the newly united colonies of British North America, it was largely a copy of a series of 1861 British statutes.

This received story of colonial shadowing of English metropolitan law and legal norms, and thus of the absence of hybridization and legal pluralism in Quebec, worked relatively well from a positivist, top-down view of the criminal law and the criminal justice system, with a focus on statutory enactments, reported case-law, and contemporary legal treatises. However, it became far harder to sustain when one began to dig down to the level of practice, and especially at the sort of low-level, everyday criminal law and justice that most ordinary people in Quebec experienced. It is from this bottom-up view that hybridization and even legal pluralism become much more evident than they are from a top-down view. To illustrate this central thesis, this text briefly addresses four topics, based largely on my own work in the field over the last two decades: the adaptation of English laws and institutions to a French colony; the influence of French norms on English penal practices; the progressive abolition of special legal status for Quebec's Indigenous peoples; and the influence of American legal precepts and norms. Each of these topics provides insight into both the possibilities and the limits of legal pluralism and hybridization in a colonial context.[10]

The adaptation of English laws and institutions to a French colony[11]

When the British conquest of the former French colony of Quebec was confirmed at the end of the Seven Years War, the new colonial masters had to decide what law was to be in force in their new possession. The colony's 70,000 or so French and almost entirely Catholic inhabitants, generally referred to as *Canadiens*,[12] had previously been subject to French civil and criminal law. What laws were they now to be subject to? After a decade or so of intense debate, the British formally restored most of pre-Conquest French-based private law, under the provisions of the 1774 Quebec Act. But this explicit openness to legal pluralism and hybridization, at least within the broader context of the British empire, did not apply to criminal law. While there was some discussion among colonial administrators of instituting a hybrid system of French and English criminal law,[13] as was the case in some other English colonies, this was ultimately rejected. The same Quebec Act which explicitly restored French civil law also explicitly maintained English criminal law, the (largely disingenuous) argument expressed in the Act being that:

> the Certainty and Lenity of the Criminal Law of England, and the Benefits and Advantages resulting from the Use of it, have been sensibly felt by the Inhabitants, from an Experience of more than Nine Years, during which it has been uniformly administered.[14]

Furthermore, at least on paper, there was no recognition of any general form of legal pluralism with regards to the criminal law: from 1763 onwards, all inhabitants of the colony, whether French, British, or even to some extent Indigenous, were theoretically subject to the criminal justice of the Crown.

When British civil administration was initiated in the colony in 1764, the legal substrate in the colony was thus undeniably unreformed English criminal law, with a single system for both the conquered *Canadien* population and more recent British settlers. Not only was the criminal law itself firmly English, so too were the criminal courts. When they were established in 1764, the new judicial institutions were largely simplified versions of the common law courts of England, much as might be found in other British colonies in North America. Hence, on the criminal side, for more serious cases, there was a Court of King's Bench, held by the colony's Chief Justice; and at the lower level, justices of the peace who held quarter sessions for lesser crimes such as assaults and petty thefts, and weekly sessions for regulatory matters.[15] The quintessential English criminal institution of the jury was also implanted, both grand juries and trial juries.

This radical shift in penal norms and institutions, it has been argued, was a prime factor in alienating the colony's *Canadien* majority. For one thing, English criminal law had little ideological resonance for them, and was also not readily available in their own language. Furthermore, the criminal courts were staffed by English judges and officials and operated in English. As a result, the *Canadien* population on the whole avoided the criminal justice system, just as they had avoided the civil law courts before French civil law was restored.[16] This alienation has also sometimes been taken up by one particularly nationalist stream of Quebec historiography which sees the Conquest as having been the ultimate disaster for Quebec's francophone population. In their view, the wholesale imposition of English criminal law and justice was yet another example of English oppression of the colonized *Canadien* majority.[17]

The problem is that empirically, the notion of particularly *Canadien* avoidance of the criminal courts is not tenable, at least in regards to the lower criminal courts, where most cases were heard. From the 1760s to the 1830s, *Canadien* plaintiffs and defendants made up the majority of those before the lower criminal courts, and showed no particular disposition to avoiding them when they could be useful. Furthermore, *Canadien* plaintiffs, both men and women, were drawn above all from the popular classes, and complained above all against other *Canadien* men and women.[18] In that respect, they were no different from *ancien-régime* populations elsewhere in Europe and colonial North America: while there is no indication that they were particularly satisfied with British criminal justice, as the framers of the Quebec Act would have it – and it is easy to find examples of individual resistance by *Canadien* men and women towards specific agents of the system, such as constables, bailiffs, or magistrates (many of whom were also *Canadiens*) – there is no indication either that there was a broad-scale popular struggle against the criminal justice system, except perhaps during the two years of active rebellion in 1837–1838. How then to explain this relatively frequent recourse of *Canadien* plaintiffs to a criminal justice system that was apparently alien to them? Part of the answer lies in its relatively plural and hybrid nature.

For one thing, although the criminal law in the restricted sense of the substantive law relating to major crimes did not change much before the early 1840s, there were many formal adaptations of the penal law more generally to fit local colonial circumstances. Local penal legislation is a case in point. This was generally ignored by those who postulated the wholesale introduction of English criminal law, or at best, dismissed as relatively unimportant. And yet, from the Conquest onwards, local legislators adopted a wide range of penal measures to address circumstances that were entirely foreign to the English context, such as trade with Indigenous peoples or universal militia service. Since English law could provide little guidance in these matters, local legislators had to fill the gap, just as had been the case under the pre-Conquest French régime. Indeed, many of the ordinances and acts adopted in the eighteenth century in particular were very similar to analogous legislation of the French régime, which rendered them all the more familiar to the *Canadien* population, and no more popular. As colonial circumstances changed, so too did this normative framework: for example, from the end of the eighteenth century, there were increasingly complex penal provisions associated with the laws on roads repairs, which had become essential to maintaining the economic growth so cherished by colonial elites. Furthermore, these laws were always published in both

English and French, making them far more accessible to the *Canadien* population than English criminal law as such (Fyson 2006, pp. 19–23).

A broader definition of what constitutes penal law must also take into consideration the legislation promulgated by the colony's justices of the peace, especially in the cities. In the absence of elected town corporations, justices were largely responsible for local administration, and as part of their exercise of this power, right from the beginning of British rule they promulgated what were known as rules and regulations of police (in the older sense of local administration). These rules and regulations became increasingly complex and interventionist over the years, as the cities grew rapidly, and addressed more and more aspects of daily urban life. By the beginning of the nineteenth century, the rules for both Quebec City and Montreal had become veritable law codes (the first true attempt at codification of law in the colony), each with more than a hundred articles divided into chapters, and bilingual to boot. These regulations addressed traditional urban matters such as the regulation of markets and rates of carriage, building norms, and hygiene, but also sought to regulate or repress behaviours that were more directly related to criminal law, such as vagrancy and begging. They also criminalized matters we would today consider to be the purview of the civil courts, notably relations between masters and servants. As colonial conditions and elite ideologies changed, so too did the regulations: for example, regulations promulgated in the first decades of the nineteenth century reflected the hardening of urban elite attitudes towards behaviours deemed disorderly or immoral, and contributed directly to growth of repression through punishments such as imprisonment. Police regulations, just like other local legislative measures, thus created a penal law that was far from static and that was adapted to the changing desires of local elites, unlike criminal law in the narrower sense (Fyson, 2006, pp. 23–32; Fyson, 2014a).

There were also other adaptations more specific to the relation of the *Canadien* population to the criminal justice system. One example concerns juries. Quebec criminal justice historians often suggested that *Canadiens* were not particularly well disposed towards this new English institution, which they knew little of.[19] My own work has shown that to the contrary, *Canadien* men participated quite willingly in criminal juries, both grand juries and trial juries, and indeed were more assiduous in attending to their duties than their British counterparts. Equally importantly, the practice adopted in the criminal courts up until the early 1830s was that grand juries were composed about equally of English- and French-speaking jurors, and that at least in cases involving *Canadien* defendants, trial juries were *de medietate*, half English, half French. As a result, *Canadien* defendants could almost always count on mixed juries.[20]

One could argue that juries *de medietate* were already part of English law and thus did not represent a significant openness to hybridization. But this was not the case for another crucial legal measure, the exemption of Catholics from English anti-Catholic penal statutes. These were potentially in force in the colony up until the 1774 Quebec Act made them inapplicable. Under the strictest possible interpretation of these measures, Catholics (and thus almost all *Canadiens*) would have been excluded not only from all positions of trust, such as the magistracy and other judicial offices, but also from legal professions such as attorneys and notaries, and even from juries. Had this been followed, *Canadien* parties could never have been represented by or dealt with legal figures who shared their religion and their language. However, colonial governors essentially ignored most of these anti-Catholic provisions, and especially those that excluded Catholics from positions of trust. Apart from the magistracy, which the governors were explicitly instructed to name only from among the few Protestants in the colony, Catholic *Canadien* men continued to act as court clerks, bailiffs, attorneys, jurors, and so on. The legal justification was not that these *Canadiens* deserved special status, but rather, that the penal statutes did not apply in the colony at all; an explicit recognition of at least weak legal pluralism within the British empire. But in fact, this was far more a political and strategic than a legal decision, and far from benevolent. In essence, it stemmed among others from the practical necessities of governing a colony whose population was overwhelmingly Catholic and whose Protestant men were far too few to fill the necessary administrative positions, and also from the desire of the colonial governors to maintain the loyalty of the *Canadien* population, or at least its elites, in the face of growing unrest in the American colonies to the south. It did, however, institute a form of special legal status for the majority *Canadien* population, setting them off from their counterparts elsewhere in British North America. The Quebec Act confirmed this special status, and is indeed sometimes included among the Intolerable Acts that helped set off the American Revolution, among others because of its enshrinement of Catholic emancipation (Fyson, 2012b; Fyson, 2013a). Like local legislation and the acceptance of juries *de medietate*, the opening of at least part of the legal profession to Catholics was another sign that the colonial legal order was open to hybridization and adaptation to local colonial circumstances, the scope of which can only be fully appreciated by a bottom-up study of the law and the justice system.

English practice, French influences

The accommodation of the *Canadien* population implicit in the measures discussed in the previous section also applied in the everyday practice of criminal justice in Quebec. This left space for the expression of French influences in penal practice in Quebec, which was reflected in how *Canadien* plaintiffs and defendants used and interacted with colonial courts.

One small example concerns bastardy cases; that is to say, proceedings instituted for illegitimate births. In England, these were penal procedures, before local magistrates, which sought both to criminalize the single mothers of these children and to force the fathers to indemnify the local parish for the additional charges that would be incurred. In eighteenth-century post-Conquest Quebec, in contrast, bastardy proceedings before the justices of the peace became a means for a number of women, almost all *Canadiennes*, to obtain support payments from the fathers of their children. This was entirely at odds with English practice, and represented instead the continuation of French-régime civil law practices. In the absence of any parish-based poor law system in the colony, this repurposing of the criminal law was tolerated by Quebec magistrates right up until the end of the eighteenth century, when an English lawyer successfully argued that bastardy laws were not in fact in force in the colony.[21]

A more general example concerns language. That the criminal courts in post-Conquest Quebec operated only in English is one of the most frequently repeated 'facts' about the system, often used to underscore *Canadien* alienation. As early as 1874, Justice Thomas-Jean-Jacques Loranger, a strong Quebec conservative legal nationalist, asserted that up until 1857, the language of the criminal law meant that it had remained 'a mysterious science for the French race of Lower Canada'; and this same view has persisted ever since.[22] In the higher criminal courts, proceedings do seem to have been largely in English, although the testimony of French-speaking witnesses meant that the courtroom remained a bilingual arena. The predominance of English was in accordance with English precepts that the language of the law must be English. However, right from the beginning of British rule, in the lower courts, and notably before the colony's justices of the peace, a kind of working institutional bilingualism was implanted, just as it was in the civil courts (Garneau, 2009). This concerned not only oral proceedings, but also court documents. Arrest warrants, summonses, bail bonds, warrants of committal, were all issued in French or in English, according to the language of the justice issuing them, the party concerned, and so on. Even lower-court registers were kept in a mixture of English and French. Only indictments and analogous documents absolutely had to be drawn up in English, under the explicit provisions of English law, and even then, they were read in translation to French-speaking accused. As a result, in these lower courts, the form was English, but the language was often French, and in no way was English the only official language of the law (Fyson, 2006, pp. 249–253). Even in the higher criminal courts, one might see motions by lawyers in French, and at least in the Montreal court, when the accused were French-speaking, sentences, including death sentences, were often pronounced in French by British judges.[23]

All of this bilingualism raised interesting issues of translation. For one thing, all legislation modifying criminal law adopted in Quebec was bilingual, although general (unwritten) practice was that the English version took precedence. Furthermore, *Canadien* legal writers had to wrestle with how to translate English criminal law concepts. For example, in his 1814 treatise *Questions et réponses sur le droit criminel du Bas-Canada: dédiées aux étudiants en droit*, Joseph-François Perrault, who among other things was the clerk of the peace at Quebec City, offered translations such as '*offense capitale*', '*assaut et batterie*', and '*reconnaissance*', all of which would have shocked the ears of a French-language purist, but were perfectly comprehensible in the context of a mixed-language penal justice system (Perrault, 1814). This early bilingualism was inspired less by a project of colonial domination than by the practical necessity of communicating with *Canadien* parties who came before the courts. But it was also due to strong representation of *Canadiens* among local magistrates and court officials (Perrault being but one example).[24] As well, many British judges and magistrates understood French. It also laid the groundwork for future institutional bilingualism in the criminal justice system in the nineteenth century. By 1874, it was definitively established that even indictments could be in French; and when the Canadian Criminal Code was adopted in 1892, it was entirely bilingual, marking the first official translation of most of the criminal law into French.[25]

One might also note the frequent equivalencies between English and French penal practices, especially in minor criminal cases. One example is the quasi-civil nature of criminal cases involving minor violence, such as assault and battery prosecutions. Essentially, as in many other jurisdictions, plaintiffs could launch a complaint, have their antagonist arrested and dragged before a magistrate, and then drop the case, without any particular consequence. This instrumentalization of the criminal justice system was not at odds with English practices; but very importantly, it was also similar to pre-Conquest French-régime practices, and in particular, the role of the *partie civile* in assault cases and the frequent decriminalization of such cases (Fyson, 2006, pp. 272–289; Leclerc, 1985; Garneau, 1995). More generally, from the point of view of the plaintiff, making a complaint for assault, for petty theft, or for other lesser crimes was quite similar under both systems, French and English (Fyson, 2006, pp. 17–19). At any rate, *Canadien* parties adapted quite well even to those aspects of English criminal law that were entirely new to them, such as defence counsel or pardons (Fyson, 2012a). Added to the bilingual nature of the local courts, this made English criminal justice, at least at its lower levels, far more palatable and understandable to *Canadien* parties, who used the lower-level criminal courts in this fashion abundantly; far more often in assault cases than the civil courts, which applied French law. And it also may explain why there was very little structured infrajustice in Quebec: recourse to the lower courts seems largely to have taken the place of customary third-party mediation. Overall, the influence of French legal practices on the colony's purportedly purely English criminal justice system helps explain why right from the beginning of British rule, *Canadiens*, both men and women, seem to have had frequent recourse to the English colonial criminal courts, and especially the lower criminal courts, even though they applied a criminal law in theory alien to them.

Indigenous peoples

The low-level adaptation of colonial criminal law and justice to the specific circumstances of Quebec's *Canadien* population provides an example of hybridization within the broader context of the British empire, and of the legal pluralism of the empire taken as a whole. However, it is not a particularly strong example of legal pluralism within the colony's legal order, for even in practice, there was no special status (positive or negative) for *Canadien* parties: other than with regards to language, they were treated no differently from their British counterparts. A clearer example of legal pluralism expressed in practice rather than through the formal law concerns the changing relationship between Quebec's small Indigenous population and British criminal law and criminal justice, as the case of Nichau Noite suggested. As elsewhere in North America, the subject has received considerable scrutiny in recent years, in connection with ongoing litigation over sovereignty and land claims; the question being whether the British Crown regarded Indigenous peoples as subjects or as allies.[26]

Under the French régime, before the Conquest, official discourse generally presented Indigenous peoples as subordinate to the French Crown and subject to French criminal justice. Nevertheless, in practice, colonial administrators applied a type of weak, informal legal pluralism with regards to them. Even members of Indigenous groups who lived on reserves in close proximity to the colony's cities, such as the Huron-Wendat of Wendake, near Quebec City, or the Kanien'kehá:ka (Mohawk) of Kanehsatà:ke and Kahnawá:ke, near Montreal, were essentially exempt from colonial criminal justice. This was not the result of any formal recognition of legal pluralism in regards to these groups but, rather, reflected strategic considerations. Indigenous peoples were essential economic partners and military allies of the French, and French officials thus hesitated to impose royal justice upon them if they did not want it. Members of Indigenous groups in turn almost never had recourse to the royal courts. In the few instances where they were accused or condemned before the colonial criminal courts, administrators generally found the means to remove them from the process. The only exceptions were the *panis*, Indigenous slaves, who like their Black counterparts were subject to the full force of French criminal law (Dickinson, 1994; Grabowski, 1996; Delâge and Gilbert, 2004).

The shift from French to British colonial rule in this regard brought little immediate change.[27] After the Conquest, as before, there was no clear formal recognition of general special status for Indigenous peoples with regards to the criminal law, although some of the treaties made between the British and Indigenous groups formerly allied to the French did stipulate that they had the right to continue the free exercise of their customs. From a positivist legal perspective, Quebec's Indigenous inhabitants, and especially those established within the European zone of settlement, should probably have been subject to European criminal law, at least in regards to more serious crimes; this was also the perspective of some British colonial administrators of the time, although not apparently Haldimand, as we saw (Delâge and Sawaya, 2001, pp. 55–61, 65–66). And yet, when actual practice has been examined, it appears that in the eighteenth century, the British continued what the French had already undertaken before the Conquest: implicit recognition of entirely separate legal status for Indigenous peoples. In all, between 1760 and 1800, there are fewer than a dozen Indigenous accused among the 800 or so defendants before the superior criminal courts of Quebec. In essence, potential criminal cases involving only Indigenous peoples were left to be dealt with by Indigenous groups themselves, even in serious cases such as homicide. This allowed for Indigenous groups to perpetuate their own legal practices, within their own customary system, and to continue avoiding the now-British colonial criminal courts. Even in criminal cases involving Europeans, colonial governors and courts very often treated Indigenous peoples differently. Hence, between 1760 and 1800, there were indeed three Indigenous defendants executed for the murder of Europeans (out of fifty non-military executions in all), but even there, as we saw in the case of Nichau

Noite, Indigenous legal norms and customs could over-ride European ones.[28] In a context where military alliances with Indigenous groups were essential to the British, among others in their struggles against the American colonies, law gave way to political and strategic expediency.

Even in the eighteenth century, not all European colonists were sanguine about the apparent openness of British colonial administrators to Indigenous legal precepts. Soon after Nichau Noite was imprisoned, a petition from three dozen prominent Quebec City residents, many from the city's merchant community (to whom his victim had belonged), urged Governor Haldimand to have him tried without delay, and unfavourably contrasted Indigenous and European legal notions:

> the smallest hesitation or even delay in punishment being so totally repugnant to the Ideas of the Savages themselves whose Law is retaliation, may be construed by them to be pusillanimous fear; while a well timed legal severity will secure their future good Behaviour.

Haldimand refused, saying simply that he would be tried 'in due course of Law', thus replying to the petitioners with an entirely European legal argument. Similar views appear to have circulated regarding Nichau Noite's execution by firing squad rather than by hanging: in his private journal, Royal Engineer James Thompson noted 'Thus he was indulged with an honor of dying that could not be granted to the first Peer of the Realm', and gave the example of Lord Ferrers (executed for murder at Tyburn in 1760), refused death by firing squad, execution in the tower, and even a silk rope, 'but must be hanged like a Common malefactor, in the common place of Execution'.[29] For Thompson, as for the merchants, English criminal law norms were clearly meant to prevail in the colony, even in cases involving Indigenous defendants.

Governors could ignore this Eurocentric positioning in the eighteenth century, but in the nineteenth century, the decline in the strategic importance of Quebec's Indigenous groups was accompanied by the decline in their special legal status and their gradual subjection to British criminal law. This was already being mooted by colonial legal officials in the late eighteenth century. Hence, in 1797, the colony's attorney general (and later chief justice), Jonathan Sewell, recommended turning down a request from the Seven Nations alliance (which included most of the Indigenous groups living in or near the European zone of settlement in Quebec) that they be exempted from colonial justice in cases that only concerned their own members. Sewell's reasoning explicitly rejected the notion of legal pluralism, for both civil and criminal law:

> In this, they ask what nothing less than an Act of Parliament can effect. They are the Kings [sic] subjects, they individualy [sic] owe him allegiance, and are in return entitled individually to that Protection in Person and Property, which His Majesty's Courts afford. If even they are to be considered, not as

> Subjects, but as temporary Residents in the Province, the case is the same; they owe individually a temporary Allegiance to His Majesty, and in Return are individually entitled to that Protection in person and Property, which our Law affords to Alien Friends.[30]

At the same time, Sewell also recognized that up until then, the practice had been not to intervene in criminal matters that involved only Indigenous parties: 'the Question, which the Seven Villages wish on this head to agitate, is well understood, and it may be perhaps better to suffer it to remain as it is undisturbed'. More clearly, in 1801, John Lees, a prominent Lachine justice of the peace, commented on an assault case brought before him by a Kanien'kehá:ka plaintiff:

> I suppose it is the first instance of an Indian prosecuting another in a judicial manner for a beating; however I think it full time that the gentry should be brought under the civil law and encourage it as much as I can.

Lees' opinion carried weight: he was not only a magistrate, but also a member of the colony's House of Assembly and Executive Council and a high official in the Indian Department; he had also served on the grand jury which had indicted Nichau Noite in 1784 (Fyson, 2006, pp. 302–304).

As well, some members of Indigenous groups began themselves to have more regular recourse to the criminal courts, even if most still resisted the implantation of local judicial institutions such as justices of the peace (Lefrançois, 2004). Although Indigenous plaintiffs and defendants remained a tiny minority of those who appeared before the colonial courts, their presence in the nineteenth century was still far greater than in the eighteenth. As well, there were more Indigenous prisoners in the colony's prisons, although again, they remained a tiny minority of prisoners overall. Although much work remains to be done to sketch out the exact contours of this transition, such as the motivations of Indigenous plaintiffs who had recourse to the criminal courts, it appears that the Indigenous peoples of Quebec were progressively coming under the sway of European criminal justice. One might be tempted to suggest that this meant that Indigenous groups were recognizing the legitimacy of the colonial courts. However, there seems clearly to have been a difference between traditionalists and non-traditionalists in this regard, traditionalists generally continuing to avoid the European criminal justice system. But certainly, by the early 1850s, it was quite possible for one Mik'maq man to be convicted for the murder of his son-in-law, in a case that turned on the testimony of the accused man's own daughter, wife of the victim. This was a case involving only Indigenous parties, all from the same family, which would have been unthinkable in the eighteenth century (Fyson, 2013b, p. 284). None of this story of the decline of legal pluralism and rise of legal centralism as they applied to Quebec's Indigenous inhabitants is visible in positive law; only the study of practice can reveal it.

American influences

A final example of how studying everyday practice can reveal the hybridization of criminal law in Quebec and its impact on the uses of justice in the colony is the influence of American models. Certainly, from a positivist perspective, it was unthinkable that American criminal law and legal precedent could influence criminal law and criminal justice in Quebec, especially after the Revolution. But they did.

One early example is the system of state prosecution for serious offences. In post-Conquest Quebec, unlike in eighteenth-century England, there was little place for private prosecutors in more serious cases heard before the higher criminal courts. Instead, all capital and serious criminal cases were prosecuted by the colony's law officers, at the (often considerable) expense of the Crown. This fundamentally changed the way that victims of serious crime interacted with the justice system. Instead of being the motors of prosecution, they were reduced to the status of simple witnesses for the Crown; at the same time, it cost them nothing. This was, however, not a Quebec invention; instead, it had already been the practice in many of Britain's American colonies and in Nova Scotia. This also represented a direct continuity with pre-Conquest French practice in the colony, which once again rendered the new post-Conquest English criminal justice system less strange and more easy to understand for the *Canadien* population. However, this did mean that *Canadien* plaintiffs had far less agency in the higher criminal courts than in the lower courts, where they themselves mainly drove the prosecutions they engaged in. Furthermore, until the middle of the nineteenth century, crown law officers were almost always anglophones (Fecteau, 1989, pp.110–111; Stenning, 1986, pp. 40–42; Morel, 1978, pp. 528–533).

Another example concerns the police. As elsewhere in the Western world, Quebec saw significant reform of policing structures from the 1810s onwards, with the gradual establishment of professional police forces. However, these police followed American more than English models, with heavy reliance on police forces controlled entirely by local administrations and municipal governments. Strong resistance to any centralized control of these forces meant that attempts to set up police controlled by the central government in the early 1840s and again in the 1870s were failures. Furthermore, unlike in England, there was no significant role for police as prosecutors in more serious criminal cases and indeed in cases where there was an identifiable victim. They did increasingly act as plaintiffs in cases involving victimless offences, such as public order and regulatory offences, but the prosecution of other offences remained the purview of crown prosecutors and, in some cases, court clerks. The relationship between police and victims of crime was thus a distant one; until later in the nineteenth century, when plaintiffs wanted to use the criminal justice system, they went to the local magistrates, not to the police. Overall, in their structures and in their practices, by the later nineteenth century, police forces in Quebec were far more apt to look south of the border for inspiration, rather than across the Atlantic.[31]

A final, later example of American influence on Quebec criminal law is the citing of American authorities in criminal cases. Michel Morin has suggested, based on a survey of the small number of reported criminal cases, that there was increasing openness to the practice in Quebec, but only in the second half of the nineteenth century.[32] A cursory examination of the circulation of American criminal law treatises and reports in the colony in the first half of the century certainly seems to bear this out. Hence, a small sample of the catalogues of booksellers and institutional libraries in Quebec from the 1780s to the 1830s, including the libraries of the legislature, contain virtually no American law books, criminal or otherwise. Likewise, a study of estate inventories of personal libraries in Montreal between 1800 and 1820, including the libraries of judges and court officials, showed many law books, but essentially none of them American. Finally, an impressionistic survey of the authorities cited by counsel and judges in the Montreal Court of King's Bench in the 1810s, 1820s and 1830s also leads to the same conclusion.[33] Although the limited production of American treatises before the 1830s is one clear reason, just as it was in Upper Canada and in Nova Scotia, the complete absence even of American case reports is nonetheless striking, and may reflect the sort of judicial conservatism that Eric Reiter has shown pertained with regards to the citing of European jurisprudence (other than French) in the civil law (Baker, 1985; Hibbitts, 2004, pp. 327–328; Reiter, 2004).

This appears to have begun to change by mid-century, at about the same time as American criminal law codification initiatives began to influence some politicians in Canada (Baker, 2008; Parker, 1981). Hence, the 1840 catalogue of the Advocate's Library of the Quebec City bar did contain a small handful of American reports and treatises relevant to the criminal law. The equivalent catalogue for the Montreal bar in 1857 had considerably more, and especially case reports, although the American component of the collection was still dwarfed by the library's British and especially English criminal law books.[34] The books in lawyers' libraries evidently both reflected and influenced their practice in court. By 1860, the majority on the bench of the Court of Queen's Bench felt it necessary to strongly decry the practice of citing American authorities in criminal cases. As Justice Joseph Duval put it, 'These foreign laws are inapplicable, and ought not to be received in criminal cases', while Chief Justice Louis-Hypolite Lafontaine went further: 'Suppose the man was convicted upon american [sic] authorities, would the government, upon the presentation of a petition on behalf of the prisoner representing this fact, consider it advisable to carry out the sentence'. But the opinion of Justice Thomas Cushing Aylwin, while also condemning the practice, also suggests that it had become quite common:

> The practice of late has been to create great confusion, by the habit which has prevailed, to too great an extent, of citing american, english and french [sic] authorities, in all cases indiscriminately, and it is time to put an end to such confusion.

And Justice William Collis Meredith, though rejecting the recourse to American authorities in the particular case at hand, summed up what was probably a more general opinion in the bar: in thorny cases, 'I must confess I would not be disposed to exclude the reasoning of able legal minds, whether in the United States or elsewhere'. Indeed, five years later, in an important habeas corpus case, he cited an American judge. Nor was he the only Queen's Bench justice to cite American authorities in the next few years.[35] Still, not all judges agreed: in 1869, Duval, now chief justice, once again pushed back firmly against recourse to American and other non-British precedents in criminal cases:

> The decision of the law of England is before me and I will look at that. The decisions of the law of England are ample upon the subject, and I do not see the necessity of travelling all over France, and other parts of the Continent and every one of the thirty-one United States, for the purpose of finding a decision favourable to the application. In criminal matters, foreign law should not be brought before the Court. When I want authority in this country I can find it in the English law, and if it is not there the Legislature should be advised to interfere.[36]

Clearly, in legal practice although perhaps not in legal theory, the frontier to the south was not entirely impervious, giving further fodder to defence counsel in criminal cases, though the exact timing and contours of this shift remain to be determined and much resistance remained. Legal hybridization was thus clearly still alive and well in nineteenth-century Quebec criminal practice, although its focus had shifted considerably, from French to American influences.

Conclusion

As the four topics considered above demonstrate, a top-down approach to understanding the contours and sources of criminal law, as is still far too often practised by some lawyerly legal historians, is insufficient. From this perspective, criminal law in Quebec from the Conquest to Confederation was indeed almost entirely English, with only a few minor local adaptations. But when it comes to legal pluralism and the hybridization of criminal law, practice, viewed from the bottom up, is often far more important than legislation or even reported case-law. By digging down into practice and low-level law, we can better judge the extent to which the criminal law was a site of multiple and sometimes and conflicting influences, which often fundamentally affected how the inhabitants of Quebec, and especially both its *Canadien* and Indigenous populations, interacted with and used criminal law and criminal justice.

Both explicit, formalized adaptations to colonial circumstances, such as the abandonment of the anti-Catholic penal provisions of English law, and informal measures, such as the recognition of *de facto* separate legal status for Indigenous peoples in the eighteenth century, helped create a criminal law and a criminal justice system that was far from a slavish copy of its English model. So too did its evidently French and, later, American influences, which helped make it somewhat of a hybrid system; though not to the extent of the civil law. The considerable flexibility in how criminal justice was practised on the ground, in day-to-day situations, also allowed colonial administrators to avoid provoking outright rebellion, and instead present the system as at least in part responsive to the needs of their colonized subjects, much as Douglas Hay showed long ago for the popular classes in eighteenth-century England (Hay, 1975). At the same time, this flexibility also had very practical implications for the groups involved. In the eighteenth century, Indigenous peoples were left largely to their own devices when it came to punishing crime; and throughout the period, *Canadien* men and women could often turn the system to their own purposes.

But ultimately, none of this meant that British rule in Quebec was any less colonial, or any less dominating, for this was never a situation of true, strong legal pluralism, and the system was always under hierarchical supervision (Ross and Stern, 2013, pp. 109–110). When push came to shove during the rebellions of 1837–1838, for example, colonial administrators did not hesitate to use their discretion with regards to criminal justice to punish the largely *Canadien* rebels, through multiple executions, mass deportations, and the suspension of fundamental rights such as habeas corpus and trial by jury; just as they had at earlier periods when colonial rule was threatened by internal unrest.[37] As for the colony's Indigenous peoples, once their military usefulness to the colonial state declined, they found themselves confronted by a system which no longer saw them as exempt from the rigours of European criminal law and punishment. When Noël François, a Peskotomuhkati (Passamaquoddy) man, was hanged at Trois-Rivières in 1825 for murdering a settler, he received none of the separate treatment accorded Charles Nichau Noite four decades earlier. Even though François protested his innocence to the end, he was sentenced to be hanged in front of the prison and then have his body dissected, just like all executed murderers at the time. At best, he was allowed to sing a long hymn in his own language, before the hangman turned him off.[38]

Notes

1 My thanks to the late Blaine Baker, Maxime Gohier, Daniel Rück, and the editors of the volume for their comments and suggestions; any errors are of course entirely my own responsibility.

2 His exact ethnicity is not entirely clear – some documents describe him as Maliseet (Wolastoqiyik) but native of Penobscot, others identify him as 'Satigan' (an imprecise term used at the time in English to designate the Beauce region). His name is also variously given as 'Charles, Fils de Nichau Noite', 'Charles Noite', or 'Charles Nishonoit'. I have adopted the name used on the indictment.

3 My translation.

4 The case has been noted by several other historians: Neatby, 1933, pp. 311–312; Stone, 2000, p.70; Delâge and Gilbert, 2002, pp. 107–108. The main sources are: Haldimand Collection (British Library Add MS 21661–21889), transcripts, Library and Archives Canada (henceforth LAC), MG21, vol. 64: 124–125, vol. 220: 151–154, and vol. 225-2: 362–365; LAC RG1 E1, State Minute Book D, 3 November 1784; LAC RG4 A1, vol. 27: 8878; Bibliothèque et Archives nationales du Québec, Centre d'archives de Québec

(henceforth BAnQ-Q) TL999, file 'Charles Nichau Noite'; BAnQ-Q TL18,S1,SS1, container 1980-09-024\43, file 'Québec 1784 #250'; BAnQ-Q P450, journals of James Thompson, 5 November 1784; De Gaspé, 1866, pp. 197–199.

5 LAC MG21 vol. 225-2: 362.

6 For the purposes of brevity, Quebec is used here to refer to the colony referred to variously as Canada (up to 1763), the Province of Quebec (1763–1791), and Lower Canada (1791–1841), as well as the eastern portion of the Province of Canada (1841–1867, known both as Lower Canada and Canada East); all of which corresponded approximately to the southern part of the modern Canadian province of Quebec. I exclude the western part of the Province of Quebec between 1774 and 1791, which is now Eastern Ontario and the Great Lakes region.

7 For overviews, see Baker, 2013; Greenwood, 1996.

8 For an overview of the historiography of criminal law and criminal justice in post-Conquest Quebec, see: Fyson, 2014b.

9 For examples of this perspective, see: Morel, 1978; Morin, 2000; Fecteau, 2004, pp. 129–131.

10 As this text is largely a summary of already published work, I have kept references to a minimum; fuller discussions and citations, especially of sources, can be found in my previous publications that I cite.

11 This section summarizes the argument in the first chapter of: Fyson, 2006.

12 In current standard usage, this refers to both men and women, though truly non-sexist style would call for '*Canadiens*' and '*Canadiennes*'.

13 These debates have long been addressed by historians; for a recent summary, see: Gilles, 2013.

14 An Act for making more effectual Provision for the Government of the Province of Quebec in North America, 14 George III c.83 (1774), s.11.

15 For a detailed overview, see: Fyson, 1997–2016.

16 This is a view expressed to a greater or lesser extent in: Morel, 1978; Morin, 2000; Knafla and Chapman, 1983. A more nuanced version, which nonetheless still emphasizes *Canadien* alienation, can be found in: Hay, 1981. See also Fecteau and Hay, 1997, p. 132.

17 On this view of the Conquest more generally, see: Fyson, 2016. The recent work of Nancy Christie perpetuates this simplistic nationalist perspective; see her forthcoming book (Christie forthcoming), cited in: Christie and Gauvreau, 2017.

18 These themes are explored throughout: Fyson, 2006, especially Chapters 5–8.

19 For example: Hay, 1981.

20 On grand juries: Fyson, 2001. On juries in the lower criminal courts: Fyson, 2006, pp. 243–245. On juries in the higher criminal courts: Fyson, 2012a.

21 Fyson, 2006, pp. 285–289. The brief recent analysis of these cases by Nancy Christie and Michael Gauvreau is unfortunately incomplete and inaccurate: Christie and Gauvreau, 2016.

22 Cited in 'Codification des lois criminelles', *La Thémis*, 1 (1879), p. 272 (my translation). For a recent example of this stance: Noël, 2000, p. 78.

23 There are many examples from the 1810s to the 1830s in the bench books of James Reid, King's Bench judge and later chief justice, in LAC MG24 B173.

24 On this, see: Fyson, 2006, Chapters 2–4, along with Fyson, 2005, 2009.

25 *R v. Chouinard* (1874), Queen's Bench, Quebec, *Quebec Law Reports*, 4: pp. 220–224; Morel, 1978, pp. 533–541. On translation of the Criminal Code in Quebec and the problems surrounding this, see: Kasirer, 1990, pp. 552–556.

26 For an overview of the literature and a more detailed discussion of my own findings, see: Fyson, 2013b.

27 For the relationship between Indigenous groups and British colonial criminal justice in post-Conquest Quebec, see among others: Stone, 2000; Delâge and Gilbert, 2002; Fyson, 2013b, pp. 281–290.

28 On executions in Quebec in this period: Fyson, 2015a.

29 LAC MG21 vol. 220: 151–154; BAnQ-Q P450, journals of James Thompson, 5 November 1784.

30 Sewell to Prescott, 17 February 1797, LAC MG23 GII17, series 1, vol. 17: 212–213. See also: Beaulieu, 2002, p.145.
31 For an overview of policing in Quebec, see: Fyson, 2012c. On the rise of public prosecution in the lower courts, see Fyson, 2006, pp. 332–340.
32 Morin, 2000, pp. 160–165. See also: Kasirer, 1990, pp. 527–529, which shows the expanding use of American authorities in criminal law treatises published in Quebec from the 1880s onwards.
33 For the bookseller and library catalogues, see Fyson, 2015b, pp. 3–4. On personal libraries: Guillemette, 1988, Appendices D, E, H, and J. On authorities cited, Reid bench books, LAC MG24 B173.
34 *Catalogue of Law Books Belonging to the Quebec Advocates Library*, Quebec: Fréchette, 1840; *Catalogue of the Advocates' Library and Library of the Bar of Lower Canada: Section of the District of Montreal*, Montreal: John Lovell, 1857.
35 *R v. Creamer* (1860), Queen's Bench, Appeal Side, Quebec, in: Mathieu, 1894, pp. 435–437; *Ex parte Blossom* (1865), Queen's Bench, Appeal Side, Quebec, in: Mathieu, 1895b, p. 418; *R v. Roy et al.* (1867), Queen's Bench, Montreal, in Mathieu, 1895a, p. 500.
36 *Notman v. R* (1869), Queen's Bench, Appeal Side, Montreal, in: Mathieu, 1896, p.418.
37 See in particular: Greenwood and Wright, 1996, 2002.
38 *Montreal Herald*, 19 September 1825 and 26 September 1825.

References

Baker, G.B. (1985). The reconstitution of Upper Canadian legal thought in the late-Victorian Empire. *Law and History Review*, 3(2), pp. 219–292.

Baker, G.B. (2008). Strategic Benthamism: rehabilitating united Canada's bar through criminal law codification, 1847–54. In: J. Phillips, R.R. McMurtry, and J.T. Saywell, eds., *Essays in the History of Canadian Law: Volume X: a Tribute to Peter N. Oliver*. Toronto: Osgoode Society for Canadian Legal History and University of Toronto Press, pp. 257–319.

Baker, G.B. (2013). Introduction: Quebec and the Canadas, 1760 to 1867: a legal historiography. In: G.B. Baker and D. Fyson, eds., *Essays in the History of Canadian Law: Volume XI: Quebec and the Canadas*. Toronto: Osgoode Society for Canadian Legal History and University of Toronto Press, pp. 3–95.

Beaulieu, A. (2002). *La question des terres autochtones au Québec 1760–1860*. Varennes: Report prepared for the Ministère de la Justice and the Ministère des Ressources naturelles du Québec.

Benton, L. (2002). *Law and Colonial Cultures: Legal Regimes in World History, 1400–1900*. Cambridge: Cambridge University Press.

Benton, L. and Ross, R.J. (2013). *Legal Pluralism and Empires, 1500–1850*. New York: NYU Press.

Christie, N. (forthcoming). *A Northern Bastille: the Formal and Informal Politics of Colonialism in Quebec, 1763–1837*. Montreal: McGill–Queen's University Press.

Christie, N. and Gauvreau, M. (2016). Marital conflict, ethnicity, and legal hybridity in postconquest Quebec. *Journal of Family History*, 41(4), pp. 430–450.

Christie, N. and Gauvreau, M. (2017). 'Freedom of the Fassions': the politics of the street in Montreal and the struggle against the British fiscal-military state. *Critical Historical Studies*, 4(1), pp. 75–106.

De Gaspé, P.A. (1866). *Mémoires*. Ottawa: G.E. Desbarats.

Delâge, D. and Gilbert, E. (2002). La justice coloniale britannique et les Amérindiens au Québec 1760–1820. II – En territoire colonial. *Recherches amérindiennes au Québec*, 22(2), pp. 107–117.

Delâge, D. and Gilbert, E. (2004). Les Amérindiens face à la justice coloniale française dans le gouvernement de Québec, 1663–1759. *Recherches amérindiennes au Québec*, 33(3), pp. 79–90; and 34(1), pp. 31–42.

Delâge, D. and Sawaya, J.-P. (2001). *Les traités des Sept-Feux avec les Britanniques: droits et pièges d'un héritage colonial au Québec*. Sillery: Septentrion.

Dickinson, J.A. (1994). Native sovereignty and French justice in early Canada. In: J. Phillips, T. Loo, and S. Lewthwaite, eds., *Essays in the History of Canadian Law: Volume V: Crime and Criminal Justice*. Toronto: Osgoode Society for Canadian Legal History and University of Toronto Press, pp. 17–40.

Fecteau, J.-M. (1989). *Un nouvel ordre des choses: la pauvreté, le crime, l'État au Québec, de la fin du XVIIIe siècle à 1840*. Outremont: VLB.

Fecteau, J.-M. (2004). *La liberté du pauvre: sur la régulation du crime et de la pauvreté au XIXe siècle Québécois*. Montreal: VLB.

Fecteau, J.-M. and Hay, D. (1997). 'Government by will and pleasure instead of law': military justice and the legal system in Quebec, 1775–83. In: F.M. Greenwood and B. Wright, eds., *Canadian State Trials: Volume I: Law, Politics, and Security Measures, 1608–1837*. Toronto: Osgoode Society for Canadian Legal History and University of Toronto Press, pp. 129–171.

Fyson, D. (2001). Jurys, participation civique et représentation au Québec et au Bas-Canada: les grands jurys du district de Montréal (1764–1832). *Revue d'histoire de l'Amérique française*, 55(1), pp. 85–120.

Fyson, D. (2005). Judicial auxiliaries across legal regimes: from New France to Lower Canada. In: C. Dolan, ed., *Entre justice et justiciables: les auxiliaires de la justice du Moyen Âge au XXe siècle*. Sainte-Foy: Presses de l'Université Laval, pp. 383–403.

Fyson, D. (2006). *Magistrates, Police, and People: Everyday Criminal Justice in Quebec and Lower Canada, 1764–1837*. Toronto: Osgoode Society for Canadian Legal History and University of Toronto Press.

Fyson, D. (2009). Domination et adaptation: les élites européennes au Québec, 1760–1841. In: C. Laux, et al., eds., *Au sommet de l'Empire. Les élites européennes dans les colonies (XVIe–XXe siècle)*. Bern: Peter Lang, pp. 167–196.

Fyson, D. (2012a). The *Canadiens* and the bloody code: criminal defence strategies in Quebec after the British Conquest, 1760–1841. *Quaderni Storici*, 47(3), pp. 776–779.

Fyson, D. (2012b). The conquered and the conqueror: the mutual adaptation of the Canadiens and the British in Quebec, 1759–1775. In: P.A. Buckner and J.G. Reid, eds., *Revisiting 1759: the Conquest of Canada in Historical Perspective*. Toronto: University of Toronto Press, pp. 194–199.

Fyson, D. (2012c). La police au Québec, 1760–1878: des modèles impériaux dans une colonie nord-américaine. In: V. Denis and C. Denys, eds., *Polices d'empires, XVIIIe–XIXe siècles*. Rennes: Presses universitaires de Rennes, pp. 95–113.

Fyson, D. (2013a). Les Canadiens et le Serment du Test. In: L. Veyssière, S. Imbeault, and D. Vaugeois, eds., *1763. Le traité de Paris bouleverse l'Amérique*. Quebec City: Septentrion, pp. 272–277.

Fyson, D. (2013b). Minority groups and the law in Quebec, 1760–1867. In: G.B. Baker and D. Fyson, eds., *Essays in the History of Canadian Law. Volume XI: Quebec and the Canadas*. Toronto: Osgoode Society for Canadian Legal History and University of Toronto Press, pp. 281–290.

Fyson, D. (2014a). La gouvernance municipale avant la municipalité: Montréal, 1760–1840. In: L. Robichaud, H. Bérubé, and D. Fyson, eds., *La gouvernance montréalaise: de la ville-frontière à la metropole*. Quebec City: Multimondes, pp. 25–41.

Fyson, D (2014b). Between the ancien régime and liberal modernity: law, justice and state formation in colonial Quebec, 1760–1867. *History Compass*, 12(5), pp. 412–432.

Fyson, D. (2015a). La peine capitale au Québec, 1759–1869: modèle européen ou spécificité coloniale? In: E. Wenzel and E. de Mari, eds., *Adapter le droit et rendre la justice aux colonies (16e-19e siècles)*. Dijon: Éditions universitaires de Dijon, pp. 229–240.

Fyson, D. (2015b). Beccaria contre Howard? La réforme pénale au Québec, 1760–1841. www.profs.hst.ulaval.ca/Dfyson/Beccaria.pdf.

Fyson, D. (2016). The *Canadiens* and the Conquest of Quebec: interpretations, realities, ambiguities. In: S. Gervais, C. Kirkey, and J. Rudy, eds., *Quebec Questions: Quebec Studies for the Twenty-First Century*. Toronto: Oxford University Press, pp. 19–36.

Fyson, D. with the assistance of Kolish, E. and Schweitzer, V. (1997–2016). *The Court Structure of Quebec and Lower Canada, 1764 to 1860*, revised ed. Montreal: Montreal History Group. www.profs.hst.ulaval.ca/Dfyson/Courtstr/.

Garneau, J.-P. (1995). *Justice et règlement des conflits dans le gouvernement de Montréal à la fin du Régime français*. M.A., Université du Québec à Montréal.

Garneau, J.-P. (2009). Gérer la différence dans le Québec britannique: l'exemple de la langue (1760–1840). In: L. Derocher et al., eds., *L'État canadien et la diversité culturelle et religieuse, 1800–1914*. Quebec City: Presses de l'Université du Québec, pp. 21–48.

Gilles, D. (2013). Peine, jury et habeas corpus: le débat juridique autour des qualités du droit pénal français et du droit criminel britannique après la Conquête du Canada (1760–1791). In: Y. Jeanclos, ed., *La dimension historique de la Peine 1810–2010*. Paris: Economica, pp. 216–242.

Grabowski, J. (1996). French criminal justice and Indians in Montreal, 1670–1760. *Ethnohistory*, 43(3), pp. 405–429.

Greenwood, F.M. (1996). Lower Canada (Quebec): transformation of civil law, from higher morality to autonomous will, 1774–1866. *Manitoba Law Journal*, 23(1–2), pp. 132–182.

Greenwood, F.M. and Wright, B., ed. (1996). *Canadian State Trials: Volume I: Law, Politics, and Security Measures, 1608–1837*. Toronto: Osgoode Society for Canadian Legal History and University of Toronto Press.

Greenwood, F.M. and Wright, B., ed. (2002). *Canadian State Trials: Volume II: Rebellion and Invasion in the Canadas, 1837–1839*. Toronto: Osgoode Society for Canadian Legal History and University of Toronto Press.

Guillemette, R. (1988). Les bibliothèques personnelles de Montréal entre 1800 et 1820: une contribution à l'histoire sociale du livre. M.A., Université de Montréal.

Hay, D. (1975). Property, authority and the criminal law. In: D. Hay et al., eds., *Albion's Fatal Tree: Crime and Society in Eighteenth-Century England*. Harmondsworth, Middlesex: Penguin, pp. 17–63.

Hay, D. (1981). The meanings of the criminal law in Quebec, 1764–1774. In: L.A. Knafla, ed., *Crime and Criminal Justice in Europe and Canada*. Waterloo: Wilfrid Laurier University Press, pp. 77–110.

Hibbitts, B.J. (2004). Her Majesty's Yankees: American authority in the Supreme Court of Victorian Nova Scotia, 1837–1901. In: P. Girard, J. Phillips, and B. Cahill, eds., *The Supreme Court of Nova Scotia, 1754–2004: from Imperial Bastion to Provincial Oracle*. Toronto: Osgoode Society for Canadian Legal History and University of Toronto Press, pp. 321–360.

Kasirer, N. (1990). The annotated criminal code *en version québécoise*: signs of territoriality in Canadian criminal law. *Dalhousie Law Journal*, 13(2), pp. 520–563.

Knafla, L.A. and Chapman, T.L. (1983). Criminal justice in Canada: a comparative study of the maritimes and Lower Canada, 1760–1812. *Osgoode Hall Law Journal*, 21(2), pp. 245–274.

Leclerc, J.F. (1985). Justice et infra-justice en Nouvelle-France: les voies de fait à Montréal entre 1700 et 1760. *Criminologie*, 18(1), pp. 25–39.

Lefrançois, A. (2004). Thomas Arakwenté: promoteur de la modernité dans la communauté iroquoise du Sault Saint-Louis (1791–1820). *Revue d'éthique et de théologie morale*, supplement, 228, pp. 357–378.

Mathieu, M., ed. (1894). *Rapports judiciaires révisés de la province de Québec*, volume 8. Montreal: C.O. Beauchemin & Fils.

Mathieu, M., ed. (1895a). *Rapports judiciaires révisés*, volume 14. Montreal: C.O. Beauchemin & Fils.

Mathieu, M., ed. (1895b). *Rapports judiciaires révisés*, volume 15. Montreal: C.O. Beauchemin & Fils.

Mathieu, M., ed. (1896). *Rapports judiciaires révisés*, volume 18. Montreal: C.O. Beauchemin & Fils.

Morel, A. (1978). La réception du droit criminel anglais au Québec (1760–1892). *Revue juridique Thémis*, 13(2–3), pp. 449–541.

Morin, M. (2000). Portalis v. Bentham? The objectives ascribed to codification of the civil law and the criminal law in France, England and Canada. In: *Perspectives on Legislation: Essays from the 1999 Legal Dimensions Initiative*. Ottawa: Law Commission of Canada, pp. 125–197.

Neatby, H.M. (1933). *The Administration of Justice under the Quebec Act*. Minneapolis: Minnesota University Press.

Noël, D. (2000). Une langue qui ne capitule pas (la justice et les tribunaux). In: M. Plourde, ed., *Le français au Québec: 400 ans d'histoire et de vie*. Montreal: Fides/Publications du Québec, pp. 72–79.

Parker, G. (1981). The origins of the Canadian criminal code. In: D.H. Flaherty, ed., *Essays in the History of Canadian Law. Volume I*. Toronto: Osgoode Society and University of Toronto Press, pp. 249–280.

Perrault, J.-F. (1814). *Questions et réponses sur le droit criminel du Bas-Canada: dédiées aux étudiants en droit*. Quebec City: C. Le François.

Reiter, E.H. (2004). Imported books, imported ideas: reading European jurisprudence in mid-nineteenth-century Quebec. *Law and History Review*, 22(3), pp. 445–492.

Ross, R.J. and Stern, P.J. (2013). Reconstructing early modern notions of legal pluralism. In: L. Benton and R.J. Ross, *Legal Pluralism and Empires, 1500–1850*. New York: NYU Press, pp. 109–141.

Stenning, P.C. (1986). *Appearing for the Crown: a Legal and Historical Review of Criminal Prosecutorial Authority in Canada*. Cowansville: Brown Legal Publications.

Stone, H. (2000). Les Indiens et le système judiciaire criminel de la Province de Québec: les politiques de l'administration sous le régime britannique. *Recherches amérindiennes au Québec*, 30(3), pp. 65–78.

INDEX

Page numbers for figures are given in *italics*, for tables they are given in **bold**.

For Product Safety Concerns and Information please contact our EU
representative GPSR@taylorandfrancis.com
Taylor & Francis Verlag GmbH, Kaufingerstraße 24, 80331 München, Germany

www.ingramcontent.com/pod-product-compliance
Ingram Content Group UK Ltd.
Pitfield, Milton Keynes, MK11 3LW, UK
UKHW021722240926
475702UK00029BA/1762

* 9 7 8 1 1 3 8 4 7 6 7 9 0 *